How things *really work in*

Tur

Living, working and doing business

The Law • The Taxes • Immigration

Buying, Selling or Renting Property • Investment

Other books in this series...

This is the first book in what, we hope, will be a long series.

Coming next...

Living, working and doing business in China

Living, working and doing business in Portugal

Living, working and doing business in the USA

See our website - **www.guides.global** - for more information.

How things *really* work in

Turkey

Living, working and doing business

The Law • The Taxes • Immigration

Buying, Selling or Renting Property • Investment

GUIDES.
GL BAL

2018

First published: 22 May 2018

ISBN 978-1-9996678-1-8

Publisher:

Guides.Global Ltd
23 Bridewell Lane
Bury St Edmunds, Suffolk IP33 1RE
England

Telephone: +44 1284 719964
Email: office@guides.global
Website: www.guides.global

Printed by Amazon's CreateSpace in various countries around the world, including the US and the UK.

Ordering Information:
This book may be bought through **www.guides.global**, from any good bookshop or via Amazon

Our Authors

Başak Yildiz Orkun

Başak is a partner at the Orkun & Orkun law firm.

Her legal speciality is advising foreign individuals and companies who are relocating to Turkey to work, retire or set up a business.

She and her team of lawyers and accountants provide a full range of legal, accounting, tax and tax planning services.

She has been qualified as a lawyer in Turkey since 2005.

Burak Orkun

Burak is also a partner at Orkun & Orkun.

Orkun & Orkun started to serve clients in 1989, under the leadership of his father Suleyman Orkun. It provides a full range of book keeping and accountancy services for both Turkish and foreign individuals and companies.

Burak is a qualified accountant in Turkey and joined the firm in 2005.

John Howell

John qualified as an English solicitor (lawyer) and worked as a specialist in international legal problems, especially problems affecting private individuals and small businesses, for over 30 years.

After retiring from legal practice, he set up **www.guides.global**.

He has written many books about international law, both for lawyers and for the general public. He speaks regularly on these subjects all over the world.

Contents

Acknowledgements

Başak would like to thank her father Sahin Yildiz, also a lawyer, who started to take her to court when she was seven and taught her all she knows!

Burak would like to thank his father, Suleyman, a wise accountant who stopped him from making lots of mistakes in his early years.

John Howell would like to thank his wife, Janie, who put up with him working through their retirement and indulged his delusion that writing guides was a business.

We would all like to thank the team at Guides.Global, and especially Francine Carrel, for their ideas, patience and hand-holding.

Disclaimer

Turkey is a large country and is very varied, both geographically and culturally.

Despite this, legal and administrative practices and procedures are pretty much the same throughout the country. Sometimes, however, they can vary a little even between officials working in the same office in the same town!

The law, practice and procedure change frequently.

It is, therefore, essential that before you take any major decisions or commit yourself to any course of action (particularly one that will be difficult or expensive to undo) you seek reliable local advice.

That advice will, in most cases, come via a lawyer, accountant or other professional located in the area where you are thinking of doing business, and specialising in the relevant area of the law.

This book is intended to be of general interest and to provide useful orientation for those thinking of moving to, living in, buying a property in or doing business with or in Turkey. It is not intended to provide detailed legal or other advice. It can, self-evidently, not take into account your personal circumstances and it is, by its very nature, a brief overview of some fairly complicated topics. **It is absolutely no substitute for taking your own legal or other professional advice**. Neither the authors nor the publishers accept any responsibility for any action taken or not taken as a result of reading this book.

This book is intended to be up to date as at 1st January 2018.

Whilst we have taken great care whilst writing this book, we do not accept responsibility for any errors in it or omissions from it.

Unless specifically stated, any reference to a person or company is not an endorsement or recommendation of their service.

Note:

Long links in the text of this book have been shortened with the bit.ly tool. Just type the short link into your web browser and it will take you to the document in question.

Written by **John Howell**
Editor & Founder of Guides.Global
www.guides.global • john.howell@guides.global

Introduction

Turkey welcomes many newcomers. They come to work, to run a business, to retire or just to enjoy a great holiday. Over 650,000 foreigners have residence permits to live or work in Turkey. In 2015, 41million came as tourists. In the last few years Turkey has also received 3.5million refugees, mainly from the terrible conflict in Syria. This book is for all of them. It is to help them understand this wonderful country and the - sometimes unusual - ways things work in it.

Turkey is a powerful country of 80million people: the regional superpower. It has the 13th largest economy in the world and deployable armed forces of 495,000.

It is also a modern secular democracy with universal suffrage and extensive human rights legislation. However, at the moment (2018), Turkey may be in transition. This transition is a story of two strong men: Mustafa Kemal Atatürk and Recep Tayyip Erdoğan.

Before continuing, I must note that many people in Turkey would be unhappy seeing these two people compared, or even seeing their names on the same page: Erdoğan is far from universally popular (unlike Atatürk), and his politics and strategy draw strong criticism from many Turkish people. Their core philosophies are also very different. Nevertheless:

Modern Turkey was the creation of Atatürk, who served as its first president from 1923 until his death in 1938. During that period, he passed an endless series of reforms with a view to building a modern, secular nation state. Atatürk is still revered in Turkey and his picture adorns most homes and offices.

Fast forward to 2003. Recep Tayyip Erdoğan became Turkey's Prime Minister and, later, president. He has an Islamist political agenda. His critics accuse him of being intolerant and he has been prone to locking up or closing down his enemies. Time will tell how far this will develop. Whatever you think of him, it is undeniable that he is hugely influential in Turkey and will be remembered in history.

Turkey has been a trading nation for well over 2,000 years and has been, and still is, a pivotal point on the world's trading routes. In 1963, Turkey reached its first agreement with the European Economic Community (now the European Union), with a view to closer cooperation between them. By 1996, this extended to tariff-free trading arrangements. Later, the EU held out the prospect of full membership.

During the early 21st century, Turkey gained popularity among European travellers, homebuyers and investors due to its growing wealth and population, laid-back way of life, abundance of history, pleasant climate and exceptional scenery.

More recently, Turkey has introduced an incentive to attract foreign investment by offering citizenship to qualifying investors.

All these new arrivals face the challenge of adjusting to a new life in a country where the main language is Turkish - which few of them speak - and where the culture, laws and business practices are a confusing but fascinating mix of the European, the Asian and the truly international.

We hope this book helps you find your feet and enjoy all that Turkey has to offer.

Turkey

Written by **John Howell**
Editor & Founder of Guides.Global
www.guides.global • john.howell@guides.global

The Basics

This is not a travel guide, so we are not going to write about Turkey's beautiful beaches, fabulous food, magnificent mountains or superb sunsets.

However, there are some things you need to know if you are going to be living in Turkey.

This chapter deals with some of the basics.

Terminology

The Country:	Turkey (*Türkiye*)
Adjective:	Turkish (*Türk*)
The Nationality:	Turkish (*Türk*)
The People:	Turks (*Türkler*)
Languages:	Turkish (84.54%), Kurmanji (Kurdish) (11.97%), Arabic (1.38%), other (2.11%). Furthermore, 17% of the population (including expats) speak English, 3% speak French and 4% speak German.

Article 42 of the Constitution of Turkey says:

"No language other than Turkish shall be taught as a mother tongue to Turkish citizens at any institutions of training or education. Foreign languages to be taught in institutions of training and education and the rules to be followed by schools conducting training and education in a foreign language shall be determined by law."

Time Zone:	UTC+2
Currency:	Turkish lira
ISO International Country Code:	TRY
Local Country Abbreviation:	TL
Internet Domain:	.tr
International Telephone Dialling Code:	+90

Geography

Capital City:	Ankara: population 4.6million.

Istanbul is (by a long way) Turkey's biggest city, with a population of well over 14million.

Area: 783,562km2 (37 out of 252 countries in the world).

Coastline: 7,200km.

Terrain: A huge variety! In Turkey you can find snow-topped mountains, rolling hills, barren rock, expanses of conifer forest, deserts and diverse coastlines.

Climate: As it's so large, Turkey has three different climate zones.

In Istanbul and around the sea of Marmara, the climate is moderate (average in winter 5°C and in summer 25°C) but in winter the temperature can drop well below zero.

On Turkey's western (Aegean) and southern (Mediterranean) coasts there is a Mediterranean influenced climate with average temperatures of 9°C in winter and 29°C in summer.

The climate of central Turkey (the Anatolian Plateau) is a steppe climate, with great temperature differences between day and night. Rainfall is low and there is often snow in winter. The average temperature is about 23°C in summer and -2°C in winter.

Fresh Water: Per capita consumption: 1,500m3 per year (US: 1,583, France: 512; Cyprus: 164; China: 410).

People

Population: 80,274,604 (20 out of 238 countries in the world).

Population growth: 0.9% per year. (US: 0.81%; France: 0.41%; China: 0.43%).

Median age: 30.5 years.

Life expectancy at birth: 74.8 years.

Urban population: 72.9% of total population.

Expat population: 0.2% of total population.

Religion: Muslim 99.8% (mostly Sunni), other 0.2% (mostly Christians and Jews).

Ethnicity: Turkish 70-75%, Kurdish 19%, other minorities 7-12%.

UN Human Development Index: 71st of 188 countries (2015).

This index attempts to measure a country's achievements in education, healthcare, wealth generation and other areas. It looks at the extent to which the people in a country enjoy a long and healthy life, a good education, and a decent standard of living. It is a useful indicator of what a country will be like as a place to live.

UN Inequality Adjusted Human Development Index:

71st of 188 countries.

This index is a list measuring the lost development potential arising from all types of inequality in a country. With perfect equality, this index and the HDI would show the same result.

Population Below Poverty Line: 16.9% (2010).

Medical System

The Turkish healthcare system went through a dramatic reform in 2003, significantly improving access to healthcare. However, Turkish healthcare still leaves a lot to be desired, especially in rural areas. Many people shun the state-run hospitals and opt to pay for private care.

Health Expenditure:

5.4% of GDP (US: 17.1%; France: 11.5%; Singapore: 4.9%; China: 5.2%).

Doctors:

2.81/1,000 people (US: 2.55; France: 3.23; Singapore: 1.91; China: 1.49).

Hospital Beds:

2.5/1,000 people (US: 2.9; France: 6.4; Singapore: 2; China: 3.8).

Peace Index

Turkey is ranked 145th out of the 163 countries included in the 2017 edition of the Vision of Humanity Peace Index. This is similar to Egypt and Colombia. Syria comes last.

The methodology may be open to some debate but this a good snapshot of criminality, conflict, political attitudes and military expenditure.

Global Terrorism Index

Turkey is ranked 14th out of the 162 countries in the 2016 edition of the Global Terrorism Index. A high number is good, so Turkey's placement is poor. Iraq is number one.

This is another interesting snapshot of risk, from the same people.

Legal System

The Turkish legal system is based on the continental European civil law system. This, in turn, has its roots in the Roman law system of 2,000 years ago, but was later heavily modified by Napoleon and, via the Code Napoleon (1804), became the accepted model for the legal systems of many Western European countries.

From 1804 until the end of the 19th Century, various nations adopted and adapted the French Napoleonic code, so civil law now exists in a number of closely related yet very distinct variants.

Because Turkey was not established until 1923, it had the pick of these various European codes of law when it came to deciding the legal system it wanted to adopt. It chose the version adopted in Switzerland as the main source for its legal system.

Importantly, the Turkish legal system currently contains no elements of Islamic law.

Turkey is ranked a poor 99/113 in the 2016 Rule of Law Index from the World Justice Project. The low ranking can, we expect, be attributed to two reasons:

- Over the last decade or so, there have been concerns that President Erdoğan has been interfering with the rule of law (for instance, appointing judges that may rule according to his wishes or who are not adequately qualified).

- The system in Turkey can be sluggish and not very transparent.

Turkey scored more encouragingly - but with plenty of room for improvement - on the 2016 Corruption Perceptions Index from Transparency International, ranking 75 of 176 countries.

Going back 20 years, corruption was an issue of concern to many Turkish people. The corruption in question was not so much major institutional or political corruption, but minor day-to-day irregularities: staff in town halls requiring 'tips' for performing their day-to-day duties, police officers seeking payment when they stopped you for a traffic offence, and so on. As far as this type of corruption is concerned, the position has improved greatly in the last 20 years.

However, there is now a widely held view that large-scale corruption - both within politics and big business - has reached unacceptable levels.

Currency

Name: Turkish lira (*Türk lirası*)

Symbol: ₺

International (ISO) Currency Code: TRY

Local Abbreviation: TL

Divisions: 1 lira = 100 *kuruş*

Today's currency is the second incarnation of the Turkish lira. The first was introduced in 1923 (after independence) and replaced the Ottoman lira. The present Turkish lira replaced the first after a period of devastating devaluation in the early 2000s.

This was a very difficult period, when the economy crashed and the value of the Turkish lira fell so far that it was measured in millions of lira to the dollar.

Reforms stabilised the position to the extent that, in 2005, the government felt able to introduce the new Turkish lira (*Yeni Türk Lirası*), which removed the last six zeros from the old currency.

The reference to "new" was dropped in 2009.

Since the troubles in Syria, the value of the lira has fallen significantly - but it is far from being out of control, as it was 15 years ago.

TRY per unit

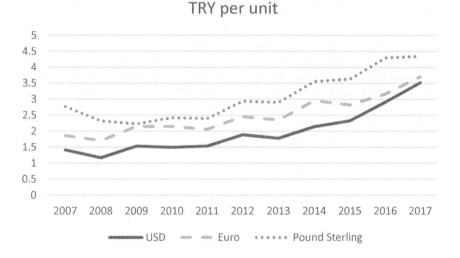

Economy

Turkey has transitioned from an economy which was, 20 years ago, heavily controlled by the state - particularly in areas such as heavy industry, communications, transport and banking. Now even these sectors have been privatised and operate as part of a free market economy.

Very large parts of Turkey remain rural and agriculture still accounts for about 25% of total employment, although it makes up a much smaller percentage of Turkey's national GDP.

Today, the biggest contributors to Turkey's GDP are industry (in particular, the construction of vehicles and shipping), the service sector, and tourism.

Turkey's GDP has, since the Syrian war, fallen a little but the economy remains the 13th largest in the world (at about US$2.13 trillion in 2017) and now seems to be growing again, probably at 3 or 4% per year.

Turkey's GDP

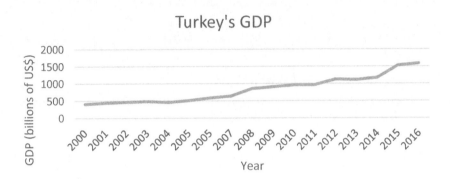

On the coast, and particularly in the area around Bodrum, the economy has benefited from the desire of wealthy Turks living in its great cities to own and enjoy property by the sea. At the same time, the demand for such properties from international buyers has fallen sharply in the light of the perceived refugee crisis and the current political uncertainty in Turkey.

Despite these changes, the economy in Bodrum (where we wrote this book) remains one of the strongest in Turkey. It is seen as a liberal and democratic refuge for people from the cities: a place where they can enjoy a high quality of life.

Inflation has remained a problem for Turkey. In 2014, Turkey sharply increased interest rates in order to slow inflation. This had limited success: inflation stood at 8.9% in 2012 and 8% in 2016.

GDP - 2017 - measured in purchasing power parity ('PPP'):	US$2.13trillion. Ranks 13th out of 230 listed countries.
GDP per capita (PPP):	US$26,500. Ranks 75th out of 230 listed countries.
GDP Growth - 2017:	5.1%. Ranks 38th out of 222 listed countries.
Inflation:	8%.
Public debt:	32.7% of GDP.
Unemployment:	General: 11.8%; youth 23%.

Further Reading

It's well worth while reading a bit - or, better still, a lot - about Turkey. It will help you settle in more quickly and it will make the whole place easier to understand. Try to fit in a chapter a day.

All the books referred to, and many others, can be bought via **www.guides.global/guides/turkey/tur-books.php**.

Facts & figures

Take a quick look at the wonderful CIA World Factbook (**www.cia.gov/library/publications/the-world-factbook**) which has incredibly detailed information about almost every country in the world, including Turkey.

History

There is a multitude of books available about Turkey's long and fascinating history. We recommend *'Turkey: a Short History'* by Norman Stone or *'Turkey: a Modern History'* by Erik-Jan Zürcher. Both are well-written and easy to understand.

Culture

Again, there are many books on the market. We like the recent (2014) *'Culture Smart! Turkey'* by Charlotte McPherson.

Tourist guides

There is a full range of tourist guides about Turkey. It's well worth reading one or two of them, especially if you don't know the country well.

Our favourite is the Rough Guide to Turkey.

Other guides are produced by Lonely Planet, Insight Guides, Dorling Kindersley (DK) as part of their Eyewitness Travel series, Fodor, Footprint, Moon, Bradt, and Blue Guides.

Politics

There is a wealth of books about politics in Turkey. Have a look at *'Atatürk: A Biography of Mustafa Kemal, Father of Modern Turkey'* by Patrick Balfour Kinross; *'Under the Shadow: Rage and Revolution in Modern Turkey'* by Kaya Genç and, again, *'Turkey: A Modern History'* by Erik J. Zürcher.

Moving to Turkey

Immigration & Residence

Written by **Başak Yildiz Orkun**
Managing Partner (Legal Department) at Orkun & Orkun
www.orkunorkun.com • info@orkunorkun.com

Transit visas

Turkey does not have transit visas.

If you arrive by plane and are immediately catching a flight to another country, you can usually remain at the airport without passing through Turkish immigration control and move from your arrival gate to your new departure gate without the need for any sort of visa. If you wish to (or need to) pass through immigration control for any reason, you will need to have the appropriate visa.

If you are arriving by sea, you will always need to have a visa.

Short-term visits

Tourists

In 2015, 41 million people visited Turkey. In 2016, largely as a result of the combination of the conflict in Syria, political uncertainty in Turkey and terrorist attacks, the number fell to about 31 million. Local reports suggest that tourist numbers have increased sharply in 2017, mainly because of an influx of tourists from Russia and the former Soviet Union.

You'll be pleased to learn that it's very easy to visit Turkey as a tourist! This is doubly useful as many people who wish to come to Turkey to work, set up a business or retire will first come as a tourist just to check out the feasibility of what they want to do. They will make their plans, return home, and then apply for whatever immigration visas that they might need.

Citizens of any nationality can visit Turkey as a 'tourist': somebody who is visiting on a short-term (less than 90-day) basis and who is not coming to Turkey to work. The length of time you can visit Turkey on a tourist visa depends upon your nationality, as the government of Turkey has reached individual agreements with individual countries when it comes to reciprocal tourism rights. Details can be found at **www.mfa.gov.tr/visa-information-for-foreigners.en.mfa**.

The only requirement is that they must obtain an 'e-visa'. This 'visa' is not a visa in the usual sense of the word. It does not involve any scrutiny of your status or application. It is, basically, a receipt for an entry tax!

You apply for the e-visa via the Turkish government's e-visa website (**www.evisa.gov.tr**). This is available in many languages. The whole process of obtaining the visa will, typically, take less than five minutes. You will need to provide information such as your passport number and your parents' full names. You will also have to make a small payment (by credit or debit card). The amount of the payment depends, again, on your country of origin. It is typically about US$20.

You can apply for the e-visa up to three months in advance of your intended travel date. Once you arrive in Turkey, your e-visa will allow you to stay in the country for a maximum of 90 days in any 180-day period. Unlike many countries, this is irrespective of whether that period bridges a calendar year.

So, for example, if you arrived for a proposed 90-day visit on 1st September 2017 you would be able to stay until 30th November 2017 (a maximum of 90 days). If you arrived on 1st November 2017, you would be able to stay until 30th January 2018 (again, a maximum of 90 days). The count does not restart on 1st January 2018 just because you are in a new calendar year.

If you wish to stay in Turkey as a tourist for longer than 90 days, you can do so, but only by obtaining a short-term residence permit. This is fairly simple. See below.

Business visitors

People wishing to visit Turkey to meet clients and/or discuss business matters can do so as tourists. There is no separate 'business visitor' visa.

However, if you want to visit Turkey for other 'business' purposes, you will need a working visa for which there are various requirements. For example, journalists have a special type of visa, people filming or conducting scientific research have a different type of visa, as do people coming to Turkey for the purposes of teaching, and lorry (truck) drivers. See below for more details.

Long-term visits

All applications for long-term visas must be made via the "Pre-Application System of Turkish Sticker Visas" (PAS). This is an online system, under which applicants enter all of their details and, once the application has been accepted, receive an appointment to visit their local Turkish consulate for the rest of the process to be carried out.

See more details or apply at **www.visa.gov.tr**.

It is essential that your online application is properly completed. If it is not, it will be rejected and you will have to start all over again.

The requirements (checklists) for visas vary slightly from country to country. The ones below are for people coming from the UK (**bit.ly/2raQHlG**). Details of the requirements for your country can be found on the Turkish consular website for your country.

Students

Turkish schools (primary & secondary education) and its colleges and universities (tertiary education) are of high quality and relatively cheap. Turkey has fairly recently embraced the idea of the international students. Most come from Western China (the Xinjiang Uyghur region, where Turkish is spoken) and other Turkic countries such as Azerbaijan, Turkmenistan, Kyrgyzstan and Uzbekistan. There are very few Western students in Turkey specifically for the purposes of education.

The main category of international students is the children of people resident in Turkey, who are treated in the same way as local students and so not considered further here. There are also international schools, where teaching is in a foreign language. See page 142 for more information.

Document checklist for a student visa:

Foreigners can only apply for a Turkish student visa *after* they've been accepted by a Turkish educational institution certified by the Ministry of Education - whether that's a school, university or language course.

A student applicant, according to the Turkish consular website for the UK, will need:

1. A completed visa application form (**www.visa.gov.tr**) (fill it in using capital letters)

2. A passport valid for at least 60 days past the intended *end* of your stay. The passport must have at least two blank pages

3. An e-visa; a visa exemption; or a residence permit

4. A passport-style photograph

5. An acceptance letter from the educational institution (one certified by the Ministry of Education) you will be attending

6. If you're coming to Turkey as an exchange student, a confirmation letter from your school in the UK

7. Non-British Citizens applying from the UK also need a one-year (minimum) valid residence permit for the UK

8. Your most recent two months' bank statements showing a reasonable amount of savings (at least £3,000 for six months' stay)

9. If you have a sponsor: a sponsor letter, the sponsor's bank statements and a copy of his/her passport

10. Accommodation details, if available

Similar requirements will apply in other countries.

Case study

Jean Gaudion

Student, French, 19

The problem

Jean wished to study on a Turkish language course, based in Bodrum, but also to work in order to fund some of his activities and save some money during his time in Turkey. He was enrolled in a nine-month course.

The solution

Obtaining a visa to come to Turkey for the purpose of studying on the language course was straightforward. He had sufficient funds to stay afloat during the course and a place to stay. However, getting permission to work was a great deal more problematic.

The first problem is that Jean's course was only a nine-month course. A person coming to study in Turkey for less than two years is not entitled to work, and even a person enrolled on a programme lasting two years or longer cannot work until he has completed the first year of his studies.

Even then, he can only work for a maximum of 24 hours per week: probably more than enough to satisfy Jean's requirements.

Jean did not wish to extend the length of his course, so he reluctantly accepted that he would not be able to work legally in Turkey.

He was very much aware that many people in his college were working illegally. This is quite common, but it does give rise to the risks set out in our chapter about working illegally. See page 204.

Duration of visa and fees (2017)

These are again quoted from the Turkish consulate in the UK and will differ somewhat from country to country. The figures will be on the website for your country.

- Student visa - up to six months - £95

- Student visa - over six months - £348

- Language course - up to 11 months - £181

Will a student visa also allow your spouse or children to live in Turkey?

No. Your student visa permits you alone to enter Turkey for the purpose of studying.

However, to live in Turkey, you also need a residence permit. This applies equally to your wife and children. If you are a student in Turkey, then there should be no problem obtaining a residence permit; and if you obtain a residence permit for yourself there should be no problem with your spouse or dependent children also obtaining permission to live with you, provided you meet the test for a Family Residence Permit. See page 27.

Can a student work in Turkey?

Foreign students can legally work in Turkey after obtaining a Student Residence Permit. However, foreign students who are enrolled in undergraduate or two-year associate programmes can start working in Turkey only after completing their first year of study. Students who are enrolled in two-year associate programmes may not exceed 24 working hours per week.

How long does it take?

Obtaining a student visa should take about 90 days if done via the consulate - but only 24 hours if done online, provided that your application has been properly completed, and all of your documents are in order when they're finally presented.

Coming to work

Just to be clear, this section does not apply if you merely wish to come to Turkey on a business trip: to meet clients, investigate the market, hold meetings etc. For those purposes you may visit on a simple tourist visa.

Otherwise, whether you just want a summer job in Turkey or you wish to settle down and work there for good, you'll need a work visa/permit. Unfortunately, work visas in Turkey are not very easy to obtain. There is a fairly high level of unemployment in Turkey (11.2% in November 2017) and much higher youth unemployment. So, naturally, the government wants to protect the employment of its own people. However, if you have skills that are needed - say, a teacher of French, a nanny or a seasonal worker in a hotel who speaks a language that is in demand - getting a visa is still fairly simple. If you have work skills that are already widely available in Turkey (e.g. a motor mechanic) it is almost impossible to obtain a work visa.

Each job for which a visa might be obtained has an eligibility criteria list and a minimum permitted wage.

The length of your visa depends upon the length of your contract: say, three months for a summer post in a hotel or 12 months for a teacher. Few companies offer contracts over 12 months, although it is allowed.

Each work permit is job-specific. It is not a general permit to work in Turkey. So, for example, you might obtain a work permit to teach French at a particular college. You cannot simply change jobs and work somewhere else; even as a French teacher. You (and your new employer) would need to apply for a new work permit.

If you have held a work permit for seven years you will no longer need to renew it: you can be given a permanent residence permit as a working resident. You are then free to change jobs as you please.

In addition to your visa allowing you to work in Turkey, you will also need a residence permit (see below).

There is a general type of working visa (which applies to almost all situations), but there are also special types of working visa.

These include visas for:

- Work involving maintenance and installation of equipment
- Academic visas for teachers
- Filming
- Scientific research
- Archaeological excavation
- Academic research
- Journalists
- Lorry (truck) drivers
- Business visits, conferences and seminars

The requirements for each of these visas can be found on the Turkish government's visa website: **www.mfa.gov.tr** or, in slightly more detail, on the Turkish consular website for your own country. For example, for those traveling from the UK: **www.turkishconsulate.org.uk/en/visa.asp**.

To apply for a general visa, you start off with the Pre-Application System (PAS). See page 15.

Once your application has been accepted, you will have to apply for an appointment to visit your local Turkish consulate.

It is important that the information in the documents you provide (below) and the information in your online application is exactly the same. If it is not, your application will be rejected and you will have to start all over again. The application must be made before the proposed start date for your employment.

The process of applying for a work permit is in two stages. The application must be made in person.

Stage 1

You will make an appointment to attend your consulate. The appointment will be confirmed to you by email. At that appointment, you will need to produce the following documents:

- A printed and completed application form. The form should be completed in capital (upper case) letters.

    o No relevant field should be left empty, even if it's not specified as "required".

    o Any mistakes, including spelling mistakes, will void the application - you'll have to start again.

    o The "duration of stay" must be filled in as 90 days, even if that's not the length of your job offer.

- A job offer letter, properly printed on letterheaded paper and with the employer's details and signature.

- Your employment contract, signed both by you and your employer.

- A clear, legible photocopy of your passport - this must be valid for the duration of your visa, plus 60 days.

- One RECENT passport-style photograph (make sure it's not crumpled, folded or otherwise damaged).

- If you're not a UK citizen, and are applying in the UK, a residence permit for the UK.

Some further notes:

- Your job title must be in Turkish and English, and must not exceed 35 characters including spaces. If you don't have a Turkish language employment contract, you must translate your job title and include it in brackets - e.g. General Director (*Genel Müdür*).

- You do not need to provide proof of health insurance for a working visa. Nor do you need to provide your criminal record history.

- If you are a dancer, acrobat or entertainer, you need to fill in ANOTHER three-page form: **www.turkishconsulate.org.uk/en/workvisa_01.pdf**.

Stage 2

One the first stage has been completed - and your forms accepted - you'll be sent a visa reference. This will take about ten days. You should forward this reference onto your prospective employer.

The employer must then lodge the employment application with the Ministry of Labour (via their website) within ten days. If the employer misses this deadline, you'll need to start all over again.

The Ministry of Labour will assess your application and respond (either to you or your employer) in four to six weeks. If you were successful, you can then pick up your visa from the Turkish consulate in your country.

Duration of visa and fees (2017)

- Work visa - up to six months - £150
- Work visa - up to one year - £432

Can you claim social security on a working visa?

As a person working in Turkey, you will be paying tax and social security payments in Turkey.

You will be entitled to Turkish social security and other benefits on the basis of the payments that you've made.

Can you use state healthcare on a working visa?

Once you registered with the Turkish Social Security as an employee, healthcare is automatically covered by your Social Security payments.

However, you may want to consider supplemental private healthcare, especially if you are going to be living somewhere remote.

Can your family or children claim state healthcare on a working visa?

Your family will be covered via your social security rights.

How long does it take?

Obtaining a work visa is, theoretically, doable in two months, but we recommend that you start the process at least three months in advance. Delays happen. Often.

Professional advice

Applying for a work visa is always complicated.

The rules are restrictive. An application expressed one way can fail; whereas an almost identical application, put in a way that takes full advantage of the rules, can succeed.

The application forms are also far from clear (particularly for someone who is not a native Turkish speaker) and the way they are interpreted will vary, sometimes significantly, from consulate to consulate.

It is, therefore, strongly recommended that you seek the advice of a specialist in immigration law before you complete and submit your application for a visa. This will make it much less likely that you make a mistake in the application (and so have to start the process all over again) and it can save you a large amount of time and frustration.

It could also open your eyes to some immigration possibilities you had previously not known about, and so not considered.

Coming to do business

People wishing to visit Turkey on a temporary basis to meet clients and/or discuss business can do so on a tourist visa.

Coming to Turkey to explore the possibilities of setting up a business can - in practice - be done using a tourist visa.

Coming to set up or run a business

People wishing to come to Turkey on a long-term basis in order to set up or run their own business will need to apply for an Independent Working Permit.

Independent Working Permits are very hard to obtain unless you are going to create lots of jobs for local people. Many people thinking of applying for such a visa might find it easier to seek one of the new (2017) residence permits and citizenship based on investment, or as a highly skilled person: see below.

Alternatively, they may decide to set up a Turkish company to carry out the business activity and then become a senior employee of that company. On that basis, they would apply for a work permit to work for that company. This is usually simpler than applying for an Independent Working Permit.

Highly skilled people ("Turquoise Card") - New in March 2017.

This new Turquoise Visa (turquoise being the national colour of Turkey) was announced on 14 March 2017.

Highly skilled people means people who are one or more of the following:

- Highly qualified
- Have a unique skill set
- Highly skilled investors
- Highly skilled scientific people
- Eminent international cultural or sporting personalities
- People who will help Turkey or its culture to be better known internationally

They will be entitled to the equivalent of an indefinite work permit.

They can be joined by their husband/wife, children and other dependants.

They are exempt from military service (otherwise compulsory in Turkey) but they can't work in the Turkish public services.

Residence permits

A person wishing to live in Turkey will, in the cases mentioned above, need a special visa authorising entry to the country for the purpose in question *and* a residence permit. However, in other cases, they will merely need a residence permit.

Any person who wishes to stay in Turkey for more than 90 days in a 180-day period requires a residence permit. This is the case whether they wish to stay in Turkey to study, to work, or simply to pass their time during retirement as people who are 'economically inactive'. See below for more details.

This need for two documents is merely a reflection of the way in which the Turkish visa system is organised. In practical terms, you will need to produce the required documentation (if any) to show that you have a valid basis to be in the country.

However, it's important to realise that if you are a person who requires a visa to enter the country (whether to work or to study) you will also need a residence permit.

Applying for a residence permit

The process for dealing with applications for residence permits was modified in 2015, and then again in 2017, with a view to making things more consistent throughout Turkey. It is not clear that it has succeeded in doing this!

Proof of income

For most categories of residence permit, you will need to show proof of adequate income.

For a single person, this is, generally, interpreted as proof that you have at least the equivalent of the Turkish minimum wage. In March 2017 this was net TRY1,404.06 per month (approximately US$400, €350 £300).

For a person with dependants it is a bit higher: usually around an additional 15% of the minimum wage per dependant.

Short-Term Residence Permits

These are the normal residence permits issued in Turkey. They can be issued for a period of one or two years.

A person wishing to stay in Turkey for more than 90 days in any 180-day period can, fairly simply, obtain a Short-Term Residence Permit.

To do this, you go to the Immigration office (*İl Göç İdaresi*) in the area where you are living. Before your visit you should book online (**www.goc.gov.tr/icerik/mailform**). You can find the list showing all the documents you need to gather together and the rules applying to residency permits on the website. *Once you have gathered the documents together*, book your appointment and show up on time to make your formal application.

General documentation needed:

- Residence Permit Application Form (must be signed by the foreigner and/or their legal representative).

- Your passport or the original and a photocopy of any passport substitute document. You need to copy the pages containing your identity information, the page containing your photo any pages with visas.

- Four copies of a photograph of yourself, which must have been taken within the last six months, against a white background and be "biometric". In practical terms, this means having a special photograph taken either by a professional photographer or in a special passport photograph booth. Do not upload family, 'selfie', unrecognizable, old, or black and white photos into the system. If you do, the residence permit document will not be issued!

- A declaration which states you have sufficient financial capacity to support yourself. Your financial means are declared in the application form, and the directorate may request supporting documents.

- Valid health insurance. The insurance period must cover the intended residence permit duration. One of the following health insurance documents is considered sufficient:

  o An electronically signed (or signed and stamped/sealed) document to be obtained from provincial social security units which states that the foreigner benefits from the health services in Turkey within the scope of bilateral social security agreements.

  o An electronically signed (or signed and stamped/sealed) provisional document received from Social Security Institution. These cover family members in Family Residence Permit applications.

  o An electronically signed (or signed and stamped/sealed) document of an application made to the Social Security Institution to become a general health insurance holder.

  o A private health insurance policy. The policy must contain the expression: "This policy covers the minimum coverage stipulated in the circular no 9, dated 06/06/2014, on private health insurance required to be taken out for residence permit applications". Present the signed and stamped/sealed original of your insurance policy during the application. For extension applications, attach only an approved (sealed, signed) copy of your policy.

It is likely to take anything up to six weeks for your visa to be issued - and that's assuming you fulfil all the criteria and provide all the correct documents.

Once you have supplied all the paperwork, you need to go to the payments (tax) office (*Vergi Dairesi*) and pay for the visa. You can also make payments to some government banks. This will include the admin fee for the visa itself and also the cost of the official visa card.

A 12-month visa currently costs around US$250.

These are the general rules. However, there are, if fact, several types of Short-Term Residence Permit. Each type requires slightly different documentation.

Foreigners owning immovable property in Turkey

As well as the general documentation listed above, you will need:

- An official, electronically signed/signed and stamped/sealed document which shows that the house belongs to the you. This is your title deed - "*tapu*".

- Any other documentation proving you own the property.

Foreigners wanting to stay in Turkey to establishing business or commercial connections

As well as the general documentation listed above, you will need:

- Invitation letters or similar documents to be obtained from the persons or companies to be contacted. Supporting information and documentation may be requested by the department's investigators when necessary (such as a Notary-approved certificate of activity, a Notary-approved tax certificate, a Notary-approved trade registry gazette, a Notary-approved certificate of signature, etc.).

Foreigners participating in on-the-job training programmes

As well as the general documentation listed above, you will need:

- Documentation which shows the duration and place of your training. This is to be obtained from the institution or organization where your training will be delivered. This must be electronically signed/signed & stamped/sealed, and on letterhead paper.

Foreigners taking part in student exchange programmes

- An education/internship document to be obtained from the institution or organization where the education/internship will be received in Turkey. This must be electronically signed/signed & stamped/sealed, and on letterhead paper.

Turkey: how things *really* work

Foreigners staying on for extended tourism purposes

As well as the general documentation listed above, you will need:

- Information or (better) documentation about your travel plan and proposed accommodation - *if* requested by the directorate.

Foreigners transferring from a family residence permit

This could be, for example, a person who has reached the age of 18 and so needs his own permit, or a couple who are divorcing.

- Submission of the original of your previous residence permit. A photocopy should be attached to your application documents.

- Depending on circumstance, the following could be required:

  o A court decision granting a divorce where the marriage has lasted more than three years *or* a court decision for divorce which reveals suffering due to, e.g., violence, in which case the three-year time period is not necessary.

  o The death certificate of your original sponsor (typically, your husband or wife). If obtained from the Turkish authorities, this must be electronically signed/signed and stamped/sealed. If it's obtained from abroad, it must be apostilled and have a Notary-approved Turkish translation. If the applicant is a citizen of a state that is not a signatory to the Hague Apostille Convention, the document must be approved by the relevant state's authorities.

Foreigners attending a Turkish-language course

As well as the general documentation listed above, you will need:

- Documentation which shows the duration and place of the language course. This is to be obtained from the institution or organization where your course will be held. This must be electronically signed/signed & stamped/sealed, and on letterhead paper.

Foreigners attending an education programme, research, internship, or course run by a public agency

- A completed residence permit application form

- Your original passport or travel document, along with a clear photocopy

- Four passport-style photographs

- Documentation showing proof of your savings/resources to keep you going for the duration of your stay

- Documentation from the (state authorised) course, internship, research or other programme organiser

- If you're under 18, a letter of consent from your parent or guardian

- Proof of valid health insurance - whether that's private insurance, or documentation showing you can use Turkish state healthcare

- The consent of your legal guardian, along with their birth and (if applicable) marriage certificates; *or* their death certificate, to be apostilled by the authorised department of your home town

Extending your Short-Term Residence Permit

Residence Permit extension applications can be submitted online up to 60 days before the expiry of the old permit.

Whilst the application is being processed you may continue living in Turkey perfectly legally, even if this takes you past the original expiry date.

The application **must** be submitted no later than the expiry date of the old residence permit. Otherwise, you will be in Turkey illegally and will have to apply again from outside the country.

Residence permit for retirement

Hundreds of foreigners retire to Turkey each year. The weather is warm, the food is good and there are already thriving communities of expats! Even better, it's really easy to do.

There is no special 'retirement visa'. You simply apply for a Short-Term Residence Permit, in the way explained above.

Residence permit to run or start a business

See our chapter on Starting a Business in Turkey (page 215) for more details about business structures.

Professional help is highly recommended if you want to apply for a business visa with a view to settlement. At the very least, it will make things a lot quicker.

Family Residence Permits

Family Residence Permits can be granted to:

- A foreign spouse (but not unmarried partner)

- Foreign children (under 18)

- Dependent foreign children over 18 (typically, disabled)

- A spouse's dependent foreign children for foreigners who have valid residence permits, and of refugees ('Sponsors')

Family Residence Permits will be issued for a maximum term of two years (renewable) but for no longer than the remaining duration of the Sponsor's visa.

In the case of Sponsors who have polygamous marriages valid in their own country, only one wife may be granted a Family Residence Permit but all of the Sponsor's children can be entitled.

If the husband and wife later divorce, the spouse who has the Family Residence Permit will have to apply for a residence permit in their own right, unless their spouse is a Turkish citizen - in which case they shall be entitled to a Short-Term Residence Permit if they had possessed the Family Residence Permit for at least three years.

When granting Family Residence Permits to children, if dual guardianship arrangements exist for that child, the consent of the other parent is needed.

Family Residence Permits held by children entitle the holder to the right of education in primary and secondary educational institutions until the age of 18 without obtaining a Student Residence Permit.

Children who resided in Turkey at least three years before reaching the age of 18 can apply for a transition from a Family Residence Permit to their own Short-Term Residence Permit.

In order to be eligible for a Family Residence Permit, the Sponsor must:

- Have resided in Turkey for at least one year with a valid residence permit
- Have a monthly income not less than the Turkish minimum wage, plus no less than one third of the minimum wage per household member
- Have suitable accommodation
- Have medical insurance covering all household members
- Not have been convicted of any domestic violence or similar crimes within five years prior to the application
- Be registered with Turkish Address Registration System

Can you claim state healthcare on a Family Residence Permit?
No.

How much does it cost?
This depends on the type of permit. Don't forget that you'll also be paying Notarial and legal fees.

How long does it take?
Simple applications typically take about three to six weeks to process.

Student Residence Permits

Student Residence Permits are granted to foreigners who will be enrolled to graduate, undergraduate or two-year associate programs in licenced Turkish higher education institutions. The period that the Student Residence Permit is valid for cannot exceed the proposed duration of education.

Foreigners who wish to study in primary or secondary education facilities can be granted Student Residence Permits for a maximum of one year (renewable).

Both groups must apply within one month of entering Turkey.

Applications from foreigners who are subject to deportation or entry ban decisions will be rejected.

Student Residence Permits do not grant any residence rights to parents or other relatives.

Foreign students can legally work in Turkey after obtaining a Student Residence Permit. However, foreign students who are enrolled in undergraduate or two-year associate programs can start working in Turkey only after completing their first year of study. Students who are enrolled in two-year associate programs may not exceed 24 working hours per week.

Document checklist

Those applying for a Student Residence Permit for the first time should have:

- A Student Visa, obtained from the Turkish consulate in their home country

- A residence permit application form

- A tax number (obtained from the tax office - see page 248)

- Four passport-size photos

- An original passport and photocopies of the following pages of the passport: the page bearing the applicant's photo, the page stamped at the last entry, the page indicating the validity and expiry dates and the page bearing the student visa obtained from the consulate

- A valid and updated student enrolment certificate obtained from the Turkish school, college or university

- A bank statement showing sufficient funds to support the student during their stay in Turkey *or* a letter of undertaking from their parents *or*, if available, scholarship documents

- For students under 18 years old, a deed of consent from their parents. The deed of consent should be translated into Turkish, notarised and apostilled.

- Proof of valid health insurance - any of:
    - A document that shows the student is entitled to benefit from the health services in Turkey under a bilateral social security agreement
    - The certificate of cover received from the Social Security Institution
    - Proof of an application made for general health insurance to the Social Security Institution
    - Proof of adequate private health insurance

Can you claim state healthcare on a Student Residence Permit?
No.

How much does it cost?
This depends on the type of permit.

How long does it take?
Simple applications typically take about four to eight weeks to process.

Refugees from Syria

Turkey is a party to the 1951 Convention on the Status of Refugees.

However, Turkey's instrument of accession to the 1951 Convention limits the scope of the Convention's application to European asylum seekers. So, asylum seekers from (say) Syria or Iraq do not qualify.

Most refugees seeking asylum in Turkey are from non-European countries.

Turkey's Law on Foreigners and International Protection (2013) instituted major changes in the country's asylum system, but most current asylum seekers are placed under what is known as 'temporary protection', expecting them (eventually) to return home or settle in another country rather than being accepted as refugees for settlement in Turkey.

On 22 October 2014, the Turkish Council of Ministers issued a regulation on temporary protection, under Article 91 of the Law on Foreigners and International Protection. According to Article 1 of the Temporary Protection regulation, the regulation applies to Syrian nationals, as well as stateless persons and refugees from Syria: including those without identification documents.

Because of the influx of migrants from Syria (well over six million by April 2017), the Turkish authorities have, over the years, expanded their rights and protections; but they remain barred from gaining regular refugee status (and so being permanently permitted to stay in the country) and, instead, are classified as beneficiaries of temporary protection.

As part of the temporary protection regime, Syrian nationals, refugees and stateless persons from Syria seeking international protection are admitted to Turkey and will not be sent back to Syria against their will.

Under the terms of temporary protection, the authorities provide for refugees' basic needs and also furnish social services, translation services, IDs, travel documents, access to primary and secondary education, and work permits. Applicants for protection may be obliged by the authorities to live in designated reception and accommodation centres or in a specific location, and to report to the authorities in a certain manner or at certain intervals.

The responsibility for registration of Protected Persons is distributed among each city district's main police stations - to avoid waiting in long lines at one central location. The documentation required to obtain the new Protected Person ID was made simple: a rental contract along with any kind of proof of identification issued from Syria, such as a national ID card, army service booklets, family registration papers, Syrian driving licenses or even expired passports. No fees are required.

Other refugees - from Europe

There are very few of these.

Because of its location, refugees have been coming to Turkey for many centuries: long before the 1951 Geneva Convention created the official status of 'refugee'. Turkey is an original signatory of the Geneva Convention.

What is a refugee?

For refugees from Europe, Turkey accepts the definition of a refugee contained in the Geneva Convention:

"A person who owing to a well-founded fear of being persecuted for reasons of race, religion, nationality, membership of a particular social group or political opinion, is outside the country of his nationality and is unable or, owing to such fear, is unwilling to avail himself of the protection of that country."

Turkey also accepts the second limb of the convention's definition of a refugee as somebody:

". . . who, not having a nationality and being outside the country of his former habitual residence as a result of such events, is unable or, owing to such fear, is unwilling to return to it."

The difference between refugee status and asylum

An asylum seeker is somebody who is applying for refugee status. An asylum seeker who has been accepted as a genuine refugee is classed as a refugee.

How can somebody claim refugee status?

If a person wishes to claim refugee status in Turkey, he or she must do so immediately upon arrival in Turkey.

In practical terms, this means that - if they arrive by conventional means - they must do so at the point of entry and at the time of entering the country. If they arrive by unconventional means (for example, in a rubber dinghy or as a stowaway in the back of a lorry) they must claim refugee status within two working days of their arrival in the country.

Failure to claim will usually result in their being sent back to the country from which they came. However, this is subject to the restriction in the Convention that a government of a contracting state may not return a refugee to a territory where:

". . . his life or freedom would be threatened on account of his race, religion, nationality or membership of a particular social or political opinion."

Because of the number of recent applications from Syria, special arrangements have been put in place. These apply to applicants arriving after 2012. The applicant is issued with a "special protection card". See above.

What is the effect of claiming refugee status?

Once an asylum seeker applies for refugee status, their presence in the country is immediately made legal until the outcome of their application is determined. This is the case even if they arrived in the country illegally.

They immediately become entitled to health and social security benefits. After six months they can apply for a work permit.

Although their presence in Turkey is legal, they are not permitted to work until their claim is accepted and they are granted refugee status.

If the claim is allowed, the refugee will be allowed to remain in Turkey for a maximum of five years. If the circumstances that gave rise to their fear disappear or reduce within those five years, they may have to return home. If the circumstances continue, they can apply for a further permit to live in the country. This will be for another period of five years. If the circumstances at the end of that period still do not permit their safe return to their own country, they will be granted unlimited leave to remain in Turkey.

Once a person has been granted refugee status they will have the right to live, work and claim benefits in Turkey. They can then either work as an employee or for themselves. They also have the right to apply for their spouse and any children under the age of 18 to join them.

What if the claim is refused?

Subject to the restriction in relation to returning people to countries where their life or liberty is in danger, a failed asylum seeker - i.e. someone who is not granted refugee status - will be returned to their country of origin.

Legal advice

It is still rare for asylum seekers to seek legal advice. Most deal directly with the immigration services. This is understandable but, perhaps, foolish.

Humanitarian Residence Permits

A Humanitarian Residence Permit may be granted:

- If the best interests of a child are in question.

- If the departure of a foreigner from Turkey is not reasonable and possible, even if the foreigner is subjected to deportation or an entry ban decision.

- If the deportation decision may not be taken due to provisions of Article 55 of the Law on Foreigners and International Protection.

- During legal action taken against deportation decisions or rejected international protection applications.

- During the (often slow) process of returning international protection applicants to the country of first asylum or to a third safe country.

- For foreigners allowed to enter Turkey on the grounds of state interests or public order and public security, if no grounds for applying for another type of residence permit are available.

- In exceptional circumstances.

Holders of a Humanitarian Residence Permit should register on the Turkish Address Registration System within 20 days of being granted the residence permit.

The remits are valid for a maximum of one year (renewable).

Can you claim state healthcare on a Humanitarian Residence Permit?

You cannot claim state healthcare unless you are suffering from the effects of an epidemic.

How much does it cost?

Approximately TRY1,000 (about US$285/€245/£220). Fees are variable depending on nationalities.

How long does it take?

Simple applications typically take about four to eight weeks to process.

Long-Term Residence Permits

A foreigner may be eligible for a Long-Term Residence Permit, valid for an indefinite period, if they meet all the following criteria:

- They have resided in Turkey legally, with a valid residence permit, and without interruption for eight years

- They have not spent more than 180 days abroad in any year

- They have not received Social Help (Social Security) within the last three years

- They have adequate funds to support themselves and their family

- They have valid health insurance

- They have no criminal convictions and are not considered a threat to public order or security

If you later leave Turkey for more than one year, for any reason except health, education and compulsory public service, your Long-Term Residence Permit might be cancelled.

Foreigners who are classified as refugees, or foreigners who have residence permits issued for humanitarian purposes (or who are under temporary protection) are not eligible to apply for Long-Term Residence Permits.

Children born in the country

A child born in Turkey is entitled to stay in Turkey for as long as the residency period of their parent. A claim needs to be made within one month from the date of birth. After six months (or less, depending on the period of the parents' residency) the application for a residency permit should be made.

Such children are not automatically entitled to Turkish citizenship at birth. This right depends upon the mother of the child being a Turkish citizen or the father (as declared on the child's birth certificate and married to the mother) being a Turkish citizen. A Turkish father of a child born to a non-Turkish mother may also be granted citizenship for the child if the bloodline is proved through the courts.

Similar rules apply to adopted children.

A child may also later apply for Turkish nationality. They will need to show:

- They are mentally competent

- They have been resident (spent more than 180 days per year in the country) in Turkey for a period of five years immediately before the date of application

- Their intent to be a long-term resident in Turkey

- They have some knowledge of Turkey

- They have no serious disease of danger to others

- They are of good character

- They can speak "sufficient" Turkish: this is open to interpretation

- They have enough income, or the ability to earn enough income, to support themselves and their dependants

- That the grant of Turkish citizenship is "conducive to public good"

Settlement (and citizenship) by investment

One indirect but very useful way to get residency in Turkey is via its citizenship by investment programme. This is not just residence but full citizenship. As a citizen you do not require any type of residence permit.

The detailed rules about how it works have yet (March 2017) to be published but, in essence, it is designed to allow Turkey to give citizenship to investors who:

Make an 'approved investment'. This can be:

- Real estate: US$1million. You must keep the property for at least three years.

- Investment in a business:

    o US$2million as a long-term capital investment in a business. The minimum duration of this investment has not yet been defined. *OR;*

    o Employ 100 people in Turkey

- Bank deposit: US$3million, deposited in an approved bank account. You must keep the investment for at least three years.

- Government securities: US$3million. This must be in approved securities and it must be invested for a least three years.

Other requirements might be added.

We will update information about this visa on **www.guides.global** as more details become available.

How long does it last?
This will, generally, last for your lifetime.

How much does it cost?
We do not yet know.

How long does it take?
We do not yet know.

Legal advice
It is likely to be particularly important to seek professional advice when obtaining citizenship by investment.

Becoming a Turkish Citizen

A person born of Turkish parents can apply for citizenship (see above).

A person married to a Turkish citizen may apply for citizenship after three years of marriage. They do not need to have been resident in Turkey during this period.

Any other person over 18 who has legally been living permanently in Turkey (meaning for at least 183 days in each year) may apply for Turkish citizenship. This will, usually, be after five years' permanent residence. Such a person needs to prove that:

- They speak "sufficient" Turkish

- They show an intention, by their behaviour, of wanting to be a part of Turkey

- They have a basic understanding of Turkish history and culture

- They are of good character: basically, you have no criminal convictions or debts and you have paid your taxes

- They are mentally capable

- They are in good health - or, at least, not suffering from diseases that pose a danger to others

- They have enough income (or the means of earning it) to support themselves and any dependants. See above for what this means

- Granting citizenship should not pose a risk to public order.

Bringing Your Possessions

Written by **John Howell**
Editor & Founder of Guides.Global
www.guides.global • john.howell@guides.global

Furniture & household goods

Can a foreigner import possessions into Turkey?

Often. It depends upon their circumstances and what they want to import.

People may import their *used* possessions, that they have owned for at least six months, for their own personal (non-commercial) use, free of all import duties, provided that:

- They have a current residence visa (and have lived outside Turkey for at least 24 months) *or*;

- They are returning to Turkey having been posted away from Turkey on an international assignment *or*;

- They are bringing an inheritance into Turkey *or*;

- They own or have rented (for at least two years) a property in Turkey *and*;

- They agree to remove the possessions or pay all the relevant import duties if any of the above conditions cease to apply *and*;

- They complete the necessary paperwork (see below).

For EU citizens, since Turkey joined the Customs Union, things *should* be simple but, in practice, they are usually not. See **bit.ly/2rSOskt** (a PDF download) or **dhlguide.co.uk/export-to-turkey** for some idea of the complexity.

Whether you are an EU citizen or not, there are lots of detailed requirements and some restricted items.

Despite this, for most people who are going to live in Turkey, importing at least some of their possessions is a good idea. Remember you only get the opportunity to do this once.

You must apply for permission to import before you arrive in the country or within six months of your arrival.

There is lots of documentation required. It is best to use a specialist customs agent to help.

What should I import into Turkey?

There are a number of things you should take into account. We would suggest:

- As far as "white goods" (domestic refrigerators, washing machines etc.) are concerned, choose items that are on sale in Turkey - or be prepared to throw them away when they break, as you probably won't be able to get spare parts for them. This is less of an issue than it used to be as few people repair white goods these days; we're used to living in a throwaway society!

- Remember that some of your possessions will be ill-suited to your lifestyle in Turkey. For example, your heavy living room chairs will probably be far too warm for use in the warmer parts of Turkey.

- Household items can be large. This means that they are expensive to transport. It can sometimes be cheaper to buy a replacement when you arrive. This could apply, for example, to beds and wardrobes.

- Turkey's domestic electricity supply operates on 230 volts at 50Hz. This is the same as the system in most European countries and Australasia, and very similar to that used in many parts of Africa (220 volts at 50Hz), so electrical items from these places should work without modification. However, if you are coming from a 120 volt at 60Hz country (such as the US and Canada), none of your appliances will work! You can buy adaptors (step down transformers) to convert the voltage. You need one per appliance. These cost about TRY100 (US$30) - TRY700 (US$200) each (depending on the power required), so it is often more sensible to replace the product.

Many people find that the most sensible arrangement is to take with them only valuable items (such as antiques) which they 'can't live without', and which it may be difficult to replace; items of personal importance; clothing and small, expensive items.

How can a foreigner import possessions into Turkey?

The best way of doing this - by far - is to use a good removal company and customs agent. They will deal with all the paperwork on your behalf (they have systems for doing this which are different from those which you would have to follow) and they will have customs clearance to pass through any countries en route to Turkey.

An added reason to use a removal company is that they are far less likely to break your possessions in transit!

If you really don't want to use a removal company, then you can import your possessions yourself. In this case, the person making the application, or somebody having Power of Attorney on their behalf - usually their lawyer or a customs agent - must attend the offices of the Turkish Department of Customs when the goods arrive.

Please be aware that there may be no, or few, members of staff at the Customs office who speak English. You will almost certainly turn up when those that do are at lunch or on leave, so it's a good idea to have this done by someone who speaks Turkish!

Remember that most people coming to turkey overland will have to take their possessions through other countries in order to get to Turkey. You may need to produce paperwork for use when going through those countries in order to satisfy their customs officers. The advent of the Schengen agreement and an almost borderless Europe makes this problem a lot less serious than it used to be, but it can still be an issue.

Who can help?

As we have already said, go to a good removal company. Prices are surprisingly low. See **www.guides.global/books/turkey/tur-contacts.php** for a list of companies accustomed to transporting possessions to Turkey.

If you are not going to use a removal company and you need help with the paperwork involved in importing your possessions, there are two main options:

- Have a friend or neighbour make the application on your behalf. They will need a Power of Attorney. This can be prepared by your lawyer. The typical cost of a suitable Power is TRY600 (US$170). They will also need to speak Turkish.

- Employ a customs agent. These can be found by a Google search but it is much better to get a recommendation from your lawyer or the estate agent dealing with any property purchase on your behalf. The cost is likely to be about TRY1,200 (US$340).

Packing

You can either pack your goods yourself or you can have your possessions packed by an international removal company. Obviously, there is a cost associated with this service. However, it's probably money well spent. They are experts and are likely to pack things in such a way that they don't break. Not only are your goods more likely to reach the destination in one piece but, if they don't, there is far less likely to be an argument with your insurance company over who is responsible for the damage.

How long does it take?

If you're using a removal company, the length of time will depend upon whether or not you have a full load (or are prepared to pay a full load price). This is quite a lot of possessions; far more than most people wish to bring with them to Turkey. If you do have a full load, the process can be remarkably quick. Clearly, the time will depend upon the distance, the next sailing of a boat and the availability of trucks and drivers at either end. If you are coming from across the ocean - say, from the US or Singapore - the time factor will be greater. For example, Singapore and New York are each about 25 days sailing time from Istanbul. In these cases, you will probably want to put all your goods into a standard container - for most people a 20ft container is more than sufficient - and ship it as a private shipment to you alone. This is the most secure solution.

A very useful quick reckoner of the shipping time (and cost) between many cities in the world can be found at **www.searates.com**. This takes account of both the charges at the origin of the trip (getting the goods and container to the docks), the ocean or on-board charges (the actual cost of shipping the goods from Port A to Port B) and the charges at the destination (the cost of transportation from the docks to the final destination).

If you do not have a full load, then most removal companies will gather together shipments from several customers and transport them all, as a full load, at the same time. They might make such a trip to Turkey weekly or, more likely, monthly. It is worth checking with the company you intend to use how long it is likely to be before your load would be shipped.

Of course, you can also ship by air freight but this is many times more expensive as well as many times quicker.

Once your goods have arrived, you've assembled all the necessary documents and presented them to the Customs Department, the customs process will typically take just a few hours. If you are bringing the goods yourself, by car or van, it is better to obtain the paperwork before you arrive with your van, but it can be done upon arrival. Once your application has been approved you will be issued with an import permit, which is presented to the docks when you arrive with your possessions.

How much does it cost?

This depends on how you choose to do the work. See above.

There are three main ways of shipping your goods to Turkey as a conventional shipment (rather than bringing them yourself).

Full container load ("FCL")

The first is to send them, by sea, as a full container load.

TABLE: COST 20ft Container - March 2017

From	To	Cost
London	Istanbul	US$730
New York	Istanbul	US$1,400
Singapore	Istanbul	US$900

These prices are just the ocean freight or on-board charges.

On top of these charges you will or may face additional costs:

- Transporting the goods to the port of exit

- Port or terminal handling charges at the post of exit

- Documentation charges

- Customs clearance at your port of exit

- Charges for security at the port of exit

- A "bunker adjustment" - a surcharge to reflect current fuel costs

- A "currency adjustment" - a surcharge to reflect changes in exchange rates

- Handling charges at the destination port

- Documentation fees at the destination port

- Customs fees at the destination port

- Security at the destination port

- Taxes and customs duties at the destination port

- Transportation of the goods from the destination port to their final destination.

To make matters worse, different companies quote for shipping work in different - and inconsistent - ways.

Part load / Less than container load ("LCL") / Groupage shipping

The second method would be to ship - again, by sea - as a part consignment. This means that you would leave your goods with the shippers or removal company, who would keep them until they received other goods from other people sufficient to make up a full load, or until their next scheduled shipment. This can be quite a lot cheaper but, of course, it could be quite some time before you receive your possessions.

This type of shipping is usually charged on a "weight or measure" basis: a charge per cubic metre or per 1,000kilos.

With this type of shipping you need to know that latest arrival date for your goods. It is not acceptable to leave them "until we have a full load".

Air

The fourth method is to ship the goods as an urgent shipment by air. This is considerably more expensive but sometimes not as ridiculously expensive as you might first expect. This is particularly so if you can take advantage of last-minute availability.

However, if you can't get some sort of discount, you could expect to pay about TRY50 (US$14) per kg from the UK and TRY70 (US$20) per kg for a shipment from the US - both of which would also be subject to limits on the weight per cubic metre which, for air travel, is more important than the physical size of the package.

Remember that you will still face handling charges etc. and the cost of getting the goods to and from your airports of choice.

Conclusions

This is all a bit complicated and it is work that, generally, needs to be done when you are busy doing other things. Keep things simple by leaving shipping to the experts and by using one company to take charge of the operation "from door to door". This is less likely to go wrong and it is often also cheaper.

Cars

In Turkey, cars and fuel are expensive. The price of a car, both new and second-hand, is likely to be much higher than 'back home'.

It therefore looks an attractive option, especially if you live in Europe, to take your car to Turkey. An added advantage is that you can use the trip to take some of your possessions with you. Can this be done? Does it actually make sense?

Bringing your car to Turkey temporarily

It is possible to drive to Turkey via Bulgaria or Greece, or via Italy (with a ferry to Turkey).

As a tourist, you can bring your car into Turkey. You can then keep it with you for up to six months, after which it must leave the country for at least six months. Only you can drive it whilst it is in Turkey.

At the border you will need to provide:

- A valid passport

- Your international driving licence

- Your vehicle licence documents

- An international green card (insurance)

- Your vehicle registration details

Your car should also have an international identification plate or sticker on its rear: e.g. a GB or F sticker. This is so even if you have a European registration plate incorporating your country identifier. See our Driving in Turkey section (page 123) for more information.

Turkey does not require a *"carnet de passage en douane"*: an international customs guarantee.

Check if your insurance is valid for the Asian side of the country.

If the vehicle belongs to someone else, a Power of Attorney will be required, under which they authorise you to drive the car. In practice, it can make your life much more complicated if you try to bring a car belonging to another person or a company.

Failure to remove the car leads to heavy fines.

Can a foreigner permanently import a car into Turkey?

In some cases, yes. However, it is not very simple.

Foreign-plated vehicles can only be brought into Turkey on an Alien Vehicles Temporary Entry Card (*Yabancı Taşıtlar Geçici Giriş Belgesi* - YTGGK). This card, also referred to as the Blue Card, can be obtained from the Turkish Touring and Automobile Union - Turing (**www.turing.org.tr**).

They are granted a 'blue plate'. Just to confuse you, the colour of the plate is no longer blue, just like an American 'green card' is no longer green.

The vehicle may only be used for your own private use. It must be registered at your (Turkish) residential address under the name of:

- A retired foreign citizen who has a temporary residence permit

- A person resident outside Turkish Customs who is in Turkey to carrying out a specific work assignment

- A person present in Turkey for the purpose of education

Required documents

Retired foreigners

- Your Residence Permit (started to be for the purposes of retirement)

- A document issued by your home state social security institution, showing that you are retired and certified by a notary public or Turkish consulate, together with a Turkish translation

- Your passport and driving license (together with photocopies)

- Your vehicle registration documents

- A delivery receipt for the vehicle, from the Customs Directorate

- A financial guarantee covering the potential liability to import duties if the vehicle is not removed, the size of the guarantee depending upon the engine capacity, and the age of the vehicle. This will require a bank guarantee from your bank. Contact **triptik@turing.org.tr** for details of what will be required

- The application form, completed and signed by owner of the vehicle. This is obtainable from the association's website

Foreign employees

- Your Residence Permit (stated to be for the purpose of working)

- Your passport and driving licence (together with photocopies)

- A photocopy of your work permit, certified

- Your vehicle registration documents

- A letter from your employer, addressed to the association, on letterheaded paper and signed, specifying your employment duties and their duration

- The employer-company's "signature circular", with a photocopy. This is the official document used in Turkey to confirm that the signatories produced are duly authorised

- A delivery receipt for the vehicle, from the Customs Directorate

- A financial guarantee covering the potential liability to import duties if the vehicle is not removed, the size depending upon the engine capacity and age of the vehicle. This will require a bank guarantee from your bank. Contact **triptik@turing.org.tr** for details of what will be required

- The application form, completed and signed by owner of the vehicle. This is obtainable from the association's website

Foreigners receiving education

- Your Residence Permit (stated to be for the purposes of education)

- A Student Certificate, issued by the school or college, addressed to the Association

- Your passport and driving licence (together with photocopies)

- Your vehicle registration documents

- A delivery receipt for the vehicle, from the Customs Directorate

- A financial guarantee covering the potential liability to import duties if the vehicle is not removed, the size depending upon the engine capacity and age of the vehicle. This will require a bank guarantee from your bank. Contact **triptik@turing.org.tr** for details of what will be required

- The application form, completed and signed by owner of the vehicle. This is obtainable from the association's website

Known issues

The YTGGK is limited to one or two years, as the term will not exceed the length of the residence permit and (if there is one), the work permit. It is very important (to avoid financial penalties) to apply for an extension before the YTGGK expires.

Certified translations by the Turkish consulate or a Notary Public are required for all vehicle licenses which are not issued in multilingual form.

The person who obtains a YTGGK from the Association should take it, first, to the

Customs Office and then to the Traffic Department Directorate for the province where the vehicle is located.

To be able to recover the deposited security, the vehicle must be definitively re-exported and the YTGGK should be returned to the Turkey Touring and Automobile Association - *after* the completion of the paperwork by the relevant Traffic Department and Customs.

Should I buy a new car to import into Turkey?

If you are thinking of buying a new car to bring with you - something we recommend - we would suggest:

- The newer the car the more valuable it will be, and so the financial guarantee you must provide will be higher.

- Choose a car with the steering wheel on the left-hand side: in Turkey they drive on the right! A wheel on the left is massively safer.

- Choose a car that is available for sale in Turkey. This will make maintenance much easier.

- Choose a car with readily available and inexpensive parts.

- If you will be driving a lot, choose a car with good fuel consumption: fuel is expensive in Turkey. An LPG (Autogas) car will be much cheaper to run.

Who can help me do all this?

If you need help with importing your car into Turkey, there are three main options:

- Have a friend or neighbour make the application on your behalf. They will need a Power of Attorney. This can be prepared by your lawyer. The typical cost of a Power of Attorney is TRY600 (US$170).

- Employ a customs agent. These can be found by a Google search but it is much better to get a recommendation from your lawyer or the estate agent dealing with any property purchase on your behalf. The cost is likely to be about TRY1,200 (US$340).

- Use your lawyers, if they offer this service. This will also probably cost about TRY1,200 (US$340).

How long does it take?

Once you've assembled all the documents and presented them to the customs agent, the process typically takes six weeks, though it can take much longer.

How much does it cost?

This depends on how you choose to do the work. See above.

Boats

Many expats keep a boat in Turkey.

There are several ways in which they can do so.

Temporary visits to Turkey

Boats must be imported via a 'frontier port': Akçay, Alanya, Anamur, Antalya, Ayvalik, Bandirma, Bartin, Bodrum, Botas, Bozyazi, Canakkale, Cesme, Datca, Derince, Didim, Dikili, Eregli, Fethiye, Finike, Gemlik, Giresun, Güllük, Hopa, Inebolu, Iskenderun, Istanbul, Izmir, Kas, Kemer, Kusadasi, Marmaris, Mersin, Mudanya, Ordu, Rize, Samsun, Sinop, Tasucu, Tekirdag, Trabzon and Zonguldak.

The entire crew must have passports valid for the length of their proposed stay in Turkey and a valid visa - either tourist or long-term.

There are no official charges on entry or departure except the purchase of a Yacht Registration Form (Transit Log) upon arrival. This contains information about the boat and its crew.

You will need to complete this form in accordance with the explanations given in it and you will need to go through the customs and other procedures as explained in it. The cost, for foreign flagged private boats, is US$35 and it is valid for one year.

This transit log allows a yacht to travel freely in Turkish waters. It may be inspected by any harbour official at any time.

As long as the captain and crew remain the same on such trips, you can sail freely to the bays and towns on your route (except forbidden areas) without the need to go through any formalities. If any change occurs between ports, in terms of your captain or crew, you must apply to the Director of Port in your area and obtain a confirmation for the change.

Foreign-flagged private yachts belonging to more than one owner, and yachts belonging to an association or a yacht club, may be used by no more than four keepers in any year.

On leaving Turkey the Transit Log is cancelled and, at the same time, an exit stamp is entered in your passport.

Staying longer

If you are in Turkey with your yacht and you wish to extend your stay, then you will need to obtain a marina or a mooring place licensed by the Ministry of Tourism. This will be your official address and place of residence in Turkey and, after you notify the authorities of the address, you will be granted an extension.

Of course, you can still use your boat to visit other places.

Foreign-flagged yachts can remain in Turkey up to five years (up to the length remaining on your residence permit) without a requirement for any other permission, on condition that they are sailed by their owners at least once every two years.

You can leave Turkey by other means of transport during this period after you leave your yacht at a marina or a moorage licensed by the Ministry of Tourism.

Tax-free diesel

Foreign-registered yachts may obtain tax-free diesel fuel:

- Tax-free fuel will be available for use only in foreign yachts and must be obtainable only from marinas and shipyards licensed by the Turkish Ministry of Tourism.

- The owner of the yachts may be Turkish or foreign but must be a person having a permanent place of residence outside Turkey.

- The yacht may be brought to Turkey with the owner or may be brought two months earlier or later than the owner's arrival in Turkey.

- The yacht may receive tax-free fuel only in the presence of the owner.

Pets

Many people worry more about how they're going to take their pet to Turkey than they do about any other aspect of their move.

Fortunately, the rules aren't complicated and most people don't experience any major problems when importing a pet into Turkey.

Coming from a country in the Pet Passport Scheme

The Pet Passport Scheme (PPS), officially known as the Pet Travel Scheme, was introduced to provide a uniform set of rules for people travelling with certain types of pet within the EU. It has since been adopted by other countries.

The rules apply to dogs, cats and… ferrets.

There will be no quarantine imposed on your pet when entering Turkey as long as the following requirements are met.

1. Your pet must first be microchipped with an ISO 11784 pet microchip that is a 15 digit and non-encrypted device. If your pet's microchip is not ISO 11784 compliant, you can bring your own microchip scanner for use by the authorities.

2. Your pet cat or dog must be vaccinated against rabies between 30 days and 12 months prior to its entry into Turkey. An original rabies certificate reflecting all of your pet's rabies vaccinations should accompany your pet.

3. In order to avoid three months of home quarantine, no sooner than 30 days after the rabies vaccination is given, your pet should have a rabies titer (blood) test, with the sample processed in an EU-approved laboratory at least 90 days

prior to entering Turkey. If your pet has not received a rabies titer test or 90 days have not passed since the date the blood was drawn for the titer test, your pet will be subject to home quarantine for the duration of the 90 day period.

    a. Although Turkish regulations clearly state that a blood titer test or other proof of anti-rabies titer level is required, presently, enforcement of this requirement appears inconsistent.

    b. You should consider your travel needs when making your decision as to whether to have the test performed, but entering with valid rabies titer test results will ease and speed customs clearance and may alleviate the requirement for home quarantine.

    c. The titer test is valid for travel to the European Union from Turkey as well as to other countries as long as the sample is processed in an EU approved lab and your pet's rabies vaccinations do not expire.

    d. Traveling with a titer test is the ultimate proof to customs officials that your pet is free of rabies, but it appears that currently, the requirement is, in effect, 'optional' when entering Turkey.

4. Within the ten days before travel, an accredited vet must complete the Veterinary Certificate for Turkey for endorsement by the Governing Authority of your country responsible for the import and export of animals. The vet should have access to the appropriate paperwork.

5. All domestic dogs and cats must be free of evidence of disease communicable to humans when examined at the port of entry to Turkey. If your dog or cat is not in apparent good health, further examination by a licensed veterinarian may be required - of course, at your expense. Your pet should arrive at customs by 11:30AM for same day customs clearance.

6. Two pets per person can enter tax-free as long as they don't arrive unaccompanied. The owner must be present at customs clearance or have issued their representative with both a Power of Attorney and either their original passport or a notarized copy, indicating that they arrived in Turkey within 30 days of their pet.

7. Puppies and kittens under three months of age can enter Turkey with their mother, provided that she meets the requirements above *or* if they come from a state in which rabies is known to be controlled, with a document which states where the puppy or kitten was born and reared and that it is an environment where it has not been in contact with wild animals. Additionally, an endorsed veterinary certificate and health declaration stating that your pet is healthy enough to travel, is free of diseases communicable to humans and is free of internal and external parasites is required. Prior permission from the Ministry is required. The owner's passport should be available at the time the import is processed.

8. Other animals

    a. Birds are permitted entry with an import permit.

    b. Invertebrates, tropical fish, reptiles, amphibia, and mammals such as rodents and rabbits are not subject to the requirements of rabies vaccination, but may have to meet other requirements and should have a health certificate to enter Turkey.

    c. Pet owners are strongly advised to seek further information from the relevant authority of their country and/or, if they are leaving Turkey, the authority of the country of destination.

    d. If your pet is not a dog, cat or ferret, and especially if it is a turtle or parrot, you should verify that it is not protected under the Convention on International Trade in Endangered Species of Wild Fauna and Flora (CITES). You will need to apply for additional permits if this is the case. Over 180 countries participate and enforce CITES regulations.

9. Turkey has adopted the EU Equine Passport Regulation for the importation of horses from the EU. For imports from non-EU countries, other rules apply. They are a little complex and, if we are to keep this book to a sensible length, must be beyond the scope of this book. Contact one of the big international horse transport companies for more details.

Bringing Your Money

Written by **Burak Orkun**
Managing Partner (Accountancy Department) at Orkun & Orkun
www.orkunorkun.com • info@orkunorkun.com

When you move to Turkey you will have a major decision to make about what to do with your money. Obviously, your day-to-day expenses will be in Turkish lira, but it will probably be that all or part of your income will be coming to you in another currency; and it will almost certainly be that your savings and investments will be in another currency.

How do you deal with this? Should you bring your money with you when you come to Turkey or is it better to leave all or part of it 'back home'?

Should you bring your money with you?

The most important factor in deciding whether or not to bring your money with you is whether you are going to be remaining in Turkey on a permanent (or, at least, a very long-term) basis.

If you are making Turkey your new home, then there is a lot to be said for thinking about your finances in Turkish lira terms. This means measuring your income, expenditure and wealth in Turkish lira rather than in the currency of your former home. This tends to be easier (and more realistic) than notionally converting your expenses back into your 'own' currency.

This way, your income and savings will be measured in the same currency as you are spending, but it doesn't solve the problem that, if your income comes in a foreign currency or your wealth is stored in a foreign currency, your spending power in Turkey will vary enormously (and over a very short period) if exchange rates change. And change they do: literally, by the minute.

If you have monthly living expenses of (say) TRY6,000 but you are receiving most of your income measured in (say) British pounds, you are very exposed if the exchange rate changes dramatically. A quick look at the last few years highlights the problem. During the last ten years, there have been times when one British pound was worth over TRY4.8 and there have been times when it has been worth as little as TRY2.2. This means that, if you enjoyed a rock-solid income of £3,000 per month, you would sometimes have had only TRY6,600 available to spend whilst, at other times, you would have had TRY14,400 available to you. This, of course, makes a dramatic difference to your lifestyle.

Now, if you are receiving a pension or a salary from another country it may be that there is little you can do about receiving it in Turkish lira - except, of course, by exchanging the money when it arrives.

However, if you are exposed to this risk, it increases the risk still further if your savings and investments are kept in British pounds: unless you think the pound is going to continue to rise in value against the Turkish lira. Predicting future exchange rates is, in my experience, all but impossible.

If you are going to be living in Turkey long-term, it seems to me to make sense to reinvest all or part of those savings in investments denominated and measured in Turkish lira. Choosing what those investments should be requires careful thought and, usually, some good advice.

Interest rates offered by banks in Turkey are considerably higher than in most Western European countries: roughly 13% if you are investing in Turkish lira, though only 4% if you are investing in US dollars (September 2017).

When making these decisions, remember the historic volatility of the Turkish lira (see page 10).

If you are wealthy enough to have a large sum to invest, then there may well be good arguments for diversifying the currencies in which you hold those investments. For example, you might decide to keep a portion of your wealth in Turkish lira but hedge against the risk of the lira falling in value against other currencies by having parts of your investments in US dollars, Euro, British pounds, Japanese yen etc.

Again, this decision has huge implications for your financial security and you should make it after taking appropriate advice.

See the section on investments on page 477 for more about these choices.

Many people decide to keep some money 'back home' even though they fully intend to make a new life in Turkey. Often, they will visit 'home' on a fairly regular basis and it can be very convenient to have a local bank account, credit card etc. Some seem to suffer from amnesia when it comes to declaring the money they receive in these bank accounts to the tax authorities here in Turkey! This is, of course, illegal.

If you do not intend to stay in Turkey on a long-term basis, then it is almost certainly better to keep all or a large part of your wealth denominated in the currency of the country to which you intend to return. This, of course, is subject to the general point that if you have substantial wealth you may want to spread your investments between various currencies as part of your general investment strategy.

One problem that arises regularly and which makes your planning more difficult is that a percentage of people come to Turkey - either to retire or to work - thinking that it is going to be a permanent move, but then find that their job comes to an end, their business does not prosper or that they do not like living in this lovely country. If they have moved their investments into Turkish lira and then move back home, they face the same problem in reverse - and so it's probably a good idea to let your plan develop over time and not to immediately jump into the process of reorganizing your entire financial life.

Case study

Peter Banks

Retiree, English, 70

The problem

This is a very recent case! When the UK held a referendum on leaving the EU - and voted for 'Brexit' - Peter found that his British pension and investments (all in British pounds) were suddenly worth a lot less to him in Turkey, as the pound plummeted in value: from £1 = TRY4.3 to £1 = TRY3.8. In fact, he had about 15% less to spend.

The solution

Sadly, there wasn't really a good way out of this mess. Acting when the exchange rates were still volatile, and everyone was panicking, would have meant a terrible deal, whatever Peter did. He would tighten his belt and wait until things stabilise before diversifying.

The only good news is that he felt it likely that, once everything has settled down, that the pound could gain a little in strength against the Turkish lira, but our analysts thought that this could take some time.

As it happened, there was a bit of a rather sad silver lining. The problems in Turkey (the Syria war, terrorism and some political uncertainty) meant that the Turkish lira fell in value even more substantially than the British pound. The rate - and so the amount of the pension he receives in his Turkish bank account - is now (at £1 = TRY4.6) even more favourable than it was pre-Brexit, so his income in Turkish lira has actually increased! Peter has still to decide what to do long-term.

This is a good lesson for our readers. When you move to Turkey, see a financial adviser and make sure you don't have all your eggs in one basket. If you are going to be living in Turkey long-term, try to make sure at least a good part of your income will come to you in lira.

What do I mean by "over time"? Typically, I would suggest that you might want to leave things for a year or two before making any major decisions as to your future investment plans. You will probably want to move some funds to Turkey during this period, but you should not leap into moving all of your money.

It can also be a good idea, if you know you're going to be moving to Turkey and that you will be dependent upon income paid in another currency, to look at fixing an exchange rate for a year or two. Of course, by fixing the rate, you may win, or you may lose, depending on what happens to the value of your currency against the Turkish lira - but you will at least have the certainty of knowing your financial position for the fixed period. A good foreign exchange (FX) dealer should be able to help you to do this and also arrange for the funds to be transferred to your Turkish bank account, monthly or quarterly, in the most cost-effective way possible.

Of course, if you believe that your home currency is going to crash in value against the Turkish lira during the forthcoming year, you might be tempted to jump ship now rather than to suffer significant loss later. Whether to do this is a decision that only you can make, and you will probably find that you can get little guidance from your financial adviser; they tend not to be in the business of forecasting the movements of exchange rates.

Probably the most important thing is that, if you do decide to allow a bit of time to go past before finalising your plan, you should make a diary note and act when that period has expired.

So much for the theory. However, when it comes to deciding whether to move your money, there may be a couple of very practical points that will have a big impact on your decision.

It is likely that you will have chosen many of your investments because they are tax-efficient in your own country. If you're no longer tax resident in that country, then those investments will probably lose all their tax benefits. Stripped bare, they could look like very poor investments indeed. In these cases, it is probably prudent to think about reinvesting as soon as possible - and the funds from these investments are probably the prime candidates for the money that you will immediately bring with you to Turkey.

You should also not forget that some of your present investments back home may simply not be permitted to people who are no longer resident in your old country. It may be illegal for somebody living in Turkey, even if they still hold their original passport, to hold those investments. These, too, will therefore need your urgent attention. This will involve discussions with your financial advisers back home. In fact, the best course of action is usually either to have your financial adviser in Turkey coordinate the whole exercise and contact your financial adviser back home on your behalf, or to have your financial adviser back home coordinate the whole exercise and contact your adviser in Turkey. Which works best will depend upon your person circumstances: usually upon where you have or will have most of your investments.

One final point when it comes to thinking about your investment plans is that you should not be worried about relocating your investments. There are many excellent investment opportunities in Turkey and, of course, whilst you are living in Turkey you are at liberty to invest anywhere in the world that takes your fancy.

The trouble is that, however canny you are as an investor and however well you understand your investment portfolio back home, you're unlikely to know very much about the options available to you in Turkey and elsewhere, and so you will need good financial advice when it comes to making these decisions.

Where do you get that advice? The most important thing is to make sure that you are dealing with a bona fide qualified and registered financial adviser. Better still, it should ideally be somebody who has already given satisfactory service to people you know. It should also be somebody with whom you feel comfortable.

Getting your money to Turkey

First of all, please don't bring a suitcase of cash with you to Turkey. Those days are long gone. Turkish Customs have imposed a limit of TRY25,000 (around €10,000) for cash taken out of the country. There is no such limit *into* the country, but it is subject to declaration, and the source of the money might be questioned by the customs authorities. There may also be limits as to the amount you can take out of your own country.

Aside from that, the most important thing to remember is that only a fool (or someone with money to burn) uses their ordinary bank to transfer money to another country. The savings you can make by using a good foreign exchange (FX) dealer can be huge: 1% or more of the amount that you're transferring.

See our chapter on moving money and foreign exchange (page 112).

If you are looking to transfer your money back *out* of Turkey, please bear in mind that bank transfers of over US$50,000 from Turkey to any other country require the sender to declare the transfer to the Turkish finance authorities. Large amounts of money transferred will also often (depending upon where you live) have to be declared in your own country.

What to do with it when the money arrives

The way in which you should reinvest your funds is, of course, entirely up to you and the best choice depends upon your personal circumstances.

Many reputable and qualified financial advisers in Turkey offer a free initial consultation so that you can explore, at least a little, some of the options that might be available to you. Just as importantly, it gives you the opportunity to decide whether you could work with this person and them the opportunity to decide whether they would like to have you as a client. These meetings are completely without obligation on either side. They will not be detailed enough to allow you to make an investment plan but they will help point you in the right direction.

Turkish sources of such advice are pretty much limited to the investment departments of the major banks. Even they tend not to have a very international perspective on your options.

There are a number of international companies that specialise in providing investment advice for people with a foot in two or more countries. Choose them with care. Some are excellent. Some are crooks. The best way to choose is by personal recommendations. Wherever possible, take references from satisfied clients.

Even if you've made the decision not to make any final dispositions of your investments until a year or so after you've arrived in Turkey, it's probably a good idea to get the ball rolling by seeing a financial adviser (in Turkey or back home) as soon as possible after you arrive in the country. Perhaps it is even better to see them before you depart your old home as there are lots of temporary and beneficial opportunities that can arise only at the moment you make the move.

What are You Likely to Miss Once You've Moved?

People miss different things, but everybody misses something from 'back home'. It is usually a food item.

Amongst British expats there is the strange cult of the Marmite lover. Even those who never dreamt of eating Marmite before leaving England claim to be addicted to the stuff. Amongst Americans, it is good old fashioned French's mustard. For Australians, it is meat pies. For the French, there is a long list but, usually, the humble baguette comes out top - often followed by semi-salted butter.

Some of these items can never be found outside their home country but, these days, you really don't need to miss out on many things as there is a wealth of shops in Turkey specialising in providing home comforts for those from different countries and - very recently - most of the main supermarkets have set up an aisle dedicated to food from around the world.

Whilst you can probably obtain almost any item that you want, you will usually find it to be considerably more expensive than back home. As a result, people tend to ask their visitors to bring supplies of these very important items.

Apart from food, most people miss other aspects of their former life: people who speak their language as natives, green spaces, a familiar administrative system etc. By the time you leave Turkey, you will miss many aspects of life in Turkey! Often, the main things missed are the tea and the organised chaos.

Living in Turkey

The Culture

Written by **John Howell** Editor & Founder of Guides.Global www.guides.global • john.howell@guides.global

Moving to or doing business in another country always throws up issues arising from the basic cultural differences between your 'home' country and the 'new' country. Turkey is no exception.

While the cultural differences between (say) the UK or the US and Turkey are nowhere near as great as they are between those places and (say) China, Nigeria or Saudi Arabia, they are still significant and they can still give rise to completely avoidable problems if you don't understand them and know how to deal with them.

Of course, these cultural differences are also part of what makes moving to or doing business in Turkey so fascinating. They should also be understood but not feared. Turks are very welcoming. All you need to do is meet them half (or even part) way!

Getting to understand another country's culture is not about learning lists of cultural facts or creating tick-lists of things that you need to do when working with people from that country. It is about gaining an understanding of the country and how it works and then proceeding sensitively in your dealings with the country and its people. However, a few paragraphs pointing out some of the key features of Turkish culture are a good starting point for this, very enjoyable, journey of discovery.

The people

Turkish people are, by nature and tradition, very friendly. Neighbours will stop in the street to have conversations. Your plumber will find it strange if you do not engage in conversation and, if he's there all day, if you don't provide some food and drink.

Despite this friendliness, they can still be reserved. I have been working in Turkey for 12 years, and doing business with the same people for most of that time: yet I have still not been invited to many of their homes.

Partly, this is because the Turks are exceptionally good hosts, and very proud of it.

If they invite someone over for the first time, it must be perfect - or they won't bother.

This means four to five main courses, with sides, desserts, soup etc.; and as many Turkish men don't know their way around a kitchen as well as our accountant partner Burak, this leaves a lot on the shoulders of the woman of the household, who may well also be working full time.

Once you've been invited over once, and this 'ceremony' is over, you will likely be invited more frequently for "tea visits" or even just to sit with some takeaway pizza.

On top of these constraints, there is a cultural difference in social norms. To explain this, I use Kurt Lewin's concept of cultural differences, which is based on the differences between the peach and the coconut.

Peach cultures produce people who are 'soft' on the outside yet, within each person, is a hard shell which prevents you getting too close to them until they are ready for you. Coconut cultures produce people who are 'hard' on the outside but - if you break through a person's outer shell - there is no further obstacle to getting to know them really well. This is not an either/or choice. There is a continuum of cultural attitudes.

The peach is a culture in which you get to know people quickly and find it easy to become connected with them.

They smile at you. You share a joke. You share a drink. You socialise. You drill through the soft fruit so that you become integrated into their lifestyle - until you reach the stone. At that point, your integration comes to an abrupt halt and it takes a long time - often a very long time - for you to be fully accepted and allowed through the hard shell of the stone into the real centre of their world.

The coconut, on the other hand, is a society where getting to know people can be very difficult at the early stage.

People do not readily socialise. They can be formal. They do not meet casual colleagues for drinks after work. They are reserved and independent. Breaking through the hard outer shell of the coconut takes time but, once you have done that, you are completely accepted and there is no further obstacle to getting to the very centre of their lives.

Traditionally, the US and Japan are considered to be 'peach' societies. Germany and Russia are thought to be 'coconuts'.

Turkey is more of a coconut society. Hence my not visiting many of my fellow-workers' homes.

I wouldn't want to take this analogy too far but it does give a convenient and easy to grasp overview of the cultural flavour of Turkey.

Of course, another vital aspect of the people in Turkey is that they speak Turkish.

Relatively few ordinary people in the countryside speak any other language.

Learning Turkish is not easy - but highly recommended if you're going to live in Turkey, and very useful if you're going to do business there. If you don't learn Turkish, it will be much more difficult to integrate into Turkish society and you will never feel quite in control of your life or your business. Nor can you enjoy life to the full.

Whilst talking about the people we should not forget that the residents of Turkey include many foreigners.

Excluding refugees, over 1.6million foreigners live in Turkey. They are found at all

Turkey: how things *really* work

levels of society and in all walks of life: bankers, gardeners, the retired, taxi drivers and waiters.

They, of course, tend to maintain the cultural values of their own country but gradually absorb some of the features of life in Turkey. One of the earliest that they adopt is a certain flexibility when it comes to timekeeping!

The number of expats in Turkey

These numbers exclude refugees.

Place of birth	Number (2015)	Place of birth	Number (2015)
Bulgaria	378,658	Turkmenistan	24,937
Germany	263,318	USA	24,026
Iraq	97,528	Kazakhstan	21,546
Syria	76,413	Ukraine	20,547
Azerbaijan	52,836	Cyprus & Northern Cyprus	20,402
Macedonia	43,400	Austria	18,609
Afghanistan	38,692	Kyrgyzstan	17,235
Iran	36,226	Libya	16,442
Uzbekistan	36,083	Saudi Arabia	14,573
Russia	34,486	Moldova	13,472
Holland	32,345	Switzerland	13,453
UK	32,140	China	12,426
France	28,507	Romania	9,512
Greece	26,928	Serbia & Montenegro	9,201
Belgium	26,531	Albania	2,488
Georgia	25,019	**Total**	**1,592,437**

Names

Turkish names consist of one or more given names (*isimler*) and a surname (*soyisim*).

Married women may, if they wish, use both their maiden name and their husband's surname.

The surname is written as the last element of the full name, after all the given names.

Official documents and indices use the format "*Soyisim, Isim*" Surname, Given Names. Or, alternatively, "*soyadı, adı*".

When addressing a Turk, traditionally the most common method was to call a man by his first name followed by the respectful '*Bey*' (pronounced bay and meaning mister or leader). So, Burak Orkun would be *Burak Bey*. Similarly a woman's first name would be followed by '*Hanım*' (pronounced ha-num and meaning lady), so our author Başak would be *Başak Hanım*.

This is now rather old fashioned, yet it's still a nice touch upon first meeting an older person. It shows some knowledge of Turkish culture and a little respect. You can quickly pick up what is expected in a particular situation by listening to what others do.

If you do not know a person's name (and when answering the phone), a generic '*efendim*' (sir or madam) is often used.

Where a person has a professional title (such as engineer: '*Muhendis*'), always use the title either on its own or before the mode of address. So, for example, "Yes, *Muhendis*, I am coming" or "Yes, *Muhendis* Bey, I am coming"

Meeting people

When meeting a person, shake hands firmly. When departing it is not usual to shake hands.

Friends and relations greet each other with either one or two kisses on the cheek.

When entering a room, if you are not approached by someone, greet the most elderly or most senior person first. At social occasions greet the person closest to you then work your way around the room or table, anti-clockwise.

Personal relationships

Despite its size, Turkey is an intimate country.

Transactions, from buying a loaf of bread to hiring a builder or signing up with a bank, are *personal*. They *matter*, and people enter into them prepared to spend a little more time on the social niceties than you might expect 'back home'. They also often do so with rather more sense that is important to behave fairly and honourably in your dealings with other people.

One consequence of the personal nature of relationships in Turkey is that, if you know the right person, you can often fix almost anything - and quickly.

Gifts

The Turks do not make a big thing about making gifts. The main exception would be if you were invited to a Turk's home for dinner. The most usual gifts to take are pastries, (especially '*baklava*') and decorative items for the home such as ornaments or vases. However, if you are a foreigner it is nice to give something from your own country.

Flowers are not usually taken to a host, but you can do this.

Turkey: how things *really* work

Turkey is, of course, a Muslim country. Before giving alcohol, be sure that they drink!

Animals

Keeping pet animals is rare amongst Turks. Historically, many might have had a working animal such as a dog or a donkey but, when they moved to the towns and cities, that did not translate into keeping them as pets. Some traditionalists would find keeping a pet - especially a dog and especially indoors - religiously inappropriate.

By contrast, about 20% of foreigners living in Turkey keep pets - mainly dogs and cats.

Most Turkish people readily accept the fact that their foreign neighbours keep a pet and they will be quite friendly towards it - if a little bemused by your wish to go to all this trouble.

Because of the number of farm animals in Turkey, and the increasing number of foreign residents, there are many vets operating in Turkey. For details, see the Turkish Veterinary Medical Association (**www.tvhb.org.tr**).

Negotiation

There are two aspects to this: when to negotiate, and how to do it.

Turkey is not like some countries, where no deal is ever done and people will be trying to change its terms right up to the moment you are signing over title to your property, or long after you have signed a contract to supply goods or services.

Yet negotiation is still important: not so much when dealing with big brands but, definitely, when buying large items from a local supplier. Incidentally, most people do not now negotiate over small items.

Most newcomers are dependent upon their professional advisers - mainly their lawyers - or their Turkish speaking friends to help them out when negotiating.

But once a deal is done, it is done.

Obeying the rules

This doesn't come naturally! Whether it is queuing or shouting at a police officer who has issued you with a parking ticket, Turks have a saying: "legal rules only exist to be broken".

Queueing

Turkish people seem not to have the queueing gene. Forming an orderly queue has, traditionally, been an alien concept. When there is competition for a service or a space, they have always seen it as a great opportunity to practice their combat skills!

However, those days are rapidly disappearing. It looks like Turks have learned the advantage of the queue from their foreign visitors and so now you will find a very orderly line of people waiting for taxis at the airport and even when waiting to buy tickets for a football match or to pay at the supermarket.

The administration

People complain about the administration in Turkey. They talk about delay. They talk about inefficiency. They talk about a bureaucratic mindset. In truth, these attributes are present in the administration of most countries and Turkey is certainly no worse than places such as Spain, Italy or the other Mediterranean countries. Even if you judge it alongside the standards of, say, Germany, it doesn't fare too badly.

It is also, rapidly, getting better. We have an e-government system on which every citizen can have their own personal account. You apply for this at the post office and it costs a massive TRY2 (about US$0.56/€0.50/£0.40). With this system you can see all of your dealings with the government: tax, fines, court cases related to you, your criminal record etc. Add to this internet banking and online services from many utility companies and the opportunity for administrative delay reduces rapidly.

Very often the remaining perceived problems with the administration result, in reality, from language difficulties. The public official doesn't quite understand what you want and therefore doesn't quite deliver the service you expect. Or you don't fully understand them.

The good news about Turkey is that it is now almost entirely free of low-level corruption. Gone are the days when you would be asked for a bribe in connection with almost any interaction with 'the authorities'. This state of affairs, highly unusual in this world, more than compensates for any slight tardiness in the administrative process. Nonetheless, when dealing with the administration, patience, tolerance and thoroughness are great virtues.

Healthcare

Healthcare has a cultural aspect far greater than you might first think.

Whilst the process of diagnosis and treatment is scientific and almost universal, the cultural overlay as to *how* that treatment is delivered varies significantly from place to place. For example, there are often three ways to administer a medicine: orally (by tablet), by injection (shot), and rectally (by suppository). In Turkey, the tablet method is the most used.

Within the state system, we use our family doctors mainly for small things. If we think it necessary, we make our own appointments directly with specialists, using the hospital's e-booking system. In other words, if I think I have a problem with my kidneys I will book an appointment with a kidney specialist. Most of the time we get it right.

For those not entitled to use our state healthcare system (like all foreigners not working and paying into our social security system), access to medical treatment will be via private doctors and clinics but we still choose who to visit and, usually, which specialists to use.

Incidentally, health insurance in Turkey is cheap. See page 102.

If you are admitted to hospital you will be expected to make far more provision for your own care than you would in many other countries. The family is expected to provide you with clean pyjamas and to do the washing of the old ones. They will often help with your personal care and feeding. The hospital will provide the food but they may expect it to be supplemented by the family and they will expect the family to make sure that you consume it. If somebody attends hospital to help look after you, the hospital will feed them too.

For more information about the system, see our section on healthcare (page 145).

Banking

Turkey has a number of good and reliable banks and they offer a full set of banking services. Almost all are now foreign owned.

However, there are probably fewer choices in the services they offer than you might have to make 'back home'. For example, there is usually only one type of general investment (deposit) account and the banks will offer far fewer ancillary services such as insurance. For more about banking, see page 109.

Language barriers

Until recently, few people in Turkey spoke foreign languages. Today it is getting better. Many younger people speak English and other languages to at least some level of proficiency. Yet language (and finding good translators) is still a problem. Most people coming to Turkey simply will not be able to undertake even simple tasks themselves: buying office equipment or household furniture, getting connected to a phone line or the water supply, etc.

For a business, deciding how to deal with this issue will be central to your business plan.

General cultural differences

Diversity

Many of the most obvious cultural challenges that will strike you when you are living in, travelling to, or doing business with Turkey stem from the sheer diversity within the country. Of course, there is diversity within every country but diversity is far more striking in Turkey than in most places.

There are several examples of this diversity. They often overlap.

Melting pot

Turkey has long been a cultural melting pot. Its core cultures have been derived from the various cultures of the Eastern Mediterranean and Central Asia - especially Thrace and Anatolia - plus, to a lesser degree, from those of Eastern Europe, and the Caucasus. Over the years, these cultures have repeatedly been mixed, partly separated and then remixed, each time resulting in a different flavour and emphasis.

These cultural components were brought together in the days of the Greek and Roman domination of the Eastern Mediterranean, in which what is now Turkey was a key player. They were re-formed in the early Christian era, which impacted and dominated Turkey until Islam took control in the 11th & 12th Centuries.

After 300 years of rivalry between the various sects of Islam, the Ottomans prevailed and controlled Turkey from 1453 until the creation of the modern Turkish state in 1923. The Ottoman Empire was, for most of that time, a multi-ethnic and multi-religious state centred upon Sunni Islam, and it became the de facto leader of the Islamic world.

The Republic of Turkey, moulded by Mustafa Kemal Atatürk, re-defined Turkey as a modern, secular and Western-focused society - albeit with a population 99% Muslim.

Now, under President Recep Tayyip Erdoğan, Turkey is again in a phase of transition. As a "conservative democrat" from Islamist roots, he seems to be trying to turn Turkey into a society that is still secular but less free and liberal than in recent years. It is too soon to tell how far these reforms will go.

Big cities and sparsely populated rural areas

With over 15million as of 31 December 2017 (officially - in reality, many more) living in Istanbul, and with millions more in several other big cities, Turkey's is a predominantly urban society. Yet 20million people - 25% of the population - live in rural areas that are sparsely populated.

Throughout the world, city dwellers differ from country-folk in the way they live and their attitude to life. This is particularly true in Turkey where, concealed within the country-city divide, there are several other important splits.

Europe v Asia

Turkey is famous for being the place where east meets west, both physically and culturally.

The part of Turkey in Europe - about 5% - feels very different from what Turks call "the Asian side" or "the Anatolian side". This is not surprising. 65% of Istanbul lies in Europe and Istanbul is Turkey's leading city, the centre of its economic life (producing nearly half of its GDP) and receiving 30% of Turkey's tourism.

For most of the last 2,500 years, coastal Turkey on the Asian side has been genetically, culturally, and commercially, fused with coastal Greece. Despite the 1923 exchange of populations (when two million Christians in Turkey and Muslims in Greece changed places), living or doing business in the Aegean facing part of Turkey - say from Çanakkale to Fethiye - still feels much more European than living or doing business in the other coastal areas or (even more so) inland.

East v West

Within the Asian side, even ignoring the Europe vs Asia issue, there is a large cultural difference between east and west. As you move into Central, Eastern and Southeast

Anatolia, life generally becomes poorer, the land less fertile, the population more traditionalist and the general culture more Islamic. The food is different, the way of dressing is different, and the way of life is different. In fact, in some ways, these areas in Eastern Turkey feel more like their neighbours (Iran, Iraq, and Syria) than they do Istanbul or Bodrum.

With the exception of some Kurds (18% of Turkey's population), the people in these areas identify strongly as Turkish. Overwhelmingly, they speak Turkish. The government, legal and administrative systems are applied in the same way throughout the country. So these differences should not be exaggerated but need to be recognized.

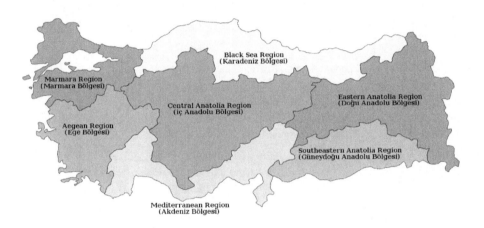

English map of the Turkish regions, by Pinpin

Traditional v modern

Mingled with the 'East vs West' divide is the 'traditional vs modern' divide; yet this divide can be seen throughout the country, not just in the east. Even in cosmopolitan places such as Izmir, you will find many traditionalists.

Some differences are, on the face of it, superficial: the style of dress, men sporting a moustache and so on. Others go deeper, often being framed as issues of personal freedom. For example, a national debate erupted in 2013 about whether unmarried male and female students should be allowed to cohabit in rented accommodation and there has been a decades-long tussle about whether women should be allowed to wear the headscarf, with the military only lifting their ban in 2017. Until 2011, wearing a headscarf was illegal, as something in conflict with the principles behind the secular state. However, by 2016, a survey by IPSOS KMG showed that 60% of women said they wear a headscarf, and nearly half of men said their wife should wear a headscarf.

As in most places, older people tend to be more traditionalist but you will also find the young and well educated who embrace general traditional values - not just traditional *religious* values.

Turks have, historically, been very accepting. The old accept the music and dress of the young. The young respect the traditions of the old. But if you are living or doing business in Turkey, you need to be aware of these cultural issues and work out which are likely to impact your business and how - if at all - to accommodate them.

Religious v secular

Related to the 'traditional vs modern' divide, but different from it, is the 'religious vs secular' split.

Constitutionally, Turkey is a secular society: there is separation of religion and the state. The current Constitution neither recognizes an official religion nor promotes any.

Yet 99% of Turks are Muslim. Some 75 % of them are Sunni Muslims, arguably the most pragmatic and flexible of the Muslim sects. Some are devoutly religious, others follow their religion in a more casual way. Few attend mosque, or pray, the prescribed five times per day.

The consumption of alcohol is prohibited in the Islamic faith but is practised widely in Turkey - mainly in the western part of the country. Many younger people cohabit, yet only 2% of births are outside marriage (OECD average 35%).

Size

With a population of 80million and 783,000km2 of land area, Turkey seems *big*, particularly if you come from Europe.

This size, coupled with relatively poor roads in large parts of the country, leads to practical problems. Yet most big companies manage to operate across the nation.

Cultural differences when it comes to doing business

A different business environment

People are attracted to doing business in Turkey for several reasons: you may wish to serve customers in the country (whilst remaining based in your own country), you may wish to take advantage of the lower Turkish labour costs to help service customers elsewhere and/or you may wish to base your business in Turkey to take advantage of its low rates of tax.

Or, of course, you might just want to access its huge market of potential customers.

Whichever your reason for doing business in Turkey, you will find that there is a very different business environment from that to which you are probably accustomed.

As with most countries, it is no good trying to fight the local reality. The best you can hope for is a compromise. To state the obvious, to compromise you and your company need to move part way towards their way of doing things!

Foreign ownership

About nine out of ten big 'Turkish' companies belong to non-nationals.

This applies to banks, supermarkets, gas (petrol) stations and in many other sectors. This is despite the names of the companies looking resolutely Turkish!

Business hours

Turks tend to be hard working: normal business hours in an office are 09:00-18:00 for private businesses, 08:00-17:00 for public officials.

Pre-planning

Most people only plan their lives a few days in advance. People would not usually arrange a business meeting a month in advance; a week would be more normal. The actual time of the meeting would be arranged closer still. The time may then move, even at the last moment. Many people just call in!

Once a time has been arranged, it is rude to be late, though quite common to be kept waiting.

Things slow down a lot during July and August (when many people go on holiday). These months, and Ramadan, are best avoided if you are visiting Turkey for business purposes.

Courtesy

Courtesy is crucial in all business dealings, even when you need to disagree about something. This is not the exaggerated and effusive false courtesy found in some countries but a genuine, measured approach based on mutual respect.

Do not mistake the need for courtesy with the idea that you cannot speak directly in your Turkish business dealings. Direct talking is appreciated and, if you know somebody, a sign that your relationship is genuine.

Maintain eye contact.

Women

Only 24% of Turkish women are employed, so the workplace is definitely male-dominated. Yet the percentage of women executives is, in some industries, higher than the Western average. In the Turkish finance industry, for example, there is a higher ratio of women executives to male executives than in Germany, Italy, or France.

Nonetheless, women - especially in traditional parts of Turkey - should avoid wearing short skirts, plunging necklines or stiletto heels in the workplace.

In some rural areas it may be unacceptable for a woman to shake hands with a man.

Many of our female colleagues in Turkey take pride in ignoring all of these 'rules', whilst being careful to avoid offending the elderly.

If you are a man meeting a Turkish businesswoman, wait for the woman to extend her hand before you move to shake it. If you are a woman, the decision will be left to you. As a foreign woman, you will certainly be given wider latitude with your dress and business customs, but you may still prefer to comply with local customs.

Business dress

In the big cities, suits and ties (and the equivalent for women) are still the norm. In the summer months and on the coast, shirts and smart trousers will be more common. For women, a certain modesty in dress is required - or, at least, appreciated (see above).

Meetings

Meetings, particularly meetings early in your relationship, may start slowly, with many questions that may seem irrelevant to the purpose of your visit. It is rude to press colleagues to get to the point!

Topics covered at the beginning of a meeting may include anything from your family to football. I find that enquiries about various aspects of Turkish life and culture are good - and very useful - topics for discussion during this opening phase.

Business cards

Unlike in places such as China, business cards are exchanged without formal ritual.

It is thought polite to use both hands to exchange cards.

It is helpful to give a business card to the receptionist when you arrive and to have others available for all the people attending your meeting.

You can have one side of your business card translated into Turkish. This is useful if you are doing a lot of business in Turkey but not essential. However, it is a simple act of courtesy to your Turkish business colleagues.

The etiquette of entertaining

Relationships in Turkey are developed over a long period, often helped by extended lunches, dinners, and social outings. Recently, Turkey has begun to suffer from the same time pressures found in the West but entertainment - and eating - is still important and time will be found for it.

Most business entertaining will take place in restaurants. Turks enjoy food and the meal is a time for relaxing and engaging in some good conversation as well as developing business relationships.

The protocol of Turkish hospitality dictates that the host always pays for the meal. The concept of sharing a bill is completely alien. You may try and offer to pay, which may be seen as polite, but you would never be allowed to do so unless your relationship is already very close. The best policy is to graciously thank the host then, a few days later, invite them to do dinner at a restaurant of your choice, making sure that you pay. As a foreign visitor, that can sometimes be easier said than done. It may be a good idea to inform the restaurant manager that under no circumstances whatsoever are they to accept payment from your guests! Even then, I have failed.

Gifts

In business relationships, gift-giving is generally not practiced. Indeed, in a world where Turks are increasingly proud of the reduction in corruption, some would see them as inappropriate. If you do decide to make a gift, avoid anything lavish. Something that relates to your home country is usually good.

If you're given a gift in a business situation and your company policy prohibits you from accepting it, be tactful when declining the gift. Do not, whatever you do, suggest that the giver has any ulterior motive! Explain your company's policy.

Negotiations

One of the most noticeable aspects of the different business environment is the different ways of negotiating and of saying no.

Most businesses in Turkey are still run by an owner-operator. This person is used to taking control of all aspects of the business and to getting his (and it usually still is a "his") own way. There is, therefore, a tendency for the owner to enter negotiations with a very clear idea of what he wants and a great reluctance to move away from it. This, of course, conflicts with the general Turkish way of solving problems by negotiation - and so one of your tasks when negotiating is to bring forward that basic cultural aspect and to work through the phase of resistance.

This will usually happen if you have valid points to make: reasons why your proposal makes more sense than your partner's and a set of proposals that fit into the Turkish legal and cultural framework.

It will also usually happen if your partner can see a clear mutual benefit in your proposal. This benefit can go beyond the mere financial.

The process of negotiating in Turkey tends to be much faster than in many other countries. You will typically make a proposal to your business partner by email and receive a quick response from them. That will, usually, be followed by a face-to-face meeting at which any differences will be discussed and resolved and the deal done. It is not common (except for the most complicated projects) for many meetings to be needed.

It is not wise to try to impose deadlines or other time pressure, especially early in a relationship.

Saying "no"

Of equal importance to the business person wanting to work with Turkey is an understanding of how to say no, and being able to tell when your partner is actually saying no while his lips are not moving.

Part of the tradition in Turkey is one of courtesy and not wanting to offend. It is therefore quite common for your business partner to prefer not to give you a straightforward answer of "no".

Suggestions of further meetings, the raising of lots of queries - especially if they're very detailed - the failure to invite you for a beer or a glass of wine after your meeting, and a distancing of your relationship or a more formal tone in your emails can all suggest that this is a project that the partner does not wish to pursue.

Turks are very used to the world of international business. They have been traders for thousands of years. They much value the directness and clarity of business thought found in North and Western Europe and in the US but you shouldn't expect them to fully reciprocate that directness, especially when it comes to saying "no".

Setting up a business

Setting up a company doesn't take long - about two days - but involves dealing with a number of different people. Setting up the business itself can be fairly simple or very complicated depending upon what licences you need. For example, setting up a hotel can take months: tourist licences, alcohol licences, hygiene licences, municipal opening licences etc. must all be acquired.

That is not the time consuming bit of setting up a new business. An outsider breaking into this world needs to establish a relationship of trust with his potential business partners. Thus, the early stages of setting up a business will involve a lot of building this trust, particularly if the business involves the active participation of a local business partner.

Whilst this process is nowhere near as extreme as in, say, China, many business people find that it is slow getting a new business off the ground.

Patience is required - and respected.

The other essential, from the point of view of your potential Turkish business partner, is that you display some knowledge not only of your industry and product but also of the way in which things work in Turkey. If the proposition is interesting enough, then your partner will help you acquire that knowledge - but he will expect you to go some way down the road by doing some research before you meet, and then by acquiring more knowledge before entering a formal business relationship.

Do remember that there are certain categories of business that are not open to foreign participation. See our chapter on starting a business in Turkey (page 205).

Advertising

Don't spend too much on advertising. This may seem counter-intuitive, but it's important if you're looking to attract a Turkish clientele. Turks are suspicious of businesses that spend lots of money on flashy marketing campaigns. Your face on a billboard is more likely to convince locals that you're a con-man rather than a high-powered business whiz. They are much more likely to use your services if they hear of you through a friend or associate. Yet another reason making contacts is so important!

Having said that, Turkish big business spends a lot on advertising: particularly construction companies, banks and supermarkets.

Of course, to start building up word of mouth exposure you need to get your name out there in the first place. A low-key campaign over social media and a few newspaper advertisements is generally the best way to go. Social media is cheap and targeted, and Turks - especially the younger generation - spend a great deal of time on Twitter and Facebook.

If you're mainly targeting tourists or expats, of course, this caution about advertising will not be an issue. Tailor your marketing to suit the group you want to attract. If there is English/German/Russian language media in your area, think about using it.

Relations with employees

If you get to the stage where you have employees in Turkey, you will need to be both flexible and culturally aware.

The employees' expectations when joining you may differ from yours at several levels.

You may come from a culture where people put in long hours when it's necessary to do so to deliver a project. In Turkey, in private businesses, they also work like this: and without paid overtime. Public sector employees are clock watchers. They also expect, at least in an office environment, to be free to go out and have coffee or a lunchtime beer with friends and other colleagues on a very flexible basis.

Generally, reaching a long-term understanding with employees involves a clear definition of their responsibilities, training about their delivery and your company's culture, and sensitive management by people familiar with Turkey's business culture.

More information

For further information about cultural differences and how they can affect your business in another country, I recommend Erin Meyer's book *"The Culture Map"*. This is available via **www.guides.global/guides/turkey/tur-books.php**.

The Language

Written by **John Howell**
Editor & Founder of Guides.Global
www.guides.global • john.howell@guides.global

Turkey is a country where a relatively small number of people speak English. They are, mainly, fairly young. Some speak it better than others. Few professionals speak it totally fluently: if you find one, value them.

A much smaller number speak German, Russian and Italian. Very few speak Chinese or the languages of many of our other readers.

Even if you speak English fluently, it will greatly simplify your life and enrich your time in Turkey if you take the trouble to learn at least some Turkish. Even a limited knowledge opens doors and business opportunities.

If you do not speak English it becomes even more important.

Unfortunately, Turkish is not the simplest of languages to learn but there are ways of becoming a Turkish speaker without too much time and trouble.

Even if you learn only a few words, it will be seen by people in Turkey as both a courtesy and a gesture of good faith. They will respond enthusiastically, correcting your errors (in a very gentle way) and helping you expand your vocabulary.

A good starting point is the '100 words' (see Appendix II).

How can a foreigner learn Turkish?

There are six main ways.

A local partner

By far the best is to find a Turkish boyfriend or girlfriend. If, however, your significant other balks at this idea, do not despair; there are alternatives!

School

You can learn Turkish before you come to Turkey or after you have arrived. Children learn very quickly - three months would be normal for a young child. Adults can take a lot longer. I know people who have been studying, regularly, for over two years and who only now feel comfortable with their ability. Of course, they may be being harsh on themselves! Most will speak basic Turkish after six months' study twice per week.

Learning 'back home'

There are lots of Turkish speakers around the world. This is a very good thing for you, because it means there are lots of people teaching Turkish.

Do an internet search for "learn Turkish in [your city]" or check out the website of your local language school.

If there aren't any official Turkish language lessons in your area, or they are too expensive for you, consider whether you know (or your friends know) any Turkish people. You can ask them if they would be willing to tutor you. This method is likely to be a little more haphazard than if you learn in a formal class, but could be very enjoyable, and it is certainly better than nothing at all.

It's a great idea to, at least, get the basics of Turkish down before you move to Turkey: it will make the whole thing a lot less scary and ensure you can get set up more quickly.

Learning in Turkey

You can visit Turkey and take intensive courses before you move (immersion is the easiest way to learn a language), continue your studies 'back home' when you arrive, or even start from scratch when you've moved to Turkey.

There are many places to learn Turkish in Turkey. Search the web and local newspapers for a private tutor or check out a local school. In some tourist areas the municipality (town hall) arranges classes for newly arrived foreigners.

Courses will vary: from evening classes over a period of months, to intensive full-time courses of a couple of weeks.

Prices also vary widely: the best thing to do is call up the school or teacher and find out what you'll need to pay for your specific needs. You can expect to pay around US$100 (TRY377/€92/£79) for a few weeks of evening classes, or $300-$400 for a three-week intensive course.

We keep a list of schools updated at **www.guides.global/guides/turkey/TUR-learning_language.php**.

The internet, DVDs, CDs and books

There are many, many Turkish language courses available online and in print.

A leading and well respected example is the Rosetta Stone courses, which are comprehensive online, audio and written lessons. A popular free course is Duolingo, which is online-only but allows you to write, listen and speak in Turkish. More below.

Websites that charge monthly will often let you 'bulk buy' months, or sign up for an extended period of time, which works out cheaper per month.

Many of these websites will also offer an app for your mobile phone.

Again, check **www.guides.global/guides/turkey/TUR-learning_language.php** for a list of what's available.

There are also hundreds of books and DVDs devoted to learning Turkish. A quick search on your favourite bookseller's website will show you. Books should be used in tandem with other, more interactive, methods of language learning.

'On the job'

Many people pick up the rudiments of Turkish whilst working. This is a slow but inexpensive way of becoming bilingual. Unfortunately, your colleagues are likely to want to use the opportunity to learn your language, and so you may find it difficult to get them to teach you much Turkish. You often end up having slightly surreal conversations with you speaking Turkish to them and them speaking English to you!

Some employers, particularly the big banks and IT companies that have now set up in Turkey, run formal tuition for their staff. This is a huge advantage and could be a good reason for taking that job in preference to another.

Friends and neighbours

Your local Turkish neighbours will be very friendly and open to forming friendships with you. They will also love it if you show that you are sufficiently interested in their country to want to learn the language and they will, often will great patience and politeness, guide your faltering steps to some level of command of Turkish. They will often, also very politely, repeat the words that you have said to them (to help your pronunciation) when replying to you whilst gently correcting your grammatical catastrophes.

Two things that are sure. One is that you will have a richer experience with your neighbours if you do speak some Turkish. The other is that your neighbours are likely to be as keen to use you as a way of learning your language as you are to do the reverse.

Your children

If you are lucky enough to have young children, especially if they are attending the local school rather than the international school, you will be amazed at how quickly they learn Turkish. They will sometimes be semi-fluent in as little as six weeks and usually skilled within six months. They can then help teach you. Just expect some face-pulling as they indulge their inadequate and stupid parents who struggle to do something that they find so simple!

Keeping up your language

Read the local newspaper (in Turkish) and listen to the local television news. Getting to the stage where you can do this takes time. In my opinion, the real test of whether you can speak any language is whether you can follow a programme on the radio, where they tend to talk quickly and where there are no visual clues.

Another great and painless way of keeping up and improving your Turkish is to watch movies on DVD. Depending on the level of your skill, you can either listen to the movie in your own language but display the subtitles in Turkish or listen in Turkish and display the subtitles in your own language. If you are really good, you can listen in Turkish and also display subtitles in Turkish! All of these methods are very effective at surreptitiously improving your skill.

The 100 words

I am a great believer in the '100 words' (you can tell, because I've mentioned it twice!). This is the idea that, with just 100 words (or short phrases) of any language, you can get by in many day-to-day situations and in an emergency.

You will also gain the respect and approval of local business colleagues: you are trying to meet them half way, not working on the basis of cultural imperialism.

See Appendix II for the 100 words. You will probably want to add a few of your own.

The Cost of Living

Written by **Burak Orkun**
Managing Partner (Accountancy Department) at Orkun & Orkun
www.orkunorkun.com • info@orkunorkun.com

The cost of living in Turkey depends entirely upon how you choose to live. Living in Turkey as an ordinary Turkish person - consuming local brands, fresh meat and vegetables and being frugal with water and power - allows you to live cheaply. Living as a Westerner - making full use of air conditioning, running a large swimming pool, and consuming your favourite brands from back home - can prove very expensive.

The cost also depends upon where you live. The following prices are for Bodrum.

Note: prices and currency conversions were correct on 1st September 2017.

Bread: standard loaf	TRY1.25 - £0.24/€0.27/US$0.33
Fresh fish: 1kg (Farm)	TRY25 - £5.50/€6.31/US$7.07
Milk: 1 litre carton	TRY2.65 - £0.58/€0.66/US$0.74
Coffee: 250g	TRY37 - £8.15/€9.34/US$10.47
Sugar: 1kg	TRY4.95 - £1.02/€1.15/US$1.36
Eggs: 6	TRY3 - £0.66/€0.75/US$0.84
Tomatoes: 1kg	TRY3 - £0.66/€0.75/US$0.84
Kellogg's cornflakes: 500g	TRY6 - £1.32/€1.51/US$1.70
Local beer: 0.5litre bottle	TRY6.60 - £1.45/€1.67/US$1.87
Imported beer: 0.33litre bottle	TRY8.50 - £1.87/€2.15/US$2.81
Local wine: 75cl bottle	TRY30 - £6.61/€7.57/US$8.49
Champagne: Moet et Chandon 75cl	TRY285 - £58.90/€66.31/US$78.29
Bottled water: 1.5 litre	TRY1.40 - £0.30/€0.35/US$0.39
Imported cigarettes: 20	TRY12 - £2.64/€3.03/US$3.40
Soap powder: 3kg	TRY30 - £6.61/€7.57/US$8.49
Shampoo: 400ml	TRY12 - £2.64/€3.03/US$3.40
Toilet rolls: 12 pack	TRY19 - £4.18/€4.80/US$5.38
Washing up liquid: 675ml	TRY4.25 - £0.93/€1.07/US$1.20
Washing machine: Bosch	TRY1,200 - £264/€302/US$339

Turkey: how things *really* work

Washing machine: local brand (Arçelik)	TRY1,000 - £220/€252/US$283
TV set - Philips: 32in/81cm	TRY1,150 - £253/€290/US$325
TV set: local brand (Beko)	TRY1,150 - £253/€290/US$325
Jeans - adult: unbranded	TRY60 - £13.21/€15.14/US$16.98
Cotton socks - unbranded: 3 pairs	TRY13 - £2.86/€3.28/US$3.68
Pullover/sweater - wool - unbranded	TRY50 - £11.01/€12.62/US$14.15
Trainers - child's - unbranded	TRY85 - £18.72/€21.45/US$24.05
Local small car - e.g. Fiat Panda	TRY57,900 - £11,029/€12,450/US$25,237
BMW 320 diesel or equivalent	TRY205,400 - £39,123/€44,172/US$54,052
Petrol: 1 litre	TRY5 - £1.10/€1.26/US$1.41
Diesel: 1 litre	TRY4.50 - £0.99/€1.14/US$1.27
Local newspaper	TRY1 - £0.22/€0.25/US$0.28
Mobile telephone (handset only -Samsung Galaxy A7)	TRY2,003 - £441/€505/US$566
Mobile phone contract per month (1,000 minutes, 4gb data)	TRY60 - £13.21/€15.14/US$16.98
Water bill - 1m^3	TRY2.50 - £0.55/€0.63/US$0.70
Electricity - 1kw/hr	TRY0.41 - £0.09/€0.10/US$0.11

Shops & Shopping

Written by **John Howell**
Editor & Founder of Guides.Global
www.guides.global • john.howell@guides.global

Shops

There is still a diminishing tradition of buying food and other goods through small, specialist shops, but the big supermarkets have made large inroads into this. Companies like Migros (owned by Walmart) are everywhere and very popular as a result of their lower prices and greater range of products.

Late night shopping

Most shops are open from 10:00 until 20:00 in the summer and 10:00 to 18:00 in the winter but are closed on Sundays. Big shopping malls tend to be open 10:00-22:00, seven days a week.

Bars

Although Turkey is an Islamic country, it has plentiful bars. Most small villages have at least one. Bigger towns have dozens or hundreds. Despite this, there is no culture of drunkenness amongst Turks. The antics of some expats and many young tourists give rise to constant hostile comment in the press.

Bars are, typically, open from 10:00 until 00:00 with some in the tourist areas remaining open until 02:00 or 03:00.

Bars range from the simple rural meeting places for locals to sophisticated, internationally-themed establishments and nightclubs.

Local beer is cheap and very palatable. A 33cl bottle of Efes will cost you about TRY9 (£2/€2.2/US$2.5) in a bar.

Local and, to a lesser extent, imported wines are also available, though not in all bars. A large glass of local red wine will cost you about TRY15 (£3.10/€3.49/US$4.12) in a typical bar.

Local spirits are an acquired taste. Turkey is famous for its *rakı*, the equivalent of Greek ouzo. Its low price belies its explosive power. Consume with caution!

Imported drinks are expensive.

A bottle of Budweiser will cost about TRY20 (£4.13/€4.65/US$5.49) and a bottle of imported wine, in a bar or restaurant, will cost a minimum of about TRY130 (£26.87/€30.25/US$35.71). A Jack Daniels and Coke will cost you about TRY40 (£8.27/€9.31/US$10.99).

Restaurants

Turks, especially in the big cities, eat out a lot. It is part of their culture. Whether as couples, groups of friends, or entire family units, they fill most restaurants.

The places they don't go are the tourist restaurants where they feel, with some justification, that the food is poor, and the price is high.

There is an expanding range of cuisine available in Turkey. From excellent (and traditional) local fish and meat restaurants to Italian, Chinese, Vietnamese, Brazilian and even Australian fusion, you will find your taste well catered to. Talk to your Turkish friends to find some great places to eat.

It's worth bearing in mind that, when a Turk decides to go out for a meal, the first question is always whether you want to eat fish or meat. Depending upon the choice will be the restaurant. Many fish restaurants do not serve meat dishes and vice versa.

Restaurant prices, of course, vary enormously, but you can get a good, simple meal for two in a local restaurant for less than TRY90 (£20/€22/US$25) and a first-class meal for two in a fancy restaurant in Bodrum will cost about TRY300 (£66/€75/US$84), including wine.

Housing

Written by **Başak Yildiz Orkun**
Managing Partner (Legal Department) at Orkun & Orkun
www.orkunorkun.com • info@orkunorkun.com

Where you live is one of the largest factors when it comes to how happy you are going to be in Turkey.

There are four main options when it comes to choosing a place to live:

Hotels

Many people who come to Turkey on what they think is going to be a long-term basis will start their time here by living in a hotel. This gives them the opportunity to look around the area - a place they may well never have been to before - and to decide exactly where they want to live and in what type of property.

Living in a hotel may look like an expensive option, but many hotels will offer very attractive rates to somebody who's going to be staying in the hotel for a month or more, particularly if it's off-season. In any case, whatever the cost of the hotel, it will be a great deal cheaper than leaping into a decision to live in the wrong property in the wrong place.

In the last few years, an alternative to the hotel has emerged in the marketplace. This is the short-term apartment rented on pretty much the same basis as a hotel - in other words, rented by the night or by the week. Companies such as Airbnb (**www.airbnb.com**) and HomeAway (**www.homeaway.co.uk**) offer a mass of such accommodation in Turkey.

Short-term rentals

There is no special law for short-term rentals. For both residential and commercial rentals, you can sign a contract up to ten years - and, even if you (as a tenant) sign an annual agreement, the law gives you an automatic renewal right up to ten years (subject to the fulfilment of contract terms such as paying the rent on time).

On Turkey's coast, very short-term (daily and weekly) rentals are now becoming very common. We call them seasonal rentals. However, we do not yet have legislation to specifically deal with this matter: hence they could be considered a trading activity by the tax office. This is of more concern to the property owner than the person renting.

House-sitting

An interesting alternative to a short-term rental is to become a house-sitter (temporary caretaker). A number of (usually expat) families like someone to live in their property when they themselves are not there. This is often motivated by the fact they have a pet which they leave behind or by a fear of burglary.

These opportunities may be advertised in local newspapers or on **www.mindmyhouse.com** - where you can also register yourself as a person looking for a house-sitting opportunity. There are, typically, only small numbers of these opportunities but they're worth exploring.

Don't expect to get paid for this work, unless you take over gardener's work or pool maintenance. You will sometimes also be expected to contribute towards utility bills for the time you're in residence.

Home exchange

Another interesting, but rare, alternative to renting is home exchange. This is an arrangement where you allow somebody to use your home and they allow you to use theirs. If you have retained a property 'back home', this may be a better way of using it than renting it out - at least, for the period until you find a permanent place to live in Turkey.

Several websites, such as **www.homeexchange.com**, list exchange opportunities. There are, typically, only about ten in Turkey at any given time.

Long-term rentals

There is a plentiful supply of rental property in Turkey and rents are, generally, low for a property of the quality that you will be occupying.

Long-term rentals are usually for one year or two years but automatically extended at the end of the term.

Many people, particularly those who are working in Turkey or setting up businesses in Turkey, will decide that rental property will best suit their long-term needs and, after a period renting short-term, may look for a long-term rental.

There is usually a signed rental agreement. The tenancy can only be ended:

1. By the tenant giving the landlord written notice. The period of notice can be stated in the contract; if it is not, one month would be considered legitimate.

2. By the landlord asking the tenant to leave and him agreeing to do so. In the absence of good cause - damage to the building, not paying the rent, illegal use of the premises etc. - contracts extend automatically for up to ten years.

3. By a court order - based on non-payment of rent, damage caused to the property or improper use of the property. This can take up to two years if the case is challenged, plus several months more for an appeal.

If you are likely to be staying in Turkey for only a few years, tenancies - long-term or short-term - are probably your best solution as the cost of buying and selling a home can be substantial and that, of course, is lost money.

See our chapter on renting a property (page 431) for more details about these contracts.

Starting off in rental property can also make a lot of sense for somebody who wants to start a business in Turkey. Finding the necessary capital to start a new business can be difficult for a newcomer and you may decide that you're far better putting your available money into your business rather than into the home in which you'll be living. Once the business has become successful you can buy a mansion! See our chapter on starting a business (page 215).

Buying a property

The attractions of owning a home in Turkey are obvious. You can buy exactly what you want, where you want it. You can modify and decorate the house to your requirements. You may find that it gains substantially in value. If mortgage finance is available to you, the cost of your mortgage repayments could well be similar to, or even cheaper than, what you would otherwise have to pay out in rent.

Yet, of course, there are downsides:

- The most important is that the price of property can go down as well as up - and, indeed, did so in the late 2000s.

- The cost of buying a property (mainly in terms of fees and taxes) is substantial: typically, between 8% and 10% of the price of the property.

- The cost of later selling a property can also be significant.

- The Turkish lira is presently (June 2017) suffering due to unrest in the region.

You, therefore, don't want to incur these expenses if you're only likely to be in the house for a short period and you definitely don't want to buy an inappropriate property and then find that you have to move again after a couple of years.

There is a plentiful supply of property of all types in Turkey. See our chapter about buying a property in Turkey (page 364).

Understanding property advertisements

With so many people from so many different nationalities buying, selling, or renting property in Turkey, it's not surprising that some confusion can arise.

The most important things to know are:

1. In Turkey, we use the UK/European way of describing floor levels: the part of the building at ground level is known as the ground floor, the floor above it as the first floor and so on.

2. Properties are usually described as having a certain number of rooms. A "one plus one" property has a single bedroom and a living room. A "three plus one" would have three bedrooms and one living room.

   It will also (you hope!) have a kitchen and a bathroom but they do not count when calculating the number of rooms. If the property has more than one bathroom, the advert will say so.

3. Generally, anything not mentioned in the advert won't be there. So, look out for phrases such as, "Central heating (*kalorifer/ merkezi ısıtma)*", "Air Conditioning (*klima*)", "Lift/elevator (*asansör*)" and, "Parking (*park alanı*)" or "Garage (*garaj*)".

Rent-to-buy

Since the financial crisis of the mid-2000s, when bank finance was almost unavailable for those wanting to buy a property, 'rent-to-buy' has become quite frequent in some countries. Owners keen to sell their property, and conscious of the pitiful interest rates available if they invest the money they receive from selling it, are often prepared to take a part of the price - normally at least 50% - at the time of sale and the rest by monthly payments protected by a mortgage over the property.

This is not usually done in Turkey.

Furniture

People moving to Turkey are split almost 50/50 between those who bring no furniture with them and those who bring at least some items.

See our section on importing your possessions (page 37) for more about this.

Those who have brought nothing, or who need to buy some furniture in Turkey, will find that there is a remarkably large number of furniture shops. Turks tend to spend quite a lot of money on furniture and replace it frequently.

Most furniture available in Turkey is new and, increasingly, the trend is to own furniture of a streamlined and modern design; rather than the heavy, carved pieces that were so popular a few decades ago.

There are a few shops selling antique furniture, often at very competitive prices, and there is also a small number of shops selling second-hand (but not antique) furniture. These are well worth a look and can allow you to provide most of the furniture for a small apartment for a couple of hundred euros.

Utilities

Written by **Burak Orkun**

Managing Partner (Accountancy Department) at Orkun & Orkun

www.orkunorkun.com • info@orkunorkun.com

Electricity

Electricity is supplied and administered by a local monopoly company, which differs from region to region. However, the electricity itself is provided by the government. There is no alternative supplier.

Most electricity is generated by (Russian) gas and by coal-fired thermal power plants. Hydro-electric is also common. Nuclear power is on the way. Solar and wind power plants are becoming more common.

Prices depend upon the amount that you use. For an average two-bedroom apartment with air conditioning but using gas heating, electricity is likely to cost about TRY150 (£33/€38/US$42) per month.

If you use electric heating, it could be TRY500 (£110/€126/US$141) in the winter and about TRY300 (£44/€50/US$57) in the summer.

Your electricity bills are paid monthly. There is no initial payment when you are connected to the service.

Few of the electricity supply companies' employees speak foreign languages.

Water

A piped water supply serves the whole of Turkey except some very remote areas. Piped water is safe to drink but can sometimes taste of chemicals, and Turkish people prefer to drink either filtered water or bottled water. Filters and bottles of water are available from almost all food shops and supermarkets. A common way to obtain drinking water for a household in Turkey is ordering by telephone: 19-litre drinking water bottles are available in almost all towns and cities.

The arrangements for the supply of piped water are similar to those relating to electricity.

It is charged by the cubic metre.

Typical cost per month for a two-bedroom house might be TRY40 (£8/€10/US$11) for combined water and sewerage.

Gas

There is a piped natural gas supply in Turkey. It covers 78 of 81 provinces. It doesn't cover some regions in the hottest climates (in the South-West), or under-developed regions (in the South-East).

Gas is subsidised by the government and, therefore, cheap.

In areas where there is no piped gas, and in many other parts of the country, people use gas cylinders. Cylinders are readily available from supermarkets and other shops.

A 12kg refill cylinder will cost about TRY85 (£19/€21/US$24), though this will vary slightly from city to city. Check your local prices here: **bit.ly/2qK1wrz** (just pick the city and size of container from the two drop-down lists).

Sewerage

Only about half of the houses in Turkey are connected to a proper system for the collection and treatment of sewage. Some of these systems (again, about half) are municipal systems. This means that they're provided by the town or village in which you live and that you can simply connect to them upon payment of any connection charge and an ongoing annual charge for the use of the system.

The cost of municipal sewerage is included with your charge for water.

Other systems were built, and are operated by, a particular development project or community. In these communities, your home will already be connected to their system and you will have to pay for the cost of running it as part of your normal community fees or charges (see page 380).

The cost of running a community sewerage system will not usually be shown separately in your community charges.

The other half of the properties in Turkey are either served by an individual septic tank or they are connected to a sewerage system which simply discharges the outflow into the sea.

Septic tanks are perfectly legal, and they can work well, but it is your responsibility to maintain them and to arrange for the periodic emptying of the tank.

Arrangements that discharge the sewage directly into the sea are now completely illegal and they should have all been replaced. However, some have not. If your property has such a system, you will need to factor in the cost of replacing it, as you will need to do so immediately. The installation of a septic tank typically costs about TRY3,000. Your lawyer should check the existing arrangement if you are buying a property.

Waste (rubbish/garbage) collection

Waste (garbage) collection is provided everywhere in Turkey and it is paid for by way of a municipal charge, paid at the same time as your normal municipal taxes. It is a very minor portion of the Real Estate Tax, which needs to be paid annually to the local municipality. It is calculated using the property's annual Real Estate Tax.

Garbage collection varies depending on the municipality. It can be a daily service, weekly, or something in between.

Recycling

General household waste collected in the usual way is not recycled. Most is placed into landfill.

Partly as a result of this, Turkey has one of the worst recycling rates in Europe, with a little over 2% of all waste being recovered.

Telephone

The telephone service in Turkey is supplied by one leading company (Türk Telekom) but other cable suppliers are now entering the market under the license and using the infrastructure of Türk Telekom.

Until a few years ago, there was a shortage of telephone lines and so you may have heard that it is difficult - and might take months - to obtain a connection to the service. This is no longer true.

You can arrange a telephone connection online (**www.turktelekom.com.tr**), by phone (tricky if you don't have a phone!) or by calling in at one of the Türk Telekom offices.

Unless you live in the middle of the countryside, you are likely to be connected within 48 hours. Even if you live in the countryside, and a new line needs to be taken to your home, you are likely to be connected within seven days.

There used to be special numbers used for special purposes in Turkey. But all the emergency lines like fire, ambulance and police recently merged under 112. However, the old numbers can still be used for those who like tradition. They are:

- 155 - emergency police line

- 156 - *Jandarma* (rural military police)

- 110 - emergency fire line

- 112 - emergency ambulance line

- 158 - coastguard

- 121 - telephone breakdowns

Mobile phones

It feels like mobile phones are available from almost every shop in Turkey. There are three main operators, of which the biggest (just) and oldest is Turkcell (40%). The others are Vodafone (38%) and Türk Telekom (12%).

There is a mass of tariffs available for mobile phones depending on your expected usage and the length of your contract. They change all the time so it's pointless setting them out here.

As in most countries, you have the choice of taking a monthly contract (typically for a fixed period of two years) or a 'pay-as-you-go' contract.

Turkey: how things *really* work

Even if you intend to use your foreign mobile phone and number in Turkey, you will almost certainly find it a good idea to take a pay-as-you-go contract with a Turkish company and use that phone alongside your usual phone. This is because the cost of making calls (both within Turkey and internationally) will be much lower. Some phones can be used with adapters to hold two SIM cards at the same time, meaning you won't need two phones to use both your old number and your new Turkish one. Alternatively, if you are in the market for a new phone, twin SIM phones are very good and much cheaper than comparable big-brand (but single SIM) products.

The contact details for the Turkcell can be found on: **www.turkcell.com.tr**.

Public phones

Phone boxes are almost impossible to find now. I have not seen one in 5-10 years. As in most countries, they have reduced in proportion to the number of people who now have mobile phones.

The few that do exist take both cash and credit cards.

Call rates are roughly twice what you would pay from your own landline.

If you can't find a public phone you will find that, if you ask nicely, most bars will allow you to use theirs - but they will expect you to make a small payment (or have a drink) in return for doing so.

Postal service

As in most countries, people make much less use of the post today than they used to, but it is still an important means of communication in what is still a very rural country. It is, in particular, used widely for the delivery of packages and parcels as there are far fewer courier companies than you might find in Western Europe.

There are regular complaints about the quality of the Turkish postal service: about the speed of delivery and its charges. However, most expats living in Turkey find it to be at least as good as the service in their own country.

There is a post office in every town and many small villages. In small places, they are often co-located with bars. You will also find them in airports and railway stations. They are normally open from 09:00-18:00, Monday to Saturday.

You can only buy stamps from a post office.

The postage charge depends on the weight of the item.

The cost of posting an ordinary letter (up to 100g) within Turkey is TRY5. The cost of sending a 500g parcel is TRY15.

The cost of sending a regular letter from Turkey to anywhere in Western Europe is TRY20 and the cost of sending a 500g package from Turkey to anywhere in Western Europe is TRY50.

Post boxes are bright yellow. They are relatively few and far between. Most people will deliver their post, in person, directly to the post office.

There are an increasing number of courier services, who advertise ever more widely and who are quite a lot cheaper than the post office so - as in other countries - the post office's future may be limited.

Turkish couriers (such as Inter and Yurtiçi Kargo) and international couriers (such as FedEx and DHL) will be able to give you specific quotes for international delivery.

Internet

Internet can either be supplied by Türk Telekom, as part of your telephone package, or by your mobile telephone operator, who will provide a 3G or 4G connection.

A Türk Telekom connection will cost you about TRY70 per month for unlimited usage. Most mobile connections are more expensive, and the charge varies with the amount you use.

The broadband bandwidth, except in the most rural areas, is a minimum of 25mbps and can rise to 50mbps, depending upon where you live (although a very high-speed connection is, of course, far more expensive). The average download speed in Turkey in 2016 was 16mbps in Istanbul, about 11mbps in other big cities and less elsewhere. Overall, an average of 14.2mbps. This is about on a par with Germany (13.9mbps) and the UK (14.9mbps) but well behind the US(18.75mbps).

Both services - broadband and mobile - are reliable. Both services tend to slow down when the children get back from school. No change there then!

Insurances

Written by **Başak Yildiz Orkun**
Managing Partner (Legal Department) at Orkun & Orkun
www.orkunorkun.com • info@orkunorkun.com

Car Insurance

Every vehicle registered in Turkey or located in Turkey must have insurance complying with Turkish law.

A vehicle registered in Turkey must have insurance from the day it is registered until the day it is officially de-registered or removed from Turkey. This will include insurance for periods when it was not being used ('off the road') or parked on private land.

The minimum insurance requirement is insurance that covers risk to third parties (people, cars, and property).

Other (and fuller) types of insurance are available and recommended because, in Turkey, third party insurance does not cover injury to your own passengers and damage to your own car.

The penalty for not having car insurance is a fine of TRY95. In addition, your car will be towed to a car parking lot and will be prohibited from being driven away until you have a valid insurance policy. Of course, the real penalty of not having insurance is that if you have an accident and cause damage or injury you will not be covered. Not only will you have to live with the consequences, but this could leave you exposed to claims of €1million or more if you cause someone permanent disability.

Insuring your foreign-registered car in Turkey

This is not possible.

Foreign cars must be insured by an insurance company in the country in which the car is registered. That company will produce proof that you have insurance valid for use in Turkey. This is the "Green Card". The card is in an internationally recognised, multilingual format and recognised in 45 countries around the world.

Types of insurance available

There are four main types of insurance available in Turkey, plus some additional extra cover that you may add on to a standard policy.

1. Compulsory traffic insurance (*Zorunlu Trafik Sigortası*)

   This complies with the basic requirements of Turkish law but offers little or nothing more than that.

2. Limited vehicle insurance (*Dar Kasko*)

This provides all the cover required by law, plus other cover. This insurance is the most comprehensive standard insurance available for vehicles in Turkey. It covers not only injury to third parties (including your passengers) but also damage caused to you and to your own vehicle, and the loss of your vehicle by reason of theft, fire, or any other cause.

3.   Intermediate insurance (*Genişletilmiş Kasko*)

In this version, on top of the limited vehicle insurance referred to above, you can add one or two additional clauses (such as cover whilst abroad).

4.   Full Vehicle Insurance (*Tam Kasko*)

This policy includes all of the above but with all the possible options for additional cover: e.g. losses caused by force majeure ('acts of God'), terrorism, or damage by animals.

Extras

Roadside assistance insurance (*Yol Asistanı*)

This covers you in the event of breakdown, and also covers you for the breakage of glass and legal expenses if your main policy does not cover them.

Additional driver and passenger insurance (*Ekstra Sürücü Teminatı*)

This covers loss or damage to the driver and passengers of the car, including loss of earnings. This is only needed if you do not have full vehicle insurance.

How long does car insurance last?

Insurance policies normally last for one year. Some companies will offer short-term policies (typically for three months or six months) but these tend to be very expensive for the cover they offer.

Who will be covered by the policy?

By default, the only person who will be entitled to drive the vehicle is the person who took out the insurance policy.

However, when you make your application for insurance (complete the proposal), you can select other options:

- You and your husband/wife
- You and your husband/wife and any children who live with you
- You and a named driver or drivers
- Any driver

Of course, the only people entitled to drive will be those who have a licence to drive that category of vehicle in Turkey. This will include people entitled to drive on the basis of their foreign driving licence.

The proposal for insurance

Insurance companies and their contracts are regulated by the Insurance Association of Turkey (**www.tsb.org.tr**). Technically, your contract of insurance is a contract like any other and, therefore, it also needs to comply with the general requirements of Turkish contract law.

However, in practice, the application for insurance is a standard form that contains all the terms necessary to comply with both the insurance and contract laws.

Once the application for insurance is sent to the insurance company, the law allows them a maximum of 15 days during which to make you an offer of insurance or to decline your proposal.

If they do make you an offer of insurance, you are not obliged to accept it.

If the company makes you an offer of insurance, they must honour that offer for a period of 14 days from the date upon which it was made.

In practice, insurance is now normally arranged over the internet and the offer is made and accepted instantly.

Until a couple of years ago, the biggest problem was that all the local insurance companies would only accept proposals in Turkish and only had websites in Turkish. Today each of the insurance companies has a website in English and a proposal form in English. Some have websites and proposal forms in other languages, too.

The insurance policy

This will be issued in Turkish. This is a legal requirement. In most cases, you will also be offered a translation into English or (more rarely) another language.

Can I obtain my insurance from a company outside of Turkey?

No. To insure a car registered in Turkey you must use an insurance company licensed to operate in Turkey.

Which Turkish company should I use?

When deciding which company to use, most people are influenced mainly by price.

They should be more concerned about what happens when they make a claim. How easy will it be? Is there a claim line in their own language? Does the company pay out quickly when a claim is made, or do they try to find excuses for non-payment?

The good news is that all the Turkish insurance companies have an excellent record for making payments without unnecessary fuss when you make a claim. They are required to do this by Turkish law.

However, this does not make them all equal. There is a huge advantage of having the application form and a claim line available in your own language. If you speak English, this is not a problem as all the companies provide these facilities but if you speak (say) Russian or Swedish the options are more limited.

As the availability of language support changes regularly, we leave you to check on the individual insurance companies' websites to see what is currently available. See the contacts section at **www.guides.global/books/turkey/tur-contacts.php**.

Cancellation of an insurance policy

Cancellation by the insurance company

The insurance company may only cancel the insurance policy in the following circumstances:

- If the insured made false statements in the proposal for insurance

- If the risk covered is increased. For example, if the person is convicted of dangerous driving or wants to use the vehicle for business purposes. In this case the insurance company must offer the insured the opportunity to pay for continuing cover for an additional premium

- If the people insured all cease to have a driving licence. In this case the cancellation is automatic. No refund is due

- If the vehicle is sold. In this case the insurance company must refund the proportionate part of the insurance premium (less an administration fee)

- If the insured fails to pay the premium when it falls due. This means that, if you pay by cheque and your cheque is not honoured, the policy will be cancelled. You will be given notification of the cancellation and you then have 14 days in which to reinstate the policy by making the payment. Note that insurance policies are automatically renewed when they expire using the same bank or credit card you originally used when taking out the policy. If the payment is not collected in this way (for example, if your card is expired or you changed banks) you will be given notice of cancellation as explained above

Cancellation by the insured

The insured may cancel the policy in the following circumstances:

- If the vehicle is sold

- If circumstances arise that reduce the risk to the insurance company and, when the company is notified of these circumstances, it refuses to revise the premium downwards. This might occur, for example, if the person was going abroad for six months and the car was to be locked up in his garage for that period

- At the end of the agreed period of insurance (by stopping the automatic renewal of the policy)

Premiums

Insurance premiums in Turkey are amongst the lowest in Europe but take into account:

- The type of insurance

- The type of vehicle. Vehicles are divided into ten categories based on their performance, the cost of repairs and the extent to which they tend to be used. Some insurance companies will offer you a reduced premium on the basis that the vehicle is only used for a limited number of kilometres each year (typically 2,000km or 5,000km)

- Your age. Drivers under 25 or over 70 will attract a much higher premium or may not be insured at all

- Your accident record

- The area where you live

- Whether the car is garaged.

No-claims bonus

Insurance in Turkey is based upon the concept of the no-claims bonus (*Hasarsızlık indirimi*). Typically, your premium will be reduced by 5% for each year that you have not made a claim up to a maximum discount of 60%.

Some companies will, for an extra premium, allow you to protect your no-claims bonus. This means that, if you have an accident and make a claim, you will not lose your entire bonus - which is what would happen if you did not take out the protection. So, for example, if you pay the extra premium and you make a claim you may only lose one year of your no-claims bonus.

If you are moving to Turkey, the insurance company must recognise any no-claims bonus that you have 'earned' in your home country. You will need to produce an officially translated letter from your insurance company confirming the size of the no-claims bonus. This does not apply if you are insuring an extra car in Turkey: for example, if you have bought a holiday home here.

Making a claim on car insurance

When you make a claim against your insurance policy you are required to notify the insurance company within seven days of the event occurring. If you fail to do this then the company can decline any benefit to which you, personally, are entitled (including any claim in respect of damage to your vehicle) but it cannot refuse to pay for any third-party claims, including claims by your passengers.

If there is good cause for the delayed claim (for example, if your car was damaged while you were away on holiday and you only discovered it when you returned, or you were hospitalised) the seven-day limit will not be applied.

When you make your claim, you must submit a copy of any accident report form completed at the time of the accident.

You must also tell the insurance company whether the police were involved and, if so, give them the police reference number.

If your car is stolen, the same rules apply, and you must report the theft to the police and supply the company with the report number.

Once you have reported the claim, the insurance company will obtain copies of any evidence (such as police reports) and then decide whether to make a payment in respect of the claim.

They will then assess the amount of loss suffered. For this purpose, they may appoint their own assessor to provide an expert report about the injuries suffered by the people concerned or the damage caused to vehicles or other items.

The insurance company will then make an offer to compensate individuals for any injuries suffered.

They will usually arrange for the repair of any vehicles or other property damaged but sometimes may offer a cash payment instead. These payments are often lower than the full cost of repairing the vehicle as they will take into account any improvements that the repairs may cause. For example, if a tyre is ruined in an accident and it is half worn they will only offer to pay half the cost of a new tyre.

The insurance company must complete its investigations and pay the compensation or do the repairs within 40 days from the date you notify them of the claim. This does not apply if there are exceptional circumstances, such as an ongoing police investigation, or if damage of a very technical nature is caused.

What happens if the accident was not my fault?

You have two choices.

You can either claim directly from the insurance company of the driver whose fault it was, or you can claim against your own insurance company.

If you claim against the other driver, he will refer the claim to his insurance company who will then deal with it in the same way as they would if you were making a claim against your own insurance company. This claim will, of course, be subject to him having adequate insurance cover.

If the insurance company accepts that their insured was responsible for the accident they will deal with the claim, normally within 30 days.

If they do not accept that their insured was responsible for the accident, you will have to establish blame. This will either involve your lawyers making representations to the insurance company or using the Commission of Insurance Arbitration. In the worst case, it could mean going to court.

Your worst nightmare is an accident that could be said to be partly the fault of both or several people. In this situation, the Turkish system does not work very well. The companies do not really cooperate with each other. If one of the vehicles involved was a foreign vehicle, insured by a foreign company, the position is even worse.

Alternatively, you can claim against your own insurance company. If you claim against your own insurance company, they will pay you and - if they think it worthwhile - take up your rights against the other driver but, in this case, you will lose your no-claims bonus unless you have no-claims protection.

Legal remedies against the insurance company

Normally your insurance company will keep its end of the deal with you and pay you fair compensation for the losses suffered by you or other people.

However, if you are dissatisfied with the offer made to you, you do have the right to complain to the Commission of Insurance Arbitration, and/or to the Turkish courts.

There is a time limit of two years for making a claim if the insurance claim did not relate to personal injury, or five years if it did.

Home & Contents insurance

Is home insurance in Turkey obligatory?

Homes must be insured against earthquakes, but private home insurance is otherwise rare amongst Turkish people, unless they took a mortgage when they purchased the property: in which case the bank is likely to insist on insurance. In fact, fewer than half the homes in Turkey are insured.

What types of home insurance are available?

There is a lot of choice.

Strangely, for a country that insists you use a Turkish insurance company to insure your car, you may insure your home (and its contents) with any insurance company that takes your fancy and is prepared to take on a property in Turkey.

There are a number of international companies that offer to insure properties in most popular destinations in the world and there are local Turkish companies offering to insure your property in Turkey.

The types of insurance they will offer you can be very different.

The international companies tend to offer less complicated policies with fewer things for you to trip over when you're applying for the insurance or making a claim.

Most international companies will offer three types of insurance:

1. Insurance for when the property is your main residence.

2. Insurance for holiday homes that are not let (rented out).

3. Insurance for homes that are rented out for all or part of the year.

Insurance companies based in Turkey tend to take a different approach, offering you a menu of insurance items from which you can choose and, for several of those items, different amounts for which you can insure.

For example, in Turkey there is usually only one home insurance policy to which you can add extra insurance if your property is going to be vacant for more than a certain number of days each year (with a different premium depending on whether it will be empty for - say - 30, 90 or 180 days per year). They will also offer you insurance, at an additional cost, if you are going to let (rent out) your property for part of the year.

How much should I insure the building for?

Many people think that if their house is worth €300,000, they should insure it for €300,000. This is wrong.

Under the insurance law in Turkey (and that in many other countries), the amount you should insure for is the cost of rebuilding the property.

In some cases, this can be less than the value of the property. After all, you will still own the land and that might be worth 30% or more of the value of the building.

However, in other cases the cost of rebuilding (including the cost of any demolition and clearing the rubble from the site), can be far higher than the value of the building. This is particularly true if you own an older 'character' property. For example, I live in a 16th century building. Where and at what cost would I find 16th century beams, doors etc. to replace those that were destroyed and where would I find the workmen skilled in the construction methods needed to rebuild such a building?

What *is* the cost of rebuilding your property? This can be difficult to assess. This is strange when you consider the fact that everybody needs to do this to arrange insurance.

Fortunately, there are some websites - but none based in Turkey - that will help you estimate the cost of rebuilding a typical property of a typical type.

For example, specialising in UK property, the Building Cost Information Service, a part of the Royal Institution of Chartered Surveyors (RICS) and working at the request of the Association of British Insurers (ABI) provides a very detailed website allowing you to estimate the cost of rebuilding properties of different types, different sizes and located in different places.

Similar sites exist in many other countries around the world. They may give you some idea of the cost of rebuilding your property in Turkey.

What is covered by the average policy?

You will need to check your proposed policy to see what is actually covered. They often vary considerably.

Reading insurance policies can be complicated and it's certainly not much fun. This is one reason why simpler policies tend to be favoured.

Typical cover includes:

Insuring a permanent residence

- Full insurance for damage by wind, flood, fire, impact etc.

- Damage by explosion

- Escape of water from tanks or appliances within the building

- Escape of oil from any oil-fired heating system

- Damage caused by riots or people acting maliciously

- Damage caused by falling trees, lamp-posts etc.

- Full insurance against theft from your property

- Alternative accommodation cover if your property becomes uninhabitable

- Cover for architectural and other professional fees if repair work is necessary

- Damage caused by infestation

- Damage caused by subsidence

Things to look out for

- Does it cover your swimming pool? Surprisingly, some policies do not.

- Is there any limit to the value of the items covered in respect to theft? Most home insurance policies will only include the theft of items such as your hot water cylinder, your cabling etc. Some impose a financial limit on the value of such items.

- Does the policy offer public liability insurance (see below)? If it does not, you will probably need to take out additional insurance.

- Does the cover include employer's liability insurance (see below)? If it does not, you will probably need to take out additional insurance.

- Is there a high excess (the amount you need to pay yourself before you can make a claim)? In some cases, this can be expressed as a percentage of the claim rather than a fixed amount and this could amount to a lot of money.

- Does the insurer require special security arrangements: burglar alarms, cameras etc? Some will require these only if the content insured exceed a certain amount.

Insuring a holiday home

You will require all the insurance you would require for your permanent residence but, in addition, the insurance policy should provide cover for periods when the property is empty.

Things to look out for

- How long can the property be empty before cover ceases? In some cases, this period can be as short as 30 days. Other companies do not impose any restriction.

- Are you required to use special security procedures when the home is empty?

Insuring a holiday home that is also rented out

In addition to the insurance that you will need for a holiday home, you will need cover for damage caused by your tenants if you rent the property out during part of the year.

You will probably also want cover for theft by your tenants.

You may also want a special clause insuring you against claims by your tenants (for example, if they cannot stay in the property because it is infested by cockroaches or if they trip over something and injure themselves). Although some claims by your tenants might be covered by ordinary public liability insurance, it is better to have the position made clear in your policy.

Things to look out for

- Does the policy cover you for loss of rental income?

- Does the policy cover your valuable items such as jewellery?

- Do different excesses apply if tenants are in the property?

Turkish insurer or an insurer in another country?

For most people, the first thing they think about when deciding which insurer to use is the cost of the policy.

This is not the right approach.

You need to think carefully about the extent of the cover being offered. This means reading the policy documents or (and this is increasingly difficult in the age of the internet) finding an experienced insurance broker to advise you as to the best overall deal in your circumstances.

Saving €50 on the cost of your policy is no good if it dramatically reduces the cover provided.

The next thing to be thinking about is how good the company is when it comes to paying out on a claim. Some of the companies have a very poor record. This applies, particularly, to some of the cheaper companies.

A Google search on the name of the company plus "problems" may produce interesting results!

Once again, there is no point in saving €100 on your premium if the company constantly quibbles and treats paying out as an optional extra.

The next major issue for most people should be language. Unless you speak fluent Turkish - and technical, legal Turkish to boot - you will find it very difficult to understand policies and claim forms written in Turkish. It is therefore worth paying a little extra to an insurance company that provides documentation in your own language and a claims department that can operate in your own language.

Finally, if something goes wrong and you get into a dispute with your insurance company, would you be happier dealing with that dispute 'back home' or in Turkey? If you deal with an insurance company based in your home country, or with many international insurance companies, you will find that the law of that country governs the policy - not the law of Turkey.

Overall, our preference is to deal with insurance companies (good, experienced insurance companies) based in your home country or, failing that, operating internationally, and speaking your language. They will probably cost you a little bit more than a local Turkish company but, in the unfortunate event that you have to make a claim, you will probably think the extra cost well worthwhile.

Can my mortgage lender insist I use their insurance?

No. This is illegal.

They **can** insist that the property is properly insured.

They can **offer** you insurance, but they cannot force you to take it.

Most insurance offered via banks is uncompetitive.

What sort of cover do I need?

This will depend upon how you intend to use the property.

If, like many people, you are going to live in Turkey but intend to be away for large parts of the year visiting friends and relatives, you will probably find that holiday home insurance suits your requirements better than permanent residence insurance.

If you are thinking of renting out the property **at all** then you need insurance that permits this and covers you during the periods when tenants are in the property. This is not necessary if you allow friends and relatives to stay in the property without charge, but any payment (whether in cash or otherwise) can invalidate the insurance unless you take this special type of insurance.

What if my home is in a block of apartments?

Under Turkish law, if your home is in a 'community of owners' - if it is part of a block of apartments or part of a group of buildings that share common facilities such as swimming pools, tennis courts etc. - the administrators of the community must insure the buildings. However, the law only requires them to insure the 'common parts' of the property: the bits such as the corridors and lifts that all the owners can use.

Exactly what these are depends upon the legal structure of your community but, in the case of a block of apartments, it is likely only to be the roof, the shared walls, the car park, the gardens, the pool etc. This leaves the rest of your home - the bit within the outer walls of your apartment, uninsured.

Some (but few) communities take it upon themselves to arrange full building insurance for all the properties in the community. You need to check whether this is so in your case and, if it is, the scope of the insurance that has been arranged.

Of course, if they arrange such insurance, the cost is shared by all the owners in the community and forms part of your community fees.

On the face of it, having the administrators of the community arrange the insurance sounds like quite a good idea. In practice, it can be very wasteful. If almost everybody in the community is a permanent resident but you are using your home as a holiday home or to rent out, you will probably find that the insurance that has been arranged is inadequate. You will then have to either find a company that will provide top-up insurance (almost impossible) or take out a fresh policy to give you what you need. This means, of course, that your share of the cost of the community's policy is largely wasted.

Making a claim on home insurance

1. Your first step is usually to telephone your insurance company to tell them what has happened. Clearly, this is easier if they have a claim line in your own language.

2. If your policy includes providing alternative accommodation and if your home is uninhabitable, you should tell them this at the time you make the phone call. Alternative accommodation should be arranged almost immediately.

3. You will then usually need to submit some type of claim form and, then or later, evidence to support the claim (for example, an estimate for repair work).

4. In all but the smallest claims, it is usual for the insurance company to appoint an assessor who will report on the extent of the damage and what is needed to rectify it. This process can take several weeks.

5. At the end of it, they should agree with you how the claim should be dealt with. For example, that they will appoint a building company to repair the damage and pay you compensation for other aspects of your claim.

Premiums

Fortunately, home insurance rates in Turkey tend to be inexpensive. This is probably for two reasons.

The first is that Turkish people are (by and large) an honest lot and so fraudulent claims are rare.

The second is that most buildings in Turkey are relatively simple in structure and at low risk of fire.

An insurance premium for an average two-bedroom apartment in a block will probably be about €200 per year.

An insurance premium for a three-bedroom villa used as a holiday home but not rented out might be €500 per year.

In both cases, these premiums do not include contents.

In both cases, they can vary dramatically from one insurer to the next.

Can I protect myself from claims and lower my premiums?

As with almost every country, there are things that you can do which will make your insurers love you and reduce your premiums.

- Install secure locks. These may be required but, even if they're not, they're likely to lower your premium.

- Install an approved burglar alarm, possibly with remote cameras so that you can see what's going on in your home whilst you're not there. These will, typically, reduce your premium by 10%.

- In the case of a holiday home, limit the value of the insured items in the property.

Contents insurance in Turkey

Why do I need contents insurance in Turkey?

Your contents will not automatically be covered by your home/building insurance.

They will probably be worth a lot of money and if, for example in the case of a fire or flood, they were all to need to be replaced, it would be very expensive.

Most people will, therefore, want to insure their contents.

What will contents insurance generally cover?

- Damage to your possessions caused by all the things covered by your building's insurance

- Theft of your possessions

- In some cases, but not all, accidental damage to your possessions: for example, dropping a valuable camera

How much should I insure for?

You should insure for the full replacement value of the contents. To calculate this there is no alternative but to go around, room by room, to see what is there and give it a value.

Don't forget to include the value of any clothes, jewellery, cameras, watches etc. and the value of any cash that you hold in the building. There is usually a maximum allowable amount for any individual item set out in the policy. If you have items worth more than this the values will need to be agreed with the insurance company and an additional premium will probably be charged.

Making a claim on my contents insurance in Turkey

The process is exactly the same as for making a claim on the building's insurance.

Premiums

Contents insurance is relatively inexpensive unless you want to have large amounts of protection for long periods when the property is going to be empty.

The premium will depend upon the value of your contents and where your property is located.

It is usually much cheaper to take out building insurance and contents insurance at the same time and from the same insurer.

Other important insurance for your home

Employer's liability insurance

Most people are surprised when I mention employer's liability insurance. After all, this is their holiday home!

It is, however, easy for claims to arise under the category of employer's liability.

This is because, under Turkish law, the owner of the property is responsible for any injury or damage caused to someone working at the property *whether or not they are technically the employee of the property owner*. The claim is treated as an employment claim.

For example, if you are employing a cleaner at your home on a regular basis then that is - clearly - an employment contract and so it is no surprise that if the cleaner is injured a claim could arise by way of employer's liability.

What might be a little more surprising is that if you're employing a contractor - for example, someone who comes to clean the pool once a month - and that person is injured then the claim that will arise will be an employer's liability claim rather than a public liability claim.

You therefore need to have employer's liability insurance to cover anybody who is going to be working on your premises.

Fortunately, such insurance is usually extremely inexpensive if it is only going to cover casual employment such as this. It can be added to your main policy for as little as €50 per year. In some cases, it's included automatically.

Public liability insurance

Public liability policies cover any claim made by a member of the public: someone who is not a member of your household, your employee, or your tenant.

If your garden wall falls on someone's car, it will give rise to a public liability claim.

If a delivery man walks up your path and trips over a hole in it, that will be a public liability claim.

If your swimming pool leaks and the water kills the plants in your neighbour's garden, that will be a public liability claim.

Insurance against such claims is very inexpensive. In most cases, cover can be added to your existing policy for €50 or €100 per year. In some cases, it is automatically included.

Health insurance

Health insurance is major concern for those moving to live in another country - and even for those taking a vacation abroad. It is a particular worry to those over 60 and those who already suffer from some ailment such as a heart condition, cancer or diabetes.

Will I be able to obtain insurance?

Fortunately, there are now many more products on the market than there were ten years ago. Just as fortunately, many offer good cover. Even better, many do so at a very reasonable cost.

Will it cover my needs?

You will need to be clear about your requirements. You will also need to make full disclosure of your medical condition to the insurance company. If you don't, they are very likely to refuse to make a payment.

In this field, each case is very different: particularly if you have an existing medical condition.

Can I keep it going for the rest of my life?

Always check to see whether you have an automatic right to renew the insurance - even if you are taken seriously ill. Fewer than half of available policies give you this. Of course, if you are taken ill you can expect your premium to increase, possibly substantially.

What will it cost?

It all depend upon your individual circumstances and what kind of cover you choose.

Health insurance as a tourist to Turkey

You should always get this.

Unless you are travelling within an area where there is reciprocal recognition of healthcare rights (such as within the European Union or in Australia & New Zealand) you really should have health insurance.

This applies for even the shortest trip abroad. Disaster can strike at any time and it doesn't make any difference that you were only going to be in the country for two days when it comes to the (often horrendous) cost of medical treatment after, say, a car crash or heart attack!

Even if you are travelling within an area (such as the EU) - where (as a fellow EU citizen) you will have full cover for urgent and emergency treatment - it is *still* a good idea to have health cover. It can cover you for a lot more than the automatic cover that you enjoy.

For example, it could cover the cost of repatriation by air ambulance if you suffer serious injuries and cannot otherwise travel. Repatriation from Turkey to the UK will cost you about €5,000!

The European Health Insurance Card (EHIC) is not valid in Turkey. The EHIC scheme allows travellers to access to state-provided health care within member countries, so visitors are entitled to the same medical treatment that citizens of participating countries could expect to receive. Turkey is not part of the EHIC group of countries. Make sure you always have adequate travel health insurance and access to sufficient funds to cover the cost of any medical treatment in Turkey and the possible cost of repatriation.

If you need to make a claim, you must notify the insurance company at the earliest possible moment: certainly before you start authorising major items of expenditure. The best insurance companies will then take over responsibility for direct payment to the doctor or hospital in Turkey, but not all companies do so. Those companies may expect you to make some or all payments and then recover the money from them.

Is Turkey counted as part of Europe for travel insurance?

If you are buying Europe-wide travel insurance, make sure that Turkey is covered. While some companies treat Turkey as though it is part of Europe, other travel insurers class it as a 'worldwide' destination - so it's vital that you check.

I have travel insurance or private health insurance at home - do I still need health insurance in Turkey?

Health insurance as a tourist is often packaged into a broader travel insurance policy, covering not just the cost of healthcare but also lost baggage, delay to your flights etc.

Alternatively, you may already have private health insurance in your own country. Check that it covers you for travel to Turkey and for some of the crazy things you might want to do whilst you are there. Many policies exclude 'dangerous activities' such as diving, paragliding - and a night on the town with my husband!

Do I need health insurance for other (non-tourist) short-term visits?

Short visits for business and other purposes are usually covered by your tourist policy, but check to make sure. As Turkey is not a member of the EU, an EU emergency medical card (The European Health Insurance Card (EHIC)) is of no use here.

What healthcare insurance do I need for a long trip to Turkey?

Many annual multi-trip travel policies limit the length of any one trip, typically to 30 days. If you want to travel to Turkey for longer, make sure your policy permits this.

Health insurance as a resident in Turkey

Unless you qualify for cover under the Turkish health care programme (basically, if you are working and paying Social Security payments in Turkey), you will need to have health insurance if you live in Turkey. In most cases, you will need to produce proof of such insurance in order to obtain your permit to live in Turkey.

In 2014, the government, through the General Directorate for Migration Management, decided that retired people would no longer need to prove that they have health insurance in order to obtain or renew their residence permit. This was, partly, because retired people were finding it difficult to obtain cover: especially if they had any pre-existing conditions.

Of course, just because you may not need to produce proof of insurance does not mean that it is not a good idea to have it!

There are many types of policies available. Choosing the right one is critical.

You may, instead of taking out a private insurance policy, be able to sign up to the state controlled insurance scheme (*Sosyal Güvenlik Kurumu* "SGK"). The SGK is the Department of Social Security. This department is only deals with the affairs of employees (either Turkish or non-nationals with a work permit) and retired elderly Turkish citizens.

However, non-nationals who are not employed in Turkey, and who want Turkish residency, can only get it if they take private insurance - unless they are over 65 or have valid national insurance from their home country which is accepted by Turkey.

The Turkish state health insurance scheme, called GSS (*Genel Sağlık Sigortası*), is applicable only for Turkish citizens.

For those who sign up to the SGK scheme, once you have been accepted the policy can only be cancelled by SGK if you are leaving Turkey for good. This is very reassuring. Membership to SGK requires a medical assessment and costs around TRY272 (around $70/€60/£50) monthly, for a person in their sixties.

What is the difference between GSS and SGK?

The GSS is a non-compulsory government health insurance scheme, available only to Turkish people.

The SGK is the social security scheme, comprising two elements: pensions (and other social security benefits) and healthcare.

The SGK scheme

Once you have joined the SGK scheme, you are entitled to healthcare in Turkish state hospitals and clinics, but not most private hospitals or clinics. Most health problems, including operations, other medical treatment and pregnancy, are covered. Some private hospitals accept SGK patients; you will have to pay towards the cost of your treatment, but at a heavily discounted rate: typically, 30% to 70%.

A married couple with dependents under the age of 18 can join the SGK scheme under one policy. The cost is approximately TRY270 per month and is an inexpensive health insurance option for many families.

You can apply to join the SGK Health Insurance Scheme at any age. However, a set of doctor's reports from a state hospital showing that you do not have any pre-existing chronic condition must be presented with your application.

If you do not speak Turkish, it may be difficult to communicate with SGK staff, as most SGK offices do not provide support in foreign languages.

Private Cover

When you calculate the cost of SGK over the course of a year, it can be more expensive than some private health insurance policies.

The private health sector in Turkey is growing rapidly. Many Turkish people and foreigners choose private cover, as waiting lists are shorter and the standard of healthcare is generally higher.

You may have to check several options before you find a local company to offer you cover. This is especially so if you are over 70 or have a history of health problems.

It is well worth seeking help from a person experienced in this field.

What are the different types of private health insurance?

Your existing health insurance

If you have existing private healthcare cover this *might* cover you in Turkey. This is, often, the simplest and cheapest solution. Check.

A policy taken out with an international health insurance provider

There are a number of such providers. See our contacts list on **www.guides.global/books/turkey/tur-contacts.php.**

The main advantage of choosing such a provider is that you can choose one that speaks your language. This means that both filling in the forms and dealing with any claim can be much simpler. However, it may be subject to a time lag because you and the claims department could be in different time zones.

The main disadvantages are that such companies *tend* to be a little more expensive than local companies and they *tend* to offer a slightly narrower range of products.

A policy taken out with a Turkish health insurance provider

There are several such companies.

Unfortunately, some only offer their policy documentation in Turkish and only offer a Turkish speaking claims department. We suggest that (unless your Turkish is fluent or you are a masochist) you avoid those companies. Dealing with claims becomes extremely stressful.

However, increasingly, local companies are offering products aimed at the (substantial) expat community. With these companies, your application can be processed in a number of languages - especially English, French, Arabic, German and Russian. So can the process of making a claim. The policy document might even be available in your language: a huge advantage.

They have the added advantages of being local; you can go to see them if there is a problem. They are also, typically, a little cheaper than their international rivals.

Remember that, whichever insurer you use, the most important thing is that they behave properly when you make a claim: paying out promptly and without quibbling in a genuine case. Sadly, some companies do not. They enjoy taking the premiums but see paying out on claims as a nuisance and an optional extra. A Google search for the company's name and "claims" can be a real eye opener!

Pay particular attention to the international validity of the policy. Will it cover you if you live in Turkey but go on holiday to, say, France or - a sticking point for many - the US, where medical bills can be truly huge? Equally, will it cover you if you make a trip 'back home'? Some won't.

What should I be looking for?

Try to follow this checklist:

- Track record of paying out without argument

- Documents in your language

- Claim line and processing in your language

- Covers you in other countries as a tourist

- Covers you on trips 'back home'

- Price - this point is firmly last

Life insurance

Life assurance/life insurance

What is the difference between life insurance and life assurance? Basically, they're almost the same thing: they pay out when you die.

Technically, insurance is a contract that pays you out if something that might not happen does happen: e.g. you crash your car. On the other hand, assurance is a contract that pays you out when something that is definitely going to happen happens: e.g. you die.

As you are, most assuredly, going to die, all life insurance should really be called life assurance but it is increasingly known as life insurance.

The only exception to this is life insurance which is limited and will only pay you out if you die by a certain date. For example, you might be covered only until your 65th or 70th birthday. This, then, would properly be known as life insurance.

Will any existing life insurance policies be valid in Turkey?

Many people will, by the time they go to live in Turkey, already have life cover. They may have had it for many years.

The good news is that these policies will almost always still be valid if you move to Turkey. In very rare cases there can be a clause that limits cover if you go to live in another country. Check your policy.

Nonetheless, it is a good idea to notify your insurance company if you are going to go and live in Turkey. This will make it easier if you have to make a claim and you can take the opportunity of confirming that the policy will continue unchanged whilst you're living there.

New life policies in Turkey

You may be coming to Turkey with no life insurance or with life insurance that is about to expire: for example, a policy that only covers you up to the age of 65.

In this case, there is nothing to stop you taking out fresh cover, if you can find a company to insure you. This will be much easier if you are still young.

Under Turkish law you may take that cover either from a life insurance company based in Turkey or from a company based anywhere else in the world.

When it comes to choosing where to insure, the two big drivers will be language and price. Most people find it helpful to deal with a company that can process any claim in their own language - this is especially important when you remember that it will not be you who is making the claim but some relative, possibly thousands of miles away. As ever, of course, price is not everything and so you need to think about the nature of the cover being offered to you.

What does life insurance cover?

In a life insurance policy, the main cover is the payment of a lump sum in the event of your death. By definition, all policies offer this.

However, other cover can be added. This is often for the commercial advantage of the insurance company, but it can sometimes be convenient for the customer to have several types of insurance covered by the one policy. Generally, though, it tends to be more cost-effective to have separate policies.

The sort of other cover that can typically be added is cover for specific types of accidental death, which might increase the sum covered by the policy or maybe cover you for a longer period than the period covered in the policy: for example, covering you for your entire life against accidental death caused by drowning, whilst the general life insurance policy might expire at the age of 70.

The policy could also be extended to cover permanent disability or serious illness.

Other life insurance policies will agree to pay the amount you have insured not only on your death but also (instead) if you're diagnosed as suffering from a terminal illness during the period covered by the policy.

You do need to be careful that you're not signing up for multiple cover in these areas as you may find they're already covered by other policies. That is wasteful.

The cost of life insurance

The cost of life insurance will vary enormously depending upon the amount you wish to insure, your age and your existing medical conditions.

Advice

If you're thinking of taking life insurance cover you really ought to see a specialist life insurance adviser who should be able to direct you to the most appropriate policies.

Alternatively, or as a preliminary step before approaching an adviser, you could try one of the comparison websites.

Banks & Banking

Written by **Burak Orkun**
Managing Partner (Accountancy Department) at Orkun & Orkun
www.orkunorkun.com • info@orkunorkun.com

National banking

There are quite a number of banks operating in Turkey. Almost all are now foreign owned. TEB is owned by the French BNP Paribas; Garanti Bank is owned by the Spanish BBVA; Denizbank is owned by Russian Sberbank; and Yapı Kredi Bank is co-owned by Italian Unicredit.

Still more foreign institutions replaced old, historic, brands entirely with their internationally recognized names such as ING Bank, HSBC, QNB and ICBC.

Some banks do remain under Turkish control: Işbank, for example, is owned by the Social Democratic Party/Republican People's Party (CHP: the party founded by Kemal Ataturk); Vakif Bank is owned by the Government and both Ziraat Bank and Halk Bank are Turkish Government controlled.

Istanbul-based Türkiye İş Bankası is the largest bank in Turkey by Tier 1 capital, with US$10.4bn of core capital. It is closely followed by Akbank, which has US$9.6bn, and Türkiye Garanti Bankası, which has US$9.3bn.

Profits at Turkish banks have historically been high: hence their acquisitions by foreign banks. However, the country's lenders are now bracing themselves for the impact of regulatory measures aimed at curbing consumer lending and fear profits may tumble.

All banks in Turkey offer a full range of 'high-street' banking services for the private and business customer. None offer investment banking.

All the high-street banks offer debit and credit cards.

International (offshore) banking

There is no offshore banking industry based in Turkey, but people living in Turkey often use the services of offshore banks based in other jurisdictions.

Regulation

Following a series of bank failures and closures, all the banks operating in Turkey have, since 2000, been subject to the supervision of the Bank Regulation and Supervision Agency (BRSA, or BDDK in Turkish). It is very strict, and the system seems to work well. See **www.bddk.org.tr**.

Deposit protection

Any money you have deposited with any of the high-street banks in Turkey will be protected if the bank goes bust. The maximum protection will be TRY100,000

(£22,000/€25,000/US$28,000) per customer in the bank. This means that whether Mr Smith has one account or several in the bank that has failed, the limit is TRY100,000. If, however, he had accounts in several banks, he would be covered to TRY100,000 for each bank.

Who can open a bank account in Turkey?

Anybody, Turkish or foreign (with some exceptions, including Iranian citizens who suffer many restrictions), resident or not, can open a bank account in Turkey. You will need:

- To produce proof of your identity and address, in order to satisfy international money laundering regulations. The proof of identity will be the original or a certified copy of your passport and the proof of address will usually be original 'official' bills from the likes of your utility company, the tax department of the place where you live, etc.

- A Turkish tax number

- Your father's & mother's names and your mother's maiden name

- For US citizens, there are further formalities to comply with US law

Internet banking

All the high-street banks offer internet banking.

The instalment system

This is an arrangement for finance that is available and often used in Turkey.

A shop will promote the facility. You pay by credit card, with payment of the full price by instalments over six, nine, or 12 months. The shop receives immediate payment of the full amount, funded by the bank. You repay the bank by the agreed instalments.

How to choose the best bank

This book cannot advise you about the strengths and weaknesses of the various banks in Turkey. However, if you are going to be living in Turkey, or if you have a holiday home there, there are four very practical considerations that will help you decide which bank and branch might best suit your needs. This assumes that you do not have a strong preference for one bank or another on other grounds.

- Choose a bank that is located near to your home or in a place you visit regularly

- Choose a bank where there are (preferably several) members of staff who speak your language

- Choose a bank which provides internet banking services in your language

- If it comes to a tie-breaker, choose a bank where there is easy parking!

These considerations tend to be far more important than a marginal difference in interest rates or banking terms, especially as the best bank today is likely to be overtaken by another bank next week.

Turkish people tend to favour government-owned banks as they feel they are safer and more thorough. However, interest rates tend to be more competitive in the other banks.

Moving Money & Foreign Exchange (FX)

Written by **Burak Orkun**
Managing Partner (Accountancy Department) at Orkun & Orkun
www.orkunorkun.com • info@orkunorkun.com

Foreign exchange (FX) is one of those boring subjects which it is so easy to overlook when planning your international affairs. Doing so is a major mistake! Using an FX company - and choosing the right company - will probably make you one of the biggest savings associated with your project.

Whether you are buying a house or a car, starting a business, making regular payments or looking to make ongoing but irregular payments in the future, you need to understand FX.

What is FX (foreign exchange)?

FX stands for foreign exchange.

The foreign exchange market is a vast global market. Every day people need to pay for container loads of goods that they have shipped from A to B. Every day people are buying houses or businesses or cars where they are paying the price in (say) Japanese yen and converting (say) euros in order to do so. Some may be making regular transfers from one country and currency to another to make a mortgage payment or provide for their children. Others may be moving their entire savings from one country to another when they retire. They may be protecting a future position; if they know that they are going to have to find €100million later in the year, they may want to buy the money now and secure a fixed (and, more importantly, known) exchange rate.

Or they may just be gambling. Do not underestimate the last category. It is by far the largest component of the FX market.

The FX market is so large that it is hard to understand. In December 2016, it reached $5.1trillion per **day**. To put this into context, the entire GDP of the US - the world's largest economy - is about $19trillion per **year**. The daily size of the foreign exchange market is larger than the annual GDP of the world's fourth largest economy (Japan), twice as large as the UK GDP and over five times as large as the annual Turkish GDP. Remember, that is every single day!

It is also increasing. In 2010 it was only $4trillion.

What is an FX (foreign exchange) company?

An FX company is a company that specialises in foreign exchange: converting money from one currency to another. Of course, banks deal with FX transactions but that is only one area of their activity. FX companies do nothing else.

Case study

Heng Leu

Bar owner, Hong Kong Chinese, 60

The problem

Heng came to Turkey to start a bar when he retired from the civil service in Hong Kong. He gets a small pension from his old job, which helps with his living costs, but it goes into his bank account in Hong Kong, in Hong Kong dollars - and the bank charges extortionate conversion rates when sending the money to Turkey.

The solution

Although FX companies are known for transferring large amounts of cash (thousands of euros), Heng was able to make a deal with one which allowed him to transfer his pension over to Turkey, and receive it in Turkish lira, every two months. His exchange rates and transfer charges are now much better. In fact, sending the money in this way has made him nearly 15% better off.

Just as importantly, he is not currently at much risk of currency fluctuation because the FX company agreed to a fixed conversion rate for the next two years. This means he won't benefit if the HKD goes up in value against the Turkish lira, but also that he won't suffer if it goes down. That gives him some sense of stability and a little comfort.

Some foreign exchange companies will deal with almost every currency in the world (there are one or two that cannot be readily exchanged) whereas others specialise in dealing with just one or two 'pairs' - for example, they might deal with conversions from dollars to euro or dollars to yen but nothing else.

What are the typical FX (foreign exchange) services offered?

Most larger FX companies will offer four main services.

1. Their analysts can advise you about likely future exchange rates and when it is a good (or bad) time to buy a particular currency. They can often set up their system so that, when a currency hits a trigger point, they automatically make the purchase for you.

2. They can buy and sell currencies for you - so-called 'spot trades'.

    These are trades where you buy one currency (say, US dollars) using another currency (say, euros) at the rate prevailing at that very moment. This fluctuates by the second, sometimes quite dramatically.

3. You can enter into a 'forward contract'. This is a contract where you agree to buy a certain amount of currency (say, US$100,000) on a certain future date (say, in three months' time) for a certain fixed price (say, €75,000).

    The way this works internally for the FX company is quite complicated but, from your point of view, it is quite simple. You will normally be expected to pay a deposit (perhaps 10% or 20%) and to make the rest of the payment on the date you've agreed to take the currency.

    It's important to note that once you've entered these contracts you do have to honour them. If the exchange rate agreed moves against you and so the purchase at that price looks expensive, you still have to buy. If you don't, at the very least, you'll lose your deposit. You may face legal action.

    Generally, the maximum period for which you can buy forward is two years.

4. They can make regular payments for you, sometimes at a fixed exchange rate covering the next 12 or 24 months. For example, if you're moving abroad you may want to transfer your pension income from your 'home' bank to your new foreign bank every month. Alternatively, you may be making payments under a mortgage in another country or by way of child support.

Why should I use these services?

Forward buying your FX (foreign exchange)

Basically, using an FX company is likely to save you lots of money and/or to give you a fixed budget to aid your forward planning.

For example, forward buying allows you to know how much you're going to have to pay in your own currency for future services being paid for in another currency.

Imagine that you live in the US but are buying a house in France for €1million. The exchange rate between the dollar and the euro is volatile. For example, on 5 May 2014 the exchange rate was 0.7212. This means that to buy €1million would have cost you $1,386,578.

On 16 March 2015 the rate was 0.9391. The cost of buying your €1million would have been $1,064,849. This is a difference of over $320,000.

You might not be prepared to take that risk and prefer to know exactly how much that €1million is going to cost you on (say) 1 July 2018. A fixed rate forward purchase contract will give you that certainty. Of course, you may do better or worse than you would have done if you had waited and taken the spot rate when the money was actually needed, but you will, this way, know the extent of your exposure and be able to plan accordingly.

Regular payments

The problem with regular payments is not only that you may not know, in advance, how exactly much you're going to have to pay but also that, for small payments (say a few hundred dollars to pay your mortgage) the bank charges can be completely disproportionate to the amount you're sending.

A regular payment plan can eliminate one or both of these risks.

You can take a regular payment plan at a fixed rate (just like a forward buying contract) that will apply for the next year or two years, or you can just make arrangements to pay the money regularly on whatever date happens to be the day. In either case, the FX company can usually arrange for the payment to be transferred free of bank charges or at bank charges very much lower than normal because they will simply include your payment along with many others in one large transfer.

Why use an FX company and not your bank?

Generally, FX companies are a lot cheaper and they have the additional advantage that they can often give you a lot of useful guidance as to when it is best to make the exchange.

Foreign exchange companies tend to be cheaper than your bank for three reasons:

1. They are specialist. They don't have to fund a whole range of banking services and so their overheads are, generally, comparatively low.

2. They are usually working on a lower margin than your bank will apply. When making FX deals you do not usually pay a fee. Instead, the dealer makes his profit by a 'margin' between what he pays for the currency and what he charges you for it. The margin tends to be a lot tighter with an FX dealer than it is from other sources.

   For example, as I am writing this article, the interbank rate for a conversion from US dollars to euros is 0.9310. You will not be offered that rate. Through an FX dealer, you might be offered a 1% spread (the difference between the buying and the selling price). This would make a rate of 0.9217. If you were withdrawing cash from an overseas ATM, you would probably suffer a 2% spread: 0.9124. If you were using your credit card there might be a 3% spread: 0.9031. If you were so foolish as to change the money at a currency exchange kiosk you would probably suffer a 5% spread: 0.8844.

In real terms this means that, at the interbank rate, €100,000 would cost you US$107,412. From your FX dealer, it might cost you $108,497. From your ATM or bank it might cost you US$109,604. From the kiosk, it would cost you US$133,065.

Clearly, there are substantial savings to be made.

3. They can often give you good advice as to timing which can, in turn, make a big difference to your net cost.

How big are the savings?

As you can see, they are substantial.

Equally importantly, there can be substantial differences between FX companies.

Comparing those differences can be difficult because of the way the rates change every second. If you phone for a quote and then phone another company for the same quote there will *always* be a difference between the two figures.

About five years ago, in my office, we carried out an experiment. We simultaneously phoned our own bank and three foreign exchange companies to get a quote for converting £100,000 into euros. The difference between the bank and the worst FX company was well over €1,000. The difference between the best and the worst FX company was also over €1,000. That was an overall saving of €2,000: 2%.

A saving of €2,000 on the transaction probably pays your legal fees on the purchase of a house. It certainly buys a lot of bottles of wine for the house-warming party!

How do I choose an FX company?

There are two main considerations. The first - but less important - is obviously price. If one company is going to charge you US$115,000 and the other is going to charge you US$114,000, you would normally want to use the second.

However, the most important consideration is security. You're going to be giving this company a large amount of your money. You want to make sure that if they go bust or if one of their people runs away with all the money, your cash is safe.

This means that you need to make sure that the company is properly regulated in the country where you're living. It's also a good idea to do one of those wonderful Google searches to see whether people are experiencing any problems with them.

There are a number of good, reliable and highly experienced FX companies.

See our contacts page at **www.guides.global/books/turkey/tur-contacts.php**.

What's the minimum I can send?

This varies from company to company. For a one-off customer, it's typically about US$5,000. For regular customers, the figure will be much lower, and for regular payments it can be as little as US$300.

FX regulation in Turkey

At present, Turkey does not come under the EU MiFID guidelines. Hence, FX brokers in Turkey are not allowed to operate in the EU without a valid EU FX broker license.

Turkey has experienced its fair share of FX broker scams during the past decade, which has resulted in the Turkish Government's introduction of the Capital Markets Board of Turkey (*Sermaye Piyasasi Kurulu*) (CMBT) into the retail FX trading industry. This organization controls the entire capital market of the Turkish economy under guidelines directly imposed by the Turkish Government.

CMBT is an independent self-regulatory organization that operates on funds generated through membership fees and fines levied on its member firms for deviation from regulatory guidelines.

By law, only CMBT regulated FX brokers can offer financial services to Turkish residents. However, these limitations lead many Turkish retail traders to become unregulated FX scam victims.

In February 2017, the government banned Turkish citizens from excessive gambling on the FX markets by imposing a leverage limit of 10:1 when dealing with Turkish registered FX companies and trying to stop them arranging FX deals via international internet sites.

FX dealers based in other countries

If you're using an FX dealer based in another country, the laws of that country will regulate it.

How do I transfer foreign exchange to Turkey?

The method varies a little from one FX dealer to another. However, you will usually need to open an account with the dealer. This is usually quite simple.

They will need:

- Your personal information (name, address etc.)

- Your bank account details

- A copy of your proof of identity (usually a passport) and proof of address

- The reason you're going to want to be making FX transfers

All this is for anti-money laundering purposes.

When it comes to making a transfer, they will need to know the full details of the bank and the person to whom the money is to be transferred:

- Receiving bank name

- Receiving bank address

- Receiving bank's SWIFT or other ID code (if the bank doesn't use the IBAN (International Bank Account Number) system)

- The full name of the account holder

- Full details of the account into which the money is to be paid - usually the IBAN

- A short reference to help the recipient track the funds (e.g. "John Smith - deposit on yacht")

- The reason for the transaction

- The date upon which you wish to make the transfer

They will then book and hold a rate for a few minutes and email you an invoice.

You then arrange for a bank transfer to the FX dealer and they will release the foreign currency funds upon receipt of that money.

If you're making a regular series of transactions, you can set the whole deal up at the same time.

Summary

FX trading 'as an investment' is gambling. It is not for the faint hearted. In my view, it is not really sensible for anyone at all, but I am old-fashioned. 'Leveraged' FX trading (where you borrow part of the money) is - again in my view - madness.

FX trading is very open to fraud.

However, FX dealing for a specific purpose - such as when moving money overseas to set up a business or buy a house - makes a lot of sense. If you choose a good FX dealer you will save yourself a lot of money. A lot of money. Maybe as much as 2.5% of the amount you are transferring and, very often, 1% or more.

So the challenge is to find a good company. There are plenty about.

See our contacts page: **www.guides.global/books/turkey/tur-contacts.php**.

Transport

Written by **Başak Yildiz Orkun**
Managing Partner (Legal Department) at Orkun & Orkun
www.orkunorkun.com • info@orkunorkun.com

International transport links

Turkey is easily accessible from other countries.

Travelling by air

Turkey has many international airports. The busiest ones are:

Airport	City	Code	Visitors (2015)
Atatürk International Airport	Istanbul	IST/LTBA	61,322,729
Sabiha Gökçen International Airport	Istanbul	SAW/LTFJ	28,112,438
Antalya Airport	Antalya	AYT/LTAI	27,724,249
Esenboğa International Airport	Ankara	ESB/LTAC	12,326,869
Adnan Menderes Airport	İzmir	ADB/LTBJ	12,139,788

You can get a direct flight into Istanbul from most places in the world. If you can't get a direct flight to another Turkish city, it is easy to take a domestic flight from Istanbul to most other cities.

Flights into Turkey are generally reasonably priced. Examples for flights to Istanbul, booked a month in advance for July 2017:

From	Airline	Price
London	Pegasus	£207/€237/US$266
Berlin	Turkish Airlines	£237/€272/US$303
Mumbai	Turkish Airlines	£306/€350/US$393
Singapore	Emirates	£544/€622/US$699
New York	Turkish Airlines	£736/€847/US$940

Turkey: how things *really* work

The main Turkish Airlines are:

- Anadolujet
- AtlasGlobal
- Onur Air
- Pegasus Airlines
- Sun Express
- Turkish Airlines

Travelling by sea

Arriving in Turkey by sea is quite rare, unless you're a tourist hopping across to Bodrum, Kusadası, Marmaris or Fethiye from the Greek islands or to the Black Sea ports from Ukraine.

A ferry from the Greek islands (e.g. Kos or Rhodes) will cost between £17/€20/US$22 and £70/ €80/US$89.

Transport within Turkey

Travelling by road

Roads in Turkey vary from modern motorways to single-lane dirt tracks. Within and between cities, roads are usually of a good quality: head into the countryside, though, and you may struggle a little more.

Driving in Turkey (see page 123) can, at any time, be a challenge if you're used to a sedate experience 'back home'. Speed limits are widely ignored, and drivers will often drive through stop signs and even red lights.

Driving at night can be stressful, as many on the road will neglect to turn on their headlights and street lighting can be patchy. Expect to find cows and carts on rural roads.

Renting a car in Turkey is easy. All of the major international companies (Avis, Hertz, Europcar etc.) have offices in the country, and most international airports will have car hire desks offering both the big international companies and a host of local Turkish alternatives.

Be careful when using very small companies. The cars can be in poor condition.

Taxis

Taxis in Turkish cities are, generally, modern five-seaters that run on environmentally-friendly liquified gas (referred to as LPG or Autogas). This helps keep pollution down, but means that boot (trunk) space is severely limited, as the tank is kept in the back.

All taxis are fitted with a digital meter. All taxi drivers are meant to use them. Sometimes they don't - but they will usually give in if you insist (and your price will usually be lower if you do).

The starting fare in a Turkish taxi is usually around TRY3 (£0.60/€0.75/US$0.80). From there, the fare will vary depending on the city - but expect another TRY3 per km.

A taxi waiting for an hour may charge around TRY30 (£6/€7.5/US$8).

'Tipping' is not expected, but a gentle rounding up is the norm: a fare of TRY37 becomes TRY40. A tip is appropriate if your driver helps with heavy luggage.

As well as conventional taxis, Uber is also available in major cities.

Travelling by train

Unlike in most countries, Turkish train travel is generally a cheaper and slower method than traveling by bus - although many long-distance travellers are happy to sacrifice a couple of hours for the additional comfort of a train. Most trains are now air-conditioned and well maintained.

A ten-hour journey on a normal train will cost you about TRY40 (£9/€10/US$11) for a single ticket.

A return ticket costs around 20% less than two single tickets would do.

A high-speed train is now in service on the Istanbul-Ankara-Konya route, and many other such routes are currently under construction (Adana, İzmir etc.). These trains are of the same high quality as high-speed trains in Europe, and the price reflects it: tickets cost twice what they do on ordinary trains on the same routes.

A single ticket on a high-speed train from Istanbul to Ankara will cost around TRY70 (£15/€17.5/US$19).

Metro

İstanbul, Ankara, Bursa and İzmir all have metro (underground) railway systems. A *jeton* - a transport token - will cost around TRY2 (£0.40/€0.50/US$0.60).

Travelling by bus

Long-distance buses

Buses are a great option for long-distance travel in Turkey. They are reasonably fast (six to seven hours between Ankara and Istanbul) and run regularly (every 15 minutes or so). They are usually modern, air-conditioned vehicles.

See a list of bus routes here: **bit.ly/2rTLq39**

Regular buses within cities

Bus systems in Turkish cities are generally reliable, frequent and well-connected. In most places, you'll have to buy a ticket in advance from a special kiosk. Tickets cost around TRY2 (£0.40/€0.50/US$0.60).

Airport buses

Most airports have buses operating to nearby towns and cities.

Dolmuş/minibus

Dolmuş are operated by licensed private vehicle owners, mainly outside of major routes and in the places where municipal transportation is not provided. Therefore, they are usually a little more expensive than buses, but they're generally more comfortable and faster. They operate on fixed routes.

They can be used to travel within or between towns. You can find *Dolmuş* stops by signs with a capital 'D' (*Durak*/Stop - used for all local public transport). They are usually located near town squares or other landmarks.

The main difference between a *Dolmuş* and a regular bus is that a *Dolmuş* will usually stop almost anywhere along its route upon the request of a passenger, even though they are not really meant to do so.

Driving

Written by **Başak Yildiz Orkun**
Managing Partner (Legal Department) at Orkun & Orkun
www.orkunorkun.com • info@orkunorkun.com

Driving in Turkey is pretty simple - especially if you come from a country where they drive on the right-hand side of the road. Simple, but not unexciting. Turks tend to drive very quickly, usually weaving through traffic and often whilst speaking on their mobile phone. Too frequently (though less often than before), they do this after consuming alcohol.

Its traffic laws are similar to those in most European countries, as are the rules about who can drive.

There are lots of police checkpoints, looking for drunk drivers, drivers with no licence or insurance and vehicles that are dangerous. They are also looking out for general criminality, wanted people and so on. If you are stopped and your paperwork is not in order, it can become very tedious.

The two things that make driving in Turkey a little more complicated - and off-putting to some people - are the poor secondary and local roads found in most of the country and the foolhardy courage of some Turkish drivers: no gap is too small, no straight too short to overtake and no speed quite high enough! However, this stereotype of the Turkish driver is getting a little out of date and standards have improved enormously over the last few years.

Licences

Driving in Turkey can be complicated not only because of the roads and the traffic but also because of the complexities surrounding driving licences.

Using your 'home' driving licence

Turkey has agreements with 50 countries (see **www.trafik.gov.tr**) permitting visitors to use their home licence *providing it includes a photograph* during visits of up to six months. If your licence does not have a photograph, it cannot legally be used in Turkey.

The period for which you can use a foreign licence depends upon the country you are from. The periods for each country are listed on the website. It is available only in Turkish, but translates quite well using Google Translate.

It covers most countries from which visitors are likely to come to Turkey.

For countries *not* on this list, or if your licence does not bear a photograph, you can *only* use your home licence in conjunction with an International Driving Permit (IDP).

An IDP is, as the name suggests, recognised internationally. This includes in Turkey.

There are two types of International Driving Permits. These are based on the two conventions under which various countries agreed to adopt them. Turkey requires what is known as a '1949 Convention IDP'. The people who issue the permit will know this, but it's worth reminding them. The agency that issues IDPs is usually the main motoring association in your country. A Google search will reveal where you need to apply in your country.

The cost of obtaining an IDP varies from country to country but is typically about €20.

Note that an IDP is not the same as an international driving licence. An IDP is not a legally recognised document giving you the right to drive. It is, rather, evidence that you possess such a licence in your own country.

An application for an IDP cannot be made more than three months before the date when you intend to use it. It is valid for 12 months. It must be used in conjunction with and presented with your own national driving licence.

Although the IDP document is valid for a period of 12 months, it can only be used in Turkey at any one time for a period of six months. So, for example, you could go to Turkey in January and remain there until April (four months) and then return in September and stay until the end of October (two months) using the same IDP as the total time spent in Turkey in the calendar year is no more than six months.

The important thing is that you do not spend more than six months in the calendar year in Turkey driving on your combined 'home' driving licence and IDP.

Converting your licence

After that, you must convert your licence and validate it for use in Turkey. This will usually apply to people who are resident in Turkey.

This is bureaucratic but relatively simple. You do it at the local traffic department. There is no driving test or health check.

You need to produce:

- Your existing driving licence

- An official translation of the licence

- Two approved biometric photographs. Get these taken by a local photographer. They will know what is required

- Your residency permit

- A health certificate, valid for one year. This can be obtained either from a state hospital or a private hospital

- A certificate showing your level of education (in Turkey only people educated to at least primary school level are allowed to have a licence)

- A certificate showing your blood group

You also have to pay a fee.

Once you have obtained a licence, there is no expiry date.

Driving a car that you have temporarily brought to Turkey

If you have brought your foreign-registered car or vehicle to Turkey on a temporary basis, you are allowed to drive it in Turkey on the basis set out above. You must be able to produce proof of ownership of the car.

This right is a strictly personal right. Only you, your spouse or your children may drive the car. It may not be used for commercial purposes.

These rules are a result more of the restrictions on importing vehicles than they are the law relating to driving licences.

Things you must carry with you

When driving in Turkey you must (by law, though many people don't) carry with you:

- Your passport
- Your driving licence
- Your vehicle registration document
- Your vehicle insurance document (usually a 'Green Card' is needed)
- Headlight converters, if your vehicle is normally driven on the left hand side of the road
- A first aid kit
- A fire extinguisher
- A tow rope
- A vehicle jack and tyre changing kit
- A portable hazard lamp
- Two European-style warning triangles, which must be placed at least 50 metres in front of and behind the vehicle if you break down
- In parts of Turkey, during the winter, snow chains
- If you're driving a foreign car you must display the internationally recognised plate showing the vehicle's country of registration.

Insuring your vehicle

See our section on car insurance (p88).

Turkey: how things *really* work

Vehicle safety test

There is no annual vehicle safety test.

Basic rules of the road

In Turkey, they drive on the right-hand side. Most of the time!

Generally, the speed limit in towns is 50kph. In some places it is 30kph

The speed limit on all other roads except motorways (freeways) and two-lane highways (dual carriageways) is 90kph.

On two-lane highways: 110kph.

On motorways (freeways): 120kph

There is a general tolerance of 10% over these limits.

There are a few exceptions (for example, near schools) but these will be clearly signposted.

There are a growing number of speed cameras - and lots of cows around blind bends!

The permitted blood alcohol level is low (but the same as in many European countries): 50mg of alcohol in every 100ml of blood. Breaking this law will result in losing your driving licence for six months.

Pedestrians have an absolute right of way on pedestrian crossings - in theory. You must stop if you see a pedestrian on the crossing or about to step on the crossing. If you are a pedestrian, don't rely on this happening!

You and your passengers (front and back) must always wear seatbelts if your vehicle is fitted with them.

Children under less than 1.35m (about 4'6") tall or under 36kg in weight must be restrained in proper child seats.

Car parks are marked with the internationally recognised 'P' symbol or *"Otopark"*.

The road signs are, in the main, the conventional European road signs. For details of the rules covering driving in Turkey, see the Traffic Sign Handbook (**www.kgm.gov.tr**).

Parking

In Turkey, parking is a cross between an art form and a type of warfare. In the towns, and in many of the developments by the sea, parking is in short supply. Finding and occupying a parking space can, therefore, be challenging and - once he's found one - any local Turkish driver would feel that he had failed miserably if he did not seize it and, somehow, squeeze his car into it.

If the space is a little too small for the car, this process can involve him gently (or not so gently) pushing the cars in front and behind out of the way.

Having said all that, there are various types of parking available:

On-street parking

In small towns, unless the road is labelled to say that parking is restricted in some way, there is no need for any permit to park on any street in Turkey. Nor is there any charge for such on-street parking.

However, in the major towns and cities, in most streets parking is restricted in some way. This is often by the presence of a parking warden, who will charge you the appropriate parking fee.

Off-street parking

Most towns and villages have off-street parking.

Some of it is privately owned and *cannot* be used by the general public.

Some of it (such as supermarket car parks) is privately owned but *can* be used by the general public upon the terms stated. These are, normally, that it can only be used by customers and only for a maximum of two hours.

Some is publicly owned and can be used by anybody upon payment. Proof of payment is almost always by displaying a voucher in your car.

The cost of parking and the length of time for which you park varies from place to place.

Fuel

Fuel is widely available. In the last few years, thousands of large new fuel stations have opened. You will seldom be more than a few kilometres from a place where you can buy fuel.

Prices vary from place to place. Typically (March 2017):

- Petrol/gasoline (*benzin*) - TRY5.16 (£1.14/€1.30/US$1.46) per litre

- Diesel/gazoil (*dizel*) - TRY4.50 (£0.99/€1.14/US$1.27) per litre

- Autogas/Gas (*LPG*) - TRY3.11 (£0.68/€0.78/US$0.87) per litre

In rural areas, tax-free diesel is also often available. It is cheaper. It may only be used in agricultural vehicles. If you're found using it illegally, you will be subject to a large fine *and* your vehicle will be seized and not returned to you.

Things to know

Bear these facts in mind...

- You will have to pay tolls for some motorways. They can only be paid using a tag/transponder (HGS). You can't pay by cash or credit card

- The speed limit is between 30kph to 70kph in built-up areas, 110kph on open roads and 120kph on motorways

- If you're caught committing a driving offence, you'll be given a fine. The fine can be paid to the tax offices and some banks. You cannot pay in cash to the police officer

- The drink driving limit is zero for commercial drivers and 50mg/100ml for other drivers. It is best if there is no alcohol in your blood when driving. The penalties are stiff and could see you held in a Turkish jail or ordered to carry out community service in Turkey

- You must use dipped headlights during the day when the weather is obscuring your view

- You shouldn't use your horn except in cases of extreme danger. This is much ignored

- Children under age ten can't sit in the front of your car

- Petrol, diesel and LPG are readily available

- If you're driving at night, or in rural areas, watch out for livestock, unlit farm vehicles and drunk drivers

- If you have an accident, you will need to fill in an accident report and may need to call the police

Motoring offences

There are many, the main ones being:

Driving dangerously

Dangerous driving is very broadly defined and very subjective. It can cover driving too quickly, driving too close to another vehicle, overtaking on bends, passing when not permitted, using your mobile phone whilst driving and all sorts of things pretty much at the discretion of the police officer who stops you. If you disagree with their assessment you can, of course, try to persuade the judge that what you were doing was not dangerous.

In most circumstances these are treated as administrative offences (and fined as such) rather than full criminal cases. Each offence has a different penalty. Typical penalties are a fine of TRY100-200. There is usually no loss of your licence.

However, if you put the public in serious danger you can be taken before the full criminal courts and punished more heavily.

Driving whilst drunk

The permitted blood alcohol level is (as of January 2013) 50mg/100ml of blood (0.5 grams per litre) for cars and 0mg/100ml for commercial drivers or those towing.

If you are stopped, breath-tested and fail the test your licence will be suspended immediately for at least six months, the vehicle will be banned from the road and there will be an administrative penalty. On a first offence the penalty is TRY876 (£193/€221/US$247).

On a second offence, the penalty is TRY1,098 (£241/€277/US$310) and the licence will be taken for two years.

On a third offence, the penalty is TRY1,763 (£388/€455/US$498), plus at least six months in jail and the licence will be taken for five years. You will also have to take a fresh test at the end of the five years.

You can refuse a breath test. If you do you will be taken to a hospital for a blood test.

Driving without insurance

As in most countries, it is a criminal offence to drive without valid insurance.

In Turkey, the fine is usually a modest TRY95 (£21/€24/US$27) but your car will be impounded until you produce proof of insurance.

See our chapter on car insurance (page 88).

Accidents

If you are unlucky enough to be involved in a road accident in Turkey, you should read our chapters on accidents in Turkey (page 305).

The police

There is a heavy police presence on the roads in Turkey and they routinely stop drivers to check on their insurance and other driving documents.

Random stops are permitted.

The police officers are invariably courteous, but they are also invariably strict. If they discover that you have committed any offence or that your car is in any way defective you can expect a fine or a summons to attend court.

Despite what many people believe, the fines levied by the police do not go into their pockets!

If your vehicle fails a safety check for anything other than the most trivial of reasons (for example, a failed stop lamp bulb) it will usually be impounded and then taken away by the police to a vehicle storage centre where it can only be recovered by an officially approved garage who will then carry out the necessary repairs to it. The fee for releasing your vehicle varies from place to place.

Marriage

Written by **Başak Yildiz Orkun**
Managing Partner (Legal Department) at Orkun & Orkun
www.orkunorkun.com • info@orkunorkun.com

Turkey still has one of the highest rates of marriage in the world: about 7.75 women out of every thousand in the population get married each year. We're also blessed with a low - but growing - divorce rate (20%).

We also have many beautiful places in which to live and get married. No wonder that so many foreigners wish to marry here!

The number of foreign grooms in 2015 was 3,566 and they comprised of 0.6% of total grooms. When foreign grooms were analysed by citizenship, Germans with 38.4% (1,368) took first place. They were followed by Austrians with 7.9% (282) and Syrians with 6.8% (241 persons).

Under Turkish law, two foreigners of the same nationality can marry either in the offices of their own country's Embassy or Consulate, or in front of the Turkish authorities. This book only deals with marriage using the Turkish system.

The system of marriage in Turkey

Marriage is only permitted between a man and a woman.

Polygamy is not accepted; monogamy is an essential principle of Turkish family law and anyone currently married may not be married again in Turkey.

Normally, you must be at least 18 years of age to marry but, if they are judged to understand the proceedings, a person 17 years of age may be married with their parent's or guardian's consent. For a person to get married at age of 16, a court order is required. There is no maximum age for marriage.

You need to have mental capacity and there are the usual prohibitions on marriage between close relatives.

In Turkey, all marriages take place in the presence of an authorized official from the local town hall: at the town hall or in a place chosen by the couple. There is no restriction on the place where you can marry.

The ceremony is carried out either in person by the mayor of that municipality (if you are important), or - more likely in most cases - by an official appointed by the mayor.

Each town hall has a marriage officer appointed to deal with all the administrative steps necessary before a marriage. In smaller municipalities, the marriage officer is often also the person who conducts the marriages but in larger towns it is a separate person: a clerical officer.

If you wish to have a religious ceremony in Turkey you can do so, but this can only be carried out *after* you've been through the civil ceremony. It is not a requirement to have a religious ceremony.

> **Late update:**
>
> As this book went to press, the Turkish government announced plans to allow *Muftü* (Islamic scholars) to conduct marriages in Turkey.
>
> It will only be state-registered *Muftü* who are authorized to do this and they will be only conduct state marriages, not religious marriages.
>
> The announcement has caused some concern amongst Turkish lawyers and women's groups who fear that it is another step towards the loss of Turkey's secular society.
>
> Concern has also been expressed about whether some *Muftis* might turn a blind eye to the minimum age for marriage, and permit the taking of multiple wives.

Documents you will need to get married in Turkey

You will need to present the following documents, in person, to the marriage officer at the town hall:

- Your passports, with official translation

- A Certificate of No Impediment/Certificate of Capacity to Marry/Certificate of Celibacy/Affidavit of Eligibility to Marry. This is known by different names in different countries but certifies that a person is legally free to be married. Where you get this from depends on which country you come from.

- A valid entry visa. This could be a tourist visa. You do not need to have been in the country for any specific period, though arranging things does take some time, so you will need to be there for some days. See below.

- Your birth certificates, with an official translation

- A health certificate. This confirms your mental capacity and shows the results of blood tests for HIV and certain other conditions

- Four photographs of each person

- If you are divorced, your decree absolute or final certificate of divorce

- If you are widowed, your former spouse's death certificate and your previous marriage certificate

- If your birth name has been officially changed, the document changing your name

- If you are adopted, your adoption certificate

- If you are under 18 and judged fit to marry, a letter of consent from a parent or guardian

- An accommodation document: foreign couples not resident in Turkey must provide a letter written by the hotel (or other place where they are staying) stating the duration of their stay and their proposed departure date

- If any of your documents are not written in the Turkish language, an official translation is required. This will be a notarised document prepared in Turkey or you can have the document translated and notarised back home - where the cost will probably be several times higher

Making an appointment at the town hall

Once you have all your documents, you need to attend the town hall where you are to be married and submit them to the marriage officer. If you are lucky, you will be able to see the marriage officer immediately but if this isn't possible you can make an appointment to see them, usually within a couple of days.

Note that you cannot submit these documents by post. Nor can you apply for an appointment to see the marriage officer until you have arrived in Turkey.

Your appointment with the marriage officer

During your meeting, you will complete, and sign in duplicate, a marriage declaration (*Evlenme Beyannamesi*).

If the office is satisfied with the application, a district alderman (*muhtar*), or a marriage officer - subject to couples applying together, in person, notarises and an authorised officer certifies the documents. The stamped and dated marriage declaration gives you permission to marry. This is valid for six months; the marriage can take place within 48 hours of this licence being issued.

The marriage officer will suggest some dates. These are usually several months in the future. A wedding within a couple of weeks can be difficult but not impossible to arrange. In Turkey, quick marriages are usually as a result of pregnancy.

Once you have chosen the date, you will be required to pay an administration fee to the municipality. This is currently (2017) about TRY100 (£22/€25/US$28), if you are not using their venue. If you want to use their venue, the charge is usually in the range of TRY100-TRY450 (£99/€113/US$127), depending upon the place and the day of the week. Weekends are more expensive. There is currently no fee for carrying out the ceremony but it is customary to give the officer a present. This is not corruption!

Pre (and post)-nuptial agreements

There are two different systems that usually govern what happens to marital property under Turkish law.

The basic (and default) matrimonial property regime is the "participation in acquired assets" which means that the spouses will benefit equally from all assets acquired during the marriage.

If the spouses do not want to be subject to these arrangements, they can choose an alternative arrangement: a separate property regime, a shared separate property regime or a communal property regime.

Under the Turkish Civil Code, spouses are able to make agreements about marital property, before, at the time of, or after the marriage.

There are two different forms of pre-nuptial agreement. Under the first, the pre-nuptial agreement can be completed at the office of a notary public. Under the second, the couple can declare to the marriage officer the regime that they want to use when they apply for the marriage.

If the spouses decide to choose a marital property regime during the marriage application, they must inform the marriage registrar in writing.

You should note that, as the institution of marriage is so important to public policy, in the course of matrimonial proceedings a judge has absolute discretion as to how to apply any terms in a pre-nuptial agreement. In reality, this means that your chosen arrangement could be modified or overruled.

The stag (bachelor) and hen(na) nights

In Turkey, it is becoming customary for both the bride and groom to have a celebration with their friends the night before the marriage. These days it is increasingly common for it to take place a week or two before the marriage.

For brides, the traditional form of this is the henna night. The bride and her friends get together and paint henna on each other's hands. This is not compulsory.

I understand that in some countries such parties tend to involve considerable public drunkenness. This is not the case in Turkey. These events are an unofficial but important part of the marriage process and drunkenness would be thought totally inappropriate.

The ceremony

The marriage ceremony will, typically, take about 15 minutes. Usually, a time slot of 30 minutes is allocated to the ceremony. Do not be surprised if you arrive and find that you have to wait until the marriage of a preceding couple has been concluded or if there is another couple waiting in the waiting room as your marriage is concluded.

Most marriages take place in the evening.

In the case of foreigners (who do not speak fluent Turkish), most town halls extend the period reserved for the marriage to one hour. There is no extra fee for this.

This extra time is because, by law, the ceremony must take place in Turkish: it must be open to any member of the public to attend. For this reason, if the parties do not each speak good Turkish, the marriage officer will arrange for an interpreter to be present at the marriage and the whole proceeding will be translated into the language of the parties. The parties will have to pay the fee of the interpreter. For most languages, this will be about TRY200 (£44/€50/US$56), although for unusual languages, where the interpreter may have to travel some distance, it can be much higher.

We have, on occasions, had to deal with a marriage where we needed two interpreters because neither of the parties spoke the language of the other very well. It made me wonder why they were getting married!

The ceremony itself is in a standard form. The marriage officer will supply you with a script when you book the wedding. The marriage officer asks each of the couple if they agree to marry the other; after a positive response from both, the marriage is declared made in accordance with the law.

Two witnesses (other than immediate family members and the translator) are required for the procedure. These can be friends or hotel staff.

Wedding photographs

Photography (including video photography) is permitted at your marriage, whether it takes place at the town hall or elsewhere. If you want professionally taken photographs, there will be several local photographers who specialise in providing this service.

Marriage certificates

Immediately after the marriage you will be issued with a certificate of marriage.

If you require further copies of this certificate they can be supplied, at the time or later, for a modest cost. People often want extra copies to supply to their bank and other institutions, so that the details of their accounts can be changed and so that they can change the legal ownership of their property into their joint names.

If you wish to use these certificates in another country then, technically speaking, they should be 'apostilled'. They may also need to be translated. The process of apostilling a document is an internationally recognised procedure established under The Hague Convention of 1961. It involves the responsible authority in Turkey applying a seal to the document confirming that it appears to be valid. In Turkey, the authority responsible is the Ministry of Internal Affairs, and the apostille is done by the governor's office of that province/town. There is no charge for the apostille. It usually takes two days to receive the document back.

Note that if either of the parties to a marriage is not a Turkish national, the law requires them to supply an official copy of their new Turkish marriage certificate to the embassy or consulate in Turkey of their own country.

Validity of your marriage

Under international law, a marriage in Turkey is legally recognised and binding in most countries. It is worth confirming that it will be valid in your country. Ask a lawyer or the office than conducts marriages in your country.

To make your life easier, it is recommended that you translate and legalise the marriage certificate for use in your own country.

Religious ceremonies

It is commonplace for people to also want a religious ceremony, and this is entirely permitted by Turkish law.

The ceremony may be of religious importance but it has no legal effect. The arrangements for the religious ceremony are made directly between the parties to the marriage and the church or mosque in question.

The ceremony *must* take place after the civil ceremony. It is a criminal offence to do otherwise. This is despite the fact that, in some traditional rural areas, people have lived together for years and raised families when they have had only a religious ceremony.

The honeymoon

It is customary for the newly married couple to go away together for at least a few days by way of a honeymoon. If you're already here in Turkey, you might not want to go elsewhere!

There are usually local companies who specialise in providing honeymoon packages, in Turkey or elsewhere.

Things to do after the marriage

After your marriage - ideally within about four weeks, but this is not compulsory - there are several things that you should do. For a foreigner, the most important is to notify your consulate about your marriage and send them a copy of your marriage certificate. See above.

You are likely to want to change the name on the wife's passport and other official documentation. It's worth spending a few minutes making a list of all the places where the name is stored and to contact them all at once.

Typical examples of people you will need to know about your marriage are your bank, your mobile phone company, your doctor and dentist, any companies who've provided loans to you, any store or credit cards that you use, the residential community of which you are a member, any professional bodies to which you are affiliated and any social groups to which you belong. It is surprising how many will end up on the list!

Next you need to decide which of these will require formal notification, including a copy of the (translated and apostilled) marriage certificate. There tend to be very few of these. For most of the people on your list, a simple photocopy of your marriage certificate and translation or even just a letter of notification will suffice.

Don't forget to notify your tax office. You may be entitled to some tax breaks!

Children

Written by **John Howell**
Editor & Founder of Guides.Global
www.guides.global • john.howell@guides.global

Your children will have a great time living in Turkey. Because of the climate and the freedom that children still enjoy in a country largely free of crime, they will probably lead a far more active and outdoor life than they would have done in your own country.

Turks, and especially Turkish children, are very friendly and inquisitive about new foreign classmates and neighbours, with the result that your children will probably make friends quickly. This is one of the advantages of there being relatively few foreign children in the country.

Of course, by making friends they will also learn the language. It is not at all uncommon for children aged four or five to be able to converse in Turkish within a couple of months of their arrival in Turkey, and to become thoroughly proficient within 12 months. Older children can expect to be speaking Turkish perfectly within a couple of years.

It is not all freedom.

Your children will have to go to school (see below). To make the transition to school as painless as possible, there are five things that you should do before you bring your children to Turkey:

- Obtain a full copy of their academic record (from back home). Exactly what your educators will be able to give you will vary depending on where you live but they will know or have access to the information about what is needed, and it is usually simple to procure this documentation

- Obtain official copies of all their examination certificates and other qualifications

- Obtain a full copy of your child's health records. The school in Turkey may or may not wish to see these. Strangely, they have the right to do so - but it seems to be exercised less and less frequently

- Investigate the schools available in the area where you think you're going to be living. You will usually not be able to make an application for a place (except at one of the international schools) until the school has met you and your child; but most schools in an area have very similar requirements when it comes to the documents you'll need you to produce for registration, so you should be able to find out what these are

Turkey: how things *really* work

- Gather together all the documents you're likely to require, erring on the side of caution. It's better to have a document and not to need it than to have to send back home for it once you have arrived in Turkey.

Should you have all these things translated into Turkish?

The infuriating thing is that there is no guarantee which, if any, of these documents will need to be translated, so it is probably best to travel to Turkey and then arrange for the documents actually requested to be translated. This is usually the cheapest solution.

You should, strictly speaking, use an official, certified translator for this purpose but this is not often necessary in practice, provided the Turkish translation is clear. However, once again, given the cost of translation and the time it takes, it is probably better to have the documents translated by an official translator. Your lawyer should be able to suggest one.

If you decide to have things translated before your move, translators are used to receiving documents by email and then translating them for people who are not yet resident in the country.

As the stack of documents you're going to want translating could be quite substantial, you can expect translation to cost you quite a lot of money. Different types of documents incur different levels of charge but if you think about something like US$30-50 per page as an average, you'll get some idea of the sums involved.

Education

Written by **Başak Yildiz Orkun**
Managing Partner (Legal Department) at Orkun & Orkun
www.orkunorkun.com • info@orkunorkun.com

The state education system (except for state universities) has not been popular over the last ten years, so there is a high demand for private schools.

This is because people believe that state schools don't live up to the highest modern European standards, and that they have deteriorated over the last ten years following various policy changes. This has led to many people putting their children into private education.

The state system's quality, inevitably, varies from place to place and school to school.

However, this doesn't mean that state education should be dismissed by foreigners arriving in Turkey. It offers a solid, if slightly old-fashioned, education suited to the needs of its largely rural community. School hours are long. Homework is required. You have one teacher covering almost all your primary school education. Exams are challenging.

For a foreigner, the choice is whether to put your children through the local Turkish state education system or to enrol them in one of the private (often international) schools in the country (see below).

The law requires all schools to make strenuous efforts to integrate foreign children.

State education in Turkey

State and private educational establishments in Turkey are both the responsibility of the Ministry of Education.

There are schools throughout the country, even in quite small places, and universities in each province.

Children must attend school from the age of five. Nursery and preschool education is also available - and encouraged - but not compulsory. The first 12 years of education is compulsory, meaning that someone could leave school at 17.

There are special types of education for students with special needs. In most cases, this special education is delivered within an ordinary school.

All state education is free (although you will pay for some materials) up to university level. State universities charge a small fee.

A person resident or working in Turkey will be entitled to use the state system. Recognised refugees are also entitled to use the system. Most other foreigners will not be able to do so.

Nursery education

Nursery education (for children from birth to the age of three) is available in limited quantity. It is not widely used by local people.

Nursery education can either be provided privately or within a state-run institution: often as part of an ordinary school. In either case, it is not free to the parent. Some companies and government offices provide nursery facilities as an employment benefit.

Preschool education

Preschool education is available for children from three to five years old. This is widely available and commonly used by local people. It is free in the state sector.

The preschool day is the same length as the regular school day: 08:30 to 16:00

Preschool education involves both elements of pure education and play. It also involves eating and, usually, a sleep in the afternoon.

First stage education

Education used to be split into three stages, each of four years. Now they are merged into one system. This could all take place in one school building or it could be on different sites.

Primary education continues from the age of five to nine. It follows a classical curriculum of reading, writing and arithmetic - plus sport, optional religious education, art, and the learning of one foreign language (nowadays, typically English).

The children have exams during this period.

Class sizes tend to be quite high. A class of 30 is not unusual.

Discipline is quite strict. Uniform is worn.

There is a culture of setting homework, even at this first stage level.

Secondary education

Compulsory secondary education

Compulsory secondary education is for students from 9-12.

Subjects taught include:

- Natural and social sciences
- History
- Geography
- Physical education
- Art

- Turkish
- A foreign language
- Literature
- Mathematics
- Music
- Technology

Religious education is an optional subject.

Each subject is likely to have a separate teacher.

There is an exam at the end of the child's time at secondary school: "TEOG".

High School

At the end of the first two cycles of education, everyone goes to a high school and stays there until they have completed their 12 years' education.

This education normally (but far from always) takes place at the same school building as the secondary education.

The subject list is expanded and children begin to specialize.

There is an exam at the end of the child's time at high school: depending upon the child's ability this will be either the "YGS" or the "LYS".

Passing the YGS admits a child to a two-year technical school (pre-university). Passing the LYS admits the child to university.

College and university

Turkey has well-respected universities and several technical colleges specialising in vocational training in a particular area of activity. They are often in the same building and even in the same faculty: for example, law degrees (taking four years) and a paralegal's qualification (taking two years) both taught in the faculty of law or a doctor (six years) and a nurse (two years) may both be taught in the faculty of medicine.

To enrol at any of these institutions, students are required to have passed the relevant exam (*YGS/LYS*) and then to apply (using a central application system) to the places of their choice - up to a maximum of 18 choices.

In Turkey, only about 7.5% of pupils go on to become students at institutes of higher education.

Post-graduate education

This is becoming more common. About 10% of graduates go on to do further studies. At state universities the fees are low and, for some students, free.

It is common for a Turk wanting post-graduate education to seek it in a foreign country. The US and the UK are both very popular.

Private education

Local schools

There are a large number of private schools operating in Turkey. They replicate all parts of the state system.

Parents choose private schools because, up to college level, the education is perceived to be better. At college level (where the state universities are seen as the best option) it is mainly because children can't get into the state system as they lack the qualifications.

These schools are still subject to regulation by the Ministry of Education. By law, they have to follow the same core curriculum as state schools, but they often provide extra activities and subjects of study. They also often employ more highly qualified teachers and they almost always operate with much smaller class sizes: typically, 20 or so.

There are some boarding (live-in) schools in Turkey.

Fees vary. Typical fees for a day high school are usually about TRY30,000-70,000 (£6,602-15,405/€7,573-€17,671/US$8,487-US$19,803) per year. For a pre-school it's about TRY15,000 (£3,301/€3,786/US$4,243) per year.

Many private schools require a test before they will allow enrolment and are selective about the level of student they will enrol.

The percentage of students from private schools who go on to higher education is about three times the national average.

International schools

There are several international schools in Turkey. They have all been there for many years and they have all grown greatly in the last ten years.

They are considered to be very good places to study.

The key identifying factor of an international school is that it follows a curriculum laid down in another country (although they must still cover the same core subjects required in other Turkish schools) and they usually teach that curriculum wholly or partly in a foreign language.

All international schools are private and all charge fees for attendance.

Some of these are Roberts College (US), the German School, Saint Joseph (French) and Uskudar American College.

In each case, most the pupils at the school are, mainly, not from the country in question. They are very popular with wealthy Turks because of the level of English (or German) the pupils will acquire and because the calibre of the education is considered to be higher than that provided in the local Turkish schools, whether state or private.

Typical fees would be TRY60,000 (£13,205/€15,147/US$16,974) or more per year.

There are also international schools aimed specifically at the children of expats: usually less selective, less highly rated and much less expensive. Some also accept local pupils.

Some consulates operate their own schools, for their own staff, following the curriculum in their own country.

Finding a school

When you are thinking of moving to Turkey with your children you will need to find a school for them.

As indicated at the beginning of this chapter, the primary choice you will have to make is whether to opt for an international school or a local school and, if a local school, whether to use the state system or to pay privately.

International schools often appeal to people travelling to Turkey with children already well into their education. They may find it difficult to adjust to a totally different curriculum and they may find it takes them longer to learn Turkish and so be comfortable in their new school.

If your stay in Turkey is only going to be brief, you may want to choose an international school so that you can more readily reintegrate the children when you return to your country.

On the other hand, exposing children - particularly children under the age of 8-10 - to the local education system will ensure that they learn the language very quickly (often in a matter of a few weeks!) and make many local friends.

Local education often broadens their horizons enormously and offers your children the gift of being truly bilingual and bicultural: one of the greatest things you can do for them.

Locals choose private education because they distrust the quality of the state system.

Distance learning

There is no officially-recognised source of distance learning in Turkey. This means that, unlike in some other countries, you cannot (say) obtain a degree without physically attending a college. Of course, many people in Turkey do take advantage of distance learning opportunities available outside Turkey, and any qualifications you obtain in that way will be recognised in Turkey in the same way as would be usual for that qualification.

The school year

The school year is decided by the Ministry of Education (*Milli Eğitim Bakanlığı* - MEB). The dates are the same for every state school in the country. The year usually runs from the first week of September to the second week of June. Private school may work to slightly different dates.

The year is divided into two semesters, with a two-week break in the first fortnight of February.

In addition to that break the school is closed for all public holidays - of which there are quite a large number in Turkey! For a list, see
www.guides.global/guides/turkey/tur-holidays.php.

School hours

Although the school year is laid down by the Ministry of Education, schools are free to decide their own hours of opening. This is to permit some flexibility in rural areas so that they can adjust to local transport availability and the working patterns of the parents.

The normal daily hours are from 08:30 to 16:30. There is a lunch break, typically from 12:00 to 13:00.

School uniform

School uniform is obligatory in schools in Turkey. This is to avoid highlighting differences in social class and religion.

School meals

Full-time schools usually provide a midday meal. Depending on the time of year, this may be hot or cold. The meal must be nutritionally balanced.

It is not obligatory for children to take advantage of the school meal.

A payment is required for the school meal.

Healthcare

Written by **John Howell** Editor & Founder of Guides.Global www.guides.global • john.howell@guides.global

Healthcare is right at the top of people's concerns when moving to - or even visiting - a new country. Will it be of a good standard? How do I access it? What will it cost? Will the doctor - and the nurses and other health workers - speak my language?

This chapter should help you answer those questions. But be warned. In any country, there is a huge variation in the quality of healthcare from place to place: between rich areas and poor, and between rural areas and the city.

Healthcare in Turkey consists of a mix of public and private health services.

There are (2016) 27,954 medical institutions in Turkey, with (2017) 1.7 doctors for every 1,000 people (US 2.54, UK 2.8, France: 3.37, Germany 4.17) and (2015) 2.7 hospital beds per 1,000 people (UK 2.7, US 2.9, France 6.2, Germany 8.2). Per capita expenditure in US$ (adjusted for purchasing power parity) is the second lowest amongst OECD countries at US$1,064 in 2015 (UK $4,003, France $4,407, Germany $5,267, US $9,451).

The state system

Turkey provides universal health care under its Universal Health Insurance (*Genel Sağlık Sigortası*) system. Under this system, all residents registered with the Social Security Institution (SGK) can receive medical treatment free of charge in hospitals contracted to the SGK.

Foreigners who are legally employed in Turkey (and so contributing to the social security system) or who have a Turkish spouse are eligible for publicly funded healthcare in Turkey. Others are not.

Most foreigners with a residence permit, who live permanently in Turkey and who do not hold relevant private health insurance, must make (compulsory) monthly payments into the Turkish state scheme. For most foreigners, this entitles them to unlimited healthcare for approximately TRY270 (US$75/€67/£58) per month. This covers you, your spouse (but not an unmarried partner) and children under 18.

The state system covers most aspects of medical care, including (in some places) dental care.

Public facilities consist of a network of government-run hospitals, supplemented by privately owned clinics and health centres that have contracted to take part in the scheme.

However, in contrast to the facilities available in the private sector, state-run hospitals are still suffering the effects of poor funding, resulting in critical shortages of medical personnel as well as outdated and poorly maintained equipment. While doctors in the public sector are well-trained, treatment options can be limited due to the lack of necessary medical supplies. Many of the doctors do not speak English, and expats who cannot speak Turkish usually arrange to bring along their own translator.

As with most public hospitals in the world, public hospitals in Turkey also have to deal with overcrowding and lengthy waiting periods.

Patients pay part of the cost of drugs prescribed.

The private system

There is also a large private healthcare sector.

Private health care often offers shorter waiting lists and higher quality services than the state system.

The quality of Turkish private hospitals varies tremendously. Istanbul and Ankara have newer private facilities, with modern equipment, but they still may not be able to deal with all medical conditions. In other cities too, particularly those that are wealthy and/or have an active foreign community, there are hospitals offering very high standards of patient care. Ask locals what the hospitals are like in the area where you are going to be living.

In fact, local medical expertise, a high-quality private healthcare infrastructure, ease of access and a convenient location have resulted in Turkey becoming a 'health tourism' destination. It is a regional hub for health and medical services for people from Eastern Europe, the Baltic states and the Middle East. Neighbouring countries such as Syria, Iran and Azerbaijan rely on Turkey's services for medical emergencies.

Increasing numbers of foreigners from Western Europe visit Turkey for (much cheaper) cosmetic surgery and dental work.

This will, no doubt, increase when such treatment becomes VAT-free for foreigners. This will be in March 2018.

Health insurance is widely available.

Foreigners in Turkey favour private medical treatment over public due to the higher quality of treatment available, access to internationally recognized English-speaking doctors and high overall standards within the sector. Many employers of expatriates provide supplementary private health insurance cover for their employees.

The private health insurance market is well developed. However, it can become expensive as you get older.

Many residents pay for private cover *as well as* contributing to the state insurance system in order to guarantee access to the best quality health services available, and to cover any extra unexpected costs or treatment not usually covered by the state.

While the cost of medical treatment is much lower than in the United States or the

United Kingdom, the expat patient without the benefit of health insurance can still face considerable expense when using private facilities, especially if there are complications. It is worth repeating that the EU health card, which allows the holder to access free medical treatment in European countries, is not valid in Turkey.

Most banks and insurance companies offer various pension and health insurance packages. Insurance companies provide a list of hospitals and doctors where people insured with them are covered for treatment.

The maximum age at which a person can begin to take part in the private health sector in Turkey is 65.

In addition to the health insurance options available within Turkey, many foreigners continue to benefit from the health insurance they have previously taken out in their own country. See page 102.

Preparations

There are no specific vaccinations required for entry into Turkey, although those coming from a yellow fever infected area should have a yellow fever certificate.

It's also recommended to have a rabies injection, especially if travelling outside of the main urban areas, as Turkey has one of the highest incidents of rabies in Europe.

Before coming to Turkey: paperwork

This section applies, mainly, if you are moving to Turkey and may seem a little over-the-top if you are only going there on holiday. However, if you intend to visit Turkey on a regular basis these precautions may still be worthwhile: particularly if you have known health problems.

- Visit your doctor. Obtain a copy of your medical records and have them (or, if they are huge, what your doctor considers to be the important parts) translated into Turkish

- Ask your doctor for a full list of all your prescription medicines, using their proper pharmaceutical names rather than any brand names. If your doctor won't do this, in most countries there are private doctors who will

- Get all your prescriptions topped up before you move to Turkey. Aim to arrive a with at least two (better three or six) month's supply of all your prescription medicines. This will give you time both to settle in to sort yourself out

- Sort out your health insurance, whether you are travelling as a tourist or going to Turkey on a permanent basis. See our chapter on health insurance (page 102) for more details

Upon arrival in Turkey

Register with a local doctor. Do this now, before you need one!

If you have a choice of doctors:

- Seek a recommendation from other foreigners who live in the area. Your needs will be different from those of local people, particularly regarding the staff's language skills

- Choose one who speaks your language **fluently**. It is not a good time to be searching for a phrase book when you have chest pains!

- Try to find one familiar with any existing medical problems you may have.

To register with a doctor, you will need to give the doctor details about you and your medical history.

You may also need to supply the doctor with two passport size photos.

Although your doctor will, no doubt, be your primary point of contact with the healthcare system, you do not need to access it all via your doctor. If you feel the need of the services of a specialist, you can approach one directly. However, the downside of doing this is that if the specialist decides that you do not need any treatment of the type they can provide, you will be charged for the assessment session. This will not happen if you are referred by your doctor.

If you have a known medical condition, and without - in any way - wanting to diminish the role of your doctor, it is also worth checking out which local specialists might be best if and when you need one. Once again, language skills weigh heavily when making this decision.

If you find no local doctor with the necessary language skills, look into the availability of translation services. Many hospitals and doctors have lists of recommended translators. If you have ongoing health problems, you could get to know your translator really well.

Emergencies

In the case of a medical emergency, call an ambulance (dial 112). The ambulance crew will assess your condition and, in most cases, take you to the nearest public or private hospital, as you specify. In some places, ambulance response times can be slow. Think about taking a taxi instead.

If you wish to be taken to a private hospital they will do this but will bill the hospital - and therefore you - for the trip.

In the case of tourists (and, by extension, all foreigners) they may be tempted to take you directly to a private hospital as they will assume that you are not entitled to the benefit of the state health care system.

If you wish to be taken to the public hospital, say so.

When you arrive at the hospital you will be asked for details of your health insurance or entitlement to state funded healthcare. If you cannot give immediate proof of either entitlement or insurance you will be treated as a private patient until you produce such proof. The hospital is entitled to ask for a deposit and/or a credit card imprint. This does not always happen.

Many doctors offer an emergency service for less dramatic but still urgent cases. Your doctor will give you details of their service. This might avoid the need for you to go to the hospital. It can be quicker and cheaper.

It is also commonplace for Turks to visit their pharmacy (*eczane*) in the case of a minor emergency. They are often capable of dealing with the problem far more quickly than the public hospital and far less expensively than a private doctor. Pharmacies can be identified by a green cross - often illuminated: very vibrant and flashing.

Treatment by your doctor

The first thing you will usually do is telephone for an appointment. A few doctors are beginning to offer an online booking service. You will, normally, receive an appointment within three days; or on the same day if you believe your condition makes seeing a doctor a matter of urgency.

The doctor's appointment will be free of charge if you benefit from the state healthcare scheme. Otherwise you (or your insurance company) will be charged for the visit. Charges are, typically, about TRY150 (£25, €30, $40). Any charges are paid at the time of the visit. All doctors are required to accept payment by credit card.

If the doctor thinks that you need any medicines, he will prescribe them.

Proof of entitlement to 'free' treatment

Every time you use the healthcare system, you will be asked for either proof of entitlement to the benefit of the state programme or proof of health insurance. It is, therefore, a very good idea to carry these at all times.

Proof of healthcare insurance takes several forms, depending upon your insurer. If you benefit from private health insurance, the doctor will usually make contact with the insurer to obtain their agreement to the treatment proposed.

If you cannot produce proof of cover by the state programme or insurance, you will be treated as a private (paying) patient. If you later produce your proof of entitlement the accounting will be undone and your 'free' entitlement backdated to the date your treatment started.

Paying patients may be required to pay a deposit towards the cost of treatment (usually by credit card) and to leave a credit card imprint. The deposit is, typically, €250-500. This is not always taken.

Treatment in hospital

This will be charged for on the same basis as treatment by your doctor: either as a state (free) patient, as an insured patient or as a private (paying) patient.

Please note that, whilst the staff and the care in Turkish hospitals and clinics are excellent, the way the system operates may well be different to what you are used to.

You may see lots of relatives around other beds, helping the nurses by feeding their family member, bringing in clean pyjamas etc. This is a normal part of the Turkish system. As a result, staffing levels in hospitals - and so the level of personal care - tend to be lower than other countries.

You should try to have some such support yourself. Clearly, if you are living in Turkey and your children are in Germany or China, this can be a problem. Fortunately, a number of the local associations of foreigners offer a support service staffed by volunteers, to help people in difficulties for this reason. Incidentally, serving as a volunteer is a great and rewarding was of making new friends! Ask about availability.

The other problem you may encounter is that of language. Even if you have learned some Turkish, it is unlikely that you will have the vocabulary or fluency to converse freely and without error with the nurses, doctors and other staff. Obviously, that can be a bit of a problem!

Until a few years ago, this was a major problem. Now, if you speak English, Russian, German or (increasingly) Mandarin Chinese and live in a large city or a place frequented by foreigners, there is likely to be at least one person on duty in the hospital who speaks your language and who has been trained to help foreigners by translating.

As already started, some associations of foreign residents also provide some translation facilities.

Longer-term medical requirements

Ongoing treatment from a specialist for longer term conditions such as (say) a heart condition or diabetes is best arranged via your doctor.

It will be charged for on the same basis as treatment by your doctor: either on a free basis, as an insurance patient or as a private (paying) patient.

Obtaining medicines

Some basic medicines - mild pain killers, cough medicines, anti-histamines etc. - can be obtained without a prescription. They can be bought at any pharmacy or from many supermarkets.

All other medicines can only be obtained from a pharmacy. Many larger supermarkets have their own pharmacy.

The price of your medicines will be heavily subsidised by the state if you benefit from the state healthcare scheme. Otherwise, you I'll have to pay the full cost.

'Alternative' medicine

Since the 2014 medical reforms, 14 alternative treatments can now be legally practiced in Turkey: acupuncture (the stimulation of points along the skin with thin needles), apitherapy (the use of honeybee products for treatment), phytotherapy (treatments based on traditional herbalism), hypnosis, leeches, homeopathy, chiropractic (massage-like treatment on the muscles, the spine and the skeleton affecting the nervous system), wet cupping, larval therapy (the introduction of live, disinfected maggots into the skin), mesotherapy (the injection of special medications into the skin), prolotherapy (the injection of irritating solutions into an injured spot to provoke regenerative tissue response), osteopathy (nonsurgical treatments of the muscle and skeleton system), ozone therapy (the introduction of ozone and oxygen mixtures into the body) and reflexology (massage-like treatment by way of pressure on reflex areas).

Only specially certified physicians and dentists can practice these treatments. Today (2017) there is only a small number of practitioners of alternative medicine in Turkey.

Most insurance policies do not cover alternative medicine.

Going 'back home' for treatment

Largely because of the language and care difficulties, many foreigners resident in Turkey choose to travel 'home' for serious, but non-emergency, treatment.

Be aware that, if you are living as a resident in Turkey, you may no longer be entitled to the use of any state subsidised facilities in your 'home country'. If you have health insurance, you need to make sure it gives you the option of going home for treatment. Many policies do not.

Politics & Voting

Written by **Başak Yildiz Orkun**
Managing Partner (Legal Department) at Orkun & Orkun
www.orkunorkun.com • info@orkunorkun.com

Politics

Turkey is a large nation with a complex political structure.

It has a unicameral Grand National Assembly (*Türkiye Büyük Millet Meclisi*). This means that, unlike most countries, there is only one house in the legislature. This contrasts with, for example, the US where you have the House of Representatives and the Senate; or the UK where you have the House of Commons and the House of Lords.

The Assembly has 550 seats, with members directly elected in multi-seat constituencies by proportional representation. They serve a four-year term. The next election is to be held in June 2019. Following the April 2017 constitutional referendum, this number will increase to 600 at the next election.

Political parties in Turkey

The main political parties are:

- Justice and Development party (AKP)
- Republican People's party (CHP)
- Nationalist Movement party (MHP)
- People's Democratic party (HDP)

At the last elections, the votes received were:- AKP 49.5%, CHP 25.3%, MHP 11.9%, HDP 10.8%, other 2.6%. In terms of seats, this converted to: AKP 317, CHP 134, MHP 40 and HDP 59.

Voting

Voting rights - Turkish citizens

All Turkish citizens over the age of 18 have the right to vote in both national elections and local municipal elections.

Turkey was one of the first countries to give women the right to vote. Full suffrage for women dates back to 1934. About 15% of Turkey's legislators are now women.

Voting rights - foreign residents of Turkey

Foreign residents cannot vote in Turkey - unless they take Turkish citizenship.

Social Security (Welfare Benefits)

Written by **Burak Orkun**
Managing Partner (Accountancy Department) at Orkun & Orkun
www.orkunorkun.com • info@orkunorkun.com

In order to benefit from the Turkish Social Security System, residents in Turkey must enrol with the Turkish Social Security Fund (*Sosyal Güvenlik Kurumu* - SGK). This was formerly known as the SSK, but the name changed after the Self-Employment Organisation (*Bag-Kur*) and Government Officers' Organisation (*Emekli Sandığı*) merged with the SSK in 2008.

Contributions

Paying into the social security scheme is compulsory for all employees. The employer and the employees both pay premiums. The employee contributes approximately 15% of the employee's salary, which is deducted at source and paid to the state. The employer contributes about 22.5%. If the employer pays all dues on time, the 22.5% drops to 17.5% and so the total drops from 37.5% to 32.5%.

Many Turkish employers consider income tax deductions (15%-35%) also to be part of their social security contribution. It is not.

The contributions made are not paid into one big central fund, but are allocated for specific purposes:

Type of contribution	Employer pays	Employee pays	Total paid
Short-term social security	2.0%	0.0%	2.0%
Disability, old age and death	11.0%	9.0%	20.0%
Health insurance	7.5%	5.0%	12.5%
Unemployment	2.0%	1.0%	3.0%
Total	**22.5%**	**15.0%**	**37.5%**

Agricultural workers, the self-employed, and people receiving benefits from other organisations in the system are not eligible for SGK social security benefits.

Refugees are covered, at least in part.

Those contributing to the social insurance scheme and their spouse (but not their unmarried partner) and children are insured for:

- Work injuries and work-related illnesses,

- Medical care, illness and pregnancy care.

Disability benefits are available only to Turkish citizens.

The unemployed, who are not students, pay TRY53 (£12/€13/US$15) per month for healthcare only.

Students pay nothing, but are entitled to free healthcare until the age of 25.

Payments & Entitlements

In very brief summary:

Healthcare

See above.

Unemployment benefits

You will receive 40% of your monthly salary (the average of the last four months' salary), up to a maximum 80% of the current base salary of TRY2,029 (2018).

The actual amount depends upon the length of time for which you have been contributing to the system.

You will need a minimum 600 days of contributions over the last three years. If you do not have these you receive only the minimum wage.

If you quit your job or are fired for good cause, there is no entitlement to benefit.

Otherwise, depending upon your contributions record, unemployment benefit lasts from six to ten months.

If you are self-employed, there is presently (June 2017) no entitlement to unemployment benefit. This will change in 2018, when self-employed people's contributions to the social security system will increase to 37.5% of their profit and when they will become entitled to unemployment benefit on much the same basis as the employed.

Sickness ("temporary incapacity") benefits

Based on medical evidence, temporary incapacity allowance shall be paid:

- For each day the insurance holder is suffering from temporary incapacity due to a work accident or an occupational disease

- For each day, starting from the third, of temporary incapacity due to sickness - provided that a minimum of 90 days of short-term insurance premium has been paid in the previous year

- During any period of inpatient treatment or any period of rest granted due to such treatment, to self-employed insurance holders, in the cases of work accidents or occupational disease or maternity and provided that any all premiums, including universal health insurance, are paid

Temporary incapacity allowance paid in cases of work accident, sickness and maternity shall be half of daily earnings for inpatient treatments and two thirds of the same for outpatient treatments.

Where an insurance holder suffers from more than one of these things, temporary incapacity benefit shall be payable at the highest level.

Being ill for more than your period of notice (between two and eight weeks) plus six weeks is grounds for dismissal.

Maternity benefits

These rules are changing in 2018.

At the moment, you are entitled to eight weeks' paid leave, paid by the state at your normal salary.

You can split this eight-week period, as you choose, before and after the birth of the child.

The new regulations will give an entitlement to an extra six months' *unpaid* leave. You will also be entitled to go back to work half time for 60 days after your first birth, 120 days after your second and 180 days after your third. There is also the option of part-time work for one of the parents until the children are of school age.

Disability ("permanent incapacity") benefits

Insurance holders whose earning power is reduced by at least 10% due to disease or disabilities caused by a work accident or occupational disease shall be entitled to permanent incapacity income.

Permanent incapacity income shall be based on the loss of earning power in the occupation of the insurance holder.

- In case of full incapacity, the insurance holder is put on an income amounting to 70% of their monthly earning.

- In the case of partial incapacity, entitlement shall be calculated on the same basis as for full incapacity bur proportional to the degree of incapacity. For example, if the it 30% you would receive 30% of 70% of your monthly earnings.

- Where the insurance holder is in need of permanent care from another person, the benefit shall be calculated as 100% of earnings

Few people have private disability insurance.

Old age pension

These rules, too, change in 2018.

Entitlement depends upon when you started work. The system is complicated.

For example:

- If you started work before 1999 and have accumulated 5,500 working days on which you have paid social security premiums, you will be entitled to retire at 58 (man) or 56 (woman)

- If you started work after 1999 but before 2008 and have accumulated 5,500 working days, you will be entitled to retire at 59 (man) or 57 (woman)

- If you started work after 2008 and have accumulated 7,200 working days (about 28 years), you will be entitled to retire at 60 (man) or 58 (woman). The entitlement age is planned to rise steadily to 65 for both men and women over the period from 2036-2048.

Private pensions are also very popular in Turkey. They will soon be compulsory. They are encouraged by the government, which (subject to a maximum) contributes 25% towards your pension contributions, even if you are unemployed.

Other benefits

There are various other benefits payable to various groups of people: e.g. breastfeeding benefits, survivors' pensions, death grants, marriage benefits and funeral benefits.

More Information

Much more information about all of these benefits is available (in several languages, including English) on the Social Security Institution website: **www.sgk.gov.tr**.

Local Press & Other Media

Written by **Francine Carrel**
Assistant Editor of Guides.Global
www.guides.global • francine.carrel@guides.global

Turkish media is varied and competitive on the surface - but much of the media, across all mediums, is owned by large conglomerates with other business interests. This means that Turkish news media, whilst it does cover stories from different angles, is somewhat restricted in its viewpoints.

Despite this, I would recommend that anybody living, working or doing business in another country makes an effort to consume local media. It is a great way to learn about the culture, as well as current events, and Turkey is no exception!

If you speak Turkish then, of course, you will have a much wider range of media and press to choose from. If you are learning Turkish then reading, watching and listening to local media is one of the best ways to improve your language skills.

Only 18% of Turks read a newspaper daily, according to the BBC, with television being by far the preferred medium.

Press Freedom

Turkey ranks 155 out of 180 countries on the Reporters Without Borders' World Press Freedom Index 2017. This is just below the Democratic Republic of Congo. It is an abysmal ranking for a democratic country.

Press freedom, which has been bad for years, has plummeted since the failed coup of July 2016. Journalists have been imprisoned in their dozens - many without trial. Journalists who *are* still practicing in the country are not having a good time of it: many have had arbitrary restrictions on their travel, or suffered seizure of their assets. For up-to-date news on the media crackdown, see this (oft-updated) page from the Committee to Protect Journalists: **cpj.org/europe/turkey**

Social media, now an important part of news distribution, is also heavily restricted in Turkey.

Newspapers

Zaman & Today's Zaman

Now closed, as they were deemed to have been publishing on behalf of the Gülen movement, which is classified as terrorist organisation in Turkey.

Turkey: how things *really* work

Hurriyet

- Circulation of around 360,000
- Owned by Doğan Media Group
- Liberal and secularist
- Classified advertisements, including many property ads
- Runs a property portal: Hurriyet Emlak
- Partnered with jobs website **www.yenibiris.com**

Contact details

Website: **www.hurriyet.com.tr**

Telephone: +90 (0) 850 224 0 222

Email: okuriletisim@hurriyet.com.tr

Hurriyet Daily

- English language
- Owned by Doğan Media Group
- Liberal and secularist

Contact details

Website: **www.hurriyetdailynews.com**

Telephone: +90 (0) 212 677 00 00

Email: ekizilkaya@hurriyet.com.tr

Posta

- Circulation of around 330,000
- Owned by Doğan Media Group
- Generally more focus on entertainment and gossip than on business or 'serious' news, but worth a look if you want to learn about Turkish culture

Contact details

Website: **www.posta.com.tr**

Telephone: +90 (0) 212 677 00 00

Email: ekizilkaya@hurriyet.com.tr

Milliyet

- Circulation of around 150,000

- Owned by Demirören Holding

- Centre-left, secularist

- Thorough coverage of international affairs

- Known for being a bit sensationalist; often shares materials with the UK's Sun and Daily Mail newspapers

Contact details

Website: **www.milliyet.com.tr**

Telephone: +90 (0) 212 337 99 99

Email: eisleyen@milliyet.com.t

Sozcu

- Circulation of around 280,000

- Formerly *Gözcü*, before being taken over by its employees in 2007 after it ceased publication

- Openly critical of the ruling party (AKP). Read by Social Democrats.

Contact details

Website: **www.sozcu.com.tr**

Telephone: +90 (212) 698 35 35

Email: net@sozcu.com.tr

Cumhuriyet

- Circulation of around 52,000

- Centre-left, social democracy, dislikes religion in government affairs

- Was the target of death threats in early 2015 after publishing excerpts from Charlie Hebdo following the notorious terror attack on the French magazine

Contact details

Website: **www.cumhuriyet.com.tr**

Telephone: +90 (0) 251 98 74 75

Email: reklam@cumhuriyet.com.tr

Television stations

Television is the main source of news and entertainment for many Turks.

Although there are rising numbers of people using the internet for television, viewer numbers for traditional television appear to still be very high.

Turkey has a large range of television channels.

Government channels

The TRT (Turkish Radio and Television Corporation) channels in Turkey are run by the government. TRT held a monopoly on radio and television until the early 1990s.

TRT channels include:

TRT World

TRT's newest channel. International and domestic news. English-language.

TRT 1

A general entertainment channel. Shows domestic and international entertainment programmes as well as sports, news and arts.

TRT Spor

A sports channel. Football and basketball hog most of the air time.

TRT Haber

News, culture and arts. Like TRT 1, you'll find a few English-language programmes.

TRT 6 / Kurdî

Kurdish-language channel.

Commercial channels

There are a great many commercial channels in Turkey. Popular broadcasters include:

- Star TV (the first to break TRT's monopoly)
- Show TV
- Kanal D
- Fox

There are two main multi-channel services.

TurkSat

A cable service. Over 50 channels; most of these are in Turkish but you will be able to find English-language programmes through the BBC, French-language programmes through TV5 and German-language programmes through German RTL.

Digitürk

A satellite service. More than 120 channels, including children's viewing, sports and entertainment. To use Digitürk, you will need a dish antenna.

Radio

As you'd expect in such a large country, the list of radio stations in Turkey is extensive.

To get an idea of the local radio stations, see this list: **bit.ly/2ffS9u6**

TRT also broadcasts a large number of channels. You can see them (and listen to some of them online) at **bit.ly/1H6EIZ5**

Social Life

Written by **John Howell**
Editor & Founder of Guides.Global
www.guides.global • john.howell@guides.global

One of the great attractions of Turkey is the rich and diverse social life enjoyed by people living here. You have access to both the facilities available to all local people and the additional opportunities created and enjoyed by foreign visitors and residents.

The best way of finding out about social activities in Turkey is to read the local press and to search local websites. See above and visit our contacts page: **www.guides.global/books/turkey/tur-contacts.php**.

In Turkey, the most important elements of social life are food, conversation and sport. These are often combined.

Food

The dinner table is one of the traditional foundations of Turkish culture. This can be a dinner table at home, shared with your children and/or friends, a larger family dinner table welcoming several generations or a table in a restaurant or cafe.

Eating out is a regular occurrence and even small towns have a multitude of cafes and restaurants.

Food also helps hold together communities. Religious holidays and social activities like the *bayram* (a nationally-celebrated festival or holiday), *iftar* (the breaking of the fast during Ramadan), and wedding ceremonies focus on food.

This is true throughout Turkey but, especially, in Anatolian culture: the culture of much of the Asian side of Turkey.

It is as true for expat communities, though the definition of food is, perhaps, extended and more focused on the liquid variety.

Sport

Perhaps surprisingly, when you see the slightly rounded shape of many Turkish men, Turks are mad keen on sport: both as participants and as spectators.

Football

For local Turks, the great sporting passion is football. But there is far more to Turkey's sporting interests than that. Basketball, volleyball, handball, track-and-field and wrestling (which is considered as the ancestral national sport) are also popular. Recently, Turkey has enjoyed important international successes in boxing, taekwondo, judo and archery.

But football *is* the focus. Most Turks support one of the top teams: Fenerbahçe, Galatasaray and Beşiktaş. Developing an interest in football, the teams and their fortunes gives you lots of opportunities to start conversations.

Golfing

Golf is popular amongst foreign residents and increasingly popular with local Turks.

The best known golfing area is Belek, between Antalya and Side. In just 20 years Belek has gone from a golfing backwater to a bona-fide big-hitter of the European game. There are now over a dozen courses in the area. However, there is also good golf available in Istanbul and many coastal towns, including Bodrum, Cesme, Fethiye, Konakli, Kuşadasi, Izmir & Marmaris.

They all operate on the basis of membership of the club concerned but they all also offer access to non-members, when space is available, upon payment of a fee.

Sailing

There are marinas up and down the coast catering to both Turks and foreigners who love to sail. These also offer some compelling business opportunities. Sailors, in Turkey, tend to be the wealthy or young professionals. Either way, they are an attractive target market.

General fitness

This has really taken off. Gyms are opening everywhere: general gyms and all sorts of specialist centres. They are, of course, again aimed mainly at the young and would-be young. As with sailing, they offer a wealth of business opportunities.

Drink & Drugs

Written by **Başak Yildiz Orkun**
Managing Partner (Legal Department) at Orkun & Orkun
www.orkunorkun.com • info@orkunorkun.com

Turkey is rather schizophrenic when it comes to its attitude to alcohol and drugs. As a substantial wine producer it is, perhaps, not surprising that social attitudes to the consumption of alcohol are very relaxed. As an Islamic country, it is perhaps equally unsurprising that their attitudes towards drunken behaviour are unaccepting and uncompromising.

As both an Islamic country and a place which, until recently, was a major trans-shipment point for drugs entering Europe, it is easy to understand why their approach to the possession of drugs is also very negative and very robust.

Alcohol

Turks do drink, the men more than women. This is true for both the religious and the secular. Drinking is less prevalent in conservative areas, such as eastern Anatolia, than in other parts.

Consumption is not high. In 2010, Turks drank an average of just two litres of raw alcohol equivalent (the measure used to average out the consumption of beer, wines and spirits) - (China 6.7, US9.2, UK 11.6, Germany 11.8, France 12.2).

Consumption is split 63% beer, 9% wine and 28% spirits.

Licences are required to sell or serve alcohol. They are administered by the Tobacco and Alcohol Market Regulatory Authority.

In 2011, all advertising of alcohol in sports was banned. In 2013, new laws banned all forms of advertising and promotion of alcoholic beverages.

Alcohol is highly taxed. This "special consumption tax" (*Özel Tüketim Vergisi ÖTV*) was established in 2002 and dramatically increased in 2010 by the AKP government, whose leadership is known for their disapproval of alcohol. This led to a significant rise in smuggling and fraud and, probably, the 2011 Turkish Riviera mass alcohol poisoning.

Legal age for consumption

The lower limit to the age for the purchase of alcohol is 18.

Availability

Alcohol is widely available. In most areas it is sold in many food shops and supermarkets. It is, of course, also available in restaurants and bars.

Supplying drink to under age people

It is a criminal offence (the penalty is a hefty fine of between TRY12,543-627,250 or six months to one year in prison) to supply alcohol to someone who is below legal age. The seller's license to sell alcohol will also be cancelled. This is an offence where 'the act speaks for itself'. It is no defence that you did not know or even suspect that they were underage.

Drunkenness

It is a criminal offence to behave in a disorderly manner ("threatening public security") whilst under the influence of alcohol. It is also a specific offence under the current State of Emergency (post-coup attempt of 2016). Fine TRY100 (£22/€25/US$28).

Being drunk can also lead to you being locked up for the night "for your own safety".

Disorderly conduct involves anything from shouting and rowdiness to vomiting in the street and fighting. The judges take the view that disorderly conduct is hard to define but they know what it is when they hear a case.

Although the minimum fine for disorderly conduct under the influence of drink is TRY100, in practice the fine rises significantly with each subsequent offence. Instead of a fine, offenders can be ordered to attend alcohol awareness classes and/or to undertake public service.

Driving under the influence of alcohol

See the section on drink driving (page 129).

Cigarettes

Attitudes to cigarette smoking are changing fast on the back of an increased awareness of the health risks and concerted government action to deter smoking. Or, maybe, it's because it is now (to Turks) so expensive: TRY12 (£2.64/€3.03/US$3.40) for 20 cigarettes.

A couple of decades ago almost everybody over the age of about ten seemed to smoke.

Today fewer than 24% of the population smokes. Mostly men.

Smoking is banned in many public places, such as airports and restaurants, and many places of work. The response to "No Smoking" (*Sigara İçilmez*) signs is variable.

Legal age

It is illegal to buy or possess cigarettes under the age of 18.

Supplying cigarettes to an underage person

The same rules apply as in the case of alcohol. See above.

Availability

Cigarettes are widely available in shops, bars and restaurants.

Drugs

Which drugs are restricted in Turkey?

The Turkey Drug Law of 1961 prohibits the possession or supply of "any chemical substance to alter states of body or mind for other than medically warranted purposes". Alcohol is specifically excluded from the scope of this law.

Turkey has strict laws against the use, possession or trafficking of illegal drugs. If you are convicted of any of these offences of supplying drugs, you can expect to receive a heavy fine or a prison sentence of four to 24 years.

'Mere' possession carries a minimum of one year in jail, and a maximum of two years. However, in the case of this particular offence, by a 2011 law the minimum jail sentence can be converted to a drug treatment order, a financial penalty, a supervision order etc. A second offence *must* receive a jail sentence.

Manufacturing or trading in the drug carries a *minimum* sentence of ten years and no maximum. In addition, there will be a financial penalty. If the drug is heroin, morphine (or morphine-based), or cocaine, the penalty is increased by 50%.

Do not mess about with drugs in Turkey!

International cooperation

The Government of Turkey has arrangements with many other countries, including all European Union countries and all North American countries, under which they share all intelligence about drug trafficking and report all convictions for drug-related offences to the government of the country of which the convicted person is a national.

Sex & Sexuality

Written by **John Howell**
Editor & Founder of Guides.Global
www.guides.global • john.howell@guides.global

As befits an old country right in the centre of the old Mediterranean civilisation, Turkey is pretty much on the centre-ground of gender politics.

Same-sex sexual activity was legalized in the Ottoman Empire (the predecessor of Turkey) in 1858 and, in modern Turkey, homosexual activity has always been legal since the day the country was founded in 1923. The age of consent is 18.

No specific anti-discrimination laws exist.

It is worth remembering that Turkey is (and has always been) a very conservative, Islamic country where, irrespective of the legal position, attitudes to all sexual matters tend to be very orthodox. Public opinion about homosexuality has generally been conservative, and LGBT people have been widely reported to experience discrimination, harassment, and even violence in recent years. This is particularly so away from Istanbul and the coast.

Displays of public affection are rare, irrespective of the gender of the people taking part. This is still true, but less so, for heterosexual couples. Affection between same-sex couples is almost unheard of except, perhaps, in parts of the largest cities.

Again, irrespective of the gender of the people concerned, 'indecent activity' in a public place is illegal. This is interpreted to include nudity. Bikinis etc. are accepted, often even if you are not on the beach.

Attitudes towards the legalization of same-sex unions in Turkey are mixed. In a 2015 poll by Ipsos, 27% of the Turkish public was in favour of legalizing same-sex marriage, while 19% preferred civil unions instead. Some 25% of those surveyed were against any form of legal recognition for same-sex couples and 29% stated that they didn't know which option to choose.

Turkey is ranked 111 of 197 countries on the Spartacus Gay Travel Index.

What are a foreigner's heterosexual and LGBT rights in Turkey?

Heterosexual activity

The age of consent is 18. The punishment for breaking this law is a minimum of three years in jail and a maximum of eight years. However, there are restrictions on the ability to prosecute people for offences against victims aged 15, 16 & 17. In these cases there is also a lower sentence than in the case of younger victims: six months to two years in jail. Sexual activity between a person over 21 and a person under 15 can result in lengthy periods of imprisonment.

The absolute minimum age for marriage is 15 but people under 17 require a court order permitting the marriage. A person aged 17 needs the consent of their parent. Marriage without the consent of your parents requires you to be 18.

Gay (homosexual, male) activity

Homosexual activity between consenting people is permitted in a private place but illegal in a public place. There is no legislation about gay sexual activity, so general interpretation is that the age of consent is the same as for heterosexual couples.

Civil partnerships are not recognised but the courts have some discretion to act to redress the results of unfairness when a same-sex relationship breaks down.

In all other respects, a homosexual has all the same legal rights as a heterosexual.

Lesbian (homosexual, female) activity

This is treated in the same way as male homosexual activity.

Transgender

This term is not recognised under local law. No special provision is made for transgender people. A transgender person retains the gender of their birth but, when an adult, is permitted to change their official gender with the benefit of a court decision.

Who can help?

If you face any issues concerning sex or gender, your first point of contact should be The Istanbul LGBTI Unity Association (**www.istanbullgbti.org**). They may direct you elsewhere.

Religion

Written by **John Howell**
Editor & Founder of Guides.Global
www.guides.global • john.howell@guides.global

Religion in Turkey is as old as Turkey itself - which is very old. Islam is still a massively important part of Turkish culture, even though increasing numbers of Turks (and, in particular, of younger Turks living in the western part of the country) are becoming more secular and less strict in their observance of religion. At the same time, many in the centre and east of the country are becoming more religious and conservative.

The statistics

In the 2010 census, 98% of the population professed to be Muslim.

More generally, people claim to be:

- Muslim: 98%

- Atheists: 0.9%

- Christian: 0.4%

- Jewish <0.1%

- Other: <0.1%

A (brief!) history of religion in Turkey

When mankind first arrived in Turkey, in about 10,000BC, they brought their religion with them. There are a number of early sites where there is clear evidence of religious observance. There appear to have been a number of gods, but little is known about the details of religion in Turkey at that time.

With the arrival of the Christian era, two out of the five centres of ancient Christianity were in Turkey: Constantinople (Istanbul) and Antioch (Antakya). Antioch was also the place where the followers of Jesus were first called Christians, as well as being the site of one of the earliest Christian churches, established by Saint Peter himself. For a thousand years, the Hagia Sophia in Istanbul was the largest church in the world.

Turkey was then part of the (Christian) Byzantine Empire. As the name suggests, this was based in Byzantium (later Constantinople and later still Istanbul).

The lands to the east, including the Arabian Peninsula, formed part of the Islamic Empire.

Tolerance, trade, and political relationships between the Arab and the Christian states waxed and waned. During this period, pilgrimages to sacred Christian sites such as

Jerusalem were permitted, Christian residents in Muslim territories were given *Dhimmi* (protected person) status, with legal rights and legal protection. These Christians were allowed to maintain churches, and marriages between the faiths were not uncommon.

By 1071, Islamic armies controlled what is now eastern Turkey. By 1453, Istanbul was captured by the Ottomans and the whole of what is modern Turkey became committed to Islam. At about the same time, after centuries of conflict and dispute, the Ottomans (who were orthodox Sunni Muslims) took control from their Shia rivals. They become the de facto leaders of the Islamic world and remained in control of Turkey until the creation of the new Turkish state in 1923.

Starting in the late 1700s, the Ottoman empire started to explore secularism and, when Mustafa Kemal Atatürk established modern Turkey in 1923, secularism was eventually embedded as a cornerstone of its constitution.

Religion in Turkey today

The Constitution of Turkey states that the country is secular: religion is a private matter for its citizens. Yet 98% of all Turks are Muslim. Of those, 75% are Sunni and 25% Shia.

Turkey is, fundamentally, tolerant of all religions and just as tolerant of those who profess none.

Religious education takes place in all schools from the age of five until 15. Increasingly, it is a multi-faith religious education in that, whilst focusing on Islam, includes the study of all the world's major religions.

In the last few years, the government - an Islamic party - appears to be steering Turkey gently towards a more religious and less secular future. Time will tell.

Main religious festivals

The two great festivals in Turkey, as in the rest of the Islamic world, are the two Ids: the first (*id al-fitr*) immediately at the end of Ramadan and the second, the greater Id (*id-al-adha*), which takes place three months after the end of Ramadan.

Retirement

Written by **Başak Yildiz Orkun**
Managing Partner (Legal Department) at Orkun & Orkun
www.orkunorkun.com • info@orkunorkun.com

Retirement age for local Turks is, officially, 58 for women and 60 for men - but many will continue to work beyond this age, either by inclination or because of financial pressure. It is not unusual to see truck drivers in their 70s or even to have your child educated by a teacher in her 80s.

Life expectancy (2014) is 75.8: for a male 72.6 and for a female 78.9, so they may be in retirement for a long time! Turks tend to be active (but not very physically active) in their years of retirement, though they also enjoy taking a coffee in a pavement café.

In 2005, a study was conducted by social security institutions to determine the life satisfaction of men in Turkey. The most popular leisure activities were audio-visual and reading. The strongest predictor of life satisfaction was the frequency of participation in leisure activities, followed by the level of satisfaction with health & income and the planning of leisure activities.

There are a number of organisations dedicated to helping older people. The Social Services department is involved, some hospitals run programmes and there are some charities operating in this field but the overwhelmingly most important help comes from the older person's family. The strong Turkish tradition is that families look after their older people. This is helped by the fact that the families tend to live near to each other.

There are growing numbers of foreigners who have settled in Turkey for their retirement. There are, probably, some 15,000 foreign retirees living permanently in Turkey (strangely, the Government does not keep official statistics on this) and there are many more who spend a part of the year - often a substantial part - in the country.

They, too, organise a wide range of activities, both sporting and cultural, for the benefit of other retirees and they, too, are a very good way of making new friends.

The main retirement organisations are featured prominently in the local media. See our section on the media - page 157.

Receiving Your Pension

Written by **Burak Orkun**

Managing Partner (Accountancy Department) at Orkun & Orkun

www.orkunorkun.com • info@orkunorkun.com

When you live in Turkey there are no restrictions upon receiving any pension to which you are entitled in another country. It is, in essence, treated just like any other income - although it is sometimes taxed at a lower rate. The policy on this changes often.

There is no income tax on pensions in Turkey.

This applies equally to pensions paid by the government of another country and to private pensions, such as pensions from your former employment or generated by your accumulated pension investments.

The main problem with receiving your pension is that you will seldom be able to persuade your employer to convert it into Turkish lira and pay it into your Turkish bank account. Many will insist on paying it into an account in your own country.

Worse still, even if you can persuade the government or your former employer to convert your pension or pay it into your Turkish bank account, you will find that you will receive a lousy exchange rate.

So, many people choose to retain an account 'back home' into which these payments are made. They will, in any case, probably go home from time to time and so can use the money to pay for things there, without having the cost of first converting the funds into Turkish lira (when you receive them) and then back again.

On the hopeful assumption that your pension payments will exceed the amount of money you spend on your holidays, you can then arrange for the remaining funds to be transferred from that account to your account in Turkey a certain number of times each year. Usually, it's better to wait until the sum to be transferred is measured in thousands rather than hundreds because this will make it easier to use an FX company and you're likely to get a much better rate from them. However, some FX companies have special arrangements for transferring small but regular payments to a foreign destination and these can be very beneficial. You could, for example, commit to transferring (say) US$500 through them every month and they can set up systems to reduce the cost of this quite significantly. See our chapter on FX on page 112.

When it comes to your pension income, you are likely to find that, occasionally, you will have to prove that you are still alive. It is all too easy for someone to move abroad and then for payments to continue to be made for decades after they have died! 'Proof of life' is usually done either by you going to the appropriate office in your home country when you are next there or by you submitting a statement (in a form that they provide) to the effect that you are still alive and then having this statement witnessed by (for example) a Notary or your doctor - as required by the company in question.

Dealing with a Death

Written by **Başak Yildiz Orkun**
Managing Partner (Legal Department) at Orkun & Orkun
www.orkunorkun.com • info@orkunorkun.com

Dealing with the death of a loved one is always distressing. It can also be stressful, time consuming and expensive. The stress, time factor, and expense are often worsened by distance, language, and differences in procedure.

If you need this chapter, it's probably too late to say that it's much better to reduce all these problems by way of forward planning. This includes speaking to the person concerned as to their wishes and speaking to a local funeral director as to what can (and cannot) be done and the likely cost involved.

This is particularly important as many foreigners still put in their Wills, or tell their relatives, that they wish to be buried 'back home'. It is my belief that many would change their minds if they knew the cost and trouble that this wish is likely to cause their loved ones.

Finally, we realise that in this chapter we use some terms - such as deceased and body - which can sound a little callous. No disrespect is intended but there are few expressions that capture the right balance between brevity and respect.

Preparation

First off, tell your family what you want: your wishes as to burial or cremation, whether you want the family to be present etc. Preferably, do this in writing so there are no misunderstandings and the recipient can show the document to doubting relatives. This saves a lot of anguish.

It is better not to put these things in your Will. When you die, these issues need to be dealt with quickly: possibly days before anyone has access to your Will. If you prefer to put these things in your Will, make sure that all the key players (such as your wife and children) have a copy of it and you tell them that it contains important instructions as to your wishes about burial etc.

If you have a pet - or dependent children - in the same document, make clear what you want to happen to them. Action will, obviously, have to be taken immediately.

Make a Will - possibly more than one (see page 461) - and tell your family where it is. Better still, send at least one of them a copy of it.

It is also very helpful if your friends and your family know the whereabouts of certain key documents.

Case study

Joy Barnaby

Actress, Canadian, 37

The problem

Joy lives in Canada. Her father David, a widower, retired to Turkey at the age of 70 and died 8 years later. Joy took a month off work to come to Turkey and deal with her father's affairs. Sadly, her father had not organized things very well: she had no idea where his passport was kept, let alone the documents relating to his various investments.

The solution

Thankfully, David's lawyer was a lot more organized than his client! He had kept copies of a lot of relevant correspondence and so was able to track down many of the missing items, albeit at a considerable cost as this was very time-consuming. The lawyer, along with one of David's friends in the area, helped Joy find David's other important documents. She realized that, without help, she didn't even know which *were* the important documents, especially if they were written in Turkish!

The bank statements that they found were clearly several years out of date, so the lawyer put Joy in contact with David's accountant, who was able to tell them about David's various current bank accounts and investments. The lawyer also sourced a copy of David's Will, which was a blessedly simple document leaving everything to Joy.

With the lawyer's help, Joy was able to sell David's assets in Turkey.

Talking to your relatives about the advantages of keeping copies of all of their key documents and an up-to-date list of their assets in one place can be delicate, but will save a lot of money on their death.

As far as the death itself is concerned, these documents will include:

- Your passport

- Any residence card

- Any medical insurance policy or card

- Your social security card

- The names of both of your parents - even if you're 90

- The name of your bank and your account number

There are other documents - many documents - that are needed to deal with the inheritance of your assets. See our chapter about inheritance (page 468) for details. It is helpful if they are kept together and the whereabouts of the documents is known to your family, your local lawyer and a trusted local friend.

I refer to the location of documents being known by a local friend because, in many cases, all your family and other relatives will be living hundreds or thousands of miles away and so be unable to act quickly at the time of your death.

Many people are nervous about entrusting information such as this to friends, even friends they have known for a long time. In this case, the best thing to do is usually to tell your lawyer where the documents are stored. Then tell your family that you have done so and give them the lawyer's contact details.

You should also give the lawyer (or the friend) the means to get access to the house when needed. This doesn't normally involve giving them a key but, more often, telling them which of your friends and neighbours has the key and giving the friend or the lawyer a letter to those neighbours, asking them to assist them and to permit them to remove the documents.

Having said all of that, the good news is that the process of dealing with a death in Turkey is always far more straightforward than it is in most countries.

Action in Turkey

Death at home

If the person who has died has been receiving medical treatment, it is customary for you to call out your family doctor to certify the death and initiate the steps needed to deal with the body. If the doctor does attend, he will complete the necessary paperwork and issue an officially stamped death certificate (*ölüm belgesi*).

This is, however, not strictly needed and an alternative arrangement can sometimes be quicker and more straightforward.

This alternative is to call out the Municipal Funeral Department (*Belediye Cenaze Isleri*). The Municipal Funeral Department performs an absolutely central task when dealing with deaths in Turkey.

Turkey: how things *really* work

As the name suggests, the Municipal Funeral Department is a part of the municipal government, and is based in your local town hall. They are paid for out of the taxes that you pay.

Once they have been called, the Municipal Funeral Department will attend very quickly: often within a few minutes.

If a doctor has not already been called, they will arrange for a doctor to attend and certify the death. This will not necessarily be your normal doctor.

When a doctor attends - whether it is your own doctor or the doctor arranged by the Municipal Funeral Department - the doctor will have to decide (based upon the facts of the case and a brief examination of the body) whether there is anything suspicious about the death. If there is, he will involve the police and the prosecutor. See below.

Assuming everything about the death appears to be routine and in order, the doctor will certify the death and the Funeral Department will arrange for the removal of the body to a local mosque.

The body will be washed. Depending on where you are, the body will be washed in a special room at the local cemetery (usually by professional body washers) or in the house or the garden of the house where the person died (either by professional body washers or by members of the family).

Various Islamic rituals are usually performed in relation to the body, but these can be dispensed with if the family indicates that the person who died was not a Muslim.

At the mosque - unless an alternative is agreed, or the washing has already taken place - the body will be washed and wrapped in a white shroud. This is in accordance with Islamic tradition. Professional washers (male and female) are, again, usually employed for this purpose.

Whilst all this is happening, the Municipal Funeral Department will complete all of the paperwork that is necessary to recognise the death so that the body can be released for a funeral.

In addition to making the arrangements for the funeral, the Municipal Funeral Department will also take care of some of the practical issues arising out of a funeral. For example, they can arrange for the funeral to be announced (often by the *hodja* - the man responsible for making these announcements - and the mosque's public-address system) and for food, chairs and a funeral car to be provided at the time of the funeral.

The Municipal Funeral Department is not permitted to make these arrangements for foreigners unless there is evidence that they have converted to Islam. In many cases, they may never have come across a deceased foreigner before, and so can be uncertain as to what needs to be done. This, sometimes, leads to them entering 'default mode' and taking the body to the mosque.

The reason the Municipal Funeral Department takes care of all of these steps is largely to do with time. Funerals in Turkey (and other hot Islamic countries) tend to take place very quickly for both religious and practical reasons. Often, if a person died in the morning, the funeral will take place after prayers that afternoon. If he or she dies in the afternoon, the body will usually remain in the mosque overnight and be buried the following morning. This works because, until recently, most of the time the deceased's family lived close to the deceased.

Increasingly, even for Turkish people, you will find that families can be widely dispersed throughout Turkey - though with the majority still in one place - and so it is acceptable for the ceremony to be delayed to allow relatives to arrive from distant parts of the country. However, this delay will seldom be more than a day or two.

Of course, in the case of many foreigners, the relatives might live on the other side of the world and so it might be necessary to delay the funeral for several days or several weeks. This can be arranged, but the body will have to be released from the care of the Municipal Funeral Department. In the parts of Turkey where there are significant numbers of foreigners, there are likely to be specialist funeral services who can provide this facility and deal with whatever other arrangements (such as a non-Islamic religious funeral) might be requested.

The funeral, whenever it takes place, will normally be attended by the deceased's family and neighbours, who will eat together after the funeral formalities have taken place.

Following the funeral, there is a period of mourning by the deceased's relatives. During this period, if there is a widow/widower, they will generally not be left alone.

Within local Turkish tradition, partly rooted in Islam and partly rooted in antiquity, there are certain special days when it comes to the mourning of the deceased. The third, seventh, 40th and 52nd day after the person dies are particularly important.

Death in a hospital

If the deceased died in hospital, then it will be the hospital doctor who certifies death and decides whether there are any circumstances that justify the involvement of the police and prosecutor.

They will then issue a hospital death certificate and report the death to the Municipal Funeral Department.

From that point onwards, the procedure is the same as if the person had died at home.

Death elsewhere

Sometimes, someone will die elsewhere: for example, at the scene of a car crash or in a restaurant. In these cases, the police will inevitably be called and the body will be taken to a hospital.

From there on, the process is the same as if the death had taken place in a hospital.

Reporting a death to the authorities

It is the duty of the doctor who attends after a person has died to consider whether the death needs to be reported to the authorities. This will usually happen if the deceased died 'out of the blue': in other words, without there being any illness leading up for the death. It will also happen if the deceased died as a result of accident or violence.

It's important to understand that the fact that the doctor refers the death to the prosecutor's office does *not* mean that he suspects foul play. It is merely because the cause of the death is not superficially obvious and so further investigation is required.

If the doctor calls in the public prosecutor, they will attend with the police and carry out an inspection of the deceased's body. Using their experience, they will then decide either to release the body immediately for burial or to arrange for a post-mortem/autopsy to help them establish the cause of death. If, after the autopsy, the prosecutor is satisfied that everything is in order, the prosecutor will release the body and the normal procedure will then be followed.

If not, it's another story!

The funeral director

For a Muslim, there is really no such thing as a private funeral service or director but, with the increasing number of non-Muslim foreigners living in Turkey, specialist services have sprung up to deal with their wishes and needs.

If you wish to have a non-Islamic religious funeral, you will need to use the services of such a company. If you live in an area with a lot of foreign residents, the Municipal Funeral Department will probably be able to point you in the direction of one that is suitable. Failing that, the deceased's lawyer or (expat) neighbours should be able to help.

It is then necessary to contact the funeral directors urgently to ask them to make the necessary arrangements. From that point onwards, they will liaise with the Municipal Funeral Department and do what is needed.

However, they will need some directions and guidance from you.

The funeral director will usually need to receive the following documents and information:

- A copy of the deceased's passport
- A copy of the deceased's residence permit
- Details of the deceased's insurance company
- A copy of the deceased's social security card
- The full names of both deceased's parents (however old the deceased)
- The deceased's place and date of birth, marital status, and permanent address

When you have a meeting with the funeral service, you need to be prepared to give the funeral director instructions as to what needs to be done.

The questions will include the following:

- If not already known, did the deceased wear a pacemaker? This may have already been removed by the attending doctor

- What type of coffin do you require?

- Do you want a burial or cremation?

- If you want a burial, in which cemetery?

- If you want a cremation, what do you intend to do with the ashes?

- Do you wish the deceased to be embalmed?

- Do you wish the deceased to be repatriated?

- Do you wish to take in any special clothes for the deceased to wear?

- Do you require a religious service and if so of which denomination?

- Your choice of music

- Whether the body is to be available for viewing prior to the burial or cremation

- Your preferred date, time, and place for the service and burial

These are a lot of things that need to be decided quite quickly, and it is obviously helpful if the family have thought about these issues in advance and if they and/or the deceased have told them what is required.

In this section, I have talked about "you" doing various things. Self-evidently, if the deceased was living in Izmir and you are living in Chicago, it is going to be impossible for you to deal personally with all of these things within the very short time frames required. In practical terms, therefore, you will have to delegate these tasks to someone more local.

Usually, this person will be a friend of the deceased or - if there is one - a local family member. They will often have been asked by the deceased to perform the task. It is helpful if you know that this has happened!

All in all, dealing with a death in Turkey - if you want to do something other than what is normal and arranged by the Municipal Funeral Department - requires quick action and that, in turn, is helped by a bit of planning and preparation.

Cemeteries

In Turkey, the norm is for a person to be buried rather than cremated. Municipalities each have one or more burial grounds. The use of these is very inexpensive when used as part of the municipal funeral facilities. However, they cannot be used for non-Muslim burials.

In places where there are significant numbers of foreigners, there is often a minorities graveyard. Your specialist funeral service will make arrangements with that graveyard and reserve a plot for the burial.

Such minority graves tend to be expensive: certainly far more expensive than a regular municipal grave. All in all, a funeral service for a foreigner (including the services of the funeral company and the provision of the grave) can cost from TRY2,000-10,000 (US$550-3,000; €500-2,500; £400-2,000). This is probably a lot less than you would have paid at home.

Crematoriums

In theory, it should be possible for a cremation to be arranged instead of a burial, but very few places will have the facilities to carry this out.

Death certificates (*ölüm belgesi*)

As already explained, the death certificate can be issued by either a hospital doctor or (if the death did not occur at a hospital) a municipal doctor.

If the public prosecutor becomes involved, then the death certificate will be issued by the court.

Unlike in many countries, the death certificate is only a certificate that the person has died. It is not sufficient to arrange a funeral.

The death certificate must be filed with the Population Registry Office (*Nüfus Müdürlüğü*) within ten days.

Burial licence

In order for a body to be buried, a burial licence is required. This is issued by the municipal doctor upon production of a valid death certificate and completion of a certain amount of paperwork. This paperwork can be dealt with either by the family or friends of the deceased or by a funeral service, if one is being used. If you're going to use a funeral service, it makes a lot more sense for them to deal with the paperwork, as the burial of foreigners is (in most parts of Turkey) a relatively rare occurrence.

Repatriation of the body

Many foreigners living in Turkey will say to their friends and relatives and/or put in their Will that they would like their body to be 'taken home'.

This can be done, but it is usually both complicated and expensive. As I said earlier, I suspect that if the person realised how complicated and expensive it was going to become, they would express their preference to be buried in Turkey.

Even if the person does say in their Will that they wish to be taken home, it is only an expression of their wish and not legally binding; so the heirs could decide to proceed by way of a burial in Turkey in any event. Unfortunately, many people are uncomfortable about ignoring the deceased's wishes in this way.

If you wish to repatriate the body, you will need to tell the specialist funeral service that you are using.

It is necessary to involve the consulate of the country of which the deceased was a national, as they will have to produce some paperwork.

The formal part of the process starts with making an application to the Municipal Funeral Department. This must be accompanied by an official request by the consulate to remove the body from Turkey.

Before you can make this application, the body must be ready to travel. There are detailed national and international requirements as to the nature of the coffin used and various other technical issues. The coffin itself has to be of a special type and completely sealed. Unless it meets the specification, the customs officer will not grant the export certificate and the airline will not allow the coffin to go into its hold.

For example, Turkish Airlines carries bodies only as cargo (not as part of the baggage of an accompanying passenger). For international flights, human remains transported inside a coffin must be enclosed in a sackcloth or canvas winding sheet, and a zinc or lead coffin or a sealed solid wooden coffin must be used. For domestic flights, human remains must be transported inside an impermeable solid wooden coffin, with a secured cover and without any cracks or breaks.

The Municipal Funeral Department will then issue a licence permitting the body to travel and, at the same time, a burial licence.

The coffin is then sealed.

The municipal doctor then issues yet another piece of paper: an export permit.

An officer from the Customs Department must then examine the sealed coffin in the presence of the municipal doctor and issue a customs clearance permitting the coffin to pass through customs and the body to be sent home.

Once you arrive back in your own country, you will of course have to go through the relevant formalities to import the body into that country and then deal with it by way of cremation or burial. In order to do that, you will, at the very least, need to have a certified copy of the original Turkish death certificate translated into your own language.

You are likely also to have to register the death with the authorities where the body is to be buried. In order to obtain the death certificate in your own country, it may well be necessary for the coroner or other official to issue a clearance certificate. Sometimes, depending upon the circumstances surrounding the death, the coroner might want to hold an enquiry (inquest) before consenting to the burial or cremation.

As already mentioned, doing all this is expensive. The cost of transportation of the body is likely to be at least US$3,000/€2,500/£2,000 and can be well in excess of that amount. The cost of the funeral service companies in the two countries can easily be twice that amount.

Repatriation of the deceased's ashes

This is a cheaper and less complicated process, if you have access to a crematorium in Turkey.

Some airlines give passengers the option of checking cremated remains as carry-on luggage or as checked baggage (just like a suitcase). If carrying the ashes onto the plane, they are subject to screening and must pass through the X-ray machine.

Other airlines require cremated ashes to be sent only via cargo. Contacting the airline will help ensure that you are not held up for unnecessary and preventable reasons.

You may also be able to send them by a courier company. Usually the smaller ones are the most flexible. DHL, UPS & Fedex do NOT accept ashes. You must declare what is in the package. The courier cost will be decided by the size of the box that you send the ashes with. A small size box will cost likely US$300/€250/£200.

Other people who should be informed

Local people to be informed

- The consulate of your country in Turkey

- The Immigration and Population office

- The president of any apartment building/condominium in which the deceased was resident

- The deceased's medical insurance company

- The deceased's bank

- Any places where the deceased had investments - e.g. shares, insurance policies, bank accounts, investment funds etc.

International people to be informed

The international equivalents in the deceased's home country of all the above agencies and organisations are likely to need copies of the death certificates

It's also a good idea to keep a copy of the death certificate for yourself.

Action 'back home'

Notifying the consulate

The first thing you should do, though it's not strictly at home, is notify your consulate in Turkey about the death. They will then remove the deceased from the list of nationals who they know to live locally and can be useful in other ways. Doing this might also serve as an official notification of the death to the government of your country.

To do this, you will need to have a copy of the local death certificate.

There is no legal requirement to do this, unless you want to repatriate the body.

Surrendering the deceased's passport

In most countries, there is a legal requirement that you surrender the deceased's passport to the local consulate or to the passport office back home.

Banks and investments

Any institutions in which the deceased held money or investments will need to be notified so that the estate can get its hands on those assets.

Reporting the death to the coroner 'back home'

The requirements here vary from country to country but, in many countries, if you repatriate the body or (in some cases) the ashes the coroner back home will have the legal responsibility of 'signing off' the death and, if it's necessary to do so, of holding an inquest.

Insurance

Check the deceased's medical and, if appropriate, travel and insurance policies. You may find that some or all the costs of dealing with the death are covered by those policies.

Wills - and dealing with any inheritance

See our chapter on inheritance (page 468) for details.

Returning 'Home'

Written by **Başak Yildiz Orkun**
Managing Partner (Legal Department) at Orkun & Orkun
www.orkunorkun.com • info@orkunorkun.com

There may, for various reasons, come a time when you decide that you want to leave Turkey and return 'home'. This is something that worries many people thinking of settling in the country but it is, in fact, a rare thing to happen. Ignoring people who have obtained employment in Turkey on a relatively short-term basis, in our experience fewer than 20% of people who settle in Turkey will decide to leave.

There are usually two main reasons why those who leave make the decision to do so.

The first, and probably the more common, is that they moved to Turkey when they retired, with their husband or wife, and that the spouse has since died. The surviving spouse wants to go back to be closer to the children and other family members.

The second main reason is ill health. Although Turkey has a good medical system and although, especially if you speak English, you will probably find that there will be people in the medical profession who speak your language, there is no pretending that everybody will do so and there is no doubt that it is more complicated to deal with doctors, nurses and other health professionals in a language which is neither their own nor your own. If you are going to have to have regular contact with doctors and hospitals, it is tempting to go back to a place where communication will be easy.

Of course, communication is vitally important. There is not much room for error if you're trying to communicate your symptoms to a doctor and the sort of subjects that you're likely to have to discuss - and the technical terminology you're likely to have to use - will challenge both your grasp of Turkish and the doctors' grasp of your language.

The good news is that, although we in Turkey will be very sorry to see you go, moving 'back home' is simple - at least from our point of view.

There are five main steps you need to take.

1. If you have a tax residency in Turkey, you need to tell the tax office in Turkey that you are leaving the country. You need only to tell your main tax office. They will then pass the information on to all other relevant government departments such as the healthcare system, your local town hall etc. You need to tell them when you will be leaving or you can delay notifying them until after you have left and tell them the actual date of your departure. It is better done before you leave. Either way, the tax office will then assess any taxes that you might owe (or any refund to which you might be entitled) and arrange payment with you

2. You need to end your tenancy by giving notice to your landlord or, if you own your own home, you may want to sell it. You're not obliged to sell it.

You could continue to own a home in Turkey which you might use for holidays or which might be used by your family and friends. The choice is yours

3.   You need to tell your bank that you are no longer going to be living in the country. You can either close your bank account or leave it open. If you choose to leave it open (and many people will, at least for a year or so), they will make a note on your account that you're no longer a resident and this will change the way in which some paperwork is dealt with

4.   You will need to notify the utilities - electricity, telephone company, water company etc. - that you're leaving, and pay any outstanding bills

5.   You should notify your neighbours and the president of the community of owners is you live in a place with such a community

So, that's all easy. Of course, in your case there may be other things that you need to do but they're all likely to be obvious and simple.

However, one thing we cannot control here in Turkey is the difficulty you might face back home when you arrive back in your own country. We would strongly recommend that you consult your own lawyer in your own country to seek advice on how you should deal with the move.

A number of problems commonly arise.

The easy ones tend to be things such as reregistering as a tax resident in your own country and the importing of any goods that you're bringing back from Turkey.

The more complicated and challenging can relate to healthcare. You will need to make sure that you are entitled to healthcare in your own country. What you will need to do will vary from country to country.

In some, you will need to take out fresh healthcare insurance and you may find that its terms are much less favourable than you had when you left because you no longer qualify for any discounts as a long-term customer and you are now older and may be suffering from an existing medical condition. In some countries (such as the UK) you will need to re-register with the health service and they may impose limitations on your eligibility to use that service until you have been resident in the country for a certain amount of time.

One thing you can do to help on the healthcare front - if you lived in and are a citizen on an EU country - is to make sure that you have an up-to-date EU healthcare card, based upon which you will be entitled to emergency medical treatment in any EU country until you again become officially resident in that country.

One practical point that it's probably worth mentioning when talking about going back home is that many of my clients have reported a sense of disappointment when they return home: so much has changed, so many things are not as they remember them and re-igniting friendships (which may have been run at a distance for many years) can be more difficult than you might imagine. They say that the transition when moving back to your old country is nearly as difficult as the transition when moving to Turkey.

Working in Turkey

Working for Others

Written by **Başak Yildiz Orkun**
Managing Partner (Legal Department) at Orkun & Orkun
www.orkunorkun.com • info@orkunorkun.com

Finding a job in Turkey can be difficult. In most cases, Turkey doesn't need foreign nationals to fill a labour shortage. It has a young population (over 40% of the population is under 25) and a very large workforce. It also has an unemployment rate of over 11%% - and 23% youth unemployment.

These figures are getting worse. There is an economic crisis. Factories are closing and, not surprisingly, the government is keen to preserve jobs for local people.

Add to this the fact that a foreign worker can cost up to five times the amount that would be paid to an equivalent Turkish worker and it's easy to understand why finding a job in Turkey is not always the easiest thing for a foreigner to do.

Yet jobs are available. Turkey has a shortage of workers in certain key fields and actively encourages foreigners to fill those posts.

In particular, there are some high-tech posts where there is a local shortage of workers and many foreign-owned companies find they need to have some foreign employees to act as a bridge to the local, Turkish work force.

The job market

There are over 30 million Turks in the local Turkish workforce and well over a million more working overseas.

The Turkish economy has, over the last 20 years, become ever more dominated by the private sector. It is led by industry and, increasingly, the service sector - which now accounts for nearly 50% of all employment.

Industry is changing rapidly. Fewer Turks are now employed making clothes and many more making trucks and cars, electronics and other more sophisticated products. About 25% of Turks still work in agriculture. They are concentrated in the Eastern part of the country.

For the foreigner seeking work in Turkey, the main opportunities lie in the service sector and the more high-tech industries.

Marriage to a Turkish person

If you are married to a Turk, when it comes to employment you will enjoy all the same legal rights and benefits that a Turkish national enjoys. For many this is a very pleasurable way of getting around the restrictions on employment in Turkey.

Of course, in the real world it might not make it much easier to find an 'ordinary' job: particularly if you don't speak fluent Turkish.

Working in Turkey as a foreigner

Turkey granted 73,584 work permits to foreigners in 2016 - a 14% increase on 2015. The acceptance rate on applications for work permits was 85%.

Seasonal work

The main opportunity for seasonal work in Turkey is in the tourism industry, which contributed US$31.5billion (6.2%) to Turkey's GDP in 2015.

Many tourist businesses, large and small, lack the language skills to service the needs of international visitors and need international input to help them tailor their product to the specific needs of their various foreign customers.

Most seasonal workers in the tourist industry are appointed for two or three months, to cover the main tourist season from the end of June to September.

Many of these jobs - an increasing number and now, probably, 80% or more - are 'official' jobs. In other words, the person employed has been employed following the usual process of an application for a work permit. There are still some jobs in this sector where people work 'below the radar'. They work, usually in smaller establishments, completely unregistered and illegally. They have no work permit or employment contract. They have few legal rights.

Many jobs in the tourist sector are at one and a half or two times the minimum wage. As of January 2017, minimum wage stood at TRY1,777.50 (€479.47) gross per month. This contrasts, for example, with €684 in Greece and €1,498 in Germany. Some employees in the tourist sector - particularly those with very good language skills (including Turkish) and previous experience can earn significantly more.

If you're seeking employment in the tourist industry, you need to start looking early. If you're going to travel to Turkey to look for work (rather than applying to large tour operators based in your own country) you probably need to be in Turkey no later than April, with a view to starting work in May or June. You would, of course, travel as a tourist. If you succeed in finding a job in this way, you will have to return to your own country to apply for your work permit.

Temporary work

There is a difference between seasonal work and temporary work. Temporary work can arise at any point during the year.

Two areas where there is often demand for temporary employment are training positions relating to the opening of hotels and other tourist establishments and teaching foreign languages. See the section on Teaching English (page 187).

Full-time employment

The basic rules

The basic rules regulating the employment of foreigners in Turkey are:

1. All employment requires a work permit. The employer obtains the permit. The permit authorises the foreigner to undertake only that employment and only for that employer. It does not permit the foreigner to go and work elsewhere or in some other role. If you want to change employers or job, you need to obtain a fresh work permit

2. The employer has to justify why he needs a work permit - for example, he might need an English receptionist because 70% of his clients are English

3. The employer must find a person and *then* apply for a permit for that person

4. If the potential employee is already in Turkey, they must have a valid residency permit in order to apply for a work permit whilst they're still in the country. If they don't, they must go to the Turkish consulate in their own country to apply

5. If their application is initially accepted, they'll receive a reference number. They should send that number to the employer. The employer does everything else (see page 18)

What are your job skills?

Because of the challenges associated with finding work in Turkey, it's well worth spending some time working out exactly what skills you have to offer, how you can improve them and how you can best take advantage of them.

In many countries, this leads people to consider whether their skills make them better suited to working as an employee or to being self-employed - i.e. running their own simple business. This is not normally the case in Turkey, where obtaining a visa to work as an independent self-employed person can be very difficult. See page 27 for visa information. In Turkey, if you relish running your own business you will, therefore, usually be forced to consider setting up a proper Turkish business (and working for it) rather than simply being self-employed. See page 215 for more information about starting a business.

Many people coming to Turkey will already have a well-defined set of job skills and, of course, many will have been invited to work in Turkey precisely because of this. If you're not in this position, I suggest that you sit down and go through the process of listing your skills.

This may lead you to conclude that there is little chance of being able to work in Turkey within your normal field of activity and that you will, therefore, have to do something else. Some people relish the idea of coming to Turkey to start a new life that will take them in a completely different direction from what they'd been doing before, but others will think that this adds one level of complexity too many.

Your qualifications

What formal qualifications do you possess and will they be accepted in Turkey?

If you're engaged in some professional activity (doctor, engineer etc.) you will probably find that your professional association 'back home' will have a database showing the requirements of Turkey (and other countries) when it comes to people wanting to work in your area of expertise.

If your qualifications are going to be of direct use, you will need to validate them and have them translated. The process for doing this varies, depending upon where you live. Once again, your professional association should be able to help by explaining what is needed. However, this is seldom easy.

In your own country, there is likely to be a government agency dealing with the recognition of qualifications from that country in other parts of the world. For example, in the US it is the Department of Education (**www.ed.gov**). In the UK it is the UK National Recognition Information Centre (NARIC - **www.naric.org.uk**).

Core skills

What are your core skills?

'Core skills' means different things in different places but, probably, would always include communication skills, numeracy, IT skills, problem solving, working with others and language skills. Others might add the ability to manage yourself and the ability to learn and develop.

It is easier to examine your core skills in an objective way if you do this with an honest and trusted friend, colleague, or partner.

You will often find that the core skills that you have developed whilst working in (say) a food factory can be directly applicable to other jobs where there are employment opportunities in Turkey.

Once you've established your core skills, it is well worthwhile talking to a Turkish employment agency (e.g. **www.stantonchase.com** or **www.kariyer.net**) to see whether those skills offer any scope for employment in Turkey. A preliminary discussion is usually free.

Improving your skills

When it comes to getting a job in Turkey, many people find that the key to success is taking their core skills and improving them, or developing them in a particular direction, to provide something specifically in-demand in Turkey. For example, a person who has worked successfully as a car mechanic in (say) Germany is likely (subject to further training) to have pretty much all the skills required to work as an aircraft mechanic in Turkey. There are no job opportunities in Turkey for car mechanics, but there are (2017) some for aircraft mechanics. However, in order to show his suitability for a job as an aircraft mechanic, he is likely to have to do some supplemental training in Germany.

The need to speak Turkish

It is, hardly surprisingly, a requirement of most jobs that you should be able to speak adequate Turkish. However, this is not always the case. For example, qualified teachers of English as a second language (perhaps surprisingly) often do not need to have any Turkish language skills, although it is helpful if they do.

You will need a very limited amount of Turkish if you are going to seek work as a seasonal worker in the tourism industry.

Finding a job in Turkey

There are a number of ways of finding a job in Turkey - bearing in mind, of course, the need for you to obtain a work permit.

These days, the most common is via the internet. Major recruitment agencies such as **kariyer.net** and **yenibiris.com** have a vast selection of jobs on offer.

Alternatively, there are more informal arrangements. Informal local advertisements appear on people's premises and a lot of importance is attached to personal contacts.

Both people seeking employment and employers seeking employees advertise in the local press.

Because of this, many people will travel to Turkey to look for work. That's also on the basis that it is much easier to persuade someone to give you a job if you've met them face-to-face. If you do this - and it's not illegal to come as a tourist for this purpose - please remember that you will have to go home whilst the employer completes your application for a work permit and there is no guarantee that the application will be successful.

Whilst you're in Turkey you might think about putting an advert in the local press. All of the main papers have a 'jobs wanted' section. You will need to think carefully about the sort of person who is going to be looking for somebody with your skills and which newspaper they're likely to read.

Advertising for a job works because many employers are impressed by people who show initiative and correspondingly depressed by the dozens of inappropriate applications they receive from employment agencies.

Restrictions on foreigners working in Turkey

Apart from the need to have a work permit, there are other restrictions on the ability of foreigners to work in Turkey. For example, they cannot work as lawyers or in medical fields. Nor can they work in industries that are considered government monopolies.

Case study

Diego Martin

Engineer, Spanish, 45

The problem

Diego was a 30-year-old mechanical engineer in Spain who wanted to start a new life abroad. He loved the idea of working in Turkey or Cyprus. However, getting a work permit in Turkey was proving difficult whereas, as another EU country, it would have been very simple for him to move to Cyprus. However, he kept on hankering after Turkey...

The solution

Diego took a long-term view and decided to retrain. He obtained a qualification, in Spain, for maintaining aircraft engines (something that had always interested him and which paid much better than his general mechanical engineering). He also started learning Turkish via a course at his local college. Now the world (or at least Turkey!) was his oyster, and he decided to move to Turkey.

He managed to find a job working on aero-engines, an area of work in which (at the time) there was a great shortage of labour in Turkey.

Years later, Diego has been promoted to a management position at a small airport for private aircraft. He enjoyed his work on the engines but is quite glad to have a less physically demanding job in his mid-40s!

Diego married a Turkish girl and became a citizen of Turkey five years ago, with help from the company he works for, and now considers the country his home.

Informal applications

When you're applying for a job in Turkey it is seldom possible simply to turn up at the place of employment and ask for a job. This may be possible in the case of work as a waiter or bartender; but for anything more sophisticated than this you will need to make a proper application, in writing, followed up by a visit.

If you are applying for a job as a waiter or bartender, remember that the employer wants to employ you (a foreigner) because of your ability to engage with and draw in foreign visitors. It will be a huge advantage if you speak some Turkish but even better if you have a great personality, are good looking and energetic! It's probably improper to say this, but attractive girls enjoy a huge advantage.

Formal applications

A formal job application is made up of two parts. The first is a covering letter, the second a CV (*résumé*).

The application is, these days, almost always sent by email but you could also deliver an application pack directly to potential employers' premises.

Unlike in many countries, the CV does not need to be in any particular format.

It must contain your contact details, including a mobile telephone number.

It should set out your relevant experience and qualifications.

It should offer the name and contact details of two references.

Again, it should, if possible, be in Turkish.

If you do not speak Turkish, consider having it translated and sending the translation along with the original English, French, German etc. document.

Job interviews

It is usual for the person applying for the job to follow up the application after two or three days to see whether it has been successful, rather than to rely upon the potential employer to get back to them with a response. Even amongst employers who would have replied to your CV, such perseverance creates a good impression.

If you're offered an interview relating to a more senior post, it is common for the employer to cover the expenses of you attending the interview - especially if you're travelling a long way, such as from (say) Russia or the US.

It is quite common for you have to attend at least two interviews; the first with a relatively junior person and the others with the decision-maker.

When attending an interview, be on time and dress formally. It is always better to be overdressed than underdressed.

Working conditions

A normal working week is 45 hours.

Working hours, holidays and overtime vary quite a lot depending on the nature of the business in which you are working and where it is located. See our chapter on employment law: page 193.

If you're working in the tourist industry, do not expect to be able to take holidays during the normal holiday season! On the contrary, you can expect to be working up to seven days per week during these times.

Unless you work for a major Western company, you should not expect to be given time off for the normal Western holidays such as Christmas.

Trade unions

There are four main trade unions in Turkey:

- Confederation of Turkish Trade Unions (TÜRK-İŞ)

- Confederation of Revolutionary Trade Unions of Turkey (DİSK)

- Confederation of Turkish Real Trade Unions (HAK-İŞ)

- Confederation of Public Workers' Unions (KESK)

In some cases, a trade union might have the legal right to negotiate terms and conditions of employment on your behalf but, in order to do this, they must represent at least 10% of all Turkish employees in that particular field.

In some industries, striking is prohibited. These include education, healthcare and hospitals, defence, and many public utilities.

Employment law

Turkish law gives you substantial employment protection but be aware: many employers (though fewer each year) try to get around the law by employing you (totally illegally) without a contract and paying you cash in hand. See our section on working illegally (page 204).

The Turkish Codes

The Turkish Tax Code and Social Security Code set out your rights and obligations when it comes to taxation and social security.

Unless specifically stated to the contrary, all the provisions of both codes apply equally to local workers and to foreign workers.

Foreign workers have exactly the same remedies available to them as Turkish workers when it comes to enforcing their rights.

Probationary period and contracts

Under Turkish law, the employer is entitled to place you on a probationary period of up to two months, during which time he can dismiss you without cause and you can leave without having to give notice.

The employer must give you a written contract setting out, at the very minimum, the following:

1. Your job title

2. A summary of your job responsibilities, if this isn't obvious from the job title

3. Your rate of pay

4. Your hours of work

5. Your holiday entitlement

6. The person to whom you report

7. The period of notice that you are required to give or be given

8. Any special or unusual terms

There is no special format required for this contract.

For a contract to work in a senior post that you think will be long term, it is a good idea (and fairly inexpensive - around €250 for a simple contract) to have an employment lawyer check it over, because the law is complex. If the contract does not comply with all the technical requirements your rights can be prejudiced.

Failure to give you such a contract is against Labour Law and so can be reported to the Ministry of Labour & Social Security - telephone them on 170 or contact via **www.csgb.gov.tr.** Failure entitles the worker to compensation for any loss suffered.

Payment

In Turkey, almost everybody is paid monthly in arrear and it is rare, except in very senior roles, for there to be any hidden 'perks' or benefits such as the company paying for your accommodation, your health insurance or your children's education.

If you're working in a casual post (such as behind a bar) it is common to be paid daily at the end of each shift: often in cash.

When they're talking about their earnings, most Turks talk about their monthly salary and not about their annual salary. In other words, someone will say that they earn TRY3,000 per month. Things can get complicated at this point because, especially in a casual setting, people will often refer to their net monthly income (i.e. after deduction of tax and social security payments) rather than their total (gross) monthly income.

When discussing pay with either your employer or your colleagues, you need to be clear about the basis being used for the calculation. The best is your gross monthly salary as the amount of tax and other deductions from it can vary from person to person.

An added complication at this point is that, in some European countries, it is customary for an employee to receive 13 or even 14 'monthly' salaries per year: perhaps one each calendar month and another at Christmas. If this is what you're used to, please note that it does not happen in Turkey. You will receive 12 monthly payments.

Relocation expenses

Except for people being transferred to Turkey by an international company, it is rare for an employer to pay anything towards your relocation expenses.

Taxes and social security

As an employee, you will usually have to pay tax and social security payments. The amount of tax depends upon your earnings. See our chapters on taxes (pages 248-273).

Social security costs of 12% are deducted from your salary each month.

Holiday entitlement

After you have been employed for a minimum of one year (unless more generous terms are agreed in your contract) you are entitled to a minimum of 14 days' paid holiday per year.

If you have been employed for five to 15 years, you are entitled to 20 days.

If you have been employed for more than 15 years, you are entitled to 26 days.

In addition, you will be entitled to public holidays. These amount to 14.5 days per year. For a list of these, see **www.guides.global/guides/turkey/tur-holidays.php**.

Discipline

If the employer has a grievance about your conduct, they must raise it with you in writing and obtain your statement on the matter.

The employer might have a written policy as to how such complaints are to be dealt with. They must then follow that policy. If there is no such policy, the Code of Employment rules apply. They are as follows:

1. The employer shall explain the grievance, ask for your statement in writing and hold a meeting to investigate the grievance.

2. You need to reply, in writing, with your explanation

Only in the most extreme cases (typically theft or violence to a co-worker) can you be dismissed as a result of a first complaint.

If the employer later has any other grievance with you, he can either repeat the above process or raise the stakes by giving you a formal written notice of the grievance. Thereafter, the procedure is the same. The main significance of the written complaint is when it comes to dismissal (see below).

Dismissal

The employer can only lawfully end your employment in two circumstances:

Dismissal without notice

Should you act immorally or similarly (e.g. if you are guilty of theft or violent); or should health conditions prevent you from working for a period in excess of six weeks, the employer can terminate your contract without giving any notice. If you are dismissed without notice, your employment comes to an immediate end and you do not receive any pay for any day beyond the date on which the dismissal takes place.

Dismissal with notice

If you are dismissed for any other reason, the employer will be obliged to give you the greater of the notice referred to in your contract (usually two weeks or four weeks) or the notice required by law. The minimum periods of notice are:

- Employed up to six months: two weeks' notice

- Employed six months to 18 months: four weeks' notice

- Employed 18 months to three years: six weeks' notice

- Employed for more than three years: eight weeks' notice

You will then be entitled to be paid for the notice period, plus any other sums due on severance such as accrued wages and holiday pay.

The employer may, or may not, require you to work during the period of notice, but even if you're not required to work you will be entitled to be paid. During your notice period, you can use two hours per day for job seeking.

Should the employer have a valid reason for your dismissal (i.e. your conduct has been found lacking as a result of at least three grievance procedures within the last six months), your contract could be terminated by the employer. In this case you will have the right to ask for your job back within one month of the dismissal, but only if you have worked for the employer for at least six months and there are more than 30 employees working in your place of employment. This is called 'Security of Employment'.

Redundancy

If the circumstances of the company change and there is no longer enough work for you to do, the employer may make you redundant. This right arises whether the lack of work is due to economic circumstances, technological development or a reorganisation of the workplace.

In any situation, any alleged redundancy must be real and not just an excuse for removing a particular employee.

Generally, if you've worked for the company for more than six months, if the company has more than 30 employees, and if you think that the dismissal or redundancy was made unjustly, you can apply for reemployment in some other role within the company within one month of your contract termination.

In some places, the redundancy will affect only one or two people. In other cases, it can involve large numbers of people. In the case of large-scale redundancies (known as 'collective dismissals') more complex procedures arise, but they're probably outside the scope of this book.

If the redundancy is a small-scale redundancy, then there is no special procedure to be followed apart from the requirement to give you written notice of the redundancy.

In the event of redundancy, you will be entitled to a payment for your period of notice and your accumulated holiday entitlement. In addition, you will be entitled to receive severance payment of one month's salary for each full year that the employer employed you, up to a certain monthly maximum laid down from time to time by the government (2017: a maximum of €1,141.37 per month).

Health and safety

Turkish law makes the employer responsible for the health and safety of their employees during their employment.

The employer is, in particular, required to:

- Educate their employees about all relevant safety risks

- If they employ more than ten people, they must engage the services of an external health and safety expert

- Ensure that the place of employment is safe

- Arrange for the place of employment to be inspected on a regular basis

- Make any organisational requirements necessary (e.g. making sure that the safety equipment is delivered to the correct place and that somebody is responsible for assessing health and safety risks)

- Have all necessary equipment in place

- Comply with a quite complex series of rules, the details of which depend upon the nature of their business. If you're starting a business, we recommend you seek legal advice on this point

Employers must also have, at the place of work, a way of recording accidents at work and ensure that any accidents is reported to the Department of Social Security/Social Insurance Institution.

Restraint of trade

The employer may place a clause in your contract preventing you from working for his competitors for a certain period of time after you leave his employment and within a certain geographical area. The clause must be limited in time (for example, to a period of two years) and regional extent (for example, restricting you taking another job in Bodrum).

Any restraint of trade clauses can only be enforced through the courts and they can only be applied if an employee has important knowledge about the business. For example, it would not normally be reasonable to impose a restraint of trade clause on a waiter or car mechanic but it might be reasonable to have such a clause in a contract with a chef or a manager.

The restriction as to the scope of the restraint - i.e. the range of people that you cannot work for and the geographical area to which it applies - must be reasonable in all the circumstances. Otherwise it will be rejected by a court.

Other employee rights

Overtime pay

If you work more than 45 hours in the week you must be paid overtime for the excess hours at 150% of your normal rate of pay. This does not apply to highly paid executives. The interpretation of highly paid is left to the discretion of the court. It is rare (and frowned upon) for senior employees in professional offices to make any claim for overtime pay, even if they might technically be entitled to it.

Weekend break

Any employee who has worked 45 hours in the week is entitled to a continuous weekend break of 24 hours.

Rest breaks

You are entitled to a minimum of one hour for your lunch.

In some industries, it is customary for there to be other allocated breaks, but there is no compulsory schedule of breaks laid down by the general law.

If there are defined breaks, they must be stated in a notice on the premises.

Minimum wage

With effect from 1 January 2017, the gross monthly minimum wage in Turkey is TRY1,777.50 (€479.47) per month. This is revised in January each year and has been increasing quite sharply. However, it is still quite low and contrasts sharply with the minimum of €684 in Greece or €1,498 in Germany.

For those who do not work full time, there is also a minimum hourly or weekly amount.

Illness

Employees are entitled to time off in the case of illness or injury.

You'll be entitled to time off for the period certified by your doctor. If that period exceeds the period of notice the employer is required to give to you, the employer has the right to terminate your contract by giving you due notice.

The employer can dismiss a sick employee after six weeks' absence on the basis that they are no longer capable of doing the job.

Sick pay

There is no entitlement to sick pay from your employer, but there is an entitlement to claim social security payments from the government if the absence can be classified as occupational (i.e. if you were injured at work or if you suffer an illness acquired as a result of work) and a lower entitlement for non-occupational absence if it was not.

Despite this, many employers, especially if you are a senior employee, continue to pay you at your normal rate during any absence due to sickness or injury, deducting from your pay the social security benefit that you are entitled to receive.

Maternity rights

An employee's maternity rights changed significantly at the end of 2016.

During the pregnancy

During pregnancy, a woman cannot be required to work for more than 7.5 hours per day or on a night shift. In addition, if their doctor certifies this to be necessary, the woman should be assigned to lighter duties. No reduction in wages must be made as a result of doing this.

The woman is entitled to paid leave for attending medical appointments during her pregnancy.

Leave before and after the birth

A pregnant woman is entitled to 16 weeks' paid maternity leave. This is usually taken during the eight weeks before the expected date of delivery and during the eight weeks following the birth.

In the case of second and subsequent pregnancies, these periods can be extended. See our chapter on social security benefits (page 153).

If a woman wishes to take additional leave, she may do so on an unpaid basis for a period of up to six months.

Half-time work

A woman shall be entitled to work for only half of her normal working hours for up to 60 days following the birth of a first child, 120 days following the birth of a second and 180 days following the birth of a third.

The employer will pay her for the hours worked and she will receive a payment from the state in respect of the hours not worked.

Nursing leave

For one year following the birth of a child, a woman is entitled to take one-and-a-half hours per day paid leave in order to nurse her child. This time may be taken in as many instalments and at such times as the woman decides.

You will not be entitled to nursing leave if you've chosen to work half-time.

Adopted and disabled children

Similar rights apply in respect of adopted children (younger than three years old) and older disabled children. For disabled children, the rules are complex. Seek legal advice.

Paternity rights

A father is entitled to five days' paternity leave following the birth of his child.

Parental rights

A parent is entitled to up to ten days' unpaid leave per year to attend to the needs of their children. These could be, for example, looking after a sick child or taking a child to hospital.

Protection from discrimination

The Turkish Labour Code prohibits employers discriminating on the basis of language, race, religion, gender or political/philosophical views. Failure to comply gives rise to a claim for compensation of up to four months' salary plus any other claim to which the employee might be entitled.

Protection from harassment

If an employee is subject to harassment, whether sexual or a more general 'affront to their honour and dignity', they may demand an immediate end to their employment and receive the full severance payment to which they would be entitled in the case of an unfair dismissal.

Employee responsibilities

The employee has the legal obligation to work diligently and honestly for the employer, to protect the employer's business secrets and to act in good faith at all times.

Working within the expat community

Working within the expat community is a tempting option for foreigners arriving in Turkey. It is, in many ways, simpler and more straight-forward than finding a job with a local employer. However, it does have its downsides...

Who gets involved in this type of work?

There are many foreigners who would like to work in Turkey. Unfortunately, most of them do not speak Turkish and would find working for a local business difficult.

Many of them may not have a visa permitting them to work in Turkey, so making it almost impossible to find a proper job there.

Yet many will have skills of great use to the local expat community. They may find a niche in a local business where the owner is himself an expat (and struggles with Turkish) and where the clientele is also almost exclusively expat (and so would find it difficult dealing with a local employee whose English was not great).

Others have manual skills that would be really useful to other foreigners living in the area. They may be a car mechanic, or a pool maintenance engineer, or a plumber, or a hairdresser. There are lots of foreign residents in Turkey who prefer to deal with people of their own nationality. It eliminates the language issue and both parties will be working on the same page culturally. So, the obvious thing is to offer your services to the expat community.

In some cases, those services can be offered via paid employment: perhaps in a bar/restaurant, perhaps in a property maintenance company or perhaps in a car hire firm. However, to work as an employee you need a work permit, and your employee is unlikely to get one for most of these jobs. In other cases, you will need to set up your own business and then offer your services to individual clients.

Working for expats as an employee

Legal position

The rights and obligations of an expat working as the employee of another expat are the same as they would be if you were working for a local person.

See the chapter on employment law (page 193).

Having said that, there is - unfortunately - a strong tendency within the expat community to seek and offer work on an 'unofficial' basis - i.e. with no contract, paying no tax or social security and cash in hand.

Often, that work is offered to people who do not have a work permit allowing their employment in Turkey: sometimes even to people who do not have a visa authorising their presence in Turkey.

In every case this type of work is illegal. Both the employer and the employee can get into quite serious trouble with the Turkish authorities.

In the case of employment offered to someone who does not have a work permit to work in Turkey or a visa to be there at all, it is not only illegal from the employment law point of view but also as a matter of immigration law.

The immigration authorities are a great deal more robust when it comes to enforcing the law than are the employment law authorities - partly because they have far more resources at their disposal.

Working illegally is not a good idea. See the next chapter.

Finding a job

Finding this type of job within the expat community tends to be quite different from finding a job in the local Turkish community.

You're far more likely to hear about employment opportunities in the local bars, or from other expat contacts, than you are to see them advertised on the internet or in a newspaper.

The employer is far less likely to require a formal job application, including a CV, prior to an interview. They tend to see you, have an informal interview with you and then offer you a job.

A good starting place when it comes to finding jobs is to look at the general advertising in the local expat press. It contains extensive advertising aimed at the expat community, and it will be obvious from the names of some of the advertisers that an expat runs the business.

Your first stage should be to contact these businesses operating in the area of interest to you. You might get lucky.

Jobs as a nanny, a companion, or a care assistant are often circulated via the local expat churches, clubs or other places serving a significant expat community. There are also specialist international online facilities for people looking to work as nannies, English teachers etc.

Often, searching for a job like this is going to involve a lot of telephone work and an even larger amount of legwork.

It is not advisable to place an advertisement saying that you are seeking work. There are two reasons for this. Very few people who have tried this have succeeded in finding a job this way and it will put off any employer looking to employ you on any 'unofficial' basis if you have raised your head above the parapet.

Dangers of working for expats

There are three main dangers when it comes to seeking employment from expats.

1. Many of them - particularly if you are offered a job as a cleaner or gardener in their house rather than via their business - will want to employ you 'unofficially'. This means illegally.

2. In these cases, you will not be paying tax or, more importantly, social security contributions. Thus, you will have no protection in the event of accident or illness. You will not be entitled to the benefit of the state healthcare system. As far as the Turkish authorities are concerned, you are simply not there.

3. Many foreigners feel no shame when abusing their fellow countrymen. They will know the delicacy of your position and will often offer you very low rates of pay. Worse still, they may simply not pay you what they have agreed. This applies just as much if you're being employed in an expat's business as it does if you're being employed in their home.

Working for expats on a self-employed basis

As we've already explained, getting a visa to work on a proper self-employed basis (as defined in Turkey) is very difficult. You, therefore, end up either working illegally (with all of the dangers and disadvantages already mentioned) or you will need to set up a proper Turkish company in order to provide your services. See page 229.

Finding customers

If you are a proper registered business, you can - of course - advertise. You can also distribute flyers in the places where you are likely to find lots of expat customers.

A cheaper and often more successful alternative to this is establishing a network of contacts and then passing around the information about your business through those contacts. Word of mouth and personal recommendation go a long way in Turkey, including within the expat community. This is particularly important as a source of work if you're going to be working in someone's house.

Many people have been successful by cold calling residents in areas which are known to have a very large expat community. People can be very helpful and, even if they don't themselves need an odd-job man or a hairdresser, they may know someone who does.

Teaching English

There is a constant demand for people to teach English in Turkey. There is also some demand for people to teach other foreign languages such as French, Spanish, Russian, or Chinese - but the bulk of the demand is for people who can teach English.

There are many types of establishments in which you can teach English or any other language. These range from large and well-known colleges to tiny private schools. Basically, the smaller the school, the less you are likely to be paid and the less demanding they're likely to be when it comes to your formal qualifications.

If you want to get a job teaching English in a good school, you will really need the following:

- A TEFL teaching certificate
- A university degree
- A work permit (applied for by the college)

If you wish to teach some other language, the details will change but these basic principles will still apply.

In addition to these formal requirements, you will need a well-written application letter and CV and good interview skills. You will need to come across to the interviewer as a good teacher.

In Turkey, you will greatly enhance your chances of obtaining a TEFL job if you are over 30 and if you have previous work experience outside of teaching.

Turkey: how things *really* work

Sadly, some colleges will not be prepared to get involved in the process of applying for work permits. In these circumstances, you will be working illegally if you take a job with them. Fortunately, some colleges *will* follow the process through and employ you legally.

Working illegally

Working illegally in Turkey is, as we have already said, widespread. As we have also already said, it is also dangerous.

Unfortunately for those involved in this activity, or thinking about getting involved, the authorities are getting a lot more efficient at catching illegal workers and they are now highly motivated to do so because of the high levels of unemployment amongst native Turkish people.

At the moment, illegal workers can be found in almost every field of activity. There are (2015) only 64,547 foreign workers who hold work permits to work in Turkey. It is likely that there are many times more than this working illegally. There are no reliable estimates of the number working illegally but it is certainly substantial, especially in Istanbul and the coastal regions. In addition to the 'regular' illegal workers in Turkey, there is now a massive influx of refugees - especially from Syria - adding to the illegal workforce. In late 2015, the Centre for Middle Eastern Strategic Studies suggested that there were probably about 250,000 illegal Syrian workers in Turkey. The number has, almost certainly, grown since.

The legal requirements for working in Turkey

It is worth repeating that, for a foreigner to work legally in Turkey, they require a work permit. See the chapter on coming to Turkey to work (page 18) for details of what is required and how to obtain a permit.

Once you have your work permit, you need to comply with the requirements of Turkish employment law. See our chapter on employment law (page 193).

Case study

Cassandra Cobb

Waitress, Scottish, 18

The problem

Cassandra sadly fell into a situation familiar to many young travellers: she agreed to take an illegal cash-in-hand job at a restaurant. She was not caught by the authorities, but got in trouble when she injured herself at work and had no legal path to seek compensation. Nor had she entitlement to free medical treatment.

Although she would still have had the right to sue the restaurant owner if the accident had been the restaurant's fault, in her case it wasn't and she had no way of claiming any benefits through the Turkish system as she wasn't officially within it.

The solution

There isn't really a solution to this problem. Cassandra's parents sent across enough money for medical treatment and a ticket back home.

We heard of her situation after the parents called us up asking if there was anything we could do. They were only slightly mollified after being told that Cassandra was lucky not to have been arrested and deported!

The restaurant was raided by the authorities about a month later, after an anonymous tip-off. That fact may or may not be connected to Cassandra's case. The restaurant was found to be employing four illegal workers and fined TRY8,848.

It is tempting to work illegally in a country where getting a work permit can be so complicated, but it is really not a good idea. Apart from the obvious risks there could be unforeseen consequences, as in Cassandra's case.

Turkey: how things *really* work

Why do people work illegally?

There are many reasons why people start working illegally in Turkey:

- People, often but not always young people, will come to Turkey, like it and want to stay on. Unfortunately, they will seldom have the qualifications required to obtain a legal work permit.

- People may want to come to live in Turkey and need to work in order to do so, but cannot qualify for any of the categories of work permit that are available.

- People come to Turkey to work, legally, as a seasonal worker within the tourist industry but find they can earn more money working illegally in some other capacity.

- People come to work as seasonal workers and then stay on, illegally, at the end of their legitimate period of employment. Such people will often leave the country by travelling to the Greek island of Kos and then return, applying for a three-month tourist visa when they do so. They will then repeat the trip to Kos as often as is necessary. This, of course, does not comply either with the rules for working in Turkey or for visiting Turkey as a tourist. Increasingly, they are being stopped at the border when they try to return to Turkey: something possible because of the increased efficiency and computerisation of Turkey's border systems.

- People retire to Turkey but find that there are job opportunities available which can supplement their income. They might work, for example, as gardeners or ferrying people to and from the airport.

The dangers of working illegally in Turkey

The main dangers of working illegally in Turkey are:

- Arrest and deportation.

  If you are caught working illegally you will almost certainly be detained and deported. Not only will this mean that you cannot come back to Turkey, it will also often mean that you will not be admitted to any other country. If you live within the European Union (EU), you will probably be able to travel within the EU Schengen area, but not elsewhere.

  How will the immigration authorities in another country know that you have been deported from Turkey? There will be a great big stamp in your passport saying so.

- You will have no social security benefits.

  This means that there's nothing to protect you if you fall ill or are injured and no entitlement to use the medical system.

- If caught, you may face a large bill for back taxes and back social security payments. Any assets you have in Turkey will be seized until this bill is paid.

  You could also be pursued overseas for this bill after you have been deported, though this is uncommon.

- You will probably be offered a very poor rate of pay.

- You may not be paid at all!

- Many of the people seeking illegal employment are vulnerable in one way or another and they are often subject to physical, sexual, or other abuse by their employer.

Tax

See our chapters on tax in Turkey (page 248).

Social security contributions

Social security payments are, in effect, just another type of tax.

All people employed in Turkey are obliged to contribute to the social security system. See page 226.

Working for Yourself

Written by **Başak Yildiz Orkun**
Managing Partner (Legal Department) at Orkun & Orkun
www.orkunorkun.com • info@orkunorkun.com

For the reasons stated, it is often difficult for a foreigner to find legal employment in Turkey and so the obvious question arises as to whether, if you can't work for somebody else, you can set up your own business and work for yourself.

The short answer is: maybe.

There are two ways of working for yourself. The first is as a self-employed person, as defined by Turkish law. You work in your own name (rather than by setting up some business entity to deliver your service) and you are taxed on the profits you generate.

The second is to set up a company (owned either by you alone or by you and other people) and then for you to work for that company.

In both cases you are, in essence, your own boss and your income depends upon the profits from your own labour.

It is, realistically, not possible for most foreigners to become self-employed in Turkey. But it is possible for them to set up a business and then work for it. See page 27. That business does not need to be a limited company or, indeed, anything fancy. It merely needs to be a tax-registered business.

Business in Turkey

Doing Business in Turkey from Outside the Country

Written by **Başak Yildiz Orkun**
Managing Partner (Legal Department) at Orkun & Orkun
www.orkunorkun.com • info@orkunorkun.com

Turkey permits foreigners and foreign businesses of any nationality to do business in Turkey. This is true whether they are selling goods or providing services. They do not need any permits to do this if their business is located outside Turkey. If they want to have a physical presence within Turkey, paperwork *is* needed. See page 215.

Depending upon where your business is based, there may be tariff and other barriers.

- **European barriers**

  In 1995, with the signing of the EU's Customs Union Agreement, Turkey began a very long and slow path towards joining the EU. It has adopted the EU's Common External Tariff (CET) for most industrial products and is committed to eliminating tariffs and quantitative restrictions on such goods. However, there are still substantial tariffs on agricultural goods and some other protected items.

  This does not mean to say that there are no obstacles to doing business in Turkey, even if you're dealing with industrial goods. There are lots of regulations with which you will have to comply: for example, as to packaging and translation. Dealing with the administration is sometimes not straightforward and the rules can change with little or no warning.

  For more information see, for example, the UK guide to doing business in Turkey (this is a PDF): **bit.ly/2sHetEM.**

- **Barriers to trade with the US and other (non-EU) countries**

  US and other non-EU companies face barriers when selling goods into Turkey. The amount depends upon the category of the item in question. These are to be found in the Turkish government's schedule of about 20,000 different items.

  Tariffs on imports from non-European countries are, typically, approximately 3% above European Union (EU) rates, but vary on a product-by-product basis. The average tariff is about 4.1%, though some sensitive items (including agricultural goods, clothing, medical devices and e-commerce) are protected by much bigger tariffs.

> For some more information, read this article on regulations surrounding business in Turkey: **bit.ly/2sH7viM.**

- **General barriers**

  Turkey is a member of GATT/WTO, so these rules will apply.

  Once goods have been imported, they will be treated in the same way as domestically produced goods as far as Turkish domestic taxation is concerned.

Of course, there are certain rules with which you must comply if you wish to do business in Turkey. This section will deal with those rules.

In addition, there are issues of business culture with which you will have to get to grips if your business venture in Turkey is going to be successful.

The rules

There are five main rules that apply to businesses that are based overseas but who want to sell their goods or services in Turkey:

1. You do not need to register the fact that you are doing business in Turkey.
2. If you are not resident in Turkey for tax purposes, you and your company will not be subject to Turkish income or corporation taxes on your business activities in Turkey.
3. You must account for any VAT and special consumption tax arising out of the sale of your goods or services.
4. You must comply with the laws, including consumer protection laws, that would apply to businesses based in Turkey.
5. You must not engage in any of the business activities that are restricted. These are usually business activities that have some implications for national security or Turkish culture, and they are often permitted only to citizens of Turkey.

Restricted businesses

There are certain restrictions as to the types of business activity that a foreigner (whether based in Turkey or not) can carry out. See the next chapter for more details.

It is important to note that these restrictions are because of you being a foreigner and not because of your business being based overseas. In other words, you would not be able to work in these areas even if your foreign-owned business was physically present in Turkey.

Business culture

Turkey has a strong business culture. If you do not understand it and try to work with and within it, it can make life very difficult for you or, in the worst case, cause your business to fail.

Of course, you're not forced to adapt to the Turkish way of doing things but if you simply conduct your business in the same way as you would 'back home', you will find that this is a high-risk tactic.

See the chapter on culture (page 56).

Choose the right business structure

This is one of the first things you need to think about. Getting it wrong could cost you a great deal of time and money.

If you're reading this chapter, your default position is probably that you wish to have no structure in Turkey but simply to provide your goods and services from your home country. Whilst this is permissible, it may not be your best solution - so it's worth thinking at an early stage about whether there is (for you) a better way of working with Turkey.

Of course, having thought about it, you may still decide that simply working from 'back home' and selling your goods or services into Turkey is best for you. You may also decide (many people do) that you will start off by 'giving it a go' - by supplying your services or goods directly - and then review the position after several months or a year or two. There is nothing wrong with doing things this way, and it has the benefit of initial simplicity, but it can make things more expensive and complicated when you do decide to set up some sort of presence within Turkey: so this might prove to be an expensive option longer term.

There are several options at to the business structures you could adopt; see the next chapter and the section on business structures.

Get to know people

Networking is incredibly important in Turkey: more so than in most countries. Many local people will be wary of doing business with you until you are a 'known face'.

Of course, if you're not physically present in Turkey, this can be a challenge and it may be something that you never successfully achieve. However, within the limits of your not being in Turkey on a regular basis, there are a few ways to make yourself well known, and therefore well trusted, in Turkey.

Most involve being in Turkey from time to time.

If your goods are being distributed via a local agent or distributor, you will find it well worthwhile making the time to go and see that person. If you're offering services in conjunction with a local 'partner' the same applies.

Those partners or distributors may expect you to contribute to a marketing fund to engage in some of the activities usual in Turkey and so raise the profile of your product or service. If they want this, it is important to understand exactly what is being proposed, its cost, and how the expenditure will be controlled and accounted for.

If you are supplying the goods or service directly to the public, making direct contact with them can also be very helpful. This could, for example, be by attending trade shows or other consumer-facing events.

Taxes

If you are selling goods or supplying services in Turkey, you will always have some interaction with the Turkish tax authorities and you are likely to have to pay some taxes in Turkey.

This is a complicated subject and the detailed arrangements are well outside the scope of this book; so you would be well advised to consult a Turkish accountant or tax adviser before you start your activities so that you can make sure that you are complying with the rules and choosing the most tax-efficient options.

There are two basic taxes that you need to think about:

VAT

Turkey charges VAT on the supply of most goods and services. A number of different rates apply: 18% for most items; 8% for basic foodstuffs, books, medical supplies etc; and a super-low rate of 1% for agricultural products and newspapers.

Your position will also depend upon the interaction between the VAT rules in your own country (if you operate a VAT system there) and those in Turkey.

Because of the growing volume of international transactions, there has been quite a lot of harmonisation between the countries that use the VAT system. These rules change fairly frequently and so you will need to keep abreast of developments, both in your own country and in Turkey. Fortunately, because the rules are harmonised, it is quite likely that any relevant changes relating to Turkey will be flagged up in the information supplied by the VAT authorities in your own country.

For the purposes of the illustrations in this chapter, I am assuming that your business is based in the UK. If you're based elsewhere, many of the same general principles will apply, but there are likely to be some differences - possibly substantial.

Goods - *VAT in the country that supplies the goods*

There is no UK (EU) VAT payable in respect of any goods sold to Turkey, whether they are sold to a business or to a private individual. Such sales are 'zero-rated' for VAT purposes.

However, you need to comply with certain rules.

You can only zero-rate the sale if you get and keep evidence of the export, and comply with all other laws. You must also make sure the goods are exported, and you must get the evidence of this within three months from the time of sale.

You mustn't zero-rate sales if your customer asks for them to be delivered to a UK or EU address. If the customer arranges to collect them from you, an 'indirect export', you *may* be able to zero-rate the sale as long as certain zero-rating conditions are met.

Goods - VAT liability in Turkey

The importation of goods into Turkey is subject to VAT. Only registered taxpayers can import the goods into Turkey and act as an importer. The importer is liable for VAT, customs duties and any Special Consumption Tax (if applicable). In a normal importation, the importer must have acquired the title of the goods.

This means that if, as is normal, you export your goods to Turkey to a local Turkish distributor, who in turn then sells them in Turkey, that distributor will have to pay VAT on the goods when they arrive in Turkey.

Services - VAT in the country that supplies the services

There is no UK VAT charge on any services supplied to Turkey if the 'place of supply' of your service is not in the EU.

For EU VAT purposes, the place of supply of a service is the place where it's liable to VAT (if any). There are a number of place of supply rules for working out where services of different kinds are supplied, for example:

- Where the place of supply of services is in a member state of the EU, that supply is subject to the VAT rules of that member state and not those of any other country.

- If the member state is not the UK, such supplies are said to be 'outside the scope' of UK VAT.

- Where the place of supply of services is outside the EU, that supply is made outside the EU and is therefore not liable to VAT in any EU member state (although local Turkish taxes may apply). Such supplies are said to be 'outside the scope' of both UK and EU VAT.

For most supplies of services, the place of supply is decided by what is known as the 'general rule'.

If you supply services to a business customer, the place of supply is in the place where the customer belongs. In this case, Turkey. Such services will be outside the scope of UK or EU VAT.

If you supply general services to a non-business customer (such as a private individual buying them for their personal use), the place of supply is in the place where *you* belong. In this case, the UK. However, some special services are treated as supplied in the place where *the customer* belongs. In this case, Turkey. These special services would, therefore, be outside the scope of UK or EU VAT.

These special services include:

- Transfers and assignments of copyright, patents, licences, trademarks and similar rights

- Acceptance of any obligation to refrain from pursuing a business activity

- Advertising services

- Services of consultants, engineers, consultancy bureaux, lawyers, accountants, and other similar services - data processing and provision of information, other than any services relating to land

- Banking, financial and insurance services

- The provision of access to, or transmission or distribution through, natural gas and electricity systems and heat or cooling networks and the provision of other directly linked services

- Supply of staff

- Letting on hire of goods other than trucks or other means of transport

The detailed rules can be very complicated and you should seek advice from your accountants 'back home' and in Turkey before deciding upon your course of action.

Services - VAT in Turkey

According to the Turkish VAT law, where services are supplied from a foreign country but used in Turkey, the transaction is deemed to be performed in Turkey and it is subject to Turkish VAT.

The VAT is payable through a 'reverse charge mechanism' if services purchased from a foreign supplier are performed in Turkey; or if services rendered abroad are enjoyed in Turkey *and* where the recipient of the payment (that is service provider) is not a tax registered entity in Turkey.

In such a case, the Turkish purchaser is liable to account for the VAT due on behalf of the foreign supplier.

Taxes on profit

If you are supplying goods from outside Turkey, you will not have to pay any tax in Turkey on any profit your company makes from the sale of those goods.

Starting a Business in Turkey

Written by **Başak Yildiz Orkun**
Managing Partner (Legal Department) at Orkun & Orkun
www.orkunorkun.com • info@orkunorkun.com

Many foreigners want to start a business in Turkey. They fall into three groups.

There are international entrepreneurs, who simply see business opportunities in Turkey. They see that there are some areas of activity where Turkey is much less developed than in the country where they live or work. They see the rapid modernisation of Turkey, its growing population, the population's increasing wealth and Turkey's increased integration into Europe. All seem like opportunities for rapid business growth, with good levels of profit. They may also see Turkey as a good stepping-off point for getting involved in business in the wider region.

Then there are the people who visit Turkey, fall in love with it and want to find a way of being able to stay there. For many of these people, there are few job opportunities and those that exist tend to be low paid. So it seems to make sense to start a business.

The third group is people who might normally have wished to operate as self-employed, without any formal business structure, but who find that it is very difficult to do that legally in Turkey.

Are there restrictions on what I can do?

Turkey is very welcoming when it comes to people wanting to set up new businesses. They realise that new business boosts the economy and creates local employment - and they also recognise that, for historical reasons, Turkey lacks some of the skills required by innovative businesses in the 21st Century.

However, certain sectors of the Turkish economy restrict the involvement of foreigners. For example, you cannot, as a foreign-owned business, start a school; be a dentist or involved in patient care; be a vet, pharmacist, hospital director, lawyer, notary or security guard; be engaged in fishing, or be a customs agent or a tourist guide.

In Turkey, there are also quite a large number of activities where a professional qualification is required. These include many activities which may not be restricted in other countries. For instance:

- Estate agent

- Hairdresser

- Pharmacist's assistant

- Tailor

- Beauty parlour staff

Turkey: how things *really* work

Despite this, in recent years there has been quite a lot of government activity to encourage foreigners to set up businesses. For example:

- Foreigners have the right to own Turkish companies and, when they do, they are (with one or two exceptions) subject to exactly the same rules as would apply to a Turkish person owning the company

- There are certain exemptions to tax and social security contributions

- Imports of certain equipment are now exempt from customs duty and other taxes and restrictions

However, also for historical reasons (now long-since irrelevant but preserved in legislation that no government has seen fit to remove), there are several main areas of business activity which are specifically closed to businesses run by foreigners unless you obtain special permission from the government.

There is no central list of these restrictions published by the government. Instead, they're to be found on the websites of the various Turkish ministries - the Ministry of Education, the Ministry of Agriculture, etc.

In Turkey, although there are a number of professions where you will need a qualification (for example, as a lawyer), there are rarely legal barriers to working within the same professional area (for example, as a legal consultant or paralegal).

Business structures

As in almost every country, there are a number of legal structures that you can choose to use when you set up a business. At the time, this choice can seem boring and unimportant but selecting the right structure will have huge implications later on, particularly if your business prospers and grows.

It will affect the taxes you have to pay. It will affect your ability to employ people. It will affect how (and if) you will be able to obtain funding for your business. It will affect the ease of selling your business.

There are many different business structures in Turkey. These include:

Working on your own

True self-employment - working on your own - means that you can run your business without the need for any special business structure. It is generally not possible for foreigners to work in this self-employed capacity in Turkey.

A registered business

This is sometimes known as "sole proprietorship" (*Şahıs Firması*). This is similar to the concept of self-employment found in many countries but different to self-employment as understood in Turkey. It's also different from a limited company, in that it does not have its own, independent, legal personality and it does not give you the benefit of limited liability. It will, however, have its own tax number and be registered as a business in the appropriate registry. This structure can allow you, as a foreigner, to run your business in Turkey.

A partnership

A partnership is a business operated by two or more people or legal entities. If it is operated by two or more real people it tends to be called a partnership. If it is operated by two or more companies working together it tends to be called a joint venture. The legal effect is much the same.

In either case, Turkish law makes the process simple.

Unlike partnerships under the Anglo-American legal system, a partnership in Turkey has its own legal personality. To this extent, they're like companies. They can, for example, sue or be sued in the name of the partnership rather than in the name of the individual partners.

A partnership or joint venture has its own tax liability, independent of the tax liabilities of its partners.

A partnership does not create any form of limited liability. However, of course, if the partnership/joint venture is between two limited liability companies, then they will each have their own element of limited liability - though you should note that each of the partners will be responsible, in full, for all the debts of the partnership if his (or its) fellow partners cannot or do not pay their share.

Partnerships are, generally, very cheap, simple and quick to set up.

In a simple case, the partnership can be set up by your accountant. If the situation's a bit more complex, you would probably have your lawyer prepare a partnership contract.

This agreement will contain the identities of the parties, how the capital of the business is to be provided, the rules for the operation of the business and a declaration of the authorised scope of the business.

Whoever prepares the contract, it will be witnessed by a Trade Registry Office (from March 2018).

When setting up a partnership, you (or your lawyer or accountant) must apply to the tax office to register your partnership. The tax office will then issue you with a tax number.

Armed with that, you can apply to register the business itself. This will, depending upon the type of business, be either with the Chamber of Merchants and Craftsmen or the Chamber of Commerce.

The cost of setting up a relatively simple partnership might be TRY5,000 (£1,100/€1,300/US$1,400). If it's a very simple partnership, prepared by your accountant, you may find that they will prepare the contract itself free of charge if they are going to be keeping the books for the new business.

In addition to the lawyer's or accountant's charges, the Notary will charge a fee of 1.5% or 2% of the registered capital value of the partnership and if, as is usually the case, you do not speak fluent Turkish, you will be charged for the services of an official translator, who will charge you between TRY100-200 *per page*.

Companies

Limited liability companies

There are two main types of limited company in Turkey.

- The limited liability company (*Limited Şirket*)

- The joint stock company (*Anonim Şirket*)

Both are governed by the Turkish Commercial Code.

A private limited liability company (*Limited Şirket*)

Most small and medium-sized businesses are private limited companies.

This type of company can be set up with just one shareholder, or with up to a legal maximum of 50 shareholders.

A private limited company is a smaller, simpler and less formal version of the joint stock company (see below). It has the same limited liability but its shares cannot be traded on the stock exchange. They can, however, be sold privately.

Because its shares cannot be traded publicly it has to file very little in the way of official returns and information to the government, and its management structure is allowed to be a great deal simpler.

A private limited company must have a minimum share capital of TRY10,000 (£2,200/€2,500/US$2,800). This amount must be paid into the company's bank account.

This share capital cannot be used to pay the expenses of setting up the company but can be used, immediately after the company has been set up, for its business purposes. So, for example, you could use the money to buy a van.

The capital is often paid into the company's bank account, in full, at the time that the company is created, but you can set a company up on the basis that only one third is paid at the time of the formation of the company and the rest over the next three years.

The paperwork creating and regulating the company (its Articles of Association) is quite straightforward. It usually takes the form of a standard document which contains some standard options (about pension rights etc.) that can be included or not as you choose.

The total cost of setting up a private limited company might, in a simple case, be about TRY5,000 (£1,100/€1,300/US$1,400).

The company is a separate legal entity from its shareholders and so pays its own taxes.

A joint stock (public) company (*Anonim Şirket*)

A joint stock company is the structure usually adopted by large businesses.

It requires a minimum share capital of TRY50,000 (£11,000/€13,000/US$14,000).

The setting up cost is more or less same as for a limited company. Running costs depend on the capital and number of employees.

The main advantages of the joint stock company is that its shares can be traded on the Turkish stock exchange and that they are capital gains tax-free after holding the shares for more than two years.

A public company is taxed on much the same basis as a limited company.

Cooperatives (*Kooperatif*)

As in most countries, in Turkey a cooperative is a group of people who have come together, voluntarily, to do something to meet their common requirements. The essence of a cooperative is that it is jointly owned and democratically controlled.

On that very simple foundation, there has been built quite a complicated superstructure, offering many different types of cooperatives and different ways in which they can be established and managed.

Cooperatives are governed by a different legal code from companies. This is the Code of Cooperatives.

We're not going to say anything more about cooperatives in this book because they are, these days, very rarely used in Turkey.

A franchise

A franchise is not, strictly speaking, an operating structure. The franchisee (the person operating the business) can operate it using any of the legal structures already referred to. However, it is convenient to refer to franchises here.

In a franchise, the franchisor (the person who had the idea behind the franchise and set the system up) usually has a set of products and a system of working which it allows the franchisee (the person who will run the business) to use in return for a payment of an annual franchise fee and/or a share of the business' turnover or profit.

Examples of franchises common in Turkey include many restaurants (e.g. McDonalds, Subway, etc.), some car repair facilities (e.g. Speedy), some Estate Agents (e.g. RE/MAX) and many other businesses.

Many people feel that starting a new business using a well-proven system takes away a lot of the risk, particularly if you are in a new business environment. However, you do lose a significant portion of your profit and some of your ongoing flexibility.

If you're thinking of operating a franchise, you need to do considerable due diligence to check out *exactly* what you're getting and what it will cost you. Once again, your accountant will be able to advise you about this.

A joint venture

A joint venture, under Turkish law, is simply a partnership operated either by two or more limited companies or an individual and one or more limited companies.

For the purposes of this chapter, it can be treated as a partnership (see above).

Preparation

Identifying an opportunity

Traditionally, foreigners have tended to look at business opportunities where (they believe) their lack of Turkish will not be a huge impediment. They open bars, restaurants and property management companies, or they set up a business offering services exclusively to the expat community.

However, this is rather narrow-minded. It also ignores the fact that, even if you're running a bar where the large majority of your customers are (say) German, you will still find it difficult if you do not speak at least some Turkish. You will need to buy your supplies and you will need to deal with local customers.

During the last five years, we have helped clients who came to Turkey to set up not only bars and restaurants but businesses such as:

- Construction companies
- Tourism-based companies
- Business consultancies
- Employment agencies
- Recycling
- Agriculture
- Property development

and many more!

In short, do not allow your options to be constrained by unnecessary fear of working in a new environment.

How should I check that my business idea will work?

Once you have had your 'eureka!' moment and seen a fantastic opportunity in Turkey, it is very tempting to race ahead and develop the business. However, before doing so, it is essential to check that your brilliant idea is actually going to work.

This process - part of your 'due diligence' - is outside the scope of this book and will be specific to your particular type of business. Discuss your due diligence requirements with your accountant and/or lawyer. See also our section about 'Buying a Business' (page 236).

Reality check!

Risk of failure

Starting and running a business in Turkey is, at the very best, no simpler than starting and running a business at home. Even in your own country, a large number of new businesses will fail. For example, in the UK, one business in four is likely to fail in its first year. Starting a business in an unfamiliar country increases this risk: which makes it *really* important to plan on a sound basis and take advice. This can help avoid the problems that (to a local person) are obvious but which (to you) are not.

Experience

It is extremely helpful if you have had previous experience working in the same area of activity. Without experience, starting (for example) a restaurant or hotel is hugely difficult and very likely to fail. Even with experience the risk of failure is significant.

Transferable skills

Even if you don't have any directly relevant experience, you may find that you have very relevant transferable skills. For example, you may have worked for many years as a car mechanic but see better opportunities as a mechanic (engineer) looking after foreigners' boats in Turkey.

Learning about Turkey

Before you commit to opening a business in Turkey, learn as much as you can about the place. Read this book - cover-to-cover! Speak to any expats you know, or even strangers (whether that's face-to-face or via online forums). People are often extraordinarily helpful.

How do I find the right business partners?

You may decide to set up a small business entirely on your own: for example, maintaining pools for foreigners of your own nationality. Probably the majority of foreigners starting a business in Turkey do so in this way.

However, quite a large number also recognise the advantage of having an experienced partner. This could be a local Turkish person (bringing a wide range of contacts and contributing both cultural understanding and language skills), or a fellow expat. Each has its advantages and disadvantages.

It's worth thinking carefully about this issue (although, in practice, most people are instinctively attracted to one method or the other and unlikely to change their mind).

If you are going to seek local Turkish partners, then there are two main ways of doing so that might occur to you. Advertising (or looking for advertisements) and recommendation (word of mouth). In Turkey, 90% of successful partnerships are as a result of recommendation. No one would be comfortable responding to an offer that has been advertised. Sometimes your accountant or lawyer will be able to suggest people he knows who might be a good match for your skill set and business idea.

Choosing the right partner can be challenging. To put it bluntly, there are many conmen looking to make money out of inexperienced foreigners wishing to do business in Turkey. Sometimes, those conmen are Turkish but, far more often, you will find yourself at risk from people of your own nationality. They find it easier to gain your confidence and they have enough knowledge of how things work in Turkey to appear plausible.

There are, of course, risks to your Turkish partner as well as to you. In many cases, they are the people who are easily accessible. In many cases, they will be the local director of the company that's going to be running the business, and so carry almost all the responsibilities. In many cases, they will speak Turkish whereas you do not and so face the additional responsibility of being in charge of all communications for the business. Often, they will be the people with the local knowledge and the local technical skills and so critical to the success of the business. Usually, they will be the people upon whom you depend for your understanding of Turkish business culture.

For all these reasons, the process of due diligence when it comes to forming a partnership or joint venture should be a two-way process: they should want to know as much about you as you do about them. You should be suspicious if it is not.

Business plans

You will, I hope, be familiar with the concept of a business plan. A business plan sets out, in writing, your objectives, why they will work, how you're going to achieve them, and how you're going to fund the business.

Surprisingly, business plans are relatively rare in Turkey: at least at the level of the businesses usually set up by our foreign clients.

Despite this, making a written business plan is (in our view), basically, essential. The process of putting things down on paper and working out all the numbers will usually identify lots of potential problems and challenges.

It is essential even if you don't need to show the plan to anybody else. Producing it is, mainly, for your own benefit as the simple acts of thinking things through and preparing the plan significantly increase your chances of success.

However, it's important to note that a Turkish-format business plan will be somewhat different from the business plan you'd produce to your bank or business partners in the US, Germany or the UK. Those plans, in turn, will usually be a little different from each other.

If the business plan is only for your own use, then this doesn't matter: but if you want to use it to seek finance, to present to a bank or to involve a local partner then it really needs to be in the format with which the reader will be most comfortable. So, for example, if you are seeking finance from the US it would be very helpful to have your business plan converted into the format with which an American would be most familiar. Similarly, if you want to present it to a Turkish bank, it will not only need to be translated into Turkish but it will also need to be adjusted (quite substantially) so that it looks and feels like a Turkish business plan.

There are two main differences - apart from the language - between a Turkish format business plan and (say) a UK format business plan. The first is that the Turkish plan lays much more emphasis on your CV (resume). Not just your experience in this sector of business, but your personal life and general experience.

The second is that a Turkish business plan (if it's created at all) will often have cash projections going forward for 12 years rather than the three or four years more common in other countries. This may make you smile. It is all a bit of a waste of time because everybody knows that it's hard enough to predict what's going to happen in 18 months' time, let alone 12 years' time! But if this projection is not there, it will cause eyebrows to be raised and you will risk a perfectly good plan being turned down.

Don't despair, though. In practical terms, once you have prepared your draft business plan, your Turkish accountant will have the experience to convert it into the Turkish format and, more likely than not, into several other 'international' formats as well.

You can download a sample business plan from
www.guides.global/books/turkey/tur-downloads.php.

Premises

Most businesses will need some premises from which to operate. Consider the options:

Rented property

There is ample commercial property available for rent in Turkey. It is of all types from the opulent to the cheap and cheerful.

For most people, renting the property from which their business will operate is the most sensible solution: although, again, your accountant will be able to advise you which is the most appropriate in your case. The main reason why renting tends to be the best option is that it conserves your available capital for use within your business. It will often be very hard for you to replace or add to that capital from any other source.

There is one major downside to operating a business from rented property, particularly if it is a business such as a bar, restaurant or garage providing direct service to the public. If your landlord cancels your lease - which he can do each year on the anniversary of the lease once the initial period stated in the lease has passed - he will be left not only with all the improvements that you have carried out on the premises but also with a ready-made business of some value. Your customers will continue to turn up to the premises that they know to be an Indonesian Restaurant or a specialist Ferrari garage.

Property you have bought (owned property)

Despite the attractions of renting the property needed by your business, many people - particularly the British - like the idea of owning property and like the idea of owning the property from which their business operates.

They have seen property prices rise a lot over the years and they see this as an extra source of profit from the business or, in some cases, as a way of offsetting any initial losses suffered by the business.

They also feel that the money they're spending on improvement to the premises is being spent for their benefit, not for the ultimate benefit of a landlord.

They find that the cost of renting is, typically, about 5% of the value of the property and - in today's climate - if they have some spare money they feel that saving this rent is a good investment, particularly after taking into account the other factors I have referred to. After all, it is effectively giving them a real return of 5% per year on their capital.

The big downside is that owning the premises consumes lots of your cash. It will be difficult to obtain mortgage finance to buy the property and so you will have to use your own capital. This may be money you need to run the business or, at the very least, money that would generate you more profit by being invested more directly in your new (and successful!) business.

There is an additional problem in that the costs of acquiring and selling commercial property are quite expensive (about 10% and 5% respectively of the value of the building) and you may find that you outgrow the premises quite quickly or that, for some other reason, they turn out to be unsuitable. That is then wasted money.

For most people, renting turns out to be the better option unless they have lots of spare cash.

Read the chapter on buying a commercial property (page 404) for more information.

Working from home

Many businesses start off by working from home. Clearly, this is not possible in all cases - it might be a bit tricky if you're running a bar - but it can be a very useful way of testing whether your business is going to succeed and to delay incurring major expenditure until it does.

In most cases, no special licence is required to work from home, but you can expect to be visited by the tax office if your business is registered at your home address. This is to check if the business is real and so that the claims and deductions that you might be making are justifiable.

However, apart from the practical restrictions on your ability to work from home, there may be other limitations on your ability to do so.

If you are renting a property, you will need the consent of your landlord if you wish to operate a business from the premises.

If you own or rent property located within a 'community of owners' (usually an apartment or a property that shares common facilities such as a pool or tennis courts that are owned and controlled by all the owners in the complex) you will need their consent before running a business from your home. Some communities completely prohibit all business activity on the grounds of noise and nuisance. By law, commercial businesses are not allowed within a community/condominium; but professions (such as lawyers or doctors) can be carried out, if your use of the building for this purpose has been approved by the community/condominium.

If you are doing anything other than office and administrative type work, you may need to apply for the property to be reclassified as business premises. This is likely to lead to a substantial increase in your local property taxes. For a number of other reasons, this might not be a good idea.

Despite these limitations, it is commonplace for businesses to be run from home for at least a few months after they have been launched.

Internet-based businesses

More and more people are basing their whole business concept around delivery using the internet and operating from home.

Turkey has, in many places, a good, reliable, and pretty quick internet infrastructure, so this is not a technical problem if you live in a city. Delivery of physical goods within Turkey is also well catered for. Delivery of physical goods to any international customers is a little more challenging, though certainly and increasingly possible.

Funding

Any new business will need funding.

It is extremely difficult - to the point of being virtually impossible - to obtain funding within Turkey for a new business venture being started by a foreigner who has recently arrived in Turkey. From the point of view of the lender, there are lots of good reasons for this. Would you lend money to a foreigner who had recently arrived in your country and who had what was, perhaps, a good business idea but no business experience, no knowledge of the culture of the country and only a few words of the language?

Having said this, it is in some cases possible to raise funds either from banks or from private investors; but this will usually only be possible if you have lots of available security and/or personal guarantees from people of some substance who are resident in Turkey.

Most people setting up their businesses will, therefore, fund them themselves or partly themselves and partly through family and friends.

Many people used to decide to fund their business by taking out a mortgage on a property that they already owned in Turkey. Often, that property would have been owned (perhaps as a holiday home) for many years and, equally often, it would have increased substantially in value during their period of ownership. They would simply approach their bank, extract the accumulated value and use the money to fund their business idea.

This was done by a 'personal needs loan'. This is a type of loan under which the banks will agree to increase the size of an existing mortgage or to grant a new mortgage on a property that had not previously been mortgaged. In theory, these loans are still available. Loan-to-Value ratios (LTVs) will be low: typically no more than 40-50%. Interest rates will typically be 1.5% per month (measuring interest on a monthly basis in this way is very common in Turkey). This is, however, still considerably more expensive than an ordinary mortgage, which might be 1% per month. Fees apply: valuations, commissions, Notaries' fees, legal fees etc.

This approach to funding is, however, now almost closed off.

This is for two reasons. The first is that it is (at the moment - September 2017) difficult to find Turkish banks who will provide this facility to foreigners newly arrived in Turkey.

The second is that it is often illegal. People would apply for the finance at the early planning stage of their new business and on the strength of their being in regular employment in their own country. Then, once they'd received the money, they would 'magically' decide to leave that employment and come to Turkey to set up a business. This broke their duty of total honesty when it comes to their dealings with their bank and could result in the mortgage being cancelled and/or (at least in theory) criminal charges based on fraud.

Employing people

Employing people in Turkey is a somewhat bureaucratic procedure and formal employment is something that most new (and many existing) Turkish businesses seek to avoid, preferring to rely on contracting with people to provide specific services on a self-employed basis.

As in most countries, such contracts of self-employment are often not legal (because they do not represent the true position) if you are really employing someone full time and dressing it up as self-employment.

Despite this reluctance to employ, very large numbers of people are properly employed in Turkey. The complexity and expense of actually employing them is not that high but the tax and social security burdens that you take on - and your ongoing liabilities to your employee - can be quite onerous.

Remember that, as a newly-arrived foreigner setting up a new business in Turkey, you are probably more exposed than most to the risk of a disgruntled rival denouncing you to the authorities for your illegal employment practices.

See our section on employment law (page 193) for more details.

Social security payments

If you choose to employ people within your business, in addition to their salary you will have to pay social security contributions to the Government of Turkey. These cover the employees' entitlements to healthcare and other benefits.

At the moment, the rate of social security contributions is 12.5% of the person's total salary package. This includes the value of any non-cash benefits you give to the employee - for example, private medical insurance or the use of a car.

As the owner of the business, you will also have to make substantial social security payments.

- The employer usually pays a total social security contribution of 22.5% of the employee's salary. This is divided into separate pools. It is deductible from the employer's profit when calculating the employer's tax.

- You will also have to pay additional social security contributions on your own behalf, to provide for healthcare and other benefits for yourself and your family.

Your social security payments are paid to the government monthly.

See page 153 for more about social security.

Taxes

See our section on taxes (page 248).

Ongoing responsibilities as a business owner in Turkey

For every type of business, except those run through public companies - where the responsibilities are more onerous - a business in Turkey must do the following:

1. Every month (or, in some cases, three months), pay the taxes that you owe. This will include any tax payable by any company you are operating or - if you're not operating the business through a company - your own personal taxes. You must employ an accountant for this

2. Pay your insurances: indemnity for directors, possible business insurance and so on

3. Every month, you must pay your social security payments (for yourself and for any employees)

4. Every month, your tax declaration must be submitted by your accountant: you will need to pay your accountant a book keeping fee to do this

These are your primary obligations but your accountant will advise you of any other things required in the case of your particular business.

Special types of business

In conjunction with **www.guides.global** we have written specific guides to opening and running various types of businesses that are commonly chosen by foreigners moving abroad.

You can see these at **www.guides.global/guides/global/GLO-selector.php**.

Don't forget the bits & pieces!

When you're setting up a new business, it's too easy to forget about some of the smaller tasks that can make a great deal of difference a few years later, or to think that (because your business is new) they're not really important and that you will get around to them later.

One of these things is to make sure that the name of your business and any relevant trade or service marks and other 'intellectual property' rights are protected. This is something you should raise with the lawyer advising you about the creation of the business. Unfortunately, this is seldom cheap - especially if (as is usually the case) you really need to protect your rights around the world. However, those rights can become hugely valuable as time goes on: think Apple, Amazon and Uber!

Who do I go to for advice?

Seeking initial advice is not likely to be expensive unless your business idea is complex. With me, an initial overview might cost you TRY1,000 (€220/$270/£210). A lawyer who was not bilingual and experienced in these international transactions might charge less.

Traditionally, the people who deal with setting up simple businesses in Turkey are accountants (rather than lawyers) and so your best source for this information is probably an accountant. The accountant will know when it might be a good idea to get a lawyer involved. Our firm provides both accountancy and legal services.

You may find you can get additional informal (and free) help from the more experienced members of the expat community. However, using them does carry three great risks: they're unlikely to be familiar with all the Turkish legislation, they could well give you incorrect advice and they might steal your idea!

Case study

Frederica Albrecht

Teacher, German, 49

The problem

Frederica wished to move to Turkey and to set up a private pre-school. She had many years' experience of running such schools in Germany.

She wished to do this in partnership with a local Turkish person and intended to set up a Turkish company owned 51% by the Turkish citizen and 49% by Frederica.

This was not permitted by the Ministry of Education, because it was a business in the education sector. They took a very tough line on the issue, to the extent that there was no way of setting up this business in a way that was both safe and legal.

Her choice, therefore, was either not to do it or to allow the company to be owned solely by the Turkish person, and for her to find a way of being employed within that company. Neither was attractive. She felt very exposed by the idea of passing the entire ownership of her company (and her knowledge and teaching materials) to a Turkish partner whom she had known for only a few months.

The solution

Six months later, the lawyers are still working on finding a solution. Sorry.

Setting Up a Company

Written by **Başak Yildiz Orkun**
Managing Partner (Legal/Accountancy Department) at Orkun & Orkun
www.orkunorkun.com • info@orkunorkun.com

Turkey is one of the least complicated places - and one of the quickest - to set up a company.

In 2016, 66,000 new companies were registered in the company registers of Turkey. Of these, 4,729 were wholly or partly foreign owned: 1,500 Syrian, 330 German, and 304 Iraqi. Some 12,000 companies were closed.

Many local people set up the company themselves but, of course, most of them speak Turkish. As a foreigner, you will probably need some professional assistance but - unlike in some countries - the cost is modest. See below.

Things to understand before you set up a company in Turkey

A limited company is a legal structure which has two key components. It has what is known as 'legal personality' and it offers 'limited liability'.

Legal personality means that it is an entity distinct from the people who created it. It can, for example, enter into contracts in its own name and be responsible for its own actions. If it does something wrong, it is the company that will be punished, not the directors or shareholders - unless, of course, they have wilfully engineered the company doing something wrong or been negligent when carrying out their duties as a director of the company.

Limited liability means that, if the company goes bankrupt, its shareholders - unless (again) they have done something that the law sees as being wrong - will not have to pay its debts if they paid their agreed capital contribution to the company. Their liability is limited to the capital share that they own in the company.

This does not mean that people running companies in Turkey have no responsibilities or liabilities. The directors of those companies have obligations. These vary a bit depending upon whether the company is a private limited company or a public limited company (see page 231) but, in the case of a private limited company, they include:

- They should act prudently

- Information and documentation for the company shall be accurate

- The actions of the director should not cause loss for the company

- They cannot be involved with fraudulent actions

- They should keep money transactions transparent and legal

In this respect, Turkey is like most countries in the world.

These advantages are the reasons why many new businesses are set up as limited companies rather than in the form of alternatives such as partnerships or sole traders, neither of which enjoy these benefits.

Types of limited liability company in Turkey

There are two types of company in Turkey:

- LTD (Limited Company)

- AS (Joint Stock Company), with limited liability

See page 216 for more about business structures in Turkey.

The process of setting up a limited company in Turkey

This is pretty simple but, of course, it's all going to be done in Turkish. For most foreigners, therefore, this will all be done by their professional advisers: typically their accountant or their lawyer.

1. **Check that the name you want is available**

   Companies are registered nationally, so only one company with a particular name can operate anywhere in Turkey.

   Certain words can't be used in a company name in Turkey. For example, *Türkiye*, certain Turkish regional names and anything offensive or that would cause confusion. Your accountant will be able to advise.

   Hardly surprisingly, after hundreds of years, many names are not available - particularly names that include common Turkish surnames or which are short and catchy. Once a name has been used, it cannot be reused.

   Checking the availability of a name can be done by your accountant online in about three minutes, using the *Mersis* central information system.

   If your chosen name is not available, you may be able to set up a company with a different name and operate the business through that company 'trading as' (say) Fantasy Fashions. That is permitted provided that people are not likely to confuse your new business with any existing business.

   You may have noticed that many Turkish companies have startlingly long names. This is because, until recently, the name of a company had to include its main trading activities (e.g. John Smith Construction, Property Maintenance, Property Development & Property Letting Ltd).

   Because of this regulation, and because people were often not quite sure about how the activities of their company might develop, they listed anything that the company might conceivably want to do in the future.

   This requirement has now been removed.

2. **Reserve the name**

This is also done online. It is a free service. Reserving the name means that it will not be allocated to anybody else within the next four days.

3. **Produce the company's Articles of Association (*Ana Sözleşme*)**

This is the set of rules that govern the conduct of the company: in essence, its constitution. The document sets out the aims of the company and what its powers are. For example, it might say that the purpose of the company is to be a builder of houses and that its powers include the power to employ people, the power to buy and own land, the power to operate bank accounts etc. It's an important document.

Unlike in some countries, where you can also produce a standard constitution online, in Turkey the constitution needs to be produced by and signed in front of a Notary. Of course, the Notary will use a computer-based bank of precedents or templates to produce the constitution but at least he will have to make sure that it contains the powers that you require.

These standard forms often have optional sections covering some commonly requested additional powers. The Notary (or your accountant, if he is taking charge of this process) will ask whether you want to include these.

Constitutions tend to be lengthy and contain all sorts of powers that you are unlikely ever to use, but putting them in at the outset is a lot cheaper than adding them later.

If you only want to set up a simple company, you can go directly to a Notary, who will prepare the Articles of Association on your behalf. If the company is more complex or (as is often the case) you're not quite sure what powers you need to include, you should go to a lawyer or your accountant.

4. **Sign the Articles of Association**

The constitution can be signed by someone who has a Power of Attorney on your behalf. This could well be your lawyer or accountant.

5. **File the articles of association at the Trade Registry**

They will put the details into the *Mersis* system and publish its existence in the official trade registry publication (the *gazete*).

That's it. Job done!

In March 2018, the system will change. The process will be started online and completed at the office of the Trade Registry. This should make it even faster.

Case study

Daniela Castro

Baker, Peruvian, 28

The problem

Daniela wanted to start a bakery in Turkey, but was unsure about the business structures available to her. Furthermore, starting a shop was looking more expensive than she'd first thought - and no bank in Turkey would provide finance to a young foreigner with no experience.

The solution

Daniela set up a meeting with an accountant to go through her options. Together they decided that the most sensible course of action was to set up a Turkish company and start a catering business from home. Doing this would mean that she would have to provide some local employment further down the line, but her accountant came up with a number of helpful ways of delaying and minimising this obligation.

Starting a company involved not only setting up the legal structure but also having her premises approved for the preparation of food on a commercial basis, but it was still a lot cheaper than renting a shop. Luckily, Daniela did not live in a house that was part of a Community of Owners, and so she only needed the consent of her landlord in order to do work in this way. Equally luckily, she had chosen to live in a place which was suited to the commercial preparation of food, and it required minimal work to obtain the necessary municipal licence.

Daniela had to do a lot of networking to build up a customer base, and lived off very little money for the first year - but she managed to build a good reputation amongst local Turks; unusually for a foreign business owner, she did not target the expat market.

After three years, Daniela teamed up with a Turkish partner and managed to secure finance for a small shop in Fethiye.

The shareholders of a company in Turkey

At the same time as you file your constitution you must file a statement listing who the shareholders of the company will be. The initial shareholders will also be named in the constitution.

Except in the case of a unipersonal company (where, as the name suggests, only one shareholder is needed or, indeed, possible) Turkish law requires that there should be at least two shareholders in a company.

Shareholders can be either individuals or other companies.

If they are individuals, they must be over 18. They can be of any nationality. They do not need to live in Turkey. They may be (and, in small companies, commonly are) the same people as the directors.

The list of shareholders must show their full names, addresses and identity document numbers.

The directors of a limited company in Turkey

At the same time as you file your articles of association you will have to file a statement saying who are to be the directors of the company. The initial directors will usually be named in the Articles of Association.

Except in the case of a unipersonal company (see above) Turkish law requires that there should be two directors of a limited company.

They must be over 18. They can be of any nationality. At least one must live in Turkey.

The list of directors must show their full names, addresses and identity document numbers. If the directors are not resident in Turkey, they must nominate a contact address in Turkey and a responsible person in Turkey to receive documentation on their behalf. This will, typically, be their lawyer or accountant.

The duty of the directors is to manage the company prudently on behalf of its shareholders. If they do this, they will not have any personal liability if the company goes bust; but if they are reckless in the way in which they control the company or if they do not comply with certain aspects of Turkish law they can be held personally responsible for their actions and for the debts of the company.

The ongoing obligations of a company in Turkey

A limited company in Turkey must:

- Every year, file a tax return with the Turkish Tax Department
- Every month, file a VAT return and pay the taxes due
- Every month, pay the interim assessment of taxes due - based on its previous tax return
- Generally comply with Turkish law

Closing a company in Turkey

A company can be closed in two ways.

Companies that are solvent

A company that is solvent (has enough money to meet all its obligations) can be closed by a Trade Registry officer filing a statement at the Mercantile Registry to the effect that the company is solvent and that it wishes to cease to trade. This statement is made by the company's shareholders. At the same time, the company must file an up-to-date tax return and proof that any taxes due have been paid.

Companies that are insolvent

These must be closed by way of an application to the High Court of Turkey Insolvency Division. This process is beyond the scope of this chapter. Seek professional advice (see below).

Effect of closing a company

Once a company has been closed it is as if a person had died. It can no longer own any assets and it can no longer enter any agreements or sign any documents. It no longer has any tax or other liabilities.

Advice

As already indicated, setting up a company in Turkey is straightforward but it is almost certainly something about which you will need to take professional advice.

Both accountants and lawyers are accustomed to dealing with this type of work. Which to choose will be, as much as anything else, a matter of personal convenience. If you are going to need the ongoing services of an accountant, it could be a good idea to get them to set up the company. If you are already using the services of a lawyer (for example, in connection with an application for immigration) it might make sense to have the lawyer set up the company.

Whoever you choose to do the work, it's important that they should not only go through the technical process of setting up the company but also advise you about whether a limited company best suits your needs (or whether you might be better off trading in some other way) and - if a company is your best choice - the best type of company for you and how best to structure it. This broader advice will involve an additional fee.

Taking Over a Business

Written by **Başak Yildiz Orkun**
Managing Partner (Legal/Accountancy Department) at Orkun & Orkun
www.orkunorkun.com • info@orkunorkun.com

Many people consider taking over an existing business rather than starting their own, new one. There are advantages to doing this but there can also be significant risk.

Almost all the advantages (below) have, on their flipside, a corresponding disadvantage.

The most important question to bear in mind when buying an existing business is *why* the existing owner wants to sell it! It will often be because it is failing or unprofitable or underperforming or simply very hard work for very little return.

Of course, there are genuine opportunities: for example, when the existing owner wishes to retire or is suffering from ill health; but, in my experience, these tend to be the minority of cases.

So, once you've answered this question, the next is how you can improve the position and make the business a success.

Advantages

- Somebody else has already done, or paid for, all the start-up work - setting up the company, finding and renting premises, employing staff etc.

- The market for your goods or services should have been established.

- The business should already have plans, accounting policies, and operational procedures in place.

- Buying a business can give you the benefit of immediate cashflow rather than forcing you to fund both yourself and the business for what can be a long time before it becomes recognised and profitable.

- The business should have a financial history.

- As an established local business, it might make it easier to obtain local finance. However, in practice, local banks and others are usually reluctant to lend to a business that is under new ownership.

- You should have an existing customer base.

- You should have an existing network of suppliers.

- You will probably have existing staff.

- You should have all the plant and equipment needed to do whatever you do.

Disadvantages

- It is an existing business. It will have processes that you're likely to want to change and it may have staff who may not meet your ongoing needs.

- The owner might decide to open a competing new business just around the corner. It is important that this is prohibited in your contract of purchase.

- Your staff may well be loyal to the old owner and leave shortly after he sells to you. In many businesses, particularly bars and restaurants, the staff are a key component and a major influence on why customers come to you.

- Turning around an underperforming business is often much more complicated and time-consuming than building a new one.

You will often be taking over not only the business but any debts or claims that might exist against it and you can never be absolutely certain that you have fully identified the risks involved. You can often guard against this risk. You must make enquiries (carry out due diligence) to try to establish what these debts and liabilities might be and the contract under which the old owner sells the business to you should contain a clause stating that he has fully disclosed these liabilities. However, none of this alters the fact that a person who has a claim against the business will, usually, still have a claim against it once you've taken it over.

The big ones that you need to think about are claims by ex-employees, by the tax office, by your landlord, by customers and by suppliers.

However, probably the most important disadvantage of taking over an existing business is that you're likely to have to pay a substantial amount for it and this will need to be funded.

If you decide to take over the business, you can either take over the business only - its name and assets - or the company that owns the business and so the business as well. If you were taking over only the business you would usually set up a new company to do so. Your new company would then buy just some or all of the assets of the old business. This can be less risky than taking over the company that owns the business (because you will probably not automatically take over its debts), but is still not risk free. See page 244 for more about this issue.

Are you the right person for the job?

Do you have the skills and attitude required to run this particular type of business? Are you better suited to developing an existing business or to creating a new one?

Do you have sufficient funds?

You will need to make a detailed assessment, not only of the cost of acquiring the business but also the money needed to turn it around and then run it.

Unless you are very familiar with business life in Turkey, speak to a local accountant when you become seriously interested in buying a business here. They will usually have some form of spreadsheet giving you all the major financial headings that you will need to think about. Some of them may be different from those which you're used to.

Finding a business for sale

Here there is a bit of a conundrum. The best businesses do not have 'for sale' signs outside their premises and they are usually not advertised in the press or even through specialist business agents. They tend to be passed on by way of personal contacts and word of mouth.

There are several specialist business sales agents in Turkey and they are well worth consulting, not just because of the businesses advertised by their companies but also because of their network of connections and their knowledge of businesses in any sector that could well be for sale if an appropriate buyer came along.

Other useful sources of useful information about businesses that might be for sale are your own personal contacts in the area, your lawyers, and your accountants.

Preparation

Once you have identified a business that you would like to buy (or possibly a shortlist of suitable businesses), there is some initial preparation that you will need to undertake. In fact, some of it is best done even before you have identified a potential purchase.

Appointing professional advisers

You will need both an accountant and a lawyer in order to buy and run your business. Trying to do without either of these is a major (expensive and possibly even fatal) mistake.

Depending upon the nature of your business, you may need other advisers. For example: a hotel consultant or a specialist tax adviser.

Checking your finances

If you've not already done so, you need to work through the spreadsheet containing your financial projections and - erring well on the side of caution - make sure that you have access to all the funds that you need.

This could well be the time when you approach local banks or other lenders.

If you are approaching lenders (other than, perhaps, your own family), you are much more likely to be successful if your financial plan is prepared in the format and with the headings that are usual in the country in which they are based, rather than those which might be usual in your own country. You will be surprised by how these differ, and by how much, from one country to another. If you have prepared your spreadsheet showing all the necessary figures in the format to which you are accustomed, your accountant will be able to convert it into the usual local format.

You will also be more successful, if any Turkish finance is involved, if your business plan and financial projection is prepared in Turkish or, at least, in bilingual form.

Obtaining finance

You will not be able to make a formal application for finance until you've identified a specific business opportunity but it is useful, at this stage, to make sure that your initial plan - which will have to be updated once you have a specific opportunity in mind - is going to meet the sort of criteria that the lender would usually apply.

Do not forget that if you are a foreigner with no previous experience in Turkey it is going to be very difficult to persuade a bank to lend to you in order either to buy an existing business or to start a new one. This is so even if you have experience in the field and lots of assets you can use as security for the loan.

A few years ago, in the crash of the mid-2000s, it was close to impossible. However, the banks are now becoming a little bit more adventurous and may be prepared to lend in the case of well-established businesses with a good financial record and where the new owner can show relevant experience and a significant asset base. They will often also seek personal guarantees, usually from someone who is resident in Turkey.

The main things that the banks will be looking for, in descending order of priority, are:

- Will you be able to service the loan?

  Will you be able to repay both the interest and any capital repayments? The bank will usually want to see this funded from the activity of the business itself but, during the initial phases of the loan, will probably be happy if the money is coming from some other authenticated source, such as your savings or other income.

  Even if they do accept this, they are going to want to be satisfied that the business will, from its own resources, be able to finance the lending and that it will be able to do so sooner rather than later. However strong your financial position and however much security you might have, they will not lend to you if the business cannot service the loan.

- Do you have adequate security?

  The bank will want to see that its loan to you is protected. Ideally, this will be by way of a mortgage/legal charge over real estate (property) that you own. In some cases, it can be some sort of legal charge over other assets that you own or over cash that you have deposited in their institution.

  In the case of security by way of a charge or mortgage over property, you can today (2017) expect banks in Turkey to lend between 50% and 65% of the forced sale value of that security. The forced sale value is usually assessed at a conservative level. This means that the loan will often equate to 50% or less of the price you are paying for the asset.

- Do you have the necessary management and business skills?

  Your CV is a very important part of your application. In Turkey, it's common for a CV to include references from known business leaders.

- Does the business have at least two fiscal years trading history? The fiscal year is the same as the calendar year.

  This is a slightly broader concept than the simple accounts of the business and it's something that is really only found in borrowing applications here in Turkey. The bank will want to see at least one annual tax return, even if shows no tax payable, as one of the items on their check list of required documents. This is why many Turkish entrepreneurs set up their companies in December instead of in January to be able to provide one. This, in effect, reduces the requirement to just one year.

  Further criteria (like business plans, business strategy, targets, analysis of opportunities, owners' skills etc) will not considered if you do not have this.

- Does the business have at least three years of accounts?

  The bank will want to see the business' accounts and tax returns for the last three years. One year is mandatory, but you'll get on a *lot* better with three. This can be a problem as, until fairly recently, it was commonplace for businesses to understate their real income because this would reduce the amount of tax they had to pay. If the seller has adopted that policy it will now come back to bite him - and, indirectly, you. It is very difficult to persuade the bank to rely on any figures apart from the official figures.

  Fortunately, this practice really came to an end almost ten years ago, so you're not likely to encounter it; but some traditional owners, particularly owners of older businesses, have stuck with this traditional (but completely illegal) way of doing things.

  One other thing to look out for is the reverse of this problem: an owner declaring artificial *profit* to keep themselves credible with the bank. These days, this is more common than an under-declaration.

- Do you have realistic profit & loss and cashflow forecasts for the next three years?

  The bank will want to see your profit & loss and cashflow forecast for the next three years but it will also want to see the assumptions you have made about any increases in income or reductions in cost and the evidence supporting those assumptions.

Even if you can meet these requirements, your application for funding will be aided greatly by the assistance of your accountant or business adviser, who is likely to know the peculiarities of the individual banks and bank managers concerned and who will be able to present your application in the best possible way. In fact, he or she may also be able to suggest better or more appropriate institutions or individuals for you to approach for finance.

Research on a particular business

Once you have found a particular business (or businesses) of interest to you, you will need to do your own research in order to satisfy yourself that the opportunities are worth pursuing. Most of this you will be able to do yourself but some parts might be aided by your accountant, business adviser or lawyer.

Checking the location

Some businesses have very specific requirements as to their location. If they're in the wrong place - even if it's only 100m away from the right place - they're not likely to succeed.

You can normally research the suitability of the location yourself: often by checking what your potential competitors are doing.

The requirements for your business will be specific to the type of business. Guides.Global have produced a series of guides about starting businesses of particular kinds and these deal with the relevant issues concerning location. See **www.guides.global/guides/global/GLO-selector.php**.

Checking the premises

Do the premises meet your requirements? Is access satisfactory? Do they have the necessary power supply? Do they have the right number of toilets? Are the terms of the lease satisfactory?

There are many issues to be considered here. You will usually consider them with your lawyer. Guides.Global has a (free) business premises checklist which may help you with this process. Go to **www.guides.global/books/turkey/tur-downloads.php**.

Your competition

Who are your competition? Why are they successful? What are they doing that is different from what the business you want to buy is doing? How can you improve your new business to better them?

Try the business' products or services

It's best if, after an initial visit yourself, you get someone else to do this for you on an anonymous basis.

Try to validate the figures produced by the business

This is particularly true of income. If, for example, a bar claims to be taking TRY10,000 per night, get someone to sit in there for an evening and work out the actual takings.

Check the business' marketing materials

You will probably want to change them - but are they aimed at the right sector of the market, and are they hitting their target?

Of course, today the website will be a main means of marketing - and don't ignore the business' activities in the realm of social media.

Check the local demographics

Is the market at which this business is aimed growing or shrinking? Are there any other upcoming markets that you will want to focus on?

Research industry and market trends

If you are new to Turkey, this is an area where you may need some help from your accountant or business adviser.

Why is the business for sale?

You will have already asked the seller this question but it's also worth, subtly, asking the business' staff, customers, and suppliers and also your own professional advisers.

Talk to the business' customers

Are they happy? What improvements would they like to see you make? Will they continue to come when the old owner has left?

Research online reviews

These are relatively new in Turkey, but they are becoming more and more important: especially if your business is servicing the tourist industry.

You don't want to buy a business that TripAdvisor has ranked as one star! These things are difficult to lift back up and usually not worth the bother.

Talk to the business' suppliers

What do they think of the business? Has it been a reliable customer? Have they paid on time? Will they still supply the business after you've taken it over? What suggestions can *they* make as to the ways the business can be improved?

Carry out some checks on the business

These would include a credit check, a check that the company is up-to-date with its filing of taxes and that it does not have any debts or court judgements registered against it. This is usually work that will be done by your lawyer.

Due diligence

Due diligence is simply the process of checking that both what you've been told about the business is true and that what you have assumed about the business is true.

It is usually carried out after the buyer and seller have agreed, in principle, to the sale of the business but before a binding contract is signed.

A lot of what we have described above is really part of the due diligence process, but there are additional things that you (and your lawyers and accountants) will need to review carefully at this time.

- Accounting records

- Tax returns

- Bank records

- Utility (electricity, water, telephone etc.) bills

- Bank and other loans

- Any work manual or system of work

- Official company records

- The seller's claims about the business, one by one

- Arrangements protecting the intellectual property of the business

- Non-competition arrangements (so that the seller can't set up next door to you)

- The staff. Are they reliable? Have there been disciplinary issues? What rights do they have? Have they been paid up-to-date?

- Stock check

- The condition of any equipment that you're buying

- Existing accounting arrangements, including internal accounting systems

- Intellectual property assets of the business - logo, trade name, website etc

- Existing contracts with customers

- Existing leases

- Credit and other checks on the business

- The seller. What is their local reputation? Do they have debts or court orders against them?

- Arrangements for any trial period. Are they adequate? It is desirable that you should be allowed access to the business, preferably working in it, whilst the due diligence is being carried out.

Making an offer

If you've not already made a provisional offer, once you've completed these steps you will need to make an offer for the business.

Turkey: how things *really* work

There is a special form of words used when making an offer for a business in Turkey. Therefore, although you may have put forward the offer to the seller and agreed it in principle, the formal offer should be made by your lawyers so that it is clear, complete and legally binding.

The offer will usually include a basic price for the business and a separate mechanism for valuing any stock or debts related to the business.

Do not be surprised if your initial offer produces a counter-offer to which you then respond and your response produces a further counter-offer. Sometimes, this process of offer and counter-offer will be done verbally, and sometimes in writing. If it's done verbally, the final offer should be confirmed and accepted in writing.

It may be obvious, but it is all too often ignored: decide - at the outset - the maximum amount that you're prepared to spend and do not go a penny above it. There will always be another business for you to buy.

Remember, when making the offer, that this is not always just about money. You may be able to tweak your offer to give additional benefit to the seller without increasing the cash cost for you. For example, it could help the seller (for tax purposes) if the sale is made over a period of several months so that part of the business is disposed of in this tax year and part in the next. Or the seller might want to preserve the position of certain members of staff, who might not be protected by law.

Some people are very good at negotiating deals like this. Others are not. If you are not naturally comfortable with it, you might want to bring in a business adviser or negotiator who is. That could be your accountant or lawyer; or it could be another person altogether, often suggested by your accountant or lawyer.

The formal purchase contract

Once your offer has been agreed you will need to prepare all the formal legal documentation relating to the transfer of the business.

At the very least, this will be a contract. It will often contain many clauses covering not only what you're buying but also indemnities in respect of any debts or problems relating to the business, clauses restricting the seller's right to compete with you etc.

This is work for your lawyer to do.

Before your lawyers can draft the contract, you will need to decide upon the basic structure behind your takeover of the business; for example, are you going to be buying the business in the name of a limited company? This, again, is something about which you should seek your lawyer's and/or your accountant's advice as early as possible.

How should you buy the business?

There are two basic ways in which you can buy an existing business.

Buy the assets of the business

When you take over a business by buying its assets, you simply buy the things that you want. These might include the lease on the premises occupied by the business, the equipment used in it, the goodwill of the business and its intellectual property rights.

You would not (at least, in theory) be taking over responsibility for any of its debts or any disputes relating to the business, but there are still concerns to consider. The most pressing of these is whether, if you are starting a new business with the old assets, the Municipality is going to grant you a licence. You must - really must - see your local Municipality before you decide whether to buy a business or its assets.

Another consideration is that buying a business in this way can cause you to have to pay a large amount of VAT (for example, on its stock and equipment). Sometimes this is so large that it is much better to buy the business outright.

Of course, you would still be responsible for any debts registered against the assets you're taking over: for example, a mortgage or charge on the business' premises; but you would not be responsible for any ordinary (unregistered) debts.

The sort of debts and claims you need to be alert to are claims by employees (or ex-employees), claims for unpaid tax, claims from the landlord of the business' premises, and claims from suppliers to the business.

Even if there are no such claims or other problems, if you take over a business in this way it is still likely that you will have to take over responsibility for the existing employees of the business or, at least, any who have been working within the business for more than 12 months. They would have the right to have their contracts transferred to the owner of the new business and so you would need to make sure that any sums due to them were paid by the old owner before the takeover. There is a contract you will need to have drawn up between the buyer, the seller and the employee - all three parties must accept the conditions of the contract.

Buy the business itself

If the business is trading in a way where it has a separate legal personality - i.e. it is a legal entity distinct from the person who is selling it - you might be able to buy that legal entity.

If you buy the business itself - this includes buying all the shares in the business - you would also be buying any debts of the business and any potential claims that might exist against it. These would include potential claims from employees, the tax man, the landlord (incidentally, usually, a rental contract for a business will include restrictions on changing the share ownership) etc., but that is not an exhaustive list of potential claims: there are, literally, hundreds of situations that could give rise to a claim.

You can do quite a lot to reduce the risk of there being any potential claims against the business, but you cannot eliminate the risk completely.

The sort of steps you would want to take would be to carry out enquiries relating to any of the more obvious potential claims and to place a clause in your contract of purchase of the business listing any potential claims of which owner is aware and confirming that there are no others. However, even if you take these steps, and even if you have a right of compensation from the old owner if any such claims arise, this is not a perfect solution as - all too often - once a claim arises you will find that the old owner has disappeared, has no money or is dead.

Which is best?

There are clear advantages and disadvantages to each of these courses of action.

There is usually a lot less risk in taking over just the assets of the business. However, there can be significant tax and cost advantages in taking over the shares in the company. These arise, in the main, because you do not need to change the legal ownership of the premises (and so avoid any property transfer taxes involved) and you do not need to negotiate transfers of leases or register the change of ownership of any of the assets of the business.

In addition, if you buy the assets of a business rather than the business itself, you will have to pay VAT on the value of all the stock in the business and on certain other assets you may buy from it.

It is very important that you take advice from your lawyers and/or accountants as to which means of buying the business will better suit your needs. There is a lot of money at stake!

Delivery of the business

This is the final stage in the process and a very important one.

In the contract of sale that you have signed there will be a date for delivery of the business. It is my personal view that it is best if this is as soon as possible after the signing of the contract, ideally on the same day. This is to stop the existing owner doing anything that might damage the interests of the business prior to delivery. However, this is sometimes not possible. For example, you may need a licence to run the business and be unable to apply for such a licence until you are the owner of it.

On delivery of the business there will be a series of further checks that you will need to make. These will include repeating the check that the business and its assets do not have any debts or court judgements registered against them; and the mundane but important task of checking that what you have agreed to buy is present and delivered to you. Don't forget to get the keys and the code to the alarm system! Accountants often work with people whose job is to carry out this sort of check on your behalf, and it can be well worth using their services because they do it all the time and know exactly what to do. However, even if you're going to employ specialists to do this, it's a good idea for you to be present while the exercise is carried out. You can learn a lot!

Employment Law

See our section on employment law (page 193).

Selling a Business

Written by **Başak Yildiz Orkun**
Managing Partner (Legal Department) at Orkun & Orkun
www.orkunorkun.com • info@orkunorkun.com

Once you have built a successful business it will (hopefully) build up in value and can later be sold. You can sell either the business alone or the business and the company running it. See our chapter on buying a business for the advantages and disadvantages of these two methods (page 236).

If you decide to sell the company, under Turkish law you will still have an open-ended responsibility for your actions during your period of ownership. This is subject to the usual legal prescription period (five or ten years), after which time your responsibilities expire. If you were a director of the company, and you did anything wrong in terms of your responsibilities as a director, your responsibility for that wrongdoing also remains, even after you've sold the business.

In order to sell your business, you are likely to need the following:

- All your business paperwork (annual reports, tax returns etc.), which must be completely up-to-date

- Accurate business accounts

  This is, for many businesses in Turkey, a problem. Historically (though much less so today) businesses never declared the full amount of their income or profit. Huge and popular restaurants declared an income of TRY50,000 per year! When they came to sell the business, and produced their accounts showing such modest profits, it was difficult to establish the proper value of the business.

  These days have, by and large, gone: but if you wish to obtain full value for your business when you sell it, you will need to make sure that your accounts accurately reflect the turnover and profitability of the business.

- Employee rights

  The rights of your employees may transfer to the new business and they will have to sign paperwork accepting or declining that transfer.

- A proper contract of sale for the business

  Depending upon the size of the transaction and the complexity of the contract, this will be prepared either by your accountant or your lawyer.

Taxes in Turkey

Written by **Burak Orkun**
Managing Partner (Accountancy Department) at Orkun & Orkun
www.orkunorkun.com • info@orkunorkun.com

Turkey is a low-to-mid-tax regime.

Tax levels, for individuals and companies, are lower than in many countries. Turkey ranks 27th out of the 35 OECD countries in its tax-to-GDP ratio. Low is less tax. According to the OECD, in 2015, it took the equivalent of 30% of its GDP by way of tax of all kinds. This was against an OECD average of 34.3%. The US takes 26.4%, France 45.4%. The UAE only takes about 1.4%!

However, the amount of tax that Turkey takes as a percentage of its GDP has increased quite sharply over recent years. It has moved from 24.2% in 2008 (a level that it had maintained for some time) to 30% in 2015.

Different countries collect their taxes from different sources and, compared to the OECD average, Turkey takes more tax by way of VAT and social security contributions and less tax from personal income and corporate income. Turkey has a rate of 64% of its tax take from indirect taxes which is much more than the OECD average rate of 46%. However, before 2005, it was over 75%: so the balance is shifting.

Turkey does not feature on any of the world's lists of tax havens, although it does come 20th on the TJN Financial Secrecy Index and it is only deemed partially compliant by the OECD Global Forum on Transparency and Exchange of Information for Tax Purposes. It is here alongside places such as Andorra, Anguilla, the Dominican Republic and the UAE. But things move on quite quickly, and Turkey is committed to full exchange of information for financial and tax purposes in September 2018.

This is significant because, for many years, foreigners living and working in Turkey have often assumed that what they do there is invisible to the rest of the world and that they can get away with not declaring their income or paying any taxes due.

As in most parts of the world, those days are well and truly over and so anyone now thinking of getting involved in Turkey really must work on the basis that it is a modern country with all of the information exchange protocols that you would expect to find elsewhere and in which they must declare and pay any taxes due.

The good news is that Turkey benefits from many so-called 'Double Taxation Treaties' (more properly called "Treaties for the Avoidance of Double Taxation"). See page 262.

These are designed to ensure that if circumstances arise where you could face paying tax in Turkey *and* in another country, you do not end up paying tax twice on any item of income or capital gain. See **www.gib.gov.tr/uluslararasi_mevzuat** for a full list of such treaties.

The bad news is that the tax system is rather complicated: you *need* an accountant. In the case of a company, the law *requires* you to have one.

There is a good general guide to the Turkish tax system on the Ministry of Finance website: **bit.ly/2yzhGsn**.

Choosing a Tax Adviser

In Turkey, it is usual for your tax adviser to be the same person (or, at least, to work for the same company) as your financial adviser.

See our section on choosing a financial adviser (page 250).

However, not everybody follows this route. There can be a case for having a separate tax adviser, especially if your tax affairs are complicated. In these cases, your tax adviser is likely to have to liaise closely with your other professional advisors in Turkey and your professional advisers in your own country as most people in this category will have a fiscal (tax) presence in both places and - in many cases - in other countries around the world as well.

There are several multinational tax advisory firms based in Turkey. See our contacts page (**www.guides.global/books/turkey/tur-contacts.php**).

Having said this, for most of our foreign residents, the services of our local tax and financial advice companies prove more than adequate and it is usually much cheaper to use their services than it is to use the services of one of the big multinationals.

As with every choice of professional adviser, you need to be sure that the company you are appointing has the necessary professional qualifications and insurance and that you are personally comfortable with the person who will be your adviser. Qualified advisers are listed by the Chamber of Chartered Accountants (**www.turmob.org.tr**). Ask your accountant for his licence number.

Taxes on Individuals

Getting a tax number

Any foreigner wanting to stay in Turkey for more than six months will have to obtain a tax number (more correctly known as a Tax Identification Number - *Vergi Kimlik Numarasi*). It is needed for many purposes, including opening a bank account and registering to have utility bills in your own name. You'll also need it (even if you're not resident in Turkey) if you want to buy a property or pay your local property taxes.

Fortunately, it's a very simple process.

To obtain your number, you will need to visit the closest tax office (*Vergi Dairesi*) for the area in which you live. You will need to take your passport with you, together with a photocopy of the page showing your photograph.

You will also need to know your mother's and father's full names, even if they are long dead.

If you have all this information, you will find that the whole process should only take a few minutes.

If you live in an area where no one is likely to speak your language, and if you don't speak Turkish, your lawyer or accountant can arrange for a number to be issued for you.

Obtaining a Turkish Tax Identification Number does not have any impact on your obligation to pay taxes. For this reason, it was, originally, called the "potential tax ID number". If taxes are due, they are due - whether or not you have obtained the number. Nor does not having a number keep you 'below the radar' in Turkey.

Who has to pay tax in Turkey?

Whether you have to pay tax in Turkey - and on what basis - depends upon whether or not you are classified as tax resident in Turkey.

Tax residents in Turkey

A person (for these purposes meaning a 'real life' person rather than a legal person such as a limited company) is treated as tax resident in Turkey if they are physically present in Turkey for at least 183 days in the calendar year. It does not matter whether those days are in one block or taken piecemeal throughout the year.

A day is counted as from 00:01 to 24:00. So, if you arrive in Turkey at 23:30 on Monday and leave at 07:00 on Tuesday, you have been in the country for two days. This can be important if you are trying to limit the number of days you spend in Turkey in order to avoid becoming tax resident.

It is increasingly difficult to hide your presence in Turkey, or the precise length of your presence, from the Turkish tax authorities. Immigration records, your telephone and your credit card give the game away.

If you are going to stop being tax resident in Turkey, you are required to file a tax declaration 15 days before your final departure.

If a person is treated as tax resident in Turkey then they will pay tax in Turkey (or, at least, be potentially liable to tax in Turkey) on their worldwide income, their worldwide assets, their worldwide capital gains, and any inheritances they receive from anywhere in the world.

At any given time, Turkish tax law may or may not actually call for the payment of taxes in all of these categories but, if it does, you are liable to pay them.

This is always subject to the relevant Double Taxation Treaties (see page 262). Under these treaties, it may be that all or part of the relevant taxable items will be taxed in another country instead of in Turkey.

Non-residents in Turkey

A person who is not treated as a tax resident in Turkey is, for tax purposes, a non-resident.

Taxes on income

Tax residents of Turkey

Tax residents are liable to tax in Turkey on their worldwide income. This means what it says. If you have a salary being paid to you in another country or investment income generated in another country, then all that income plus whatever you might earn in Turkey will be taxed in Turkey.

The main exception to this is that overseas pensions are not generally taxed in Turkey. There are conditions to this. You will need to have a Turkish residence permit and you will need to have certain paperwork prepared by the tax authority in your own country, confirming the status of your pension payments. This form is then approved by the Turkish tax authorities, following which your pension income will no longer be taxable in Turkey. This provision is hugely beneficial to retired people living in Turkey as, often, their pension will be taxed neither 'back home' nor in Turkey.

This rule about your worldwide income being taxable in Turkey could produce cases of unfairness, but these are mitigated by the effects of the Double Taxation Treaties referred to above. These ensure that you do not, generally, pay the same tax on the same income in two different places.

Each person is taxed as an individual on their own income, so a husband and wife have two tax numbers and file two tax returns.

The amount of tax you pay will depend, mainly, upon the size of your income.

For the tax year 2017:

Income from employment

Tax bracket		Tax rate
From TRY1	To TRY13,000	15%
From TRY13,0001	To TRY30,000	20%
From TRY30,0001	To TRY110,000	27%
From TRY110,001	To [no limit]	35%

Other types of income

Tax bracket		Tax rate
From TRY1	To TRY13,000	15%
From TRY13,0001	To TRY30,000	20%
From TRY30,0001	To TRY70,000	27%
From TRY70,001	To [no limit]	35%

Other income includes interest received, dividends, rental income and any taxable capital gains.

When calculating rental income, you can offset all of the expenses that you've actually incurred in providing the rental property (including mortgage interest) or you can claim 15% of the gross rent received as a 'no questions asked' deduction. Until recently this was 25%. If you claim the actual expenses, your claim is subject to the possibility of an inspection by the tax authorities, whereas claiming the 15% deduction is something you can do as a right. You cannot combine the two claims and you cannot change your preferred way of claiming more than once in any two years.

In either case, the first TRY3,900 of rental income is exempt from tax.

In Turkey, there is no general tax-free amount of income or general tax-free allowance. However, there are various deductions that can reduce the tax that you have to pay.

These include:

- Premiums paid to a Turkish company for medical and disability insurance (up to a specified limit)

- Contributions to the social security system in your own country, if your country has an agreement with Turkey

- Certain charitable contributions (up to specified limits)

- A subsistence allowance in respect of the tax payer and, if applicable, his or her non-working spouse and children

Turkey: how things *really* work

- Deductions for health and education expenses actually incurred in respect of the taxpayer, his or her spouse, or dependent children

The provision of a car allowance or the use of a company car is taxable.

Meals provided by the employer on his premises or, up to a certain limit, by luncheon vouchers, are not taxable.

Income tax is declared on 25th March for the previous financial year (1st January to 31st December). The tax can be paid in two instalments or as one payment, as you prefer.

If you pay in two instalments, the payments are due on 31st March and 31st July.

If you are late in filing your tax return, there is a small penalty.

If you're late in paying your tax but you do eventually pay it before you are challenged by the tax authorities, there is an automatic surcharge of 50% of the tax you owe, plus interest at 16.8% per annum from the date when the tax was due to the date when it is finally paid.

If the tax authorities realise that you have been late in paying and challenge you on the point before you pay, the surcharge increases to 100%.

In the case of a company, the surcharge can rise to 300%!

If you are self-employed, you will file an interim (provisional) tax return every three months and pay the amount shown as due at that time.

If you're employed by one employer, your employer will, every month, automatically deduct the tax that is due from your salary and pay it to the tax authorities. If you have multiple employers you need to file an annual income tax return on 25th March.

Case study

Bob Richards

Marketing manager, American, 53

The problem

Bob took a job in Turkey in January 2012. He'd previously been employed in the US and, before that, in Germany.

Obviously, he had to pay tax on his earnings in Turkey, but he was very pleasantly surprised with the overall amount of tax he had to pay, which was considerably less than the income tax he'd been paying in the US or in Germany.

This was partly because of the much lower tax rates that prevailed in Turkey and partly because of the very generous tax allowances to which he was entitled.

However, co-workers told him that there were even more tax savings available, so he consulted a local accountant specializing in international taxation.

The solution

He discovered that, because he still had to spend up to 30 days per year working in the US and up to 60 days per year working in Germany, he could deduct from his taxable earnings in Turkey the full amount that he earned in respect of these periods. This came as a great surprise as this flexibility was not something he'd experienced before.

The result was to reduce his tax bill by nearly TRY25,000 per year - a good return for the TRY1,000 he paid the accountant!

The accountant is now advising him about ways of restructuring his investment portfolio to take full advantage of his situation in Turkey.

People who are not tax resident in Turkey

People who are not tax resident in Turkey pay income tax in Turkey on:

1. Any income they earn from working in Turkey

2. Any income they earn by renting out any real estate (houses, apartments or land) located in Turkey

3. Any income they generate from investments in Turkey

For non-residents, there is no tax-free allowance in Turkey. There is a tax-free allowance for rental income (see above) and capital gains tax for non-tax residences.

The Turkish tax rates for non-residents are the same as for residents. So are the penalties for late payment.

You must file your tax return and pay the taxes due in the same way as a resident (see above).

Taxes on capital gains

Capital Gains Tax is the tax you pay when you sell an asset that has grown in value since you acquired it.

The tax is payable on the sale of assets of all kinds. The rules are quite complex but, in summary:

Tax residents of Turkey

Tax is payable on the worldwide capital gains made by a person who is tax-resident in Turkey.

Real estate

If you own real estate for a period of at least five years, any increase in value is tax free.

Until then, you benefit from a general exemption allowing you to generate a tax-free capital gain of up to TRY11,000 (2017) in any one year.

When calculating the amount of your gain, you can adjust the price you paid for the property for inflation since you bought it and then deduct that adjusted amount from the price for which you sold it. Inflation in Turkey has been substantial over the last few years, so this is a valuable adjustment (though this is applicable only if the inflation rate is over 10%).

For the purpose of calculating tax on the sale of real estate, it does not matter if the property is your main home, a secondary home, an investment property or some other type of building.

Stocks and shares

If you have owned the stocks or shares of a public limited company (*Anonim Şirket*) for a minimum period of two years, any gains are tax free. Otherwise, the gains are taxed as part of your other income.

Financial instruments

This includes bank products. There is no tax exemption. Tax will be deducted automatically at source by your bank. The gain you make is taxed as part of your other income.

Gold, works of art, etc.

There is no exemption from Capital Gains Tax although, strangely, few people seem to remember to report the money they make from the sale of gold bars or paintings to the tax department.

This, and the traditionally lax enforcement of tax collection on the sale of gold and jewellery, perhaps explains why Turkey is the world's fourth largest gold buying nation, with an estimate of over 3,500 tonnes of gold in private hands. In case you are wondering, that is worth over US$225 billion! It's also nearly half of the total holdings of the US Central Bank and well in excess of the amount of gold owned by the IMF.

However, the government is concerned about all this dead money and, in June 2017, announced plans for 'gold bonds' to deflect investment cash away from physical bullion, plus 'gold lease certificates' offering a rate of interest to gold owners who put their metal on deposit instead.

Legally, any profits from the sale of gold, art etc. are taxed as part of your general income. The general TRY11,000 exemption is also applicable for this type of profit.

Foreign exchange (FX) gains

There is no exemption. The gain you make is taxed as part of your other income.

People who are not tax resident in Turkey

The same rules apply as for people who are tax resident, but only in relation to their assets in Turkey.

Capital losses

Capital losses cannot be offset against your other income.

Taxes on property (real estate)

Buying real estate - the Land Registry (*Tapu Ofis*) charge

Tax is payable each time the ownership of land (including within the definition any house, apartment or other real estate) or any part of the ownership of land is transferred (for example, if you're selling your half share of an apartment in Turkey).

The taxable value is the *greater* of the price for which the property is sold (as recorded in the deed of sale - *tapu*) or the official tax value (cadastral value) of the property. The cadastral value is the assessed value of the land, as recorded by the local municipality.

This means that if you sell your property for far below market value, there will still be a significant amount of tax to pay.

The tax is 4% (from October 2017). The cost of this is often shared equally between the buyer and the seller but the liability can be split in whichever way the parties agree. In the absence of any agreement, the full amount is paid by the buyer and it must be paid before the change of ownership of the property can be recorded at the *Tapu Ofis*.

If property transfers as a result of an inheritance, no property transfer tax is payable. Instead, inheritance tax is due.

If property changes ownership as the result of a gift, inheritance tax is again payable instead of property transfer tax.

If property changes hands as a result of a court order, no tax is payable.

Owning real estate

There are annual taxes arising out of the ownership of real estate (land and buildings) in Turkey. These taxes are payable to the municipality in which the property is located and are used to pay for all the services that they provide: e.g. garbage collection.

The tax payable depends upon the official tax value (cadastral value) of your property, as determined by the municipality.

- Buildings outside a designated metropolitan area pay tax at 1% per year of the official registered value

- Buildings within a designated metropolitan area pay tax at 2%

- General land pays tax at 3%

- Agricultural land pays tax at 1%

Selling real estate

Property transfer tax applies any time a property or land changes hands. See above.

While the parties are free to agree who pays this tax, it is normally split equally between the buyer and the seller.

There is no separate tax payable on the sale of land: though, if it has increased in value, there could be a liability to capital gains tax.

Taxation of cars, boats, planes, etc.

There is an annual motor vehicle tax.

The amount of the tax depends upon the type of vehicle, the year it was manufactured, and its engine size. The list extends to over 100 pages! You can see it at **bit.ly/1rWn2Jj**

By way of example, the tax payable on a four- to six-year-old 1599cc saloon car is TRY750 (£140/€160/$200) per year, payable in two instalments (January and July).

This is not paid as part of your normal tax return but, instead, it is paid online directly to the tax office.

Taxes on wealth

Wealth tax, for those not familiar with the concept, is a tax charged each year and calculated on the basis of your total accumulated wealth.

There is no wealth tax in Turkey.

Gift tax

Gifts, apart from modest gifts on birthdays, weddings etc., are subject to a tax. The tax-free amount is limited to a total of TRY4,068 (£770/€860/$1,100) per donee.

Gift amount	Tax rate
Up to TRY210,000	10%
The next TRY500,000	15%
The next TRY1,110,000	20%
The next TRY2,000,000	25%
Anything over TRY3,820,000	30%

The tax is paid by the recipient of the gift.

There is plenty of scope for sensible tax planning here: giving away small amounts, tax free, each year and - for larger gifts - making sure that individuals do not receive overly large amounts.

Taxes on death (inheritance tax)

The first and most important thing to understand here is that the question of who inherits what and the taxes that need to be paid upon an inheritance are two entirely different questions.

For information about who inherits what in Turkey, see page 468.

Turkish inheritance tax applies in two different circumstances.

1. If the person who inherits the property is legally resident in Turkey

2. If the property being inherited is in Turkey

There is no inheritance tax in Turkey in relation to assets that are not located in Turkey unless the person who receives those assets is resident in Turkey.

The tax is payable by the person who inherits the property.

So, for example, if you move to Turkey and have a bank account in Turkey containing

€1,500 and a bank account in (say) Switzerland containing €10million and then, on your death, you leave all your property to your son:

- If your son is NOT resident in Turkey, he will pay inheritance tax in Turkey only on the €1,500 in the bank account in Turkey, not on the €10million. Of course, that €10million may be caught by taxation in (in this case) Switzerland or in the country where your son lives. That is a separate issue.
- If he is resident in Turkey, he will pay tax in Turkey on both accounts: €10,001,500.

This also gives lots of scope for valuable tax planning.

When it comes to inheritance tax, there is a general exception of TRY176,600 (£33,500/€38,000/€47,000) for each heir. In other words, if you leave your assets on your death equally to your wife and three children, there will be four heirs and so 4xTRY176,600 by way of exemptions from tax.

If you have only one heir, the exemption doubles.

Over and above the tax-free amount, the tax payable is as follows:

Inheritance amount	Tax rate
Up to TRY210,000	1%
The next TRY500,000	3%
The next TRY1,110,000	5%
The next TRY2,000,000	7%
Anything over TRY3,820,000	10%

The value of land and buildings (real estate) is assessed at the official cadastral value, as recorded in the municipal tax registry. The value of money in bank accounts and other investments is calculated at their true market value.

Values are assessed after deduction of debts. So, for example, a house valued at TRY1million but with a TRY700,000 mortgage is valued at TRY300,000.

VAT

In Turkey, VAT (sales tax - *Katma Deger Vergisi* (KDV)) is charged at rates of 0%, 1%, 8% and 18%. For almost everything you are likely to want, the rate is 18%.

VAT applies to all goods and services provided by way of business. There are no exemptions such as those enjoyed in some other countries. What might otherwise be exempt items are subject to the 0% or 1% rate. Nor is there any threshold allowing small companies not to charge VAT.

When you register your business, you will also register it for taxation and receive a unique VAT number. This must be quoted on all bills sent out by the business and shown on any website operated by the business.

If you run a business in Turkey, you will have to file a VAT report every month and, at the same time, pay the VAT shown as being due to the Turkish Tax Department. There are both interest and penalties due for late payment. These are calculated as the same way as for income tax. See page 265.

The way the VAT due is calculated in Turkey is pretty much the same as under any VAT system: namely the total VAT that you have paid out on your allowable expenses (purchase of materials, administrative costs etc.) is deducted from the total VAT that you have charged for your goods or services. This leaves a net amount payable to the Turkish government.

Special Consumption Tax (SCT)(*Özel Tüketim Vergisi or ÖTV*)

Special Consumption Tax (sometimes confusingly referred to as 'excise duty') is, in some ways, similar to VAT. The main differences are that it only applies in the case of specified categories of goods and that it is only paid once in relation to any particular item. VAT, on the other hand, is paid each time the item changes hands commercially. See page 266.

Other taxes

Community Fees

These are not, strictly speaking, a tax but a fee payable to the Community of Owners (Residents Association/Home Owners Association) in which you live. Nonetheless, it seems to make sense to refer to them here.

Generally, you will only have to pay community fees if you live in a block of apartments or in a group of houses that shares common facilities such as a pool, gardens, parking areas etc.

See our chapter on Communities of Owners (page 380).

There is usually no community fee if you live in a self-contained villa.

The amount of any community fee can vary greatly depending upon the range of facilities made available to you. For a small apartment block, where the charge only covers communal electricity and cleaning the hallway, it could be TRY3,000 per year. For a large property, in a complex with lifts and a golf course, it could be thousands!

If you do not pay your community fees your property can (eventually) be seized and sold by the community. Don't forget about them!

Social security payments in Turkey

Social security payments are, in effect, just another type of tax.

See our chapter on employment (page 186) for more details.

Other taxes in Turkey

There are a number of small taxes in Turkey, many of which have been there for

Turkey: how things *really* work

decades or centuries, but which are unlikely to affect most of our readers.

Taxation in your own or other countries

It is, obviously, beyond the scope of this book to look in detail at the taxation systems of the 195 or so countries of the world. See **www.guides.global** for information about tax in many other countries.

The most important thing to stress is that your tax obligations in your home - or, indeed, other - countries will not necessarily end just because you are now living in Turkey.

If you have income arising from those countries, you will probably find that that income continues to be taxable in those countries.

If you sell things at a profit and so make a capital gain, that gain could well be taxable in those countries. In some places this will be by way or a separate capital gains tax; in other places the gain will be taxed as part of your annual income.

If you inherit property in another country, you are likely to have to pay some form of inheritance tax on what you inherit in that country.

If you have property - real estate - in another country, you are likely to have to pay some annual taxes relating to that property.

If you come from the US (or, strangely, Eritrea), you will even face tax based not upon your residence there but the mere fact of your nationality of that country.

In many of these cases, if you are tax-resident in turkey, the tax laws in Turkey would also include those items gains as part of your taxable income or gains in Turkey.

Do you have to pay twice?

Most countries recognise that it is essentially unfair to tax people twice on the same piece of income, capital gain, inheritance etc. To get around this problem, most countries in the world enter into treaties with other countries to make it clear who pays what, where and in which circumstances. These are usually bilateral treaties: treaties between country A and country B. They only affect citizens of those countries.

These double taxation treaties should, more properly, be called treaties for the *avoidance* of double taxation.

They differ in scope: some may just cover income and corporate taxes, some may cover income taxes and capital gains taxes, some may also cover inheritance taxes.

Double Taxation Treaties in Turkey

Turkey has signed Double Taxation Treaties with 78 countries around the world. They are:

Albania, Algeria, Australia, Azerbaijan, Austria, Bahrain, Bangladesh, Belarus, Belgium, Bosnia and Herzegovina, Bulgaria, Canada, China, Croatia, Czech Republic, Denmark,

Egypt, Estonia, Ethiopia, Finland, France, Germany, Greece, Hungary, India, Indonesia, Iran, Israel, Italy, Japan, Jordan, Kazakhstan, Korea, Kuwait, Kyrgyzstan, Latvia, Lebanon, Lithuania, Luxembourg, Macedonia, Malaysia, Moldova, Mongolia, Montenegro, Morocco, the Netherlands, New Zealand, Northern Cyprus, Norway, Oman, Pakistan, Poland, Portugal, Qatar, Romania, Russia, Saudi Arabia, Serbia, South Africa, Singapore, Slovakia, Slovenia, Spain, Sudan, Syria, Sweden, Tajikistan, Thailand, Tunisia, Turkmenistan, Ukraine, the United Arab Emirates, the United Kingdom, the United States of America, Uzbekistan and Yemen.

It means that - if you are tax resident in or have to pay taxes in any of those countries and, under the rules of those countries, you are due to pay tax on any particular item of income, gain etc. in that country - where and how much you will actually end up paying and in which country will be decided by the treaty.

Let us use an example of a person who is not resident in Turkey and who earns some income from renting out their home in Turkey.

If they are resident in (say) the US, that income will form part of their worldwide income and so it will (on the face of it) be taxable in the US.

However, under the law of Turkey, income generated by a non-resident from letting a house in Turkey is taxable in Turkey.

This could give rise to them having to pay tax twice on the same income. This is clearly unfair. This is where the Double Taxation Treaty helps.

Under the US-Turkey Double Taxation Treaty, it is agreed that any income arising from renting out real estate (a house or apartment) in Turkey is to be taxed first and foremost in Turkey.

Let's say that the tax you had to pay in Turkey was TRY3,000 (US$850). You would pay that tax to the Government of Turkey.

If the tax you would have owed in the US on the same income was, say, US$2,000 you will then be able to deduct the dollar equivalent of the tax you've already paid in Turkey from your tax obligation in the US. In this case, you would therefore have to pay a further US$1,150 of tax to the US Government.

In some cases, it could be that the tax you have to pay in Turkey is greater than the tax you would have to pay back home on the same item of income. In this case, you would pay the full amount of tax due in Turkey and this would eliminate your tax obligation in the other country. It would *not* usually mean that you would be entitled to a tax refund in that other country.

Although most of the Double Taxation Treaties contain similar provisions, there are a large number of detail variations between them and so you need to study the treaties concerned in any particular case to determine your tax liability.

Copies of the Double Taxation Treaties can be downloaded from the Turkey Tax Department website. In every case, they are available in both Turkish and the language of the country concerned.

Turkey: how things *really* work

Although I have used the example of someone renting out a property in Turkey, the Double Taxation Treaty (in almost all cases) will apply to all types of tax. In each case, it will tell you where any tax due will be payable.

The numbers I have used are purely to illustrate the point, not a real-world example of what might be payable.

Taxation of Companies

Written by **Burak Orkun**
Managing Partner (Accountancy Department) at Orkun & Orkun
www.orkunorkun.com • info@orkunorkun.com

Some businesses operate as sole traders. These businesses are not taxed separately as businesses (but do have to account for VAT). The profits that they make are simply treated as the income of the sole trader.

For the reasons already explained, these are seldom used by foreigners.

However, many businesses operate through partnerships or separate limited companies and these are taxed in Turkey on their own account.

There are two bases upon which they can be taxed. Some businesses have the right to choose which method will apply but, once they've chosen, they can't change their mind for a period of five years.

VAT

VAT (*Katma Deger Vergisi* (KDV)) operates pretty much in the same way in every country that uses the VAT system, and Turkey is no exception.

A company based in Turkey or selling goods or services in Turkey must charge Turkish VAT on the total value of those goods or services. Currently the general rate of VAT is 18%, but many services or goods are subject to the lower 8% or 1% rates. These include hotels and restaurants (8%); clothing (8%); and staple foods (1%).

The business will then submit a VAT tax return to the Government of Turkey every month and pay all the VAT due to the tax authority.

To calculate the amount of VAT due, the company will deduct any VAT that it has paid in connection with its business. This will include the VAT it has paid to the suppliers of the goods that it has sold and the VAT it has paid on all its incidental expenses such as rent, telephone charges, delivery charges etc.

Having said this, there are three main points that foreign businesses need to consider when planning their affairs in Turkey.

The first is that there is no VAT minimum limit or threshold. In some countries, the law does not require a business to register for VAT until its turnover during the year reaches a certain mount. Until then, it does not need to collect any VAT and so, of course, it doesn't need to pass it onto the government. Of course, it also can't recover any VAT on any goods or services it pays for.

In Turkey, even if your business only generates TRY100 per month, you will need to charge VAT on that amount and pass that onto the government, less any permissible VAT deductions.

The second point is that, in the case of small businesses, you will often find that the VAT that you have spent on providing the goods or services that you have supplied might be higher than the amount of VAT that you have gathered. In this case, the rest of the allowable VAT deductions will be transferred to the next month (or months - it's an unlimited period) instead of you being entitled to a cash refund from the government, as it is in most EU countries. *However*, the government has said that the VAT refund process will be coming soon.

The final - and perhaps most important - point is that Turkey imposes heavy penalties on those who are late in filing their VAT return or who do not pay the VAT that is due. These penalties are much higher than in many other countries. For example, failure to file your VAT return on time incurs a penalty of TRY1,400 (£270/€300/$370) **plus** a surcharge of between 100% and 300% of the VAT due.

Special Consumption Tax (SCT)

This is, in international terms, an unusual tax but very important to Turkey. In 2015, 25.98% of the General Budget Tax Revenues came from SCT - totalling TRY105,902,496,000 (over US$27.5billion)!

SCT is levied only once in the consumption process of goods, so it is different from VAT, and it is only levied in respect of the goods listed in the four annexes to the SCT Law.

It is listed in this part of the book because the ultimate payer of this tax is the business making or distributing the goods.

Which goods are taxed?

There are four main groups of products that are subject to SCT at different tax rates:

- List 1 is related to petroleum products, natural gas, lubricating oil, solvents and derivatives of solvents.

- List 2 is related to land, air and sea vehicles (cars and other vehicles, motorcycles, planes, helicopters, yachts etc.).

- List 3 is related to alcoholic beverages, and cola/soda drinks, cigarettes and other tobacco products.

- List 4 is related to other luxury goods (caviar, furs, mobile phones, white goods and other electrical household machines etc.).

Who pays the tax?

The taxpayers for SCT are, generally:

- For Lists 1, 3 & 4, the manufacturers and importers of the goods

- For List 2, the traders of the vehicles

How much tax is paid?

The rates vary with the type of goods concerned. For example, on petrol (gasoline) it is between TRY2.37 and TRY2.49 per litre. On cars it is between 60% and 160% of the vehicle's base price. For cigarettes, tax is TRY3.75 per pack of 20.

The tax is declared electronically and paid monthly.

Taxes on profits

Corporation tax is the tax paid by companies on their profits.

How much depends upon whether the company is fully tax resident in Turkey, partly resident or full non-resident.

A company wishing to generate income taxable in Turkey must register in Turkey for tax purposes.

Tax residents

There are two bases upon which a company can have to pay tax in Turkey.

Full taxpayers

Companies whose main business premises or legal base, as stated in their articles of association, are in Turkey are treated as tax resident in Turkey.

The profit is based upon the worldwide income of the company (although, in practical terms, income earned by the company outside Turkey is likely to be taxed first and foremost in the country in which it is earned, with tax being due in Turkey only if the tax rate in Turkey is higher than the tax rate in the country concerned). In many cases, this will mean that no tax is paid in Turkey on earnings generated outside Turkey.

Limited taxpayers

These are companies whose main base is not in Turkey but which have a presence such as a branch office in Turkey.

These companies pay tax only on their activities in Turkey. This means that any revenue they generate in Turkey is taxable in Turkey. If they have income which is not normal business income, this may be subject to a withholding tax.

Companies who are not tax resident in Turkey

Companies that are neither full nor limited tax payers in Turkey have no liability to Turkish corporate taxes, even if they trade with Turkey.

Calculation of profit

The profit is calculated by deducting from the gross earnings of the company all legitimate expenses. There are a mass of regulations governing what can and cannot be deducted as companies find ever more ingenious ways of trying to get around the rules.

Basically, you can deduct from the gross income of the company:

1. The usual operating costs such as salaries, rent, electricity bills, the purchase and maintenance of equipment and professional fees incurred in running the business

2. Depreciation, at rates published by the Ministry of Finance

3. Any capital losses

4. Interest paid for business purposes, unless it is paid to acquire fixed assets, in which case it must be capitalised

Special cases

Dividends received by the company from another company, or paid out by the company, are subject to 15% withholding tax.

Controlled Foreign Company (CFC) rules apply in Turkey, where the Turkish company has at least a 50% interest in a non-resident company. In these cases, tax will be paid in Turkey on part of the profits of the foreign company. The details are beyond the scope of this book: talk to your accountant.

Tax rates & payment

The remaining balance - the profit - is taxed at a flat rate of 22% (2018).

Any losses can be carried forward for five years, but cannot be carried back to allow for a refund of tax already paid.

The company must file a tax return by 25th April each year, covering the period up to 31st December of the year before. Any tax due is payable by 30th April.

Failure to file a tax return by the due date incurs a penalty of TRY1,400.

Failure to declare the taxes by the due date incurs a penalty of between 100% and 300% of the tax due, plus interest at 16.8% per year until paid. If there is a proper declaration on the due date, any late payment will be only surcharged with 16.8% interest per year (calculated on a daily basis).

Taxes on money earned abroad

A company based in Turkey must declare, for the purposes of Turkish corporation tax, the full amount of its earnings in Turkey and overseas.

Of course, the money it earns overseas will usually be subject to taxation in the country where it's earned. In this case, the provisions of any double taxation treaty between Turkey and the country in question will apply.

However, in general terms, even if there is no specific double taxation treaty, these companies will be granted a foreign tax credit in Turkey so that they can deduct from their Turkish tax bill the full amount of their Turkish tax liability attributable to their non-Turkish income.

Other taxes

Companies, like private individuals, will end up paying a number of incidental taxes in Turkey. These will include taxes on motor vehicles, charges for the collection of garbage and so on. See our chapter on the taxation of private individuals (page 251) for more details.

Does the company have to pay tax twice?

As in the case of private individuals, the government recognises that it would be unjust and counterproductive if companies had to pay tax on the same income both in Turkey and in another country. Thus, they have entered into many Double Taxation Treaties. See the list of countries on page 262.

Tax Inspections

Written by **Burak Orkun**
Managing Partner (Accountancy Department) at Orkun & Orkun
www.orkunorkun.com • info@orkunorkun.com

The Tax Department has the legal right to inspect any person's or any company's tax affairs at any time.

They do not have a regular cycle of audits and inspections for every tax payer. Instead, the decision of who to inspect is partly intelligence-led and partly based on the Department's risk assessment software.

Sometimes that risk assessment will relate to a particular sector of the economy (e.g. bars or restaurants).

Sometimes it will flag up a specific issue (e.g. people making large claims for travel expenses, issues relating to transfer pricing, or companies that appear to be thinly capitalised).

Sometimes, the inspections appear to be quite random.

Tax returns may be inspected at any point up to the end of the five-year statute of limitations created by the Turkish Tax Procedure Law.

Tax Planning

Written by **Burak Orkun**
Managing Partner (Accountancy Department) at Orkun & Orkun
www.orkunorkun.com • info@orkunorkun.com

Many people and companies moving to Turkey or doing business here are very concerned about tax planning. Indeed, you could almost say that they are obsessive about it. Their worries are, generally, unfounded in that Turkey has relatively a low-tax regime and displays considerable flexibility when it comes to dealing with your tax affairs.

However, some degree of tax planning is usually a good idea and it can, surprisingly often, allow you to make substantial savings in tax by making some relatively small adjustments to the ways in which you might otherwise have organised your affairs.

What is tax planning?

Tax planning is the analysis of your financial situation - or your proposed plans of action - from a tax perspective. Its purpose is to ensure tax efficiency. Ideally, it is part of a broader financial or business plan which works to deliver what you want to do in the most tax-efficient way possible. It is about arranging your affairs to produce the smallest amount of tax liability.

In a way, you can think of tax planning as being a means of avoiding tax wastage. Governments intentionally create many legitimate opportunities for you to reduce the amount that you pay in tax. They may give you incentives to make investments of certain types or they may allow you to claim allowances for doing things that align with their policy - for example, giving to charity, research and development in a company or educating your children.

Two examples applicable to Turkey, at the opposite ends of the tax planning spectrum, would be:

- Opting for a small engine in a car to avoid paying more car tax

- Investing millions in a government-supported industry for big tax exemptions

In every country, even local people are not familiar with these quite legitimate opportunities. For example, in the UK in 2016 official estimates indicated that about €5billion of tax was paid to the government by people who didn't need to pay it or who wouldn't have had to pay it if they'd known about all the allowances they could have claimed.

The position is even worse for people who have moved to a new country. They will very rarely know about all the opportunities that exist in that new country and they will usually not be familiar with the other opportunities (often just as big) that exist because of the interaction between the tax rules in their new country and those in the place where they used to live.

Some of these tax planning opportunities arising because of the interaction of tax systems are transient: they may only be available for a short period as you make your move from your original country to Turkey, so to take advantage of these it is important to take prompt advice.

So, tax planning is about arranging or rearranging your affairs to take advantage of all these things.

What tax planning is NOT

Tax planning is not about concealing your activity from the tax authorities. Nor is it about lying to the tax authorities about your affairs. Both are illegal and can be heavily punished.

Tax avoidance vs tax evasion

Tax avoidance

Tax avoidance is arranging your affairs to reduce the amount of tax that you must pay. Extreme examples would be choosing to have more children to reduce the overall inheritance tax payable or paying your employees more to reduce your profit and so your taxes. There are countless examples of tax avoidance used on a day-to-day basis.

In Turkey, as in most other countries, tax avoidance - more sensibly called tax reduction through planning - is perfectly legal and considered to be part of good business planning.

Recently, politicians around the world have started to talk about 'aggressive tax avoidance'. This is pushing the existing rules up to their very limit and sometimes beyond. The Turkish Tax Department is concerned about this and spends some time trying to clamp down on it.

Generally, with the relatively simple tax regime in Turkey and the relatively low rates of tax payable, aggressive tax avoidance should not be necessary.

Tax evasion

Tax evasion is not paying the taxes that the law requires you to pay.

This might be by not declaring part of your income. It might be by claiming more expenses than your business legitimately incurred. It might be failing to tell the Tax Department when you sell your Picasso for a large profit or when you win a lot of money at the casino.

Tax evasion is illegal.

The enforcement division at the Turkish Tax Department employs many people checking people's tax returns and chasing tax evasion. For foreigners, they also work closely with the tax departments in the foreigner's own country.

If you are caught trying to evade your taxes, then the following will happen:

1. You will have to pay double the tax originally due.

2. You will have to pay interest at 16.8% per year from the date when the tax should have been paid to the date when it actually was paid.

3. If the issue is considered an organised tax fraud by the tax inspector, the case will be taken to the local criminal court for sentencing, which is likely to result in imprisonment.

When you first arrive in Turkey and you start talking to all the 'old hands' - particularly, the old hands who you meet in bars or at the golf club - they will probably tell you that you don't need to bother with the tax man. They will tell you that they have lived in Turkey for 20/30/40 years, that they've worked illegally for much of that time, and that they don't tell the tax man about any of their earnings, at home or abroad.

They will tell you that there is no way that the tax man can know how much time you've spent in Turkey or what you have earned whilst you've been there.

This might have been true 20 years ago, but it is definitely not true today.

The advent of the computer and a greater emphasis on collecting tax has changed everything. The Tax Department is under great political pressure to collect the taxes due from foreigners. Remember that no politician ever lost votes by taxing foreigners!

It is now very simple for the tax man to know whether you are in the country or not. Your mobile phone record will disclose this in a few minutes. The tax department also has the power to require you to produce your bank account and credit cards records, which will also show where and when you have withdrawn money.

Turkey has a sophisticated tax computer system so that the information received from businesses and individuals on the island is collated and any discrepancies identified.

It is simply not worth taking the risk of evading paying the taxes that you owe, particularly when the tax system is so generous and the taxes due so small.

Remember that the difference between tax avoidance (legal tax planning) and tax evasion is the thickness of a prison wall.

Tax savings

Do not underestimate the amount of money that can be saved by simple but effective tax planning. Private individuals can often save hundreds of thousands by minor adjustments to their plans and the savings for companies could easily run into millions. This is why tax advisers are well-paid!

Financial planning

Tax planning is a part, and a very important part, of financial planning - but financial planning is a much broader subject. For example, your financial plan would deal with things such as making sure that you are likely to have enough in the way of savings to see you through your retirement and investing your savings in ways that reflect your personal attitude to risk and reward.

Your tax advice should complement your financial plan but it should not dominate it. In other words, your broader financial objectives must take priority and the purpose of the tax planning is to tweak those objectives and the ways of delivering them to make sure that you do not pay more tax than is absolutely necessary - either in Turkey or in any other country.

The Law in Turkey

The Legal System

Written by **Başak Yildiz Orkun**
Managing Partner (Legal Department) at Orkun & Orkun
www.orkunorkun.com • info@orkunorkun.com

Turkey has a very effective legal system: sometimes slow, but fully functioning.

Unlike in some countries, you do not need to 'buy' the judges, but you do have to be diligent and pursue your case to make sure things happen without any unnecessary delay.

Recent changes following the 2016 'coup' have not helped either its efficiency or credibility.

Making laws in Turkey

Turkey is unusual in that its legislature has only one chamber. This 'unicameral' approach means that the Grand National Assembly of Turkey (*Turkiye Buyuk Millet Meclisi*) deals with the entire legislative process. In most countries, there are two chambers - for example, the Senate and House of Representatives in the US or the House of Commons and the House of Lords in the UK.

The Assembly has 550 seats (which, following the April 2017 constitutional referendum, will increase to 600 at the next election). Members are directly elected in multi-seat constituencies by a proportional representation vote and serve a four-year term.

Laws may be proposed by members of the Assembly or by Council of Ministers.

The Council of Ministers (*Bakanlar Kurulu*) otherwise known as the Cabinet of Turkey (*Türkiye Kabinesi*) is the body that exercises supreme executive authority in Turkey. It is composed of the heads of the major ministries. Ministers are appointed by the President on the advice of the Prime Minister.

Proposed laws are debated and then submitted for the approval of the Prime Minister. The Prime Minister accepts or declines the new law within 15 days and, if approved, it is published in the Official Gazette (*T.C. Resmi Gazete*).

The Official Gazette is published every weekday and contains new legislation (laws, decisions of the Council of Ministers, regulations, communiqués etc.), certain case law and various official notices, especially those relating to public administration appointments and public tenders.

Laws become effective 45 days after being published in the Official Gazette or, if the

Assembly has decided to implement a law on another date, on the date stated.

Once passed, laws remain valid indefinitely or until they are specifically repealed (cancelled) by the Assembly or by a clause in the law itself.

Different types of laws in Turkey

In Turkey, laws are classified as falling into different types. The type that applies to any particular law is stated clearly in the law itself.

Criminal laws

Criminal laws are laws that punish certain types of conduct. It is the existence of a punishment (rather than a simple right to compensation) that distinguishes criminal laws from all the other categories of law.

The punishment could be a fine, imprisonment, compulsory public service, loss of civil rights etc. A person found guilty of a criminal offence can be ordered to suffer one or more of these penalties.

Criminal laws usually also give rise to the right of compensation to the victim.

All criminal laws in Turkey are set out in the Turkish Penal Code so any proposed new criminal law is in the form of an amendment to that code.

Commercial laws

Turkey's commercial law is set out in the Turkish Commercial Code, revised in 2012.

The new law was drafted in response to Turkey's negotiations for full-membership of the European Union (which required its laws to be harmonized with those of the EU) and its World Trade Organization membership obligations (which required better regulation of competition).

Employment laws

These are set out in the Turkish Labour code. See page 193.

Administrative laws

The Turkish judicial system makes a distinction between issues between private individuals or companies and issues in relation to the Government or the State and their various administrative entities.

Disputes between individuals or businesses and governmental bodies are dealt with under a special set of rules and a special court system.

Civil laws

Civil law covers the relationships between people. For these purposes, "people" means both real human beings and companies that have a separate legal identity or personality. Typical areas of civil law are the Law of Obligations (covering contracts and other duties) and the general Civil Law covering Family Law, Personal Law, Property Law, Inheritance Law, etc.

The key characteristic of civil law is that is gives rise to the obligation to compensate the other party if a person does not comply with the requirements of the law. It may also give rise to the power of obtaining a court order forcing somebody to do something they would not otherwise do - or to refrain from doing something they should not be doing.

The Civil Code was introduced in 1926 (replacing the earlier Sharia law that applied during the Ottoman Empire) and was based on the Swiss Civil Code: in turn influenced by the French civil codes. As such, it has a very European feel to it.

Insurance laws

In Turkey, the insurance sector is regulated by different types of laws, primarily the Commercial Code (for insurance contracts), the Insurance Law itself (for corporate, regulatory and operational matters) and the Turkish Obligations Code (for general contract law provisions).

Why are there these different systems of law in Turkey?

The law is, pretty much, a coherent whole and - from the end user's point of view - you do not need to get too excited about these administrative divisions. However, you need to know they exist and understand a *little* about them or you will not understand the advice given by your lawyers and the processes you will be following.

The divisions are mainly for administrative convenience. These various types of cases each have similarities with other cases of the same type.

You should note that a particular set of circumstances can fall into a legal category other than that which first seems obvious and, sometimes, into two or more legal categories. For example, if a person is seeking a divorce on the basis that their husband has been violent towards them, this will be a matter of family law (and so dealt with under the Civil Code) but the violence will probably also constitute a criminal offence and so could be punished under the Penal Code.

Police

In Turkey, there are several different types of police officers.

Each performs a different task and each has different powers.

On a day-to-day basis, this won't affect you very much. They're all police officers, most of them carry guns and they all expect you to do as they tell you!

However, there are important differences between them: for example, differences in the places where you will contact them and differences in the way you will pay any fines or penalty notices imposed.

Municipal Officers

The most junior people you may encounter are the municipal officers. These are appointed by the municipality and are only found in some towns and larger villages. They are not, strictly speaking, police officers and have very limited powers and responsibilities. They are, basically, there to enforce merchants' licences, parking regulations and similar matters. They have no power of arrest.

They are contacted via the town hall.

Police (*Polis*)

The national police cover the urban areas of Turkey. There are detachments (some of only two or three people) in most towns.

The national police deal with the work we traditionally associate with the police: the investigation of crime, the maintenance of public order and the control of traffic.

There is a national police station in each area. Its address is widely publicised. It will have its own individual telephone number but, in the case of emergencies, you can contact them via the national 112 emergency number.

Rural Police (*Jandarma*)

The *jandarma* have roots in the military. They are a branch of the Turkish Armed Forces and are responsible for the maintenance of public order in areas that fall outside the jurisdiction of the police forces (generally rural areas). They also deal with internal security, border control and other specific duties. They have the same powers and responsibilities as the *polis*.

Prosecution

In Turkey, the decision to prosecute and the process of prosecution is dealt with by a branch of the judiciary (known as the *savcı* or *Cumhuriyet savcısı*) rather than by the police. This public prosecutor directs the police as to any enquiries that they require to be made in connection with the investigation of the case and then assess the information gathered by the police, by their own investigations and by their questioning of any suspects to decide whether a prosecution is justified.

This is an arrangement common in many countries but alien to the Anglo-American tradition. See our chapter on criminal cases (page 331).

Lawyers

The main source of professional legal help available in Turkey is the lawyer (*avukat*). There are about 95,000 practising lawyers in Turkey. About 90% are generalists, covering most or all aspects of the law. All of them are professionally qualified and regulated by the Union of Turkish Bar Associations (*Türkiye Barolar Birliği* or TBB).

Their main duties are:

- To secure justice in public life

- To act in the best interests of their clients

- To avoid conflicts of interests

Unless the case is very small, the lawyer is required to give you an estimate of their likely fees and expenses. However, you should bear in mind that, perfectly genuinely, it is often impossible to give any sensible estimate of the total fees for dealing with a transaction until you know quite a lot about it. In these cases, you would expect a general indication of likely overall fees, plus a firm fee for dealing with the first stage of the transaction.

In many cases, the minimum fees are fixed by the lawyer's local bar association. They are, for court cases, typically fixed as a percentage of the value of the court case (10%, for example).

In other types of work the lawyers' fees depend upon the experience of the lawyer. They, typically, vary from TRY500-1,000 per hour (US$150-250, €125-225, £110-200).

Fees are subject to VAT (currently 18%) and you will also have to pay for any expenses incurred by the lawyer on your behalf. These will include things such as Land Registry fees, court fees and travelling expenses.

It is possible to agree a fixed fee for certain types of work. This is a fee that does not depend upon the amount of time it takes the lawyer to complete the task.

'No win, no fee' deals are illegal under Turkish law.

Legal Aid/Subsidized Legal Assistance

There is a system of Legal Aid (public assistance towards legal fees) in Turkey.

For criminal cases, a lawyer will be appointed for you if you cannot afford to appoint your own. These are, typically, junior lawyers who have gone onto a rota to provide this service. They are paid (at a very modest rate) by the state.

For civil cases, you must ask for legal aid. It is rarely available. It is means tested and also only granted where needed. It is administered by the local Bar Association.

In addition, some lawyers do undertake work 'pro bono' (in the public interest and without a fee). However, inevitably, these occasions are rare. They usually arise where there is a perceived great injustice, especially in a high-profile case.

Choosing a lawyer

If you need to see a lawyer, you need to see a good lawyer: not just someone who's going through the motions and racking up fees.

To do this, you will need to do some research. The research will take you a little time, but if the case is important it is worth spending some time to make sure that you have the best person dealing with it.

A full list of practising lawyers can, for most places, be found via the TBB website (**www.barobirlik.org.tr**). This gives you access to the website of the bar association in your area. However, far better than simply seeking the name of a lawyer from the TBB list is to have a lawyer recommended to you by someone who has already used their services and was happy with them.

If you need something done in another part of Turkey but have already used a lawyer elsewhere in Turkey, that lawyer will usually be able to recommend someone in the area - even if the work is not of a type that your lawyer normally undertakes.

If you do not know anybody in Turkey or, at least, if you don't know anyone who has used a lawyer, you may find some lawyers listed on the website of the embassy or consulate of your own country in Turkey. They will be lawyers who speak your language and have some experience of dealing with people from your country.

Alternatively, your lawyer back home may have connections and be able to make a recommendation. Or, of course, you could contact the authors of this book!

For international clients, international experience is really important. This allows your lawyer to draw to your attention the ways in which things are different here.

If you're buying a property, be very careful about accepting the recommendation of the estate agent who is selling it. You will never know whether that lawyer is really working for you or whether he's looking after the interests of the agent (possibly his cousin or brother) who introduces a large part of his work to him.

Law firms in Turkey tend to be small - typically only two or three people. Many lawyers even work on their own rather than as part of a firm, however small.

Most do not have a sophisticated web presence but an increasing number do have a website containing useful materials. If you can't understand the documents on their website, you're not likely to be able to understand documents they prepare for you. Communication is a key requirement in your relationship with your lawyer, so those lawyers are probably best avoided.

Once a lawyer has been recommended to you, or you've identified a likely candidate, don't be afraid to contact their office and speak to them. They will not think this is in any way surprising.

If you feel comfortable with the lawyer, sense he or she knows what they are talking about and find that they can communicate with you in a way that you understand, you may appoint them to act for you. This is normally done by way of an exchange of emails. Some sort of payment on account of fees will also usually be expected.

Notaries

Notaries play an important role within the Turkish legal system. This will be of no surprise if you come from a mainland European country but quite surprising if you're used only to systems in places such as the US and the UK: the so-called Anglo-Saxon legal tradition.

What is a Notary?

In Turkey, as in most European countries, the profession of Notary is an independent profession. It is related to but independent of the general profession of lawyer.

Notaries are in the odd position of being independent professionals, running their own business and generating their income from the fees they earn but, at the same time, being appointed by the State and an essential part of the State administrative system.

They start their training by taking a law degree and then continue, not by going into practice as a lawyer, but by applying to be a Notary and then taking the specialist Notarial exam.

Thus, they are a far cry from the Notary in the US or some other countries, where the Notary may have no legal qualifications at all but exist only to witness the authenticity of signatures.

What work does a Notary do?

Article 1 of the Notary Public law says that being a Notary Public is a public service. A Notary Public documents operations (for assuring security and preventing disagreements) and carries out other duties given by the law.

They perform a number of tasks including:

- Producing 'official' copies of documents

- Documenting vehicle sales

- Preparing Wills

- Preparing Powers of Attorney

- Preparing declarations and undertakings

- Preparing joint venture agreements, especially in simpler cases

- Preparing contracts for the sale of land or buildings - but not advising the parties about the transaction

- Producing certain company documents

- Producing a whole range of contracts, Powers of Attorney and other documents.

Notaries are not engaged in dealing with court cases or in advising about criminal law or family law.

They are not there to advise the parties. Their role is to make sure that the appropriate procedures are followed when a document is produced and that the document contains all the information required by law.

How do you find a Notary in Turkey?

There is at least one Notary in most towns in Turkey, however small. You can approach a Notary directly or you may be introduced to a Notary by your lawyer, accountant or adviser.

Whichever way you make contact with a Notary, his duties to you remain the same.

What happens in a Notary's office?

When you need to approach a Notary, there are various steps that will always be taken.

The first thing that will happen is that you will be asked to produce proof of your identity. In the case of a foreigner, identity is always proved by their passport. The Notary will usually take and retain a copy of your passport. This process of identification will normally be done by one of the Notary's assistants (rather than by the Notary him or herself), who will then register your case. If you go to the Notary ten times for ten different things you will still have to go through this process every time and the office will make ten different registrations.

An assistant in the office will then usually establish your requirements. For example: if you want to make a Will, what do you want to do with your assets?

When you see the Notary's assistant in this way - or even if you see the Notary himself - it is important to note that he will be establishing your wishes. He is not there to give you legal advice.

It is only in very rare cases that you will see the Notary himself at this stage. If you do see him, it is usually because the assistant has identified something unusual or difficult about your case.

Usually - though this varies a little from Notary to Notary - the assistant will then go through with you the documents that have been prepared to make sure that they are correct and properly reflect your wishes. They will then make any alterations necessary.

If you do not speak fluent Turkish, the assistant will - as required by law - arrange for an official translator to be present to translate the documents that have been prepared into your language and get your confirmation that you have understood them.

As the assistants often have the power to sign documents on behalf of the Notary, you may not - certainly in simple cases - see the Notary during the entire process! For those used to dealing with Notaries in other countries, such as France, this comes as a great surprise. Do not be worried. The system works surprisingly well.

The law requires the Notary (or the assistant authorised to sign the document) to read to you the document you are about to sign. This can often cause difficulties because, in the age of the word processor and very cautious lawyers, some of these documents can extend to many pages. Usually they hand the document over to you - if a translation is not required - before signing, for you to read it through. When you are ready to sign you will confirm that you have read and understood the document yourself, or that it has been translated to you.

One thing you will notice, whether you speak Turkish or not, is just how quickly someone can read a document aloud. If you think of the speed of the 'terms & conditions' at the end of a radio or TV ad and then double it, you'll be about right!

Once the document has been read, the Notary or their assistant will ask you to sign it in their presence. Occasionally - for example, in the case of Wills - the law will require additional witnesses. If so, you will have been told to bring them with you or the Notary will provide them.

Once you have signed the document, if there are any taxes to pay or any expenses (such as the fees of the translator), you will be asked to pay them. You will also have to pay the notary's fees. You will always be given a receipt.

Usually, payment will be required in cash. Banks know this and there is usually a nearby ATM. Take note that that no Notary in Turkey takes credit card payments. Nor do they take cheques.

Sometimes these fees and taxes can be substantial, well beyond the amount you can draw out at an ATM on a normal debit or credit card. Obtaining the funds can, therefore, require some advance planning - such as drawing them out from the ATM on several different cards or over a couple of days or withdrawing them from a bank.

What happens to the documents?

The Notary will take two hard, signed, copies of any documents and then return one original to you. In case of a Will, an original is sent to the Notaries' headquarters, to be eventually sent to the 'first instance' court (the court where your case starts) upon your death.

He will then keep the other original documents that he has prepared, together with all the copies of your documents that he has taken, as part of his official records known as his 'archive'.

He will prepare copies of any documents that need to be registered and they will go to the relevant registry.

He will also prepare a copy of the documents he prepared for you and, in the case of a sale, the other party.

He will prepare additional copies if you ask him to do so, but this will be at a modest additional cost.

How much are the Notary's fees in Turkey?

It is almost impossible to give you any sensible guidance on this because they depend upon the type of document being prepared *and* how long it is. For example, the fee for preparing a Power of Attorney document in connection with transferring the ownership of a property will vary depending on the number of the words used and, if you sign a promissory agreement for purchase, the value of the property.

Who controls Notaries?

The Association of Notaries (*Türkiye Noterler Birliği*) regulates Notaries in Turkey in accordance with the Notary Law of 1972.

What happens if I have a complaint about a Notary?

Your complaint should be made to the Association of Notaries, who will investigate it and give you a written response to it.

Mediation & Arbitration

Mediation

Mediation was developed as a much cheaper and faster alternative to going to court. It was very seldom used in Turkey. However, lawyers with over five years' experience are now taking compulsory courses, followed by an exam, and becoming a qualified mediator registered with the Ministry of Justice. In some court cases, parties will be obliged to apply for mediation before proceeding with a court case. This is to save both time and money. The system is still under development!

In mediation, the parties agree to an independent person being appointed to help them find a solution to their problem. The objective is the same as when you and the person have a face-to-face meeting, but you're helped by someone who has a lot of experience in bringing people together, bridging gaps and finding workable solutions to problems. They can also help by explaining the legal background to the parties so that they can understand the likely consequences of not reaching a settlement.

The mediator has no legal powers and cannot force either party to accept any solution. The effort will either work or it will not work! Whichever is the outcome, it will have been fast and (relatively) inexpensive. The cost and timescale involved will depend upon the seriousness of the dispute and the value involved.

The mediator will be a lawyer who has received special training in these skills, as explained above. Expect to pay about €1,000 for a half-day mediation meeting, including the preparatory work that the mediator must do to understand your dispute. For a complex dispute, involving many documents, it could be a lot more.

The process will often involve separate meetings with the two parties before bringing them together for the mediation meeting itself. If the parties agree, a percentage of the amount of dispute will be paid to the mediator separately by way of his or her fees.

You cannot force the other party to agree to mediation.

In Turkey, the Bar Association will give you preliminary advice about how to go about arranging mediation - it is, after all, specially licenced lawyers who can provide this service - and whether it is likely to be suitable in your case.

This is a recent development, but it's going to be more common: it is a requirement that, for some types of court case, you must first try mediation. Examples include employment and minor criminal cases.

Case study

Dean Perry

Architect, Australian, 40

The problem

A local Turkish building company consulted an Australian architect, Dean Perry, in connection with the design of a swimming pool and changing room complex. The company later alleged that the design did not comply with local construction regulations and refused to pay the balance of the architect's fee.

The contract between the developer and the architect used a standard international contract which was silent on the question of the standards to be incorporated into the design. It was also silent on the question of the Australian architect's responsibilities and the point at which his work would have to be approved by a local architect in order to be accepted for official purposes.

The solution

Rather than going to court, the parties (then unusually in Turkey) agreed on arbitration and the arbitrator found that it be an implied term of the contract that the design would meet local construction standards and that the architect, on the face of it, had therefore failed to deliver an adequate service. However, the arbitrator also found that the alleged breach of local construction standards was trivial (involving the thickness of insulation around some pipes) and, even if it was accepted that there was a breach - which it was not - the defect could be remedied easily and for a few hundred dollars.

As a result, the architect was entitled to be paid his fee, less the cost of any remedial work needed. This whole process took less than six weeks, rather than the minimum of five years that it would have taken through the courts - and it cost a *lot* less, as well.

Arbitration

Arbitration can also be seen as a less formal, more flexible, cheaper, and faster alternative to a court case.

It can follow on from a failed mediation.

The main difference between mediation and arbitration is that arbitration can be legally binding upon the parties.

Arbitration is not common in Turkey, except in the case of disputes with insurance companies and major construction contracts.

Because of this I will not deal with it further here.

The court system

As we have already said, there are two main types of courts in Turkey: criminal and civil. In addition, there are military courts and a state security court, which we do not consider further in this book.

The criminal courts, as you might expect, deal with all criminal cases while the civil courts deal with almost everything else.

In both cases, the court is divided into two parts: one that deals with smaller (less important) cases and the other which deals with more important cases.

Criminal Courts

The basic criminal courts (*asliye ceza*) have a single professional judge. They deal with minor cases. There is one in every city and in every district.

The other criminal courts deal with crimes with a maximum penalty of over ten years' imprisonment. They have a presiding judge and two other members. They are aided by a public prosecutor.

Civil Courts

The lower civil courts (peace courts or *sulh mahkemeleri*) also have a single professional judge. There is at least one in every district. It covers all types of cases assigned to it by the Code of Civil Procedure and other laws.

The other civil courts of first instance (*asliye hukuk mahkemeleri*) cover all civil cases other than those assigned to the lower civil courts. There is one in every city and district, sometimes divided into several branches dealing with different types of cases, according to the size of the place and its requirements.

See our chapters on crime and criminal cases (page 331) and disputes and court cases (page 320) for more information about how this works.

There is a right of appeal if either of the parties to a case is dissatisfied with the result.

Judges

All judges in Turkey are law graduates, except administrative judges (who can be graduates from another social science).

They take an exam and, if they pass, they undertake a further one year's (previously two years', but recently reduced) specialist training.

At the end of that period they will usually be appointed to a junior judicial position and then, over the years, they may be promoted into more demanding roles, usually in the larger towns and cities.

The judges in Turkey are of high calibre but - as in many countries that have adopted the Napoleonic system, where judges are appointed direct from law school - it is very often obvious in the junior courts that they lack experience. This is sometimes reflected in their being rather timid in the decisions that they will make and, on other occasions, it leads them to go too far.

As a result, far more cases are taken to appeal in Turkey (about 90%) than you would expect in a country where the judges have many years of practical legal experience before they are appointed as even junior judges.

There is no feeling within Turkey that judges are corruptible.

Juries

Juries are not used in Turkey.

Powers of Attorney

Written by **Başak Yildiz Orkun**
Managing Partner (Legal Department) at Orkun & Orkun
www.orkunorkun.com • info@orkunorkun.com

A Power of Attorney is a legal document that authorises another person to do something such as signing a document, opening a bank account, or attending a meeting on your behalf and with your full (or, at least, some limited but defined) authority.

The contents of a Power vary a lot depending upon what it is to be used for. However, the process of making one is always the same.

Here in Turkey we use Powers of Attorney a lot. This is to save our clients from having to come here, often at inconvenient times, to do things that might be just procedural. Fortunately, the process is quite simple, at least at our end!

We use Powers mainly for people setting up businesses or buying houses in Turkey and for dealing with court cases in Turkey. However, they can be used for lots of other purposes.

The Process

Granting and signing the Power in Turkey

Your lawyer will, working with a local Notary, prepare the Power of Attorney. They will make sure it contains all the necessary clauses to allow your transaction to proceed smoothly.

They will make an appointment for you to attend at the Notary's office to sign the document. They will often accompany you at that appointment.

The Notary will then register a copy of the Power in his archive and give you an original copy of it.

You then give the document to the person you have appointed to sign for you. This will, often, be your lawyer.

That's it. Simple! Better still, it's (relatively) cheap.

Granting and signing the Power in another country

Sometimes it might not be convenient or possible for you to be in Turkey to sign a Power of Attorney.

Turkey is a signatory to The Hague Convention of 1961 - 'The Hague Convention Abolishing the Requirement of Legalisation for Foreign Public Documents'. If you live in a country that is also a signatory (and most are), the process of granting a Power of Attorney is quite straightforward.

Case study

Kosta Buros

Property investor, Greek, 32

The problem

Kostas was buying a property in a new development near Bodrum.
He's a very busy man, so he wanted to set up a Power of Attorney with
his Turkish lawyer. He didn't know whether it would be better to do
this from Cyprus or to fly out once to Turkey and arrange it there.

The solution

After working out the costs, it turned out to be far more sensible to fly
to Turkey and sort out the Power of Attorney with a local Notary,
rather than trying to arrange it from Greece.

Not only was the cost less (cheap enough to justify a budget flight from
Athens), but the afternoon's process and one overnight stay was going
to be far less trying on Kostas' patience than the long rigmarole of
waiting for documents from Turkey, meeting with a Greek Notary,
legalising the Power and then sending the completed Power of
Attorney back to Turkey. Better still, he got to spend a couple of days
in Turkey with his girlfriend!

He also took the opportunity to meet his lawyers and discuss with
them the best ownership structure for the property, taking into
account his forthcoming marriage. As they would both be on the island
he could then adjust the proposed Power of Attorney so that it took
into account the decisions made. In this case, they ended up needed
two Powers as they decided to buy the house in both their names.

If you need to produce any documents (such as a Power of Attorney)
that will need to be Notarised, it is often cheaper to take a long
weekend in Turkey and produce them whilst you're in the country,
instead of going through the process of preparing them 'back home'.

You can find a full list of the Hague Convention signatories on the relevant Wikipedia page: **bit.ly/2DMDZfY**

The Starting Point

Your lawyer in Turkey will draft the necessary Power on your behalf. This will be after discussing your requirements.

It is important that it contains all the necessary clauses and so this is not something you should do yourself.

The terms of the Power - the authorities it gives to the person appointed to take steps for you - are usually quite wide, to make sure that everything that we might need to do is covered. The authorities here are quite strict in the way they interpret Powers of Attorney and so, if something is not specifically and clearly authorised, they are likely to refuse to accept the Power for that purpose.

The Power must be in Turkish. My firm always prepares Powers in dual language form - in Turkish and in your language - so that you will understand what they say!

Your lawyer will send you a draft of the Power. We do this in Microsoft Word format so that you can send it on to your local Notary (see below).

If you live in a Hague Convention Country

When you receive the Power, contact a convenient local Notary and arrange the Notary to incorporate the text we have sent you within a document that meets the needs of your country. Notaries will know what this is. They are very familiar with the whole process.

They will also need certain information about you: proof of your identity, proof of your address etc. Exactly what varies from country to country.

The Notary will then ask you to come to sign the finished document. This will usually be the next working day.

When you attend to sign the document, you must take proof of your identity (your passport) and of your address (typically, two documents such as bank statements or utility bills in your name), together - sometimes - with four passport size photographs: required for Powers to be used for transferring the ownership of land. The precise documents that you will need to take with you will vary depending upon the country in which you are signing the Power. The Notary will tell you exactly what is needed.

Once the document has been signed it will need to be 'legalised'. This process involves sending it to the appropriate body in your country. They certify that the Notary is qualified to deal with this document and that his signature on the document matches that in their records. Your Notary will usually arrange for this to be done on your behalf.

The Notary's fee for doing all this varies enormously from country to country. It is seldom cheap. Allow €250. Make sure you ask for an estimate.

This can all take some time. Allow two weeks until you get the document back.

Once the Power has been signed and legalised, send the original to us **by courier** (UPS, DHL, DPD etc.). Our postal service is quite good but things can get lost and it takes time and quite a lot of money to replace a lost Power.

Allow a week for the Power to reach Turkey.

If you *don't* live in a Hague Convention Country

The process is more complicated. You will have to ask your local Notary exactly what is required. They will be familiar with the requirements.

Once all the formalities required to permit the use of the Power in Turkey have been completed, send the original to us **by courier**, as above.

Do you really want to use a Power of Attorney?

The cost of preparing Powers of Attorney is quite high. For many people - provided they have the time - it can be cheaper to come out to Turkey for a few days to sign the documents here in person rather than appointing someone to do so on their behalf using a Power of Attorney.

There are some downsides to doing this: for example, if the arrangements change at the last minute (for example, the signing is delayed for a week) you may no longer be available and you can be in some difficulty. This does happen: quite often. Also, as the transactions will be in Turkish, you may not feel confident about signing, even with a translator, since you most likely would not understand the process.

If you decide to sign in person and, having come to Turkey, for some reason you cannot remain until the document is finally ready, you can still prepare a Power of Attorney whilst you are over here, at a fraction of the cost of doing so in your own country because the document does not need to be legalised.

Contracts

Written by **Başak Yildiz Orkun**
Managing Partner (Legal Department) at Orkun & Orkun
www.orkunorkun.com • info@orkunorkun.com

Most countries in the world use one of two basic systems when it comes to contracts: the Continental European (Roman Law/Napoleonic Law) system or the Anglo-American system. The system in Turkey is modelled on the Continental European system but has been updated and (in some respects) simplified.

Does the contract have to be in writing?

As explained above, contracts don't *have* to be in writing, except for some special types of contract (e.g. contracts for the sale of property).

However, as in any country, it is much better if contracts are in writing. Though the centuries, wise lawyers have said that verbal contracts are usually not worth the paper they are written on! It is too easy for misunderstandings to occur and too hard to prove what was agreed.

There are two ways in which contracts are, generally, produced in writing.

The first is the 'simple' written contract. See below for the formalities.

The second is a contract prepared by or witnesses by a Notary public.

Does the contract have to be in Turkish?

No - but it is, in practical terms, highly desirable for the contract to be either in Turkish or in dual language format (Turkish in one column and your chosen language in the other). If it is in dual language format, you should make sure that the legally binding version is declared to be the Turkish version.

The reason that this is so desirable is that if there is a dispute, and the contract has to be interpreted by a judge, it will be much harder for the judge to do this if the contract is not in Turkish. The judge will probably require the intervention of an official translator. Not only is that potentially quite expensive but it also introduces a level of uncertainty in that you can never be quite sure that the interpreter's translation will precisely reflect the subtlety of what has been agreed.

Do you need to use any special type of contract in Turkey?

Generally speaking, no. Turkey, like many countries, allows what is called "freedom of contract". This means that the parties are - with a few exceptions - free to agree the terms, the format, and the jurisdiction to apply to their contract.

The exceptions may require special formats. For example, some might require the contract to be in writing, some might require it to be signed in front of a Notary, or some might impose the use of Turkish law and the jurisdiction of the Turkish courts to transactions of that type.

Examples of contracts that, under Turkish law, must be in writing include:

- Contracts entitling estate agents to commission

- Promissory contracts for the future sale of property (which should also be produced by the Notary)

- Marriage contracts (which must be signed in front of a town hall official)

- Vehicle sales (which must be signed in the presence of a Notary)

- Employment contracts

- Buy-back agreements for land (which must be signed at the Land Registry *Tapu Ofis)*

- Contracts for the sale of land (which must be signed at the *Tapu Ofis)*

For most of our clients, the most important exception to there being no requirement for any special form of contract relates to the sale of land located in Turkey. For this purpose, 'land' includes not only the land itself but also any buildings on it. Although there is no restriction as to the content of such contracts, they must be in writing. To be fully enforceable, they should be signed in front of a Notary and the contract *must* eventually be formalised by the signature of the property transfer document (*tapu*) at the Land Registry (*Tapu Ofis*). See our chapter on buying property (page 364).

Even when they are not a legal requirement, written contracts will make a huge difference to your ability to prove your claims in the event of a dispute; therefore, written contracts are highly recommended by our firm, even when they are not legally required. See the various sections of this book for further relevant details.

These different types of contract look different and contain different clauses. They also often require the people entering the contract to go through different formalities for the contract to be legally valid.

In many cases, even where there is no specific legal requirement, it makes sense to use a Turkish format contract in preference to a document drawn up in accordance with the law of another country. There are several reasons for this:

- The main subject matter of the contract is likely to be in Turkey and so, if there is a dispute, it may be most appropriate for it to be dealt with by the courts of Turkey.

- In some cases, the law requires you to make the contract subject to Turkish law. The most common example of this is a contract for the sale of land (including houses and other buildings built on land).

- If the contract is to be dealt with in Turkey in the case of a dispute, the judge will be much more familiar with the Turkish form of contract (and language) than he would be interpreting a different form of contract, especially if it is stated to be subject to the law of another country.

Are there any taxes payable when a contract is signed?

This depends. So-called 'private' contracts (contracts signed by the parties but not in front of a Notary) will not give rise to any obligation to pay Stamp Duty, but they might not be fully enforceable. 'Public' contracts (contracts signed in front of a Notary) will usually give rise to the payment of Stamp Duty (in 2018 0.189% to 0.948%).

In some cases, a contract could relate to an item that is subject to VAT (sales tax) or property transfer tax. In these cases, the VAT (typically 18%) or property transfer tax (usually 4%) would also be payable.

If you want to use a Turkish-style contract, what is required?

For a contract to be valid under Turkish law there are five main requirements. These are set out in the Turkish Code of Obligations and various other codes. They are:

1. The free and informed consent of the parties to the contract

   This means that the parties must be clear that they are agreeing to a legally binding contract.

2. The parties each having the legal capacity to enter a contract

   This means that they must be of legal age (18) and of sound mind.

3. A certain and clear object

   The contract must be clear about what the parties intend, and you must be able to work this out at the time when the contract is signed.

4. The contract must be to perform an act that is possible and lawful

5. The contract must not be to do anything immoral or contrary to public policy

Thus, you will see, the formal requirements are very flexible. In particular, readers who are from an Anglo-Saxon background should note that there is no precise equivalent to the Anglo Saxon concept of consideration: i.e. that the promises made in the contract must be in return for something.

Contracts can be made by way of offer and acceptance. In this case, once an offer has been made, the contract will become binding when it is accepted by the other party.

Limitation periods

Whatever rights your contract may give you, they're likely to expire after a certain period of time. The date when this happens is variously known as the "limitation date" or the "prescription date".

The general limit is ten years from the date when the action occurred and five years from when you learn about your rights to take action under the contract; *or* when you should have become aware of your rights to take action under the contract. However, claims based upon certain rights have different periods. For example, a claim based upon an allegation of unjust enrichment must be made within two years, and a claim in respect of employment payments due to you must be made within five years.

Case study

Andy Young

Website Designer, English, 27

The problem

Andy had taken on a job with a Turkish jewellery maker. He built them an attractive but simple website listing their services, contact details, and featuring plenty of pictures.

The company, though, wanted a custom shopping facility added to the website, which would take Andy quite a lot more time, and was not in the contract. The company said they would pay Andy for all of the work once he added this functionality.

The solution

Andy had had bad experiences in these circumstances before, and was reluctant to do any more work unless he had a contract to cover it and a price agreed. This was particularly important with clients such as this, who understood very little about the things he was being asked to do.

He therefore set up a casual face-to-face meeting with the woman he'd been communicating with most often. He explained to her the process of adding custom code for an online shop. She was surprised that it involved so much work!

As the company could not afford many more hours of Andy's time, they came to a compromise: Andy would use one of the several open-source shopping add-ons and add it to the website for free; and the jewellery company would include an advertisement for Andy's services in their next email campaign.

After the meeting, Andy made sure to send an email - and get a response - confirming this agreement. It all went smoothly!

Formalities for 'private' written contracts

There is no special formality.

The contract can either be in the handwriting of one of the persons making the contract or it can be produced in some other way. Typed contracts (produced on a word processor) are now almost universal.

A written contract needs, in any case, to be signed by or on behalf of the parties. See the section on Powers of Attorney (page 288) if it is proposed that one of the parties will not sign in person.

Signatures do not need to be witnessed, though it can be useful to do this for important contracts so that there is no doubt that the signature is authentic.

Signatures on behalf of a company are authenticated by the production of an official "signature circular", confirming that the person signing is authorised to sign on behalf of the company in question.

It is desirable that the bottom of each page should be signed by both parties.

Formalities for 'public' notarial contracts

A Notarial contract is a contract either prepared by or signed in the presence of a Notary. These contracts are usually prepared by the Notary.

It's important to reiterate that, in Turkey, a Notary is a highly respected professional who started off as a fully-qualified lawyer before undertaking extra studies and being allowed to practice as a Notary. It is not at all the same as a Notary found in the US, or some other countries, whose sole job is to witness the signature of documents and who may have no qualifications at all.

In the case of a Notarial contract, the parties' wishes will be conveyed to the Notary's staff - often by way of a draft document - and they will produce a contract that incorporates those wishes whilst being clear and complying with any required formalities.

When the time comes to sign the contract, the parties must produce to the Notary proof of their identity (usually their passport) and any supporting documents for the contract: e.g. the ownership document for the promissory sale of a property.

Once the Notary is satisfied as to the parties' identity, he will allow the parties to read the contract but he must then read it to them himself: word by word. This is a hangover from the days, not so long ago, when many people were illiterate.

If one of the parties does not speak Turkish, the Notary must arrange for an official translator to translate the contract for that person's benefit. Notarial contracts are always in Turkish.

Once the contract has been signed, a fee is paid to the Notary and the original document is stored with the Notary's archive.

One original is supplied to each of the parties. If required by law, the Notary will also arrange for a copy of the document to be filed with another specified entity. If requested by the parties he will also, at a small extra cost, produce additional copies of the document.

Powers of Attorney

Sometimes it is not convenient for a person to attend in person to sign the contract.

In this case, they can appoint someone else to do so on their behalf. To do this they need to sign a Power of Attorney. See page 288.

Which court deals with any dispute?

If the contract relates to the sale of land or buildings in Turkey, any dispute must be dealt with by the courts of Turkey and the contract must be interpreted in accordance with Turkish law.

In any other case, the parties to the contract are free to choose whichever way they like for dealing with any dispute and to make the contract subject to whichever legal system they prefer. So, for example, a contract for the sale of a business could be governed by the law of Turkey, the law of the US State of Maryland or by the law of England or Germany. Sometimes this can be useful, especially if both the parties to the contract are based in that place.

Generally, any dispute about the contract will be dealt with by the courts in the country whose law governs that contract but this is not a requirement. The parties can (in most cases) make whatever arrangements they choose. For example, it is possible to have a contract subject to the courts of Turkey but to the law of another country. However, this is generally not a good idea because of the expense and the complexity it brings into the case.

If the court is subject to the jurisdiction of the Turkish courts, it will be dealt with by the civil court.

Consumer Problems

Written by **Başak Yildiz Orkun**
Managing Partner (Legal Department) at Orkun & Orkun
www.orkunorkun.com • info@orkunorkun.com

Most countries have laws intended to protect the consumer. Turkey is no exception. The need for consumer protection arises because of the usual imbalance between the power of the trader and the power of the consumer. A consumer contract is usually prepared by the trader, not freely negotiated. There is little disclosure of background information and so little possibility of effective due diligence. To make matters worse, the value of the goods or services is often quite low, making recourse to the courts an uneconomic and ineffective remedy.

Consumer protection law is less developed in Turkey than it is in many other countries.

The advent of many international visitors and businesses has also meant that the position is now less satisfactory. Some foreign-owned businesses based in Turkey may not operate to the level of ethics and honesty traditional in Turkey and, sadly, some local Turkish run businesses seem to have learned lessons from the unscrupulous practises of their worst international competitors.

Equally, international visitors - especially those from Europe and the United States - have expectations when it comes to consumer protection and are surprised and disappointed when they are not met in Turkey.

Having said that, Turkey has a consumer code, which governs the rights of consumers.

Consumer contracts are defined as contracts between a person selling as part of a business activity and either a private individual *or* a business not entering a contract for business purposes. What they are selling could be goods or services. Thus:

- A contract between you and your neighbour (two private individuals) under which you buy the neighbour's car *is not* a consumer contract.

- A contract under which you but a car from the local Ford dealer *is* a consumer contract.

- A contract between a supermarket and ABC Architects Ltd under which ABC Architects Ltd buys a kettle for use in its staff room *is* a consumer contract.

- A contract between ABC Architects Ltd and XYZ Developers Ltd under which ABC Architects Ltd agrees to provide architectural services for XYZ Ltd's new development *is not* a consumer contract.

A contract between two businesses where one of them is not entering the contract for the purposes of their business - for example, as goods to trade - *is* a consumer contract and so protected by consumer law. For example, if ABC Lawyers purchase sofas from

XYZ Furniture Ltd, if there is a problem with the sofas this will be a consumer contract and the dispute will be subject to Consumer Rights.

What consumer protection rights does a foreigner have?

Exactly the same as a Turkish person.

Rights under the general law

Most consumer protection issues arise out of contracts, whether written or verbal.

Under the general law of Turkey there is no distinction between a consumer contract and any other type of contract when it comes to the obligations of the parties. The only distinction concerns how any disputes are to be dealt with.

Specific consumer protection legislation in Turkey

There are various pieces of legislation in Turkey specifically aimed at consumer protection. They give the consumer various rights:

The right to return goods

Consumers may return any goods that they have purchased, within 14 days, without having to give any justification for their decision to do so. The goods must not be damaged.

They are entitled to a full refund.

This right does not apply to certain things such as underwear and perishables.

Internet sales and other 'buying at a distance' contracts

There is a specific regulation relating to 'buying at a distance' contracts: i.e. contracts for the provision of goods or services that are not made on the premises of the trader.

Who can help?

If you need help with a consumer protection problem in Turkey, there are two main options:

- You can contact the Consumer Commission and report the problem to them.
- You can take the matter up through your lawyer and the courts.

In either case, you should have first notified the other party about the nature of your dispute and given them a reasonable time (usually interpreted as 14 days) to put the problem right.

The Consumer Commission

Turkey has a special arrangement - the Consumer Commission - to deal with small consumer disputes, meaning disputes where the value is less than TRY3,000. In fact, disputes involving amounts less than TRY2,000 are dealt with by the Commission in the town concerned, and disputes involving amounts between TRY2,000 and TRY3,000 are dealt with by the provincial commissioner.

The Commission is set up by the provincial governor and comprises four people: one a lawyer, one from the municipal council, one from the local chamber of commerce or merchants, and one from a consumer organization.

Any issues falling within its jurisdiction are submitted to the Commission on a special form, which can be downloaded from its website: **tuketici.gtb.gov.tr**.

The Commission then asks the business for a response to the complaint. It then decides whether the complaint is justified. There is no trial or public hearing.

This is a simple and quick procedure, which can resolve lots of small problems.

Special Court of Consumer Rights

Disputes involving more than TRY3,610 must be dealt with by the Special Court of Consumer Rights. These are not available in every town. If there is no Special Court of Consumer Rights in a particular place, disputes will go to the regular civil courts.

There are no court charges for cases brought before the Special Court of Consumer Rights.

The process followed in this court is similar to that followed in any civil court trial.

The Court's powers allow it to order that the goods should be returned to the seller or that the price of the goods or services should be refunded or reduced. It cannot order general compensation (for example, for damage caused to your clothes by a defective washing machine). For that you would have to go to the ordinary civil courts.

How long does it take?

The Consumer Commission has a target of dealing with cases within six months of a complaint being received. The Commission may extend the period for another six months - but only once. The claim of a foreigner who is not resident in Turkey will be solved as a priority.

How much does it cost?

There is no charge for using the Consumer Commission or for using the services of the specialist Consumer Court.

If you are going to use your lawyer, seek an estimate of likely fees.

Defective Products

Written by **Başak Yildiz Orkun**
Managing Partner (Legal Department) at Orkun & Orkun
www.orkunorkun.com • info@orkunorkun.com

In Turkey, defective products are dealt with under the general law and, in particular, under the Code of Obligations and the Consumer Code.

However, there are some issues regarding claims arising out of defective products which are worth grouping together and it is those issues that form the substance of this section.

What is a defective product?

For the purposes of this chapter we mean any item that you buy but which turns out not to work properly or which causes you loss or damage because it is defective, or any product belonging to some other person that causes you loss or damage.

For example, if you were unlucky enough to have an artificial hip fitted and it were to snap as a result of fault in manufacture, you can imagine how painful and expensive that could be. That would be a defective product. Similarly, if less dramatically, a watch or a car could break down very soon after purchase.

As to products that don't belong to you, if you suffer injury as a result of a defective product belonging to somebody else you would also be able to claim compensation. For example, if you were sitting in a restaurant and a chair collapsed under you because of defective design you can file a claim against both the restaurant and the designer or supplier of the chair.

The basis of liability in these cases is usually that the person you're claiming against did not comply with the terms of their contract with you or that they were negligent in the way they dealt with you.

Under Turkish law it is an implied term of every contract that anything you buy is fit for the purpose for which it was sold. This is a term that you cannot sign away.

So, if the hospital sold you the defective hip or the garage sold you the defective car you may well have a claim against them under this general principle of law.

What are my general rights?

Generally, if you receive defective goods, you will have the following rights:

- Return the goods and receive a refund

- Keep the goods and ask for a reduction in the price

- Ask for the item to be repaired

- Ask for the goods to be exchanged

- Seek compensation - through the civil courts - for any losses you have suffered (e.g. if a defective tyre causes your car to crash)

What sort of injury or damage can I claim for?

You can claim for any injury or damage caused to you or your property as a result of being supplied a product that was not fit for the purpose for which it was sold, or which was sold to you negligently.

An example of a negligent sale of a product would be if you described to the shop what your requirements were and they advised you to buy a product that was not suitable for those requirements - e.g., if you bought a jack to lift up your 3-tonne Land Rover and the shop recommended one only suitable only for a 1-tonne Mini. Then, when it collapsed, you would be able to claim from the shop on the basis of their negligence.

The claim could involve injury to you or your family, damage to your goods, pain, inconvenience, or unnecessary expense.

Who can I claim against?

The claim will lie against the supplier of the product. In some cases, you may have a claim against the manufacturer of the product. Your lawyer will be able to advise you of the best approach in your case.

Deemed defect

If a defect occurs within six months of the date of delivery of a product, it is assumed to have been there when the product was delivered and so your right to take action is preserved.

When can I make my claim?

Generally, a claim must be made within two years of the date when you suffered any damage but there is a five-year limitation period for any claims arising out of a dwelling or holiday home.

If the defect was hidden (a legal term that can be quite difficult to understand - and the meaning of which can vary quite a lot depending on the type of product - but which will generally mean a defect that could not have been discovered by a reasonable inspection of the product) then the time during which you can make a claim can extend for up to 20 years or for two years from the time when you discovered the defect.

How much will it cost?

It is impossible to say as so much depends upon the individual facts of each case. Your lawyer should be able to give you an estimate but it will be only an estimate.

There is no form of public legal assistance in Turkey for this type of case.

Turkey: how things *really* work

Note also that 'no win, no fee' arrangements are illegal in Turkey.

How long will it take?

Again, it is very hard to predict. Sometimes the facts will be so obvious that the company concerned, or its insurers, will agree quite quickly to a payment in settlement of the claim. In other cases, the case will have to go to trial, in which case it could take two or three years.

Even in a simple case, the process is not likely to take less than six months.

What happens if I lose?

As with all court cases, if you bring a case against somebody and lose, you are likely to have to pay their legal expenses. These can amount to a lot of money.

You should, therefore, seek guidance from your lawyers as to the strength of your case and the prospects of winning. Do not be afraid to push them quite hard to give you clear advice on this point.

Note that in Turkey it is not possible to insure against the risk of having to pay such expenses.

Dealing with Accidents

Written by **Başak Yildiz Orkun**
Managing Partner (Legal Department) at Orkun & Orkun
www.orkunorkun.com • info@orkunorkun.com

Unfortunately, accidents happen. When they do you need not only to take the correct action but also to do so swiftly.

This chapter focuses on road accidents, but many of the principles apply to accidents of all kinds.

Accidents on the road are an all-too-frequent occurrence, particularly in Turkey where the combination of poor roads and a scant regard for the traffic laws leads to a higher-than-average accident rate.

In 2016, there were 1,182,491 road accidents in Turkey, of which 185,128 involved death or injury. Some 7,300 people were killed and 303,812 were injured. This is the equivalent of 8.9 fatalities per 100,000 inhabitants - that's compared with 2.9 in the UK, 4.3 in Germany, 5.1 in France and 10.6 in the US.

How can a foreigner deal with an accident in Turkey?

Immediate action

As soon as the accident happens there are some obvious things that you need to do.

This is not a first aid manual (though it's always a good idea to have and read one) but the most important thing to do at the scene of any accident is not to make it worse. Generally, this means not moving the person who has suffered the accident unless it is vital: for example, if they are in the middle of the road or in a burning building. Moving them can make minor injuries life-threatening.

In most cases, you will need to call an ambulance. In some cases, you will also want to contact the police and the fire department. Call 112 for all of these services. When you do phone, you may well find that the operator does not speak your language. If you speak English, there is a reasonable chance that someone can be found who will speak it to some extent but if you speak another language the odds are not good. Therefore, it's a good idea to find a person at the scene of the accident who is able to speak Turkish and make the call on your behalf.

Use your judgement about calling the police. In the case of road accidents where there is some injury you have the legal obligation to do so, but otherwise and in the case of most general accidents it is not necessary.

Whatever the type of accident, you should also try to take photographs of the scene of the accident before anything is moved. Fortunately, most of us now have mobile phones capable of doing this. Take lots of photographs from different points of view.

If there is any obvious cause of the accident, photograph that both close up and from a distance.

Also try to make a rough plan of the scene of the accident. Show on the plan approximate measurements. As you are unlikely to have a tape measure to hand, remember that a long step is about 80cm and the height of things can be shown by having a person stand in front of them.

Some accidents directly involve two or more people. Others happen because of some failure where there is no other person present. If there is no other party, the insurance company may seek a police report as proof that you were not drunk.

If your accident involves two or more people, you are likely to encounter your first problem. They will speak Turkish and you may not. In this case, it is very important that you neither say, nor could be understood to have said, anything accepting responsibility for the accident. Even if the accident was your fault it is probably not a good idea to make any formal admissions at this time. This does not mean that you are going to try and wriggle out of responsibility; just that these things are better done when the situation is a little calmer. In fact, it is if things are getting a bit too excited that you will normally think about calling the police in the case of an accident where it's not compulsory to do so.

Bear in mind that when the police turn up they, too, are (in many parts of the country) unlikely to speak your language.

If there are any people who have witnessed the accident and you are able to do so, it is a good idea to take their names and addresses and - if you speak their language - to ask them what they think happened and write it down in brief form.

Next steps

If the accident was not your fault

If you do not think that the accident was your fault and that it was not a pure accident - just one of those things that happens where nobody is to blame - go to see a lawyer as quickly as possible. The sooner you do this the higher your chances of success in making any claim.

Before you see your lawyer, write down, to the best of your memory, exactly what happened immediately before, during and after the accident. Do remember that witnesses are very unreliable. There is lots of evidence that shows that three different people seeing the same event will have three very different accounts of what they saw, so don't be surprised if your version differs from the accounts of the other witnesses. This does not mean that they are lying or out to get you.

Take this account to your lawyer. Take also the accident report, photographs, sketch plan, names and addresses of witnesses etc. that you took at the scene.

Take also copies of any insurance policies that you think might be relevant to your case. These could include your motor vehicle insurance, if a vehicle is involved, your healthcare insurance and any travel insurance that you might have.

Your lawyer will then be able to advise you on whether there appears to be any possibility of obtaining compensation for your accident. Do not expect this advice to be immediate. It will often require some research and investigation before the lawyer can form an opinion.

At the same time as the lawyer gives you an opinion, they should be able to give you some sort of estimate as to how long it is likely to take to deal with your claim and the likely cost of doing so. Expect these estimates to be very imprecise. This is not because the lawyer is being difficult but because it is impossible to give you much idea at this point.

This is because, occasionally, the other person involved might immediately accept responsibility and offer compensation. In other cases, you might have to go to court, the loser might appeal and the process could take years. Clearly, these things have an impact not only on the length of time the case will take but also the cost of pursuing it.

From this point on you will be guided by your lawyer as to the steps that will be needed. Some of them will be very different from the steps that might be required in your own country. It is human nature to think that something done differently from what you're used to is something done worse. This is, usually, not the case. It is just different. It is part and parcel of being in another country.

If you think the accident was your fault

Go to your lawyer. Lawyers love accident work because both sides need their services!

Take all the items referred to above.

If you think the accident was your fault, then it is important to establish whether this is, indeed, the case as quickly as possible and, if it was, to pass the case to your insurance company or settle it without delay. Delay makes the whole thing much more expensive and frustrating.

Medical treatment

You may well require ongoing medical treatment following an accident. You will need to tell the lawyer about the progress of such treatment and to give the lawyer the details of the doctors who are treating you.

That could be treatment in Turkey, treatment back in your own country or both.

Lasting disabilities or scarring

If you are unlucky enough to suffer either of these, you will again need to liaise closely with your lawyer, as medical and other reports will need to be prepared.

Court Cases

Unless you and the other person involved (or your lawyers and insurance companies) can reach a friendly settlement of any claim, the questions of who was responsible for your accident and how much compensation should be paid has to be dealt with by the courts. See our section on dealing with disputes and court cases (page 320).

How long will it take to settle my case?

These cases take time. There are two main reasons for this.

If the case involves injury, it often takes quite a long time for the true extent of the injuries or long-term consequences of them to become clear. You would not want to settle the case and then find that there was some hidden, but serious, problem for which you could have received substantial compensation.

The second reason there is often delay is that the court system in Turkey, like in most other countries, is overworked and under-resourced. This is particularly so if (as will often be the case with a foreigner) the accident occurs in some rural or seaside location and not in a major town. The courts responsible for that location may have almost no resources at all as the staff allocated to them were allocated, perhaps, 15 or 20 years ago: before the tourist boom and when the local population was measured in hundreds, not thousands.

As a general estimate, if your case is serious and must be settled through the courts, it will take a minimum of two to three years. Unfortunately, the culture in Turkey (and many other Mediterranean countries) is that a very large percentage - perhaps 75% - of the people who lose court cases go on to appeal against the decision. This can add a further two years to the process.

Bringing your case to a conclusion

As I've already said, this will take time - it will also take some commitment from you.

This can be a particular problem if you are a tourist rather than a resident, as you may have to take legal steps when you are no longer in the country. It is worth discussing this issue with your lawyer at an early stage and get a rough and very provisional timetable for what is likely to be necessary and when.

You may need to return to Turkey at some point: for example, for medical examination or to appear before the court.

Levels of compensation

The legal system in Turkey has a number of rules governing the compensation that the victims of accidents are likely to receive.

Broadly speaking, if the accident was not your fault but can be shown to be the legal responsibility of some other person, you will be entitled to compensation for your direct losses (e.g. damage to your car or clothing); compensation for loss of earnings (though this is often subject to a cap imposing a maximum daily amount that will be awarded - tough if you're a banker or a pop star!); and compensation for any injuries that you have suffered.

The compensation for injuries is often calculated by reference to scales and/or age.

For example, if the movement of your right arm is limited by 10%, you receive TRY X, if the movement is limited by 30% you receive TRY Y and if it is limited by 70% you receive TRY Z. This makes the preparation of medical reports of great importance. These are normally prepared by court-appointed experts but your lawyer will feed information to the expert to help them decide the appropriate level for your case.

Of course, if the accident *was* your fault then it will be you or your insurance company who has to pay this compensation. It is important to have good insurance when living in or travelling to Turkey. See our chapters on insurance (p88) for more information about this.

Car accidents - special points

There are three main components to dealing with a road traffic accident in Turkey:

- Dealing with any injuries

- Complying with your legal obligations

- Dealing with any claim for compensation

We will deal in detail with only the last two points.

It is worth repeating that dealing with even a simple road accident in Turkey is a lot more complicated if you do not speak the language. In Turkey, you have a reasonable chance that the other driver might speak some English but very little chance that they will speak any other language apart from Turkish. Except in main tourist areas, you have almost no chance that any Turkish police officer attending will speak anything but Turkish: or, at least, that they will speak it to the extent that they will be able to deal with you effectively.

Your legal obligations in Turkey

Can you move your vehicle after an accident?

In some countries, it is illegal to move your vehicle after an accident until the police have attended the scene. This is **not** the case in Turkey, unless injuries have been caused by the accident.

Even if you are legally permitted to move your car, if you do think that it's necessary to do so you should try to get the consent of the other driver before taking any action. If you are going to move the vehicle, you should not do so until after the accident report form has been completed (see below).

If you do have to move your car you should always try to take photographs of the scene of the accident *before* anything is moved.

If you move your car before you call the police or without the consent of the other driver you may find it impossible to make a claim against your insurance.

Turkey: how things *really* work

Do you have to call the police to an accident?

It is a legal requirement that you call the Turkish police if any person involved in the accident has suffered any "significant injury". In practise, this means if they are bleeding (other than superficial scratches), have a suspected broken bone or have any other symptoms that mean they cannot immediately continue with their journey.

In all other cases - which means in the vast majority of minor traffic accidents in Turkey - there is no need to call the Turkish police and doing so can prove counter-productive. This is because, if the police attend, a whole chain of bureaucracy and paperwork is set in motion and can take a long time to deal with.

While you're waiting for the police to arrive:

While you are waiting for the police - or if you don't call them:

- Get the names and addresses of any witnesses
- Take photographs
- Prepare a plan of the scene
- Write down why you think the accident occurred
- Complete the accident report form

Accident report forms in Turkey

In your car, you should have an 'accident report' form. The law requires you to carry a copy in the vehicle at all times.

In Turkey, the accident report form is provided by your insurance company as part of the annual renewal process. It is in a standard design and - very importantly - the instructions are always written in both Turkish and English. Some companies also provide a translation into other languages but that is not a legal necessity.

An accident report form is available for download at **www.guides.global/books/turkey/tur-downloads.php**. It has been translated into English. It's perhaps worth downloading a copy 'just in case'.

The form contains spaces to record the essential information about the accident. This way nothing is forgotten.

The information includes items such as the registration numbers of the vehicles, names and contact details of the drivers, names and contact details of any witnesses etc.

It also provides a space for you to make a sketch plan of the scene of the accident. This is rather meagre and there is nothing to stop you making additional sketch plans and attaching them to the form.

The form also contains a place where you and the other people involved can make an agreed statement of who you think is responsible for the accident. Equally, if you can't agree who was responsible, there is a place for each of you to state your opinion of what caused the accident.

You can record your opinion in any language. This is not a perfect solution because it means that the other people involved in the accident will probably not understand what you're saying and therefore they won't be able to comment on it in their version of events.

Once you have completed the accident report form, you may move your vehicle. Once again, it's a good idea to get the consent of the other driver(s) involved beforehand.

Most lawyers in Turkey would advise you **never** to admit responsibility for an accident on this form.

However, if the accident was clearly your fault - for example, if you pulled out of a side road and ran directly into the side of a passing vehicle or you ran into the back of a vehicle that was stopped at a red traffic light - it can create a lot of good will if you admit your responsibility at the scene of the accident. It also minimises the time and expense of later dealing with any claim.

If you are going to admit responsibility - or if you think the accident was your fault but don't want to admit it at the time - it is important to take photographs of any damage that has been caused to your vehicle and to any other vehicles or property. If you haven't got a camera, make notes but (obviously) this isn't nearly as good.

When (if) the Turkish police attend

- They will make sure nobody has been injured and call for any medical assistance necessary
- They will take the remaining people to the police station: both the driver(s) and any witnesses
- They will ask you for a copy of the accident report form. If you have not finished filling it in they will wait for you to do so but will not get involved in that process
- They will take their own measurements of the scene of the accidents and, these days, will probably also take photographs
- They will make arrangements for the road to be cleared
- They will take a statement from you and any other drivers and witnesses still at the scene
- They will ask for proof of your insurance, particularly if you are insured overseas
- They will prepare a 'fault report'. This will indicate whether, in their opinion, the accident is all the fault of one driver or whether - for example - it is 80% the fault of one driver and 20% the fault of the other. They might also

> conclude that the accident was the fault of neither driver: perhaps the fault of
> the road's surface, or the weather, or an animal crossing the highway

Expect this to take a long time, particularly if anybody has been injured.

What happens next?

If the police think that the conduct of any driver (or other person) deserves criminal
prosecution, they will report the facts to the prosecutor for a decision as to whether
charges should be brought. This will usually mean you have to attend the prosecutor's
office for interview. Fortunately, very few accidents are reported for prosecution.
Those that are usually involve drink, hugely excessive speed or serious injury.

If you are prosecuted (and convicted), depending on the offence with which you are
charged, you are likely to be fined and/or banned from driving for a period of time.
More serious cases can result in a sentence of imprisonment.

If you are convicted, the court will *not* notify the authorities in your own country about
your conviction. It has, at the moment, no mechanism for doing this.

If the police do not report the accident, the parties will be left to sort out the question
of any compensation payable. This will usually be done by their insurance company or
lawyers.

Reporting the accident to your insurance company

You only need to report the accident if:

- You are going to make a claim against the other driver

- You think that the other driver is going to make a claim against you

- You may want to make a claim against your own insurance company for what
  would otherwise be irrecoverable losses. An oddity of the Turkish system is
  that you can claim compensation for the loss of value of your vehicle even if
  it is repaired by the insurance company. This is because vehicles that have
  been damaged often have a lower post-accident value (even when repaired)
  than a vehicle that has never been damaged

If in doubt, report it.

If you are going to report the accident, do so by telephoning your insurance agent or, if
your company has one, use its claim line and then follow their instructions. This is
where you discover the benefit of dealing with an insurance company with a claim line
in your own language!

Remember that, even if you don't report the accident, you will (in most countries) have
to declare the fact that you had the accident when you apply for the renewal of your
insurance 'back home'. If you do not do so, the policy is likely to be void: i.e. of no
effect. This will make you guilty of the criminal offence of driving without insurance
and, of course, be catastrophic if you are later involved in an accident which is your

fault and which injures someone or damages property.

Seeing your lawyer

Dealing with the aftermath of a road accident is not something you should do yourself, even if you speak good Turkish.

You should see your lawyer as quickly as possible. The sooner you see him the more satisfactory the outcome of the case is likely to be.

What compensation can you claim?

You can claim compensation for:

- Material loss, e.g.:
    - The loss of an arm or ongoing restricted movement in your neck
    - Damage to your car
    - The reduction in value to your car, even when repaired
    - Time off work
    - Future losses such as loss of earnings as a result of injuries sustained
- Psychological damage, e.g.:
    - Pain and suffering
    - Family problems caused by the accident

    Payments for psychological damage tend to be small.

Other consequences of a road accident

If you cannot prove your ownership of your vehicle and/or that it has insurance, the vehicle will be impounded. Getting it back can take weeks.

If you are convicted of any motoring offence arising out of the accident, your insurance premium will rise dramatically. This is because, in Turkey, only the most serious conduct is prosecuted.

How long does this take?

If there is a criminal case, it could well take two to three years to be resolved, plus another one or two years if the person is convicted and chooses to appeal.

A civil case for compensation will be started at about the same time as any criminal case but is likely to take one or two years from the filing of any expert's report in the criminal proceedings.

Accidents at work - special points

The number of workplace accidents is increasing quite rapidly in Turkey. In 2017, over 2000 people were killed and 200,000 injured.

If you are an employee who has suffered an accident at work, there are three main things for you to bear in mind:

1. The legal requirements

2. The requirements of your employer

3. Looking after your own interests

If you are an employer whose employee suffers an accident at work in Turkey, you only need to worry about the first and third of these categories!

The legal requirements

Although certain aspects of health and safety seem not to be pursued with great vigour in Turkey, there are very strict legal requirements as to what you must do following an accident at work.

An accident at work is any accident in which you suffer any injury, however small. If you stab yourself with a paperclip and a drop of blood oozes from your fingertip that is, legally speaking, an accident at work and you must follow all the rules by reporting it etc. In practise, for trivial injuries of that kind, most people will (very sensibly) take no action.

However, you don't need to go much further up the severity scale before you really ought to report the incident, and there are many who would argue that every accident ought to be reported: after all, what happens if your paperclip has been contaminated and you are taken seriously ill? Apply common sense but err on the side of caution. It is in both the employer's and the employee's best interests to do so.

Your employer is under a legal obligation to notify the police about the accident (immediately) and the Social Security Department (within three working days). The second requirement is because, in Turkey, it is the Social Security Department that makes payments to people injured in accidents at work.

These obligations extend to any accident as a result of which there could be a claim for either physical or mental damage. Whether this is the case is a matter for the judgement of the employer.

The report can be made over the internet.

In deciding whether to report, the employer may well be influenced by the fact that there is a fine of TRY2,500 for nor reporting any accident that should have been reported and, perhaps more importantly, because if the employer does not report the accident, the Social Security Department may recover some payments they make as a result of the accident from the employer.

In many countries, there is a requirement for employers to maintain a written record of all accidents that occur on their premises. This can sometimes be in the form of a physical accident book and sometimes can be in the form of a digital record. There is no such legal requirement in Turkey but some employers - especially the larger ones - do have an internal requirement for reporting and recording accidents suffered at work.

The employer's requirements

These will vary from employer to employer.

In the case of larger companies where there is a first aid facility, it is often a requirement of the employer that is you suffer an accident at work - however small - you must report for treatment.

You should be told about the employer's requirements in the case of accidents at work when you are first employed by the company.

Looking after your own interests

If you suffer an accident at work which was not your fault and in which you suffer any sort of injury, you should see a lawyer as soon as possible. Prompt action is most likely to be successful and easier (and so cheaper) than action taken months after the event.

Claiming compensation

If you suffer an accident at work and it causes you any injury or to have to take time off work you are likely to want to claim compensation from your employer. The law requires all employers to have insurance against accidents at work.

If you do suffer an accident at work and wish to claim compensation you will need to see a lawyer. You should make sure that the lawyer has experience of dealing with accidents at work. Even in Turkey, where most lawyers cover quite a large range of areas of legal practice, there are some who do not deal with accidents at work.

The claim that you make will be a civil claim. There could also be a criminal liability in certain cases.

The civil claim is made via the specialist employment court. These courts exist in larger towns. If there is no employment court in your area, the claim will be made via the ordinary civil court; but the judge in that court will act as if it was an employment court and follow its procedures.

Taking time off work

If you suffer an accident at work you may need to take time off work.

Your employer cannot fire you if you take time off work because of an accident.

Normally, your doctor will advise you for how long you should stay off work and the doctor's opinion will be respected.

If you take time off because of an accident at work, unlike in many countries, it is not the employer who must pay you for the period when you're not working. These payments are made by the Social Security Department.

The amount of time you have to take off work will also be a factor in the amount of any compensation you receive for the accident.

Accidents in public places or due to defective premises - special points

Many people are injured each year as a result of defective premises in Turkey. Some of the injuries can be extremely serious: even life-changing. Others can be less dramatic but still cause you significant pain and financial loss. For example:

- People dive into swimming pools and break their necks because the depth is not marked

- People fall through unsafe windows

- People slip on wet surfaces in bars and restaurants

- People fall down hidden steps or on uneven surfaces

- People are injured when things fall onto them

- People are injured or killed as a result of badly maintained gas heaters

Can a foreigner claim compensation for such an accident?

The law applies equally to Turkish people and to foreigners and so, at least theoretically, being a foreigner should make no difference to your chances of success when claiming for an accident in Turkey.

However, you should remember that you are likely to be making a claim against somebody who is not only a Turkish citizen but also who may be well known (and a big employer) in the area of Turkey where the court is located. Even worse, as the owner of a local Turkish business, he or she is likely to be influential. In these circumstances, particularly if the accident claim is being made in a small town in Turkey, it is sometimes suggested that foreigner making the claim will be rowing uphill.

This is partly countered by the fact that, as mentioned below, a very large percentage of accident cases in Turkey end up passing on an appeal from the local court to a more distant appeal court, where any such influence is unlikely.

In our experience, the obstacles to foreigners making accident claims against local people are generally overstated. Foreigners can, and regularly do, make successful claims.

How can a person claim compensation for such an accident?

In Turkey the owners of premises - hotels, restaurants, shops, apartments, offices etc. - are legally responsible for the safety of people using those premises. They are also responsible for any dangerous defects in those premises. In these cases, claims are made against the owner via the ordinary civil courts.

Similarly, at least theoretically, the Turkish government (at whichever level) is responsible for any injuries or losses caused by defects in roads, pavements and other public areas owned by them. A fall in the street might result in a claim against the municipality. An accident as the result of a defective inter-city road may result in a claim against the Department of Traffic.

If your child (under 18) is injured, it will be the parents who make the claim on the child's behalf.

It is important to establish, at the beginning, whether the defect that injured you or caused you financial loss was one that would trigger the right compensation in Turkey. This is one of the first pieces of advice that your lawyer should give you.

It is not every defect or every accident that will give rise to a claim for compensation in Turkey.

The duty to pay compensation in Turkey will only arise if the defect was something that the owner actually knew about or which he should reasonably have known about. It also only arises if the risk is one that, in Turkey, is thought of as a risk sufficiently serious to demand protection from it.

It will come as no surprise that different countries have different standards - and levels of acceptance - for risks of all kinds. In many places around the world you may see high, unguarded drops off the edge of pavements - or hotel balconies with safety rails set at such a low level that they are more likely to cause you to fall over the edge than to protect you from doing so!

You must not assume that, just because (for example) stairs in public places are always marked with a white strip in the country where you live, failure to do so in Turkey will give rise to a claim for compensation if you suffer an injury.

In Turkey, the safety standards required are, generally, moderate.

Does the owner have any other responsibilities?

In certain cases, the owner will not only have the responsibility to pay compensation for damage caused as a result of his defective premises (this is called 'civil responsibility'), but he could also face the prospect of criminal responsibility if the standard of his conduct fell far below what could reasonably be expected.

This is important for two reasons.

Firstly, if there is criminal responsibility, the accident claim might be pursued by the Turkish police or other enforcement agency (in which case it costs you nothing).

Secondly, and more significantly, if a Turkish property owner feels he is at risk of criminal prosecution - and therefore at risk at going to jail - he might be more inclined to settle any civil claim for compensation, if that is going to make his problem go away.

Turkey: how things *really* work

So the tactics employed in making your accident claim in Turkey can have a large impact on your prospects of recovery, as well as the speed and costs of your case.

What can you claim for?

Claims against private individuals and companies in Turkey

Generally, you will be able to claim for compensation for any physical injuries you suffer and for compensation for financial losses directly and clearly attributable to those injuries.

For example, if you break your arm and are unable to work for six weeks, you will be able to claim for the broken arm and the pain and suffering associated with it plus your medical expenses and loss of earnings for the six-week period.

If a defective chimney collapsed on top of your car, the level of compensation would be the reasonable cost of repairs to or the replacement of the car.

In some cases, you may also be able to claim where there is no physical injury. For example, if you have suffered mental stress or other problems as a result of the accident.

If you are part of a group - such as your family - who are all injured as a result of the same defect, each person will have a separate claim against the owner. The parents of children will have a claim on the children's behalf.

If you are unlucky enough to be killed as a result of a defect in premises, your heirs will have a claim on your behalf.

Claiming against the Turkish government

If your claim is against the Turkish state - either central government for facilities controlled by them, or local government for items they have allowed to become defective - your rights are different.

The test of whether the defect was sufficiently serious and sufficiently obvious to justify a claim becomes more difficult to prove.

Any potential claim against the Turkish government, for example, as a result of a defect in a road, needs to be very carefully considered by your lawyers. They should advise you about the legal prospects of the claim as well as the length of time the claim is likely to take - and whether you are likely to ever receive any money, even if your claim is successful.

What if the accident was partly your fault?

If the accident was partly your fault - for example, if you fell through a window or off a balcony whilst drunk - at the very least, the amount of compensation that you receive will be reduced. The extent of the reduction will depend upon the extent to which the accident was your fault.

In some cases, the Turkish courts can find that the cause of the accident was so much the responsibility of the person who suffered it that they will not make any award against the owner of the premises.

How much am I likely to receive?

Compensation for death can be a very large amount of money. How much will depend upon the age, previous health and status of the person who was killed. The Court will calculate the person's loss of earnings over the rest of their working life. It is very expensive to kill a 35-year-old lawyer!

Compensation for injury rather than death is rather less generous but payments can still be substantial.

Compensation for psychological damage and the like tend to be low: almost nominal.

Again, if the accident is deemed to be partly your fault, the compensation will be adjusted accordingly. This is a common scenario.

Is the owner of the premises likely to have insurance?

In many cases the owner will have insurance of some kind.

What are the time limits for claiming?

A claim for compensation in respect of an accident causing injury must be made **within five years** of the date of the accident.

If you fail to make a claim within this period you will lose all right to do so.

You should not fall into the trap of thinking that it is alright to leave things until the last moment before making a claim. Gathering the evidence to support your claim can take some time and, after a few years, the evidence may well have disappeared or be impossible to find. Therefore, it is good advice to start a claim as soon as you are aware that you may have a case.

Dealing with Disputes & Court Cases

Written by **Başak Yildiz Orkun**
Managing Partner (Legal Department) at Orkun & Orkun
www.orkunorkun.com • info@orkunorkun.com

Disputes occur in any country.

Often, they are the result of genuine misunderstandings. Very often, they are the result of poorly prepared contracts. Occasionally, they are the result of bad faith. Very infrequently, they are the result of fraud or other criminal activity.

The good news is that Turkey has a good legal system that can help you resolve disputes reasonably quickly and at a price that is not too exorbitant.

Despite this, it is worth bearing in mind that it is far better to avoid disputes arising in the first place than it is to solve them once the problem has been revealed. Any lawyer will tell you that avoiding disputes is better than dealing with disputes and that a bad settlement is often better than a good court case.

Dealing with disputes is always time consuming and expensive. The expense is not just monetary. It includes the distraction and effort required to deal with the dispute: effort that could be much better employed getting on with your life or your business.

Preventing a dispute

There are four golden rules when it comes to avoiding disputes.

1. Deal with trustworthy people.

   Disputes tend to fall into three categories. Disputes in relation to business (for example, when you buy a car); disputes between neighbours; and disputes with your family.

   You can't choose your neighbours or your family but you can choose the people with whom you do business.

   Before you enter into any business relationship it's worth finding out a bit (or a lot) about the person or company you are going to be dealing with. The internet can help greatly. It's surprising how often a Google search for the name of the person or company and "problems" will produce some very interesting information.

   If the other person or company is engaged in an activity that requires a licence or regulation, make sure that they are duly licensed and regulated. If you can't readily find that information on the internet, it is worth consulting a lawyer to ask that very specific question. Often - if the lawyer thinks you are a client who will bring further business - there will be no charge for that preliminary advice. On other occasions, it might cost you €100 or so.

Very often, when you are discussing a project with the other person, you will feel uneasy. There may be something about either the project or the person that you do not like or which just doesn't seem quite right. Trust your instincts. You will frequently be right.

Do not be afraid to ask for references. A few words with a previous customer who received good service or a current 'partner' or supplier is very reassuring. Giving references is common practice in Turkey.

2. Clear contracts.

When you are entering into any business relationship it is worth having a clear contract - almost always in writing - and then making sure that you understand and follow the contract.

The main purpose of the contract is to allow both parties to understand what they have agreed and then to remember it, sometimes many months or years later.

When you read the contract make sure that it covers all aspects of your relationship and the situations which are likely to arise during the contract. Make a list of what you need to achieve and how you are going to do it and then make sure the contract covers those points. Make a list of the things that might go wrong and make sure that the contract covers them.

See the Guides.Global checklist of the things that should be covered in a contract: **www.guides.global/books/turkey/tur-downloads.php**.

If your agreement relates to something particularly valuable or important it is worth taking legal advice about the wording of the contract and any background checks necessary. It will cost you a great deal less than sorting out any dispute that might later arise.

3. Keep in contact.

During the whole period in which you are dealing with the other person, make sure that you stay in contact. A few telephone calls to check that everything is still in order, that a delivery date is still going to be met etc. gives the opportunity to deal with any lurking problems quickly, easily and without too much embarrassment before people's positions have become entrenched.

During these phone calls or, better still, during face-to-face visits, be friendly, be inquisitive and be prepared to reach common sense solutions to any problems that emerge.

It is much more difficult to get involved in a serious conflict with someone if you know them and like them.

Keeping in contact is important in almost every country, but it is particularly important in Turkey where good business is often built upon personal contacts and connections.

4. Nip disputes in the bud.

If a dispute arises take immediate action to solve it.

Usually, disputes arise because of the unexpected. Perhaps a cost has arisen in a project that had not been anticipated, or the person supplying a service to you has been let down by somebody supplying him. Sometimes there's a genuine disagreement as to the meaning of the words in your contract.

In either case, you will do yourself a favour by taking action as soon as a disagreement appears and before it turns into a full-blown dispute.

Once again, the secret is to discuss the problem with the other party and then to try to find a practical, cheap and common sense solution to it. This will require flexibility and compromise from both parties but any cost is likely to be way less than the cost of dealing with a fully-fledged dispute.

Whatever you do, if you reach an agreement to solve a problem, document it thoroughly. Otherwise you'll find yourself in the same position in six months' time!

Initial stages of a dispute

If all this fails and it seems likely that a real dispute is going to arise, the first thing to do is to discuss the problem with the other party to see if you can - even at this late stage - find a solution acceptable to you both. If possible, this meeting should be face-to-face. Failing that, a Skype video call can work well. A telephone call as a last option.

If you really are unable to reach a compromise at that meeting you should write to the other party setting out the problem and asking how they think it should be dealt with. You could also make your own suggestions as to how you think the dispute can be solved. This should be a non-confrontational letter (these days, usually an email): an attempt to find a solution to a problem between two 'partners' in a project.

If you're writing such a letter you need to reach a balance between protecting your legal position and being open enough to reach an agreement if possible.

Lawyers will tell you that you should make it clear that your discussions are non-binding and not to be used in court. However, you may find that being more open and running the risk that later, in court, the other person says "but he agreed that..." is a better way forward.

You should, depending upon the urgency and complexity of the situation, allow the other person between seven and 14 days to respond to your letter. The latter is better.

If you have made an informal approach that has not produced the desired result you will probably need to escalate things by sending a formal letter. This is best drafted by your lawyer.

The letter could be sent through a Notary. What you are proposing is more a notification than a formal letter, but if you send it via a Notary, you will have the ability to prove that you informed the other party and also, if the other party doesn't deal with the letter, to show that the other party has not taken advantage of this attempt to settle the dispute.

If you do not make any progress as a result of this exchange of letters, then you really have little option but to 'go legal'.

Settling a dispute outside of court

See our chapter on alternative dispute resolutions (page 284).

Settling a dispute through the courts

Turkey has quite a complicated court system. It has courts of first instance, District Courts, and a Supreme Court with a subdivision between courts for civilians and courts for the military. We do not consider the military courts in this book.

Some cases may immediately proceed to these main (civil) courts and some might be directed to the Court of Settlements.

*Court of Settlements (*Sulh Hukuk Mahkemesi*)*

The work allocated to this court is decided by its category, not by its financial value. So, for example, all disputes relating to rental agreements or disputes within a condominium will go to the Court of Settlements. So will disputes relating to the distribution of assets between partners, probate (the administration of a deceased person's assets), and claims for the possession of buildings or other assets.

In general terms, the procedure for dealing with a court case in the Court of Settlements is:

Petition

This is the statement of your case, covering all of the legal and factual points necessary. It will usually be drafted by your lawyer after consultation with you.

The reply

This is the response from the person against whom you're claiming, usually drafted by their lawyer. It is supposed to contain all of the legal and factual matters relevant to their case.

The hearing

In the Courts of Settlement, your case will be dealt with by one judge. With luck, it will be the same judge throughout the case (which might go on for a couple of years) but it is common for judges to leave and be replaced by other judges, especially in the case of inexperienced young judges working in 'lower degree' places (like towns instead of big cities) - who tend to be promoted elsewhere.

In Turkey, when people refer to the 'trial' of a case, they mean something different from what is meant in the Anglo-American legal systems. They are not referring only to an appointment in open court where the evidence is heard and the parties argue the case, but to any appointment or interim hearing arranged by the judge to progress the case.

Hearings will often include meetings with the judge where the individual parties are not present, but their lawyers are. There can be many hearings in the course of a court case.

At an early hearing, the judge will usually decide whether any expert reports should be commissioned by the court and then make arrangements for this to be done.

Also at an early hearing, the judge is likely to make directions as to the documents and other evidence the parties should produce.

The judge might decide to visit any place relevant to the dispute, such as the site of an accident or a property subject to a claim.

The judge tries to maintain the momentum of the case by arranging a series of hearings, typically at intervals of two or three months.

At these interim hearings, the Court will perform a number of tasks, such as:

- Sorting out why things that have been ordered have not happened

- Ordering official records from, for example, the Land Registry or the Companies Registry

- Interviewing witnesses

Eventually, there will be what could be called the 'main hearing' of the case, or the trial, at which the parties or their lawyers present their case to the judge and make any relevant legal arguments.

The decision

This is the decision of the judge. It may be issued weeks or months after the trial of the case. It is issued in writing and sets out not only the decision itself but also the reasons why the judge reached the decision he did.

Enforcement

These are the steps that may need to be taken to enforce compliance with the order that has been made.

Appeal

There is a right of appeal against the decision of this court. This must be exercised in the time specified, which is usually from seven to 15 days after the date of the decision. The appeal will be lodged by your lawyer.

The Civil Courts of First Instance (Asliye Hukuk Mahkemeleri)

Despite the existence of the Court of Settlements, most cases will end up in the civil courts of first instance, which are to be found throughout Turkey.

The Civil Courts have rules which allocate various types of cases to various courts.

They are, in turn, subdivided according to the particular roles that they are fulfilling.

All cases start in a court of first instance, but may be allocated to a specific subdivision of that court, dealing with, for example:

- Employment disputes (Labour Courts)

- Commercial cases (Commercial Courts)

- Land disputes (Cadastral Courts)

- Family problems (Family Courts)

- Intellectual property rights (Intellectual Rights Courts)

- Enforcement of judgements and collection of debts (Enforcement Courts)

- Consumer Problems (Consumer Courts)

The exact procedure varies somewhat depending upon the court to which the case is allocated.

It is similar to that employed in the Courts of Settlement. The main difference is that there are likely to be more stages. For example, after the reply to the petition, there will be a supplemental petition dealing with any point raised and then a final reply dealing, in turn, with the supplemental petition.

All the judges in these courts are professional (legally qualified and paid) judges.

It is not obligatory to use a lawyer to deal with a court cases in Turkey but - especially for a foreigner - it is virtually impossible to deal with a court case without a lawyer.

Appeal

There is a right of appeal from the civil courts of first instance. The appeal, generally, lies to the Appeal Court (*İstinaf Mahkemeleri*) and then (if the parties are still not satisfied), for some cases (depending on the dispute amount and subject of the dispute) from the Appeal Court, to the Supreme Court *(Yargıtay)*.

The procedure on the appeal is similar to the procedure used for dealing with the case at first instance.

Witnesses can be recalled to give further evidence.

How long does it take?

The length of time it takes to deal with a court case will, obviously, depend upon the complexity of the case but between one and two years would be normal in anything other than the simplest of cases. In addition, there will be a further period - typically at least a year - if there is an appeal.

How much does it cost?

Generally, when you start a court case you will have to pay a court fee. This is, typically, about 1.5% of the amount at stake.

The fees charged by your lawyers will depend upon the complexity of the case. You should always ask for an estimate of likely fees and expenses at the outset of a case but you must bear in mind that it is often impossible to give you any realistic estimate because the lawyer simply does not know how the case is going to develop.

The best you can hope for is a range of costs reflecting a simple case and a more complicated one.

If you win the case, the Court will usually order the loser to make a contribution towards your court costs, but these Court-awarded fees are very low and they are treated by the lawyer as being a sum *in addition to* the fee that has been agreed with you. So, even if you win a case, you can expect to have to pay significant legal costs. This should influence your decision as to whether it is worth bringing a case.

There is no 'no win, no fee' system in Turkey. In limited circumstances, it can be possible to get subsidised legal assistance. See page 279.

Case study

Tasos Papadakis

Wine merchant, Greek, 60

The problem

Tasos had been supplying a bar in Fethiye with wine for ten years: in fact, almost from the time he started to live in Turkey. In 2010, the restaurant started falling behind on its account. Keen to maintain a good relationship with a long-standing customer, Tasos did not take legal action until the bill had reached almost TRY30,000.

The solution

After informal attempts at mediation failed, Tasos felt he had no option but to take the bar's owner to court. He hired a lawyer, who felt that Tasos had a good chance of winning the case.

The court case was fairly cut-and-dry - Tasos had plenty of paperwork proving that the bar owner had signed for, and been invoiced for, TRY30,000 worth of wine. Tasos could also prove that he had not received any money. The real problem seemed to be that the bar owned had money problems.

Despite the simplicity of the case, it still took over three years before it was finished - by which time, the bar had gone out of business. Tasos' bill was, eventually, part paid for out of the liquidated assets of the bar. Unusually, the bar owner did not appeal - if he had, Tasos would have had to wait another year or so to receive his money. The bar owner was also ordered to pay part of the legal costs - which were never paid and so had to be paid by Tasos.

Tasos now makes sure that his business stops supplying customers as soon as their bills are overdue for payment.

Debt & Bankruptcy

Written by **Başak Yildiz Orkun**
Managing Partner (Legal Department) at Orkun & Orkun
www.orkunorkun.com • info@orkunorkun.com

Debt

In Turkey, debt is no longer treated as seriously as it perhaps was in years gone by. It is perfectly socially acceptable to incur debt, and most businesses or individuals have debt of some kind, but people are still very cautious about incurring debt and there is great social disapproval if people do not repay their debts when they are due.

There is a large amount of debt collection and enforcement carried out through the courts.

If you are owed money, or if you have won a court case and the person has not done what the court ordered, you will make an application to the Enforcement Department.

If you have an existing court order

You can go directly to the enforcement process. See below.

If you have no court order but 'valuable paper proof of debt'

If you have valuable paper proof of the debt (for example, a bounced cheque or a written acknowledgement of the debt), there is an accelerated process by which you can proceed to enforcement.

Non-payment of a cheque has been a **criminal** offence since August 2016.

If you have a debt claim without a paper acknowledgement of debt

These are, typically, unpaid invoices. These are treated as an ordinary debt, you can still proceed to enforcement but the process will be more challenging than in the case of a debt with valuable paper proof.

You can also resolve such cases through the civil courts. Once you've obtained a court order confirming that the money is due to you, you proceed to the enforcement operation.

Your lawyer will advise which is likely to be better/cheaper/faster in your case.

Enforcement operation

When enforcement proceedings are started, the Enforcement Court will issue a summons to the debtor and ask for the debt to be paid. The debtor has five, seven or 30 days (depending on the type of the debt) in which to reply to this summons.

If she does not reply, or if the Department of Enforcement decides that her objection to payment has no legal validity, the Court will decide how to collect the debt.

For money debts, the basic remedy is to seize assets (a car, a boat, a house, the debtor's entitlement to salary, the balance in his bank account etc.) and then, if necessary, sell them by auction. The auction is arranged by the Enforcement Department.

For obligations that cannot be measured in cash (such as surrendering possession of a building or handing over a child to the other parent), the Enforcement Department is entitled to use force.

How long does this take?

The time will vary dramatically.

How much does it cost?

A fee will be payable to the Department of Enforcement. For money debts, this is typically 4.5-9% of the amount claimed.

In addition, you will incur the fees of any lawyer that you appoint to deal with the case. These will not be recoverable.

Bankruptcy

Turkey is unusual in that only businesses can be made bankrupt and, by doing so, relieved of their debts. An individual person cannot seek relief from debt: the debt will follow them forever.

If a business is unable to pay its debt, it can be made bankrupt.

They can either apply for their own bankruptcy or someone who is owed money can apply for them to be made bankrupt compulsorily. The application is made to the Commercial Court. Bankruptcy proceedings are normally quite quick.

Last year (2016) there were 12,000 companies declared bankrupt in Turkey.

The effect of bankruptcy

Once an application has been made then, unless the sum claimed is paid or the debtor can show a good legal reason for non-payment, a bankruptcy order will be made. The result of such an order is that the court appoints a lawyer as the company's bankruptcy administrator.

The bankruptcy administrator takes control of all of the business' assets and either sells them or allocates them directly to the creditor.

Recovery rates

Recovery rates on a bankruptcy in Turkey are low. By the time things get this far, most people will lose their money.

Alternatives to bankruptcy

Turkey has an arrangement whereby a business in financial difficulty can apply to be placed in protective measures. This is called 'Postponement of Bankruptcy' and is similar to the concept of Chapter 11 in the United States. If the application is granted, nobody will be able to take enforcement proceedings against the company for a period of one year. That period can be extended up to a maximum of four years.

Criminal Cases

Written by **Başak Yildiz Orkun**
Managing Partner (Legal Department) at Orkun & Orkun
www.orkunorkun.com • info@orkunorkun.com

In each country, the criminal system is unique: probably more so than any other part of the law except for family law. In both cases, this is because the law in these areas goes right to the heart of a nation's values, traditions, and culture.

Do not be surprised if the criminal law in Turkey is very different from the criminal law in your country. Just because it is different, does not mean that it is worse.

There is a long tradition in Turkey of impartial justice and the protection of the individual's rights. However, in recent times and as a result of some of the changes to the law - and the way it is enforced - that have been introduced by the government, there have been questions about Turkey's ongoing commitment to the protection of human rights.

The Turkish Penal Code

The Turkish Penal Code regulates most aspects of the criminal law in Turkey. It is quite a lengthy document - extending to well over 100 pages - but short by international standards. The Spanish *Código Penal* is 189 pages, the French *Code Penal*, 387.

It deals with both some basic principles and the detailed definitions of the various activities that are declared to be criminal offences in Turkey.

An English version of the code can be found here: **bit.ly/2s9aiRr**.

The Code applies both to Turkish citizens (sometimes even in relation to things done in other countries) and to foreigners present in Turkey.

It's probably worth mentioning some of the key general provisions, though they shouldn't really come as a surprise to people familiar with the criminal law of other advanced countries:

- Nobody should be subject to any penalty for any act which is not clearly declared by law to be a criminal offence.

- Penalties should be proportionate to the gravity of the offence.

- There should be no discrimination on the basis of race, language, religion, nationality, colour, gender, political ideas, etc.

- Ignorance of the law is no defence.

- The law shall apply to all criminal offences committed in Turkey.

- Criminal responsibility is personal. No-one shall be deemed culpable for the conduct of another person.

- No act should be a criminal offence unless it is committed with intent - i.e. knowingly and willingly committing the things specified in the definition of a criminal offence.

- There is a right to proportionate self-defence.

- The age of criminal responsibility starts at 12, but somebody between the age of 12 and 15 can only be convicted if they're capable of appreciating the meaning and consequences of what they did. However, although they cannot be prosecuted, various 'security measures' can be applied to minors who have committed criminal offences. These are defined in the relevant statute creating the offence.

- An act carried out by a person suffering from a mental disorder which means they cannot understand the meaning and consequence of the act will not count as a criminal offence.

- A person who, because of the effects of drink or drugs, *taken involuntarily*, is unable to understand the meaning or consequences of their actions, shall not be subject to penalty.

- Attempts to commit criminal offences shall be punished.

- If two or more people jointly commit an offence they shall all be guilty of the offence.

- Foreigners who commit offences in Turkey may, at the discretion of the Ministry of the Interior, be deported either immediately after their conviction or upon completing any sentence in Turkey.

- A person who assists another person in the commission of an offence shall be guilty of the offence and maybe sentenced (generally) to half of what would otherwise be the penalty for that offence.

Other provisions may be a little more surprising:

- Where non-citizens commit an offence to the detriment of Turkey in a foreign country - something that would be an offence under Turkish law, and subject to a penalty of more than one year of imprisonment - and the non-citizen then goes to Turkey, he will be subject to penalties under Turkish law.

  The offences to which this rule applies are limited and defined in the code, but they include things such as hijacking, dealing with counterfeit money, dealing with drugs and other serious matters.

- Turkish law permits, in most cases, extradition for offences committed outside Turkey; but this power is limited in respect of offences committed by

Turkish citizens.

- Penalties shall not be imposed upon legal entities (e.g. companies).

Penalties

Offences may be punished by either imprisonment or by a fine, depending upon the provisions of the law creating the offence.

Periods of imprisonment

The length of the period of imprisonment is defined for each offence. Periods of imprisonment are specified in days.

Any period spent in custody pending judgement shall be deducted from whatever sentence is imposed and, where a fine is imposed instead of imprisonment, the fine shall be reduced by TRY100 for each day of custody prior to sentence.

If a person would otherwise have received a short period of imprisonment, the Court may substitute one or more of the following:

- A fine

- An order for payment of compensation

- Admission to an educational institute for at least two years

- Restriction on movement or on carrying out certain activities

- Confiscation of a driving licence or any other licence giving permission to do various things

- Deprivation of the right to carry out a certain profession or occupation

- An order to do work for the public good

- A sentence of imprisonment for a term of two years or less may be suspended. Conditions may be imposed upon this suspension (such as the payment of compensation) and the sentence will only be suspended once that condition is met. People benefiting from suspended sentence shall also be placed on probation.

Fines

A fine is an amount that the Court orders to be paid to the State. The maximum amount of any fine is specified in the provisions creating the offence.

The amount payable is calculated by multiplying a number of days (more than five, less than 730) specified by the Court by a daily amount (not less than TRY20 or more than TRY100) specified by the Court after taking into account the convicted person's personal circumstances.

The Court may order the fine to be paid immediately, or it may allow payment by instalments, or permit a respite period before the payment has to be made.

Other orders

At the same time that the Court makes an order of imprisonment or imposes a fine, it may make other orders. These might include:

- If the penalty was imprisonment, deprivation of the right to do certain things. These include being part of the government, voting, acting as a guardian or trustee, and conducting certain professions or trades

- Confiscation of property used for the purpose of committing the offence

- Confiscation of any gains that have been made as a result of committing the offence

Criminal offences in Turkey

The Turkish Penal Code sets out all the activities that are considered crimes in Turkey and the penalties for committing those offences.

Note that, for many offences, there is a minimum as well as a maximum penalty.

It will be no surprise that there are large numbers of potential offences and we cannot deal with them all in this book. They are enumerated in the Penal Code.

There are certain offences with which we, as lawyers, come into contact all the time and so, in this chapter, I will give you a brief indication of the penalties associated with them. Bear in mind that the precise definition of the offence may be different from what you are used to at home and so, if you or your family or friends are in any way involved in allegations of criminal activity, you should contact a lawyer without delay. This can greatly shorten the process and the length of time that the person concerned spends in pre-trial custody.

Assault

Between one and three years' imprisonment. However, if the injury is minor and can be cured by simple medical treatment the sentence may be reduced to between four months and one year, or replaced by a fine.

If the person injured is a member of your family, or disabled, or acting as a public official, or is injured by the use of a weapon, the penalty shall be increased by 50%.

Driving - dangerous

The minimum penalty differs depending on the type of the dangerous action. Maximum penalty of two years' imprisonment.

Driving - under the influence of alcohol

The minimum penalty for a first offence is a fine of €210, a disqualification from driving and banning your vehicle from being driven for six months.

For a second offence: a fine of €250, a disqualification from driving and banning your vehicle from being driven for two years.

For a third offence: a fine of €450, a disqualification from driving and banning your vehicle from being driven for five years. After the five years, you will need to take a psychological test.

Driving whilst drunk (rather than merely over the breath-test limit) is a criminal offence, and you will be subject to a criminal case with a maximum penalty of imprisonment for two years.

Drugs - possession

Turkey takes a tough line on drugs. Possession of class A drugs (heroin, cocaine etc) carries a minimum penalty of two years in prison and a maximum penalty of five years in prison.

Drugs - dealing (supplying)

This offence carries a minimum penalty of 1,000 days in prison, and a maximum of 20,000 days.

See our chapter on drink and drugs in Turkey (page 164).

Fraud

Between one and five years' imprisonment, *and* a fine of up to 1,000 days.

Murder (intentional killing)

Imprisonment for life

Reckless killing

Imprisonment for between two and six years or, if more than one person has been killed, a period of between two and fifteen years.

Theft

Between one and three years' imprisonment. If the offence is committed during the night, the penalty is increased by half.

Rape

No less than 12 years' imprisonment.

Sexual assault

Between two and five years' imprisonment.

Other

We must stress that, in Turkey, you may find criminal offences that are unfamiliar to you. For example:

- Causing insult
- Insulting the memory of a person
- Insulting the Turkish state
- Abuse of trust
- Causing an atomic explosion!

Time limits

No criminal case can be started and, if it has started, it should be discontinued after a fixed period of time. The period depends on the nature of the offence. For the worst offences, it can be up to 30 years and it can be as little as eight years for minor offences.

Similarly, if a person is found guilty of an offence and a penalty is imposed, the right to enforce that penalty is also time limited. Again, the time limit varies with the nature of the penalty. For example, a sentence of aggravated life imprisonment expires after 40 years, whereas a fine expires after ten years.

Types of criminal court in Turkey

There are three types of criminal court.

- The Settlement Criminal Judge /Police Judge (*Sulh Ceza Hakimliği*)
- The General Criminal Court (*Asliye Ceza Mahkemesi*)
- The Court for Serious Crimes (*Ağır Ceza Mahkemesi*)

The authority of these courts to deal with a particular crime is defined in the legislation.

Appeals

Whichever court your case is tried in, you will have the right of appeal.

Appeals from the General Criminal Court go to the Court of Serious Crimes, and appeals from the Court of Serious Crimes go to the Court of Appeal.

In certain cases, there is a final appeal to the Supreme Court.

Arrest

Arrest by the police

The police have the power to arrest any person who they believe to have committed any criminal offence. They may detain a person only if the offence is serious, or if there is a risk of further trouble, or to protect the person concerned.

If you are arrested, you will be taken to a police station.

For offences potentially punishable by a period of imprisonment, the police have the right to detain the person for a maximum period of 24 hours (or longer in serious cases, such as cases involving organised crime), during which they will take from the person a formal statement in which they answer the specific allegations made against them.

The actual length of time for which you are detained will be determined by the prosecutor (who is the independent person in charge of the investigation and the conduct of criminal cases).

The person detained is not legally required to answer any questions. Generally, a lawyer will be present when they are interviewed and, indeed, a lawyer must be present if their statement is to be admissible in court.

If the person detained does not speak adequate Turkish, an official interpreter must be present when they answer these questions.

If the person does not know a lawyer or cannot pay for one, a lawyer will be provided for them at public expense. However, if it later turns out that they have the means to pay for a lawyer, they will be required to reimburse this cost.

It is important to note that, at this stage, the lawyer is not there to defend the suspect. He or she is there to make sure that the police follow the proper procedure, that the arrested person's constitutional rights are respected and that the allegations made are clear and properly presented.

As a consequence, the lawyer will not normally discuss the case with the detained person prior to them making their statement - though, in an increasing number of cases, this is done as it can speed up the whole process to everybody's advantage.

Bail (release from custody pending trial)

Once you have given your statement to the police, the prosecutor may decide to release you on the basis that there is clearly no case for you to answer *or* they will refer your case to the Court.

You will make an initial appearance before that court. That will normally be within 24 hours of your arrest.

At that initial appearance, the court will establish your identity and ask you to confirm or deny the initial statement made to the police.

During this appearance, you must be accompanied by a lawyer.

After this brief appearance, the Court will decide whether there is at least the basis of a case to answer or whether you should be released without any charges.

If there is a case to answer, they will decide whether you should be given bail (released from custody pending the investigation of the case) or kept in custody.

This decision can be appealed by either the prosecutor or the suspect.

The grounds upon which you can be refused bail are that:

- You are dangerous

- You may run away (as an alternative to refusing bail, the court may put a note on the system and classify you as forbidden to go abroad)

- There is a risk of further offences or trouble (for example, an ongoing blood feud)

- There is real evidence of your guilt

- The crime is punished by a long period of imprisonment

It is not obligatory for you to be represented by a lawyer at this hearing but it is very wise for you to be represented. If the Court decides to keep you in custody, you could be there for a very long time pending your trial.

The criminal trial

The investigation phase

Strictly speaking, this is not part of the trial system as, at this point, you are still just a suspect and not a person formally accused of a crime, but it is convenient to cover it in this chapter.

A prosecutor is placed in charge of the investigation of the alleged crime. He is assisted by specially appointed police officers. The prosecutor will interview and take formal statements from the suspect and any witnesses, and will arrange for the preparation of any drawings, photographs or expert evidence required.

There is a maximum period during which the suspect may be held in custody whilst these investigations continue. This can be up to five years in serious cases.

This process of investigation by the prosecutor is critical and requires the active participation of your lawyer. Even if you have taken advantage of the publicly funded lawyer up to this point, now is a good time to consider who you want to represent your interests in the longer term. You can continue with the publicly funded lawyer but they tend to be under great pressure of time and they tend to be relatively junior and inexperienced.

The police and your lawyer can each ask the prosecutor to investigate specific aspects of the case. For example, you might want the prosecutor to investigate any alibi that you have put forward.

The prosecutor is under a legal obligation to act fairly and to respect the suspect's rights.

The decision to prosecute

At the end of the investigation phase, the prosecutor will decide whether the evidence is strong enough to justify formal charges being laid against the suspect and the case going to trial. If so, they will lay charges before the relevant criminal court.

At this point the status of the suspect officially changes to that of an accused person.

Either party may appeal this decision.

Basically, at this stage the suspect will receive one of two written court orders:

1. There is no, or insufficient, evidence of the accused committing any criminal offence and so the file should be closed, the case discontinued and the suspect released.

2. There is evidence that a criminal offence has been committed by the suspect and the case should proceed to trial at the Criminal Court.

Lawyers

See our chapter on lawyers (278).

The trial

Once the case is referred to the relevant criminal court, the trial phase will commence.

In the General Criminal Court, there will be one (professional, paid) judge who will deal with the trial, which will usually involve several hearings. The judge will collect the evidence that the prosecutor and parties referred to. If he needs to, he will carry out a visit to the crime scene, possibly with some court appointed experts.

Witnesses' testimonies will be taken by the judge during this phase.

The Court for Serious Crimes will follow the same process but there will be three judges and the prosecutor will be present at the hearings.

If you are in custody you can ask for bail (liberty until your trial) from the court to which the case is referred.

Legal Aid (assistance with the cost of a lawyer)

As we've already seen, if you do not have sufficient money to pay for your own legal representation the state can appoint a lawyer to represent you.

The lawyer will be a lawyer appointed by the Bar Association. Lawyers register in order to do this work and, inevitably, most of the lawyers registered are those at the beginning of their career and so relatively inexperienced.

Of course, you are perfectly entitled to appoint your own lawyer to represent you throughout these proceedings but, if you do this, you will be responsible for the payment of that lawyer's fees.

Turkey: how things *really* work

In practise, it is very common for the lawyer to be approached by members of the family of the person who's been detained and then for the lawyer to confirm with the person detained that they would like that lawyer to act on their behalf.

Family Problems

Written by **Başak Yildiz Orkun**
Managing Partner (Legal Department) at Orkun & Orkun
www.orkunorkun.com • info@orkunorkun.com

Separation

What is separation?

Separation is where two people who have formerly been living together 'as man and wife' decide to go their separate ways but without (in the case of a married couple) divorcing and so bringing the marriage to an end.

Despite the expression 'living together as man and wife', the same arrangements apply in the case of unmarried and/or same sex couples.

The concept of 'living together' requires some level of physical intimacy. These arrangements do not apply to people merely living together as friends.

There is no specific provision for dealing with such separations in Turkey, but people can bring a case before the Family Court under its general jurisdiction and the Court will apply much the same rules as it would apply in the case of a divorce except, of course, it would not end a marriage.

Divorce

Depending upon where you come from, it's likely that somewhere between 10% and 70% of all marriages end in divorce. In fact, this number is more commonly measured as either a crude divorce rate (the number of divorces per 1,000 of the population) or as a divorce-to-marriage ratio (the ratio between the number of marriages in any year and the number of divorces). Both methods are rather unsatisfactory. However, they can give an indication of where a country stands in the world.

Turkey has a relatively low crude divorce rate of 1.6 divorces per 1,000 of the population and a divorce-to-marriage ratio of 20%. In Germany, the figures are 2.0 and 41% respectively; in Spain, 2.2 and 61%; in the UK, 2.0 and 47%; and in the US, 3.6 and 53%.

We know that divorce is the second most stressful life event (behind the death of your spouse - but before both imprisonment and the death of a close family member). It is the same in Turkey.

Whilst there are various steps that can be taken to reduce the stress of divorce, probably the most important factors overall are how difficult your partner tries to be and the attitude of the legal system to divorce, as reflected in the way in which your divorce will be dealt with.

Terminology in this chapter

- Access (*görme hakkı*): the right of a parent who does not normally look after the Child to see the Child

- Child/Children (*evlat*): a child/the children of the marriage **or** the child/the children of one of the parties and adopted by the other **or** a child/the children adopted by both parties

- Custody (*velayet*): the right of a person to have day-to-day care and control of the Child

- Financial provision (*Mal Paylaşımı*): arrangements agreed between the parties (and, if necessary, adopted by the court) or arrangements ordered by the court as to what should happen to the assets of the parties to the marriage and as to ongoing financial support for either of the parties to the marriage or the Children

- Maintenance (*Nafaka*): ongoing financial provision by one of the parties of the divorce to the other or to any children

- Petitioner (*Davacı*): the person applying for the divorce

- Respondent (*Davalı*): the person against whom the divorce proceedings have been started

Will my existing divorce be recognised in Turkey?

Turkey is a signatory to the Hague Marriage Convention (the 'Hague Convention on the Celebration and Recognition of the Validity of Marriages') of 1978, which entered into force in 1991. Turkey is unusual in adopting this Convention. So far only three other countries (Australia, Luxembourg and the Netherlands) have actually agreed to abide by it (become 'contracting states')! As the Convention only applies to marriages conducted in another contracting state then the practical effect of this is, at the moment, somewhat limited but this should improve over time.

More importantly, therefore, Turkey is also a signatory to the Hague Convention of 1970 (the 'Hague Convention on the Recognition of Divorces and Legal Separations'). Some 20 other nations are parties to this convention. Most of these are in Europe. The US is **not** a party to the Convention.

Divorce in a country that signed the 1970 Convention

Under The Hague Convention of 1970, a divorce or legal separation will be recognised provided that it has been performed in accordance with the legal process required in the state where it was obtained *and* one of the following applies:

- The Respondent was resident in the state where the proceedings were started at the time the proceedings were started. For these purposes the term 'resident' has its normal, common sense meaning. The person must have been associated with that state for a significant amount of time and, where necessary, have the necessary official permission to be resident in that state *or;*

- The Petitioner was resident in the state where the proceedings were started at the time when the proceedings were started and had been so resident for at least a year *or;*

- The Petitioner was resident in the state where the proceedings were started at the time when the proceedings were started and had been so resident for any period of time together with the Respondent *or;*

- The state where the proceedings were started is the state of which both parties were citizens *or;*

- The state where the proceedings were started was the state of which the Petitioner was a citizen and where he lived or where he had lived for at least one year in the past two years *or;*

- The state where the proceedings were started was the state of which the Petitioner was a citizen - and where he was, at the time the proceedings were started, physically present - and the state in which the parties had, immediately before the presentation of the divorce petition, had their joint residence does not provide for divorce

This all sounds a bit complicated but almost all overseas divorces will be recognised. If, as is normally the case, you obtained a divorce in the country in which you and your ex-spouse had been resident for some time, your divorce will be recognised.

It will also be recognised in the other circumstances set out in the Convention.

Divorce in a country that did not sign the 1970 Convention

In these circumstances, Turkey applies its own law of what is known as 'comity'. These are the rules that apply in a country when considering whether to recognise the validity of legal and judicial acts that took place in another country. These rules apply in all sorts of situations other than divorce. For example, the recognition of contracts or debts recognised by the courts in another country.

In Turkey, the laws of comity are very generous.

Most countries will respect the legal, judicial and executive acts that took place in another country only if the recognition is reciprocated. Turkey presumes that *any* legal, executive and judicial act that took place in *any* other country and in accordance with the law of that country is valid. The only exception to this is if the act in question is one that it would be repugnant to recognise in the light of the basic and fundamental laws of Turkey. For example, if the act is a request for extradition it will not be accepted if the person would face the death penalty. If the act is a judgement of a foreign court relating to defamation (slander or libel) it will not be recognised if the country making the order does not recognise the right to free speech.

However, when it comes to the question of divorce the position, in practice, is that any divorce legally valid in the country where the divorce was granted will be recognised as valid in Turkey.

As a foreigner, can I obtain a divorce in Turkey?

Yes. In many cases you will be able to do so.

Visitor in Turkey

You will not be able to apply for a divorce during your visit to Turkey! You can safely take your holiday here.

Resident in Turkey

If you are officially resident in Turkey - there is no minimum period of residence required - you can bring a case in the Family Court and obtain a divorce. Of course, you will have to show that you have grounds for divorce under the law of Turkey.

Note that it is only you who has to be resident in Turkey. It is not necessary that your spouse has ever been resident in Turkey. This, of course, only relates to seeking a divorce from the Turkish courts. There may well be other countries where, whilst you are resident in Turkey, you could seek a divorce. For example, you could normally start divorce proceedings in the country in which your spouse was residing.

This gives rise to questions as to (depending on your approach to life) which jurisdiction is going to be fairest, which jurisdiction is going to give you the best result, which jurisdiction is going to be fastest, which jurisdiction is going to be the cheapest, and so on.

Finally, please note that, as Turkey is not a member of the European Union (EU), the 'Brussels II Convention' does not apply.

What are the grounds for divorce in Turkey?

A court in Turkey can only grant you a divorce if you can show that you have legal grounds for obtaining a divorce.

There are two types of divorces in Turkey: fault divorces and no-fault divorces.

Fault divorces

In the case of divorces sought on the grounds of fault, the Court will only grant a divorce if it is satisfied that the spouse who is applying for the divorce has proved that the other spouse has been guilty of at least one of the types of conduct specified below.

Your spouse has committed adultery

Not surprisingly, this is defined as voluntary sexual intercourse between the spouse and a third party. The application for divorce must be filed within six months of discovering the adultery and within five years of it being committed.

If you have pardoned your spouse's adultery (verbally or in writing) you will lose the right to apply on this basis.

Your spouse has engaged in behaviour which puts your life at risk

This is self-explanatory.

Your spouse has maltreated you

Maltreatment includes beating your spouse "in a ruthless way" - but not all violence may be sufficient to justify a divorce on this basis. This heading can also include more subtle means of maltreatment such as failing to provide food, preventing your spouse from leaving the house or seeing their family, and so on.

This ground is subject to the same provisions as to pardoning and time limits as apply in the case of adultery.

Your spouse has humiliated you

Significant humiliation by your spouse is grounds for divorce. What is significant humiliation is open to interpretation by the Court, but as well as the making of abusive comments (verbally or in writing), humiliation can also result from your being thrown out of the family home.

This ground is subject to the same provisions as to pardoning and time limits as apply in the case of adultery.

Your spouse has committed a crime

The crime must be a serious crime such as to cause humiliation to the other spouse and so that the other spouse can no longer reasonably be expected to live with the criminal. The definition of a "humiliating crime" is contained in the Turkish Constitution but includes things such as theft, fraud, corruption, bribery and the like.

Your spouse has behaved unreasonably

This is the most common reason for fault divorce actions. Unreasonable behaviour is behaviour that is disrespectful of the morality and honour of the other spouse or of society in general. It must be such conduct that the other spouse finds it intolerable to continue living with the person who committed it.

This ground is subject to the same provisions for pardoning and time limits as apply in the case of adultery.

Your spouse has deserted you

If a spouse willingly deserts the other for a minimum of three months, this will constitute grounds for filing for divorce. Absence as a result of imprisonment, business, military service or the like will not count.

If you wish to apply for divorce on this basis you need to serve notice on your spouse asking them to come back and giving them reasonable time in which to do so.

Your spouse suffers from a mental disease

If your spouse suffers from an incurable mental illness (confirmed by a medical report) and you find the continuation of the marriage intolerable, you may apply for a divorce.

Irretrievable breakdown

This is a very general concept and subject to the interpretation of the Court. The Court must be satisfied that the conduct of the other spouse is such that the petitioning spouse genuinely finds it impossible to live with them. If the marriage has lasted for more than a year and both parties agree to a divorce then the court will consider that the marriage has broken down irretrievably. As in the case of adultery, the Court will insist on hearing the evidence of the parties in person before agreeing to end the marriage in this way. The same applies if the parties have lived apart for a period of more than three years, whether or not they both agree to the divorce.

No-fault divorces

These cases are cases where the parties agree to obtain a divorce and have both recorded that agreement in a form accepted by the Court.

Matrimonial regimes

In common with most countries where the law is based on the continental European legal system, Turkey has clear rules about what should happen to the assets of the couple after their marriage. These rules make up what is known as the matrimonial property regime.

There are various 'standard' matrimonial property regimes from which the couple can choose at the time when they get married or which they can adopt, by agreement, after the marriage. In addition to these standard regimes, the couple can also specify a special arrangement which they have reached and properly documented.

The standard regimes include the 'separate property regime', the 'shared separate property regime', the 'communal property regime', and the 'participation in acquired assets regime'.

In a marriage, the 'participation in acquired assets regime' applies unless a different regime is chosen.

Separate property regime

Under these rules, the couple's assets are not shared. What belongs to the husband belongs to the husband, and what belongs to the wife belongs to the wife. So any money earned by the husband during the marriage would remain his property, as would any assets that he acquires: whether by purchase or in any other way. The same would apply to the wife.

Shared separate property regime

Under this arrangement, any of the couple's assets acquired after the date of their marriage will belong to them equally unless they were acquired as a result of inheritance, in which case they will belong solely to the person who inherited them.

Any assets acquired before the marriage will remain the property of the person who acquired them.

Communal property regime

Under this arrangement, all income coming into the household, and all assets acquired by the couple (before or after the marriage), will belong to them equally.

Participation in acquired assets regime

Under this arrangement, which is the one which will apply if no other arrangement is chosen, the couple will benefit equally from any assets acquired during the marriage but they will each remain the sole owner of the assets that they owned at the time of the marriage.

The validity of pre-nuptial or post-nuptial agreements

Pre-nuptial agreements

Pre-nuptial agreements are recognised in Turkey if they have been reached in accordance with the proper formalities.

For a marriage conducted in Turkey, those formalities require either that the agreement is made and signed in front of a Notary *or* that the proposed arrangements are declared to the officer conducting the marriage and recorded as part of the marriage documentation.

For marriages that did not occur in Turkey, the application of pre-nuptial agreements should, in principle, pose no problem, but, in practice, the application of these agreements seems to be a little patchy.

Post-nuptial agreements

A couple can change the matrimonial property regime that should apply to them at any point after the celebration of the marriage.

For a marriage carried out in Turkey, to do this they must inform the registrar of marriages, in writing, of their wish to do so.

For marriages conducted outside Turkey but where the parties are resident in Turkey, the position is more complicated. The ability to change the financial arrangements relating to the marriage will depend upon the wish of the parties and the applicable law that governs the marriage. In some cases, this can be Turkish law (see above) but in others it could be the law of the country where the marriage was celebrated or even the law of the country in which both of the parties are permanently resident. As a result, a person wishing to change the financial arrangements governing their marriage, and who married outside Turkey, should seek legal advice.

Case study

Gulay Gozetan

Retail worker, Turkish, 54

The problem

Gulay had given up her job in 2002 to look after her husband Yusuf, who had been injured in a work accident. She received financial support from the Turkish government during this period.

Yusuf was able to return to work (in construction) in 2012, but Gulay found it very hard to return to the workforce herself: she had worked in IT and technology had changed dramatically in a decade.

Yusuf left Gulay in 2014 and filed for divorce. Gulay could not support herself.

The solution

The Court ruled that Yusuf must provide financial support for Gulay until she re-marries, as she had given up her career to look after him. In addition, the family home was to be sold and the proceeds split unevenly, so that Gulay was able to buy an apartment.

Gulay took on a low-paying retail job to supplement the ongoing support, and hopes to reach a management position. As her position improves so financial support may come to an end.

As is usually the case, both parties were worse off financially after the divorce but Gulay feels that she has been provided for adequately and feels much happier outside the relationship.

This was all helped because Yusuf cooperated throughout, was very sensible, and recognised what his wife had done for him.

Divorce is always stressful, but it can be made far worse if the parties decide to turn the divorce into a battleground.

The process of divorce in Turkey

Mediation

Mediation is not widely used in relation to divorces in Turkey.

Until very recently, mediation was not widely used at all in Turkey. Lately, though, improvements have been made in the process, and it is being encouraged by the government.

As of January 2018, it is compulsory to apply for mediation in employment cases before a court process is started - and the government will pay for two hours of the mediation.

Plans are also being made to make mediation compulsory in divorce cases, although they have not yet come to fruition.

Application for divorce

In Turkey, applications for divorce are made to the Court.

Under the Turkish Code of Civil Procedure, the court which has jurisdiction to deal with a divorce case is generally the court of the place where the defendant is domiciled. For these purposes, "domicile" means the place where they reside on a fixed and permanent basis.

In some cases, it can be argued that another court might have jurisdiction. Where this is so, the person starting the divorce proceedings can decide which of the two courts to use for the divorce.

When it comes to property disputes that arise out of a divorce case, different rules may apply. If the parties have, by the time of the property dispute, different domiciles (i.e. they're permanently resident in areas covered by different courts), then the property dispute may be dealt with in the court where either of the parties is domiciled but, generally, the court that first took charge of the case will have priority and deal with the whole of the case.

The process in the case of an agreed no-fault divorce

If the Parties are applying for a divorce on the 'no fault' basis, and they've been married for at least one year, the process can be very quick.

There will usually be a written agreement between the Parties consenting to the divorce and setting out what should happen to the couple's assets and their children.

The judge may accept the terms of this agreement and simply grant the divorce, or may vary the terms of the agreements insofar as they relate to what should happen to the Children: where they live, financial arrangements for them, etc. The judge may not vary the terms agreed about how the matrimonial property should be divided.

An agreed divorce may be dealt with in as little as two weeks. Despite the fact that it is agreed, the Parties may appeal against the decision within 15 days. Parties need attend only one hearing to confirm their will to divorce.

The process in the case of fault divorces
Fault divorces are also dealt with by the courts in Turkey.

The Court that has jurisdiction is determined by the same rules set out above.

During the course of the divorce hearing, the Court will decide whether the alleged grounds for the divorce exist and justify the divorce in legal terms and it will also decide what shall happen to the couple's assets and children. The Court can also award the 'innocent' party compensation for the behaviour they have suffered or the stress they have been caused.

What happens to the children?

Under the law of Turkey, the interests of the Children are the Court's primary concern when dealing with any divorce.

In order to give effect to this, the Court will consider the issues below.

If there is agreement by the parties on these issues the Court will consider whether the agreement appears to be fair and reasonable when looked at from the perspective of the Children.

If there is no agreement between the parties or if it feels that that agreement is unreasonable, the Court will make such orders as it sees fit.

The issues to be considered are:

1. **Guardianship**:

    Which of the parents should be responsible for making all the major decisions regarding the Child's life? These include the type of schooling to be received, major healthcare decisions, religious observance, the country of residence etc. It is normal (and where possible) for these decisions to be made by the parents together, even after divorce. In cases where the relationship between the parents has deteriorated to the point where this is not possible, the Court will give this responsibility to one of the parents.

2. **Residence**:

    With which parent will the Child reside on a day-to-day basis? This is the parent who will also have the responsibility for making the day-to-day decisions regarding the Child's life.

3. **Access/visitation**:

    What arrangements should be made for the parent with whom the Child does not live to see the Child? These arrangements are normally expressed in general terms rather than as specifics. For example, the Child is to live with the other parent for one weekend a month and to see the other parent on one day per week. It is then for the parties to make the detailed arrangements.

If it is not possible for them to agree these then the matter can be brought back to the Court. The Court does not want to see this and, if a parent is seen as being unreasonable, they are likely to be penalised heavily when it comes to the question of court costs.

The parent being granted visitation rights has the right to see the child alone: i.e. not in the presence of the other parent.

4. **The home**:

Generally, in the case of children under the age of about six, the Court is likely to order that the Child should live with its mother, unless there is something unsatisfactory about the mother's lifestyle.

For children older than six it is still statistically more common for the child to live with its mother but there is no legal reason why the order could not provide for the child living with its father.

5. **Financial provision**:

Who should pay to look after the Child, and how much?

Generally, the Court will expect the Parent with the income - typically the father - to pay to support the children or (if both of the parents have an income) to contribute to the support of the children. This will generally continue until the age of 18, or until the Child's earlier marriage, or until some other date agreed by the Parties.

The amount to be paid depends entirely on the means of the person making the payment. In a typical case, where there are, say, two children, the mother is a teacher, and the father is the assistant manager of a bank, you might expect to see child support of TRY1,500 per month.

What happens to the money?

Assets

As we've already seen, in Turkey the courts apply the 'matrimonial regime' to the assets owned by a couple at the time of a divorce or legal separation.

Those assets can either be distributed 'in kind' - for example, the wife retaining the matrimonial home and the husband the Ferrari - or they can be sold and the proceeds of sale divided accordingly.

Given that the couples freely choose their matrimonial regime at the time of their marriage and that they can change it later, the Court is reluctant to interfere with the decisions that the Parties have made and documented.

Ongoing support

Whether there should be ongoing support and, if there is, for how long it should remain in place, depends entirely upon the circumstances of the case and - in particular - the financial circumstances of the parties. The general position is that the person with money should support the one without. Even in modern Turkey, this still results, typically, in payments from the husband to the wife but in principle it could equally work the other way around.

Once payments are ordered, they will generally remain in place until the remarriage of the person receiving the payments.

How does this affect non-married couples?

It doesn't. There is no provision for the 'divorce' of such couples. However, they do have the right to go to the Court for their affairs to be untangled. The orders that will be made are based on the twin principles of fairness and recognising the contributions made by the two parties to their relationship.

How does this affect same sex couples?

They are treated exactly the same as non-married heterosexual couples.

The Turkish population system (*MERNIS*)

Since 2001, Turkey has used a central online system to deal with many aspects of recording details of its population. The Central Population Administrative System (*MERNIS*) makes data readily available online on what is close to a real time basis. It is a comprehensive system: registering births, marriages, divorces, and deaths, as well as when people are entitled to vote and when they change address. But not all of the information is available to everybody.

It is relevant in the case of divorces for two reasons.

First, when it comes to serving your application for a divorce on your spouse, their address should be recorded in the *MERNIS* system and accessible by the Court. Thus, it is the Court that serves the papers, by post.

It is a legal obligation to notify the system when you move house: there is a fine if you fail to do so. As a result, the system is treated as authoritative to the extent that if the Court sends the documents to the other person, by post, to their recorded address they will have been deemed to have been received.

The second consequence is that, when a divorce is granted, the Court will record the granting of the divorce on the *MERNIS* system. The fact that you are divorced will, therefore, be accessible to those with access to that part of the system. However, if you ever need to prove that you are divorced, you will still need to submit your court order.

Many people were sceptical about whether this would work in a very large and populous country, parts of which are fairly basic in terms of their administration but (perhaps to most people's surprise) it has worked well.

How long does a contested divorce take?

A typical case will be resolved in about one year, but there is then a right of appeal, and the process of appeal can take a further one year.

How much does it cost?

This depends upon the complexity of the divorce.

Divorces are not cheap in Turkey. Legal fees and expenses would, in a relatively simple contested divorce, probably amount to about 15% of the couple's assets and would be at least about TRY6,000.

In a complicated case, it can cost a great deal of money!

Paternity & child support

Paternity disputes

Despite our reputation for lustiness and romance, paternity proceedings in Turkey are few and far between.

If a person alleges that a child is the child of a particular person, the issue shall be determined conclusively by DNA testing and the Court has the right to order the parties to undergo such testing.

If the person refuses to take the DNA test, the court will make an order that he be tested and, if the putative father resists, the prosecution office may get involved. In this case, they are likely to lose their case and to be found to be the father of the child. They can also be found to be in contempt of court. In this case, the Enforcement Court has the right to have you physically removed to the hospital for a test to be carried out.

In terms of procedure, the process is much the same as any other case brought before the Family Court.

A person found to be the father of a child will be ordered to make financial provision for that child. The amount depends upon the father's means.

In addition to the right to ongoing support, the child also benefits from the right to inherit from its parent and all of the other social consequences that flow from recognition.

Adoption

Formal adoption is rare in Turkey, but it is recognised under Turkish law.

Informal adoption is also seen in Turkey. This is very often between close family members and it is done without the intervention of the Court or any other state agency.

International adoptions to people habitually resident in Turkey are subject to a one-year trial period.

Turkey: how things *really* work

As in almost every country, a person formally adopting a child in Turkey acquires full parental responsibilities for that child and the adopted child is treated as the natural child of that person and acquires all such a child's rights, including full inheritance rights.

Parents wishing to formally adopt a child in Turkey must first register with the Turkish Department of Social Services and be cleared as suitable adoptive parents. They must be over 30 years of age and, if a couple, must have been married for five years. Single people can also apply to be adoptive parents.

Once the parent has been accepted as a suitable candidate for adoption, a child is selected by the parents. They will be given access to the register of children available for adoption but may find a child in another way. There is no attempt to match racial or cultural backgrounds.

The process is documented and the final certificate of adoption is dealt with by the Family Court .

The process of adoption typically takes about 12-18 months.

Child abduction

The abduction of a child is every parent's worst nightmare. Not only is it extremely distressing but you know it is also going to be difficult to fix the problem, particularly when you may be living many thousands of miles away from the place to which the child has been taken.

With the increased mobility we find in the modern world and the increasing number of relationships formed between people of different nationalities and different cultures, it is not surprising that problems arise.

During an 'ordinary' divorce, where both parents continue to live in the same town or area, the question of who should have primary responsibility for looking after the children and the arrangements for giving the other parent the right to see them often cause endless trouble, heated arguments and much expense.

It is, of course, much worse when one of the parents will be living on the other side of the world and where, obviously, the opportunities for the parent who does not have day-to-day control of the children to see those children will be few and far between. If you add the problem that there may be cultural and religious differences between the parties - and a strong tradition in some places that the father has an inalienable right to bring up his children - then we can understand how these huge problems are amplified still further.

So it is not surprising that some parents, dissatisfied by the arrangements dictated by a court (or fearful of what they could be) decide to take matters into their own hands. This is wrong and dangerous but, sadly, it happens all too often: about 250,000 cases per year around the world.

Fortunately, international law has kept pace, to a certain extent, with these developments and there are well-established remedies available where a child has been abducted. Sometimes those remedies work well; sometimes not.

Who is entitled to the protection of the law?

In the case of international child abduction there are at least two, often three and sometimes four legal systems involved.

Sometimes a child is taken away to a foreign country even when both parents are of the same nationality and were resident in the same place. This is done in the somewhat desperate, and usually ill-founded, hope that distance will make it more difficult for the other parent to get the child back.

In this case, there will only be two legal systems involved: the law of the parents' country and the law of the country to which the child has been taken.

In other cases, a child might be taken where the parents (and the child) are all of different nationalities. In this case, the legal systems governing each of the parents and the child will be relevant and if (which is relatively rare) the child has been taken to a country which is not any of these countries, the legal system of that country will also come into play.

You can imagine that these different legal systems could well take a very different view of what is in the best interests of the child and which parent should have the right to have the child live with them.

This is where international law steps in.

In 1980, after years of debate and thousands of heart-breaking cases of abduction, an international convention was adopted to regulate how these cases should be dealt with around the world.

This is the 'Hague Convention on the Civil Aspects of International Child Abduction'. It has been adopted by 93 states, so only roughly half of the countries in the world. Turkey has adopted the convention.

It's important to understand that the convention does not change any of the legal rights of the parents or of the child. It only decides which country should decide the outcome of any dispute and provides for the return of the child to that country.

The convention requires the courts in all the countries that have signed up to it - including, of course, Turkey - to return the child to the country which is allocated jurisdiction under the terms of the convention.

Where a child was 'habitually resident' in a country that is a signatory to the convention immediately before a 'wrongful action', the courts must order the child to be returned to that country. It also requires them to do so quickly, with a decision being made within six weeks.

Needless to say, that does not always happen in practice and the situation in Turkey is less than satisfactory.

'Habitually resident' has its common sense meaning. It means that the child was normally resident in that country. If a child spends 40 or 50 weeks per year in a country and only goes away on holiday they will be considered to be habitually resident in that country. The test will be applied by looking at a period of several years but if, for example, the child spent the first ten years of their life in Spain and then the family moved to, say, Germany then - after a relatively short period - the child would be considered to be habitually resident in Germany. Evidence of the permanent move to Germany would include having a long-term home there, being registered in school etc.

A 'wrongful action' is defined by the convention. Being a legal definition it is lengthy but, basically, the removal or retention of a child is 'wrongful' when it is in breach of the rights of custody that a person has under the law of the State in which the child was habitually resident immediately before the abduction.

Note that the law covers both removal and retention. In other words, if one parent *allows* the child of which they have custody to travel to another country in order to see the other parent and that parent refuses to return the child (retains it), the rules in the convention will still apply.

The rest of this chapter assumes that the child was resident in one of the countries that has signed up to The Hague Convention immediately before the abduction. See **bit.ly/2gPzFEh** for a list of those countries.

It is important to understand that, with very few exceptions, if a child is taken unlawfully then they must be returned to their home country and the authorities in the place where the child is physically present must act swiftly to arrange this.

What should you do if you're worried?

Many parents fear that the other parent will do something rash and abduct their child or, more often, refuse to return the child at the end of an agreed period of visitation. Fortunately, these fears are often ill-founded and derived from a combination of the natural desire to protect the child and excessive caution. However, they are natural.

However, if you fear that the other parent might take the child there are some precautionary steps that you can take. These include:

- Having high-quality, up-to-date photographs of the child readily available

- Taking copies of the child's passport. Better still, take a certified copy. How you obtain a certified copy will depend upon where you live but, in most countries, it involves having the copy marked as a true copy by a notary, consulate or lawyer

- Having a copy of any court documents or agreements relating to your separation or divorce

- Having a copy of any custody order (the order saying who the child should live with) and any documents relating to visitation (access) rights

- Keeping the lines of communication with the other parent open. Discuss your fears with the other parent

- If you think there is an imminent danger of abduction, notifying the police

Other steps that can be taken some time in advance of any trouble are to make sure that, in any court order relating to the custody of the child, you expressly acknowledge that the Hague Convention should apply and agree the arrangements for visits.

You might also consider an order that places the child's travel documents in safe custody when they are not legitimately needed for travel.

If you have a court order of any kind, you will need to have several copies of it, preferably certified.

If you are worried about the child being taken to a particular country, it is worth getting all the documents officially translated into the language of that country. This can be quite expensive and it can usually be done quickly if a problem arises, so it might be better left until then. However, translating them in advance can save several days if a problem arises.

You also need to have as much information as you can about the child. This might include:

- Full name (with alternative spellings) and any nicknames
- Date and place of birth
- Address
- Height (specifying the date upon which the measurement was taken)
- Weight (again specifying the date)
- Colour of eyes
- Colour of hair. Keep a few strands for DNA analysis if the need arises
- Identifying features (scars, glasses, braces etc.)
- Any relevant medical information (for example, if the child is diabetic)

You also need to have information about the other parent. This might include:

- Full name (with alternative spellings) and any nicknames
- Date and place of birth
- Nationality and place of residence
- Full details of their passport or other travel documents. If the parent has more than one passport, make sure you have details of all of them. The details will include passport number, date and place of issue and expiry date. Ideally, you should have a copy of each of the passports
- Occupation
- Employer
- Qualifications
- Current address and contact details
- Names, addresses and contact details of relatives, especially those whom they would be likely to visit
- Details of your marriage or relationship including the date of marriage or the commencement of the relationship
- Date and place of separation or divorce and copies of the court documents involved
- Current marital status
- Height, weight and colour of eyes

- Colour of hair: again, a few strands for DNA testing would not be a bad idea

- A recent photograph, with the date on which it was taken

- Identifying features

If you are worried about abduction, it is probably a good idea to download both a copy of the relevant law in your own country and The Hague Convention - and, of course, to read them!

If you are worried about the child being taken to a particular country, you might also want to download the relevant law in that country, if it available online.

Of all these things, the most important as a way of preventing abduction is to keep the lines of communication open. If you discuss your worries you may be reassured or you may have cause to worry further - in which case, further action can be taken before the event happens.

It is not uncommon for the other parent to *threaten* to abduct the child, sometimes as part of a strange and dangerous game. It is wise to take such threats seriously but also to realise that they might not signify a serious and immediate risk of an abduction occurring. If threats are made you should contact a specialist lawyer in your own country or the child protection services in your country. They can then advise you as to the steps open to you. These might involve going to court and would almost certainly involve warning your child's school and other relevant people that there might be a risk of abduction.

In almost all countries, if there is a problem or potential problem over child abduction, you should be able to get an appointment before a judge very quickly: a matter of hours or days, not weeks.

What should you do if your child has been abducted?

The first thing to say is that you should try not to panic. You will, of course, do so. However, fortunately, most children who are abducted are recovered quite quickly.

The first thing *to do* is to seek help. How you should do that will depend where you live.

In most countries, there are associations or self-help groups for people whose children have been taken away without their consent. Contact them but do not depend exclusively upon them. Self-help groups are a useful source of information but you will probably need to go to other people in order to recover your child. The group will probably be able to recommend people near to you who have experience in this field.

If you fear that your child has been abducted, or fear that this is about to happen, a good first point of contact is the police. In many countries they will act immediately: in some they will simply refer you to the "Designated Central Authority", often just called the "Central Authority". Here, for brevity, we will call them the "DCA".

The reason for contacting the police is that they *may* be able to issue an immediate arrest warrant and so prevent the removal of the child from the country.

If you have already been engaged in court proceedings, you might want to go back before the civil court for an order prohibiting the removal of the child from the country - even if this might be too late.

You may want to contact the police or civil courts via a lawyer, who will probably be able to get to the heart of the problem more quickly than you would on your own.

If you think that the child has already been removed from your country or retained in another country, your first contact should be with the DCA in *your* country. This is whether or not removal to a Hague Convention country is involved.

The process and terminology can seem complex, but it is worth wading through it.

Under the Hague convention, a parent who has 'lost' a child (called a "left behind parent") must generally submit an application for return to the DCA in the country where the child was usually living before the removal or retention.

This country is called the "requesting state".

Each country that is participating in the Convention has a DCA. This network of DCAs transmits and receives applications on behalf of the left behind parents. They assist the left behind parents in bringing their application to the attention of the competent authorities (usually a court) in the "requested state". i.e. the country to which the child has been removed or where it is being retained.

For example, the United States' DCA is the US Department of State Bureau of Consular Affairs Office of Children's Issues. In the UK, it is (for England and Wales) the Foreign Process Section of the High Court in London. In France, it is the Ministry of Justice in Paris. The point of mentioning this is that the nature of the designated authority varies quite a lot from country to country.

A full list of Central Authorities can be found at
www.hcch.net/en/instruments/conventions/authorities1.

However, the main point is that the DCA you should contact is the authority *in the country where you are living*, even if you know or suspect that the child has already been taken abroad.

If the child has been taken *from* Turkey, the DCA in Turkey is the Ministry of Justice:

Ministry of Justice
General Directorate of International Law and Foreign Relations
Adalet Bakanlığı Ek Binası Namık Kemal Mah. Milli Müdafaa Caddesi No:22
Kızılay - Çankaya
ANKARA

Telephone: +90 (312) 414 84 05 / +90 (312) 414 87 24
Fax: +90 (312) 219 45 23
E-mail: **uhdigm@adalet.gov.tr**
Website: **www.uhdigm.adalet.gov.tr**

The designated authorities are used to dealing with these applications and will usually have guidance leaflets and other materials available to assist you.

Taking action in these cases needs to be done quickly and it needs to be done correctly the first-time round. For these reasons it is usually a good idea to involve a specialist advisor - usually a specialist lawyer - to assist with your application and guide you generally at a very stressful time.

The law here is complicated and you will be dealing with multiple jurisdictions; often where there are language issues.

How does this procedure work in Turkey?

As I've already said, Turkey is a signatory to The Hague Convention but, unfortunately, the courts here seem to be less than cooperative when it comes to observing the requirements of the Convention and, in particular, when it comes to doing so quickly.

The European Court of Human Rights (ECHR) has found that Turkey has several times violated the rights of parents by not returning children who have been abducted and taken to Turkey by the other parent. The actions taken as a result of these findings have, sadly, been rather toothless.

- In 2012, the ECHR found that Turkey had violated the rights of a father in the United States. The man's Turkish wife had taken their child for a visit to Turkey and, subsequently, refused to bring her back to the States. The Turkish courts ruled (on first instance and on appeal) that it was best for the child to stay in Turkey. This was in clear violation of the Hague Convention.

  Five years of litigation led to an unsatisfactory conclusion: Turkey was forced to pay damages to the left-behind father in the US, but the abducted child stayed in Turkey.

- Another case saw Turkey violate the rights of an Icelandic mother, whose children were kept from her by their Turkey-resident father. The woman had travelled from Iceland to Turkey more than 100 times, but each time the father had hidden the children. The Turkish authorities failed to take any "meaningful measures" to assist her. Again, Turkey was fined, but no further action was taken.

Whether through lack of training, lack of experience or for other reasons the judges often adopt the wrong approach to such cases. They insist on carrying out an often lengthy 'best interests' evaluation. This means that they consider whether it is in the best interests of the child to remain in Turkey or to be returned to the country in which they were resident.

This is completely against the provisions of The Hague Convention, which makes it quite clear that it is the responsibility of the courts to order the return of the child to the country in which they were habitually resident. It is then for the courts in *that country* to decide the child's long-term future.

Because of this tendency, it is very important that you engage the services of a lawyer who is experienced in dealing with cases of this type so that this point can be made, very forcibly and very early in the proceedings. This can be done in writing or, if that fails, ideally by the lawyer appearing in person at the first hearing of the case. That will normally occur within four weeks of the complaint being made. Once the Court has made a bad decision it is hard to get it changed.

Sometimes it might require an emergency application to our Administrative Court to *order* the court to apply the law properly.

If you go down the route of a 'best interests' evaluation then it can take a year or more for a decision to be made. With every day that passes, it is easier for the other parent to argue that the child (particularly, a young child), has a strong connection with Turkey.

Under the provisions of The Hague Convention you should start your quest for the return of your child in your country via the DCA. However, this does not stop you also engaging a lawyer in Turkey and the central authority will usually respect your wish to use the services of that lawyer, particularly if they're known to be experienced in the field of child abduction.

Delay

I have mentioned several times the need to take action quickly and, usually, a parent who has lost their child is more than keen to do this. However, you do need to be aware that delay can seriously damage your case. If you wait more than one year after the date of the abduction of your child, your rights under The Hague Convention will be seriously limited.

What if the other parent ignores the local court's order?

As we have seen, there have been cases where Turkey's enforcement of parents' rights has been unsatisfactory but - if an order is made and the other party does not comply with it - the parent who has obtained the order can apply for enforcement of the order via the Enforcement Court.

How long will it take to get your child back?

The target timescale set out in The Hague Convention is six weeks but this will very seldom be achieved in Turkey.

If all goes well and the judge accepts the fact that he or she should not be undertaking a 'best interests' evaluation you should think in terms of about two to three months.

If the other parent wishes to be difficult (and, especially, if they can persuade the Court to do a 'best interests' evaluation), the time spent by the courts of Turkey is likely to be well over a year and, if the case then needs to be appealed, it can take as long again. During this time the child will, almost certainly, be kept in Turkey.

How much will all this cost?

It is impossible to predict the cost of taking legal action in these cases.

The Designated Central Authority will not make any charge for its work but it only administers the process and cannot give you legal advice.

Some lawyers feel so strongly about the issue of child abduction that they will do this type of work either pro bono (free) or at a greatly reduced cost but, in the worst scenario, cases of this kind can be hugely time consuming and therefore expensive.

Therefore, the bills can amount to many thousands of euros, pounds or dollars.

There is no form of subsidised legal assistance (legal aid) available for this type of work in Turkey.

Buying a House in Turkey

Written by **Başak Yildiz Orkun**
Managing Partner (Legal Department) at Orkun & Orkun
www.orkunorkun.com • info@orkunorkun.com

General Issues when Buying a Property in Turkey

A property is always an expensive item, so you do not wish to risk losing your money. This is true whether the house in Turkey or elsewhere.

Transferring the ownership of a house is also, inherently, complicated. It gives rise to legal questions, issues about the condition of the property, and the need for a number of administrative steps.

It is also something that has been happening for hundreds, if not thousands, of years: so a lot of lessons have been learned about risks and how to avoid them.

Thus, the process - if done properly - is bound to be a little time consuming and very detailed.

It is also a process that is likely to be very different from the process of buying a property in your own country. More than ever, this chapter is an introduction to help you understand some of the issues that arise when you're buying a property in Turkey and to let you have a sensible conversation with your professional advisors: estate agents, lawyers, the Notary etc. It is not intended to be a do-it-yourself manual!

Can a foreigner own property in Turkey?

Yes. However, Turkish law makes a distinction between the rights of a foreigner and the rights of a local person when it comes to owning property. It does not matter from which part of the world the foreigner comes. The same restrictions will apply.

Certain areas of Turkey are designated as military zones. A foreigner will, generally, not be permitted to own land (including houses, apartments or other property built on that land) within a military zone.

The position is made more complicated because it is often not obvious why a particular piece of land has been designated a military zone. They are sometimes located in places where the most uneducated person would recognise the military importance of the site but, sometimes, they seem to be located at random.

For many years, the process of establishing whether a piece of land was located within a military zone - and so whether a foreigner would be able to buy it - was time-consuming. You had to make an application to the Army, who would then issue a certificate confirming that the land was (or was not) in such a zone. This could take months.

Recently, the position has become a lot simpler.

If, since 2012 (when the new arrangements were put in place), a person has already obtained a declaration that the property is not in a military zone, that will be recorded at the Land Registry and you will automatically inherit that ruling and so don't need to make an application yourself.

If you will be the first foreign buyer (or the first buyer since 2012) of that land, you need to carry out the process of obtaining military permission via the Land Registry. Basically, you apply for the purchase of the land in the usual way and the Land Registry takes care of the issue of military permission. It typically takes four to six weeks and costs around an additional TRY300.

Some foreigners fall in love with a plot of land or a house located within a military zone and which they would, therefore, not be able to buy. In the old days, they would simply set up a Turkish company (in which they would own 100% of the shares) and then own the land through that company. This didn't count as foreign ownership. However, the law has now changed and this would now require the Turkish company to have more than 50% Turkish ownership and to be managed by a Turkish-resident person or entity. A company owned solely or mainly by foreigners will no longer work.

There are people who advise that there is a simple solution to this: set up a Turkish company where most of the shares are owned by a Turkish national (for example, your estate agent or your lawyer) and then have them execute a document saying that they hold those shares 'in trust' for you. **We think that this is really bad advice**. There is great potential for this to go wrong and, if it does go wrong, it will be hard, time-consuming, expensive and/or impossible to fix the problem. Trusts of this type are not recognised in Turkey, so you have few legal rights. We think that it is better to recognise that if the State does not want you to own this piece of land, you will just have to accept that limitation. There are many other beautiful plots and houses!

There is one further restriction on the rights of foreigners to own land in Turkey. That is that no foreigner may own a piece of land in excess of 30 hectares (74 acres). That is quite a lot of land! If this is not enough for you, you can make an application to the Council of Ministers, and the limit can be increased to 60 hectares. Whether this application will succeed will depend upon where the land is located and the commercial rationale behind what you're doing. This rule was put in place, basically, to protect Turkish agriculture from foreign intrusion.

One other matter that may cause you concern is that, for many years, the only foreigners who were allowed to buy land in Turkey were people who came from countries that gave Turkish people the reciprocal right to buy land in their country. This was not a problem for people from most European countries or the US (which granted those reciprocal rights), but it was an issue if you came from some Middle Eastern or Far Eastern countries (which did not). We mention this 'problem' only because people are likely to mention it to you but, in fact, it isn't a problem at all any more. When the financial crash came in the late 2000s, Turkey wanted to sell land to people from the Middle East to replace the buyers from the UK and Germany who had dried up. As a result, this rule was revoked. It now doesn't matter which country you come from; you will be able to buy land in Turkey unless it is in a military area.

Is buying a property in Turkey a good idea?

For many clients, buying a property in Turkey is a great decision. They buy for several reasons: as a permanent place for them (or, increasingly, for their children being educated in Turkey) to live, as a holiday home or as an investment.

Quite often the person buying a holiday home sees a huge lifestyle benefit - and sometimes becomes so comfortable in the area that they later decide to relocate or retire here.

You may enjoy a better climate, a lower cost of living and, often, a more active social life than you experienced at home.

Of course, there may also be all sorts of career and business opportunities in Turkey.

There's also a chance of making money, as property values can increase substantially. However, you probably need no reminding that there is no guarantee that properties will increase in value. You will have seen, over the last few years, that in bad times their value can fall dramatically.

Prices have increased since the dreadful years of 2008/9/10, but there is political and security uncertainty in Turkey at the moment, which is making many foreign people question whether now is the time to invest here. Of course, often, those who invest when nobody else is doing so are the ones who make real killings - but sometimes they get badly hurt when things don't go as they'd hoped.

So, buying a property in Turkey is not for everyone: none of us have a crystal ball to see whether the property market will improve or deteriorate. Yet if you want to retire to Turkey or enjoy the benefits of a holiday home in this unique country, it can still look like a very attractive option.

It is seldom economically attractive to buy a home if you are only going to live here for a year or two. You are usually better off renting. This is because the acquisition and disposal costs when buying are both quite high.

Nor is buying a property in Turkey entirely risk free from a purely technical point of view. It isn't in any country. There are always risks associated with buying a property, wherever in the world you are looking at, and Turkey is no exception. Do not over-estimate or fear the risks. The vast majority of transactions turn out to be danger-free. Making sure you get expert guidance will dramatically reduce your risk and similarly increase your chances of a good buying experience - whether you're buying a holiday home, an investment property or buying as a means of relocating to Turkey.

In fact, one of the few things that all the experts agree on is that buying a property in Turkey really does require some specialist advice.

Ignore them at your peril!

Horror stories and dangers

Let me start by repeating that, generally speaking, as long as the appropriate checks are carried out, there is no more need to worry when buying a property in Turkey than there is when buying one in your own country.

Unfortunately, many people buying property in Turkey (and in other foreign destinations) take little or no legal or financial advice and are far too casual both about the purchase of property and about the signing of legal documents. If they go about things this way, it can turn out badly. Sometimes very badly.

They may find that there is no title to the property, that it was built without planning permission - or, sometimes, that it does not even exist!

They may find that what they were told by the seller or the estate agent is just not true.

At the moment, the problems we come across most commonly are:

Kat irtifak title

Kat irtifak title - or a *kat irtifak tapu* - is a provisional title deed relating to a property in a project which has not been fully completed. There is nothing in itself wrong with a *kat irtifak tapu*. You will often receive one when buying into a new development but, once the development is completed, it needs to be upgraded into a full, permanent title (*kat mulkiyeti tapu*). It's important to make sure that there is no apparent obstacle to this being done, and that the seller has an obligation to assist in that process.

If you do not do this, you can find that it becomes very hard to sell the property.

Excess construction

This is still a problem, though much smaller than it was a few years ago. A developer will obtain a perfectly valid building licence to construct, say, six 150m2 houses on a site. He will then built eight 200m2 houses. Needless to say, the building licence will no longer be valid. It will then be impossible to obtain proper title to, and the right to use, those properties.

This remains a problem even after the property has been completed and you've taken delivery of it.

Fortunately, there are two fairly simple solutions. The first is to obtain a survey of the property you're buying. This will confirm its size and that it has been built in accordance with the permission granted. The second, in some ways cheaper, is to take a mortgage on the property. If you do this, the bank will make the necessary checks, at no extra cost to you, and refuse the mortgage if all is not in order.

Under-declarations

For many years, there has been a tradition in Turkey of stating in the title deed (selling the property to a new buyer) a price well below the real price being paid for the property. There are two reasons for this. The main one is to save paying tax, which is calculated upon the value declared in the title deed. The second, in some instances, is a desire for privacy.

Either way, under-declaration is illegal and if you assist the seller to reduce his tax liabilities in this way, you merely create an instant, completely artificial and taxable capital gain for yourself. Unless you can find somebody who will, in turn, under-declare the value paid when you sell the property to them, this can prove very expensive; particularly if you're tax resident in a country with a high rate of capital gains tax.

Under-declaration is foolish and illegal. It should be avoided. Fortunately, it is happening less and less frequently.

Bad contracts or the lack of proper contracts

This is, in particular, a problem when you are buying a property under construction, but should also be avoided in any property purchase.

Some contracts presented to buyers are simply bad contracts: they are unclear, unfair, non-compliant with legal requirements, or all of the above! These contracts, which do not make clear the seller's obligation to you or your obligations to the seller (for example, in terms of payment of the price), are highly likely to give rise to problems later on.

Fortunately, there is again a simple solution to this problem. Have your contract inspected by your lawyer before you sign it.

Problems with the building

Whether you buy a property that has already been completed, or one still in the course of construction, you can find that problems emerge with the fabric of the building after delivery.

This is true in every country and it is a problem that cannot be completely eliminated. However, a properly drafted contract (providing for the opportunity to inspect the property before taking delivery of it and a mechanism for dealing with any problems after delivery) and making sure you do arrange an inspection will greatly reduce the likelihood of this happening.

Resale properties

If you buy a second-hand (resale) property, the risks associated with the state of the property will usually (but not always) be your responsibility. You should, therefore, think seriously about having the property surveyed (inspected) before you sign a contract to buy it.

New properties

If you are buying a new property from a developer, it is important that the contract provides for the inspection of the house before you take delivery of it, and that it makes clear the obligation of the developer to rectify any problems that arise.

If no other periods are specified, the law imposes an obligation for the developer to repair any large problems that arise (such as sinking foundations or structural cracks in the walls) within 20 years of the date of delivery of the house and any small problems (such as a broken door, but not including problems caused by wear and tear) within five years (see our section on buying a new property for more information: page 395).

Because fixing problems costs the developer money, they are often reluctant to do so and if you have to go to court to enforce your rights it can often be uneconomic as a case could easily take three years.

The principal solution to these problems is, again, to have the property inspected before you take delivery and, ideally, to make sure that any issues found are rectified to your satisfaction before you take delivery.

Is the house the one you thought you were buying?

Strange as it may seem, we have come across instances where buyers have been shown and agreed to buy House A (say, unit 26 in a development) but when the contract arrived it sold them House B (say, unit 50 in the same development - or even a property in a different development altogether). This is more often due to clerical error than malice but, as you can imagine, it can cause massive problems; especially if the problem is not identified immediately, or if the house you actually wanted to buy has, in the meantime, been sold to somebody else.

The solution to this problem is to make sure that you identify the property you think you are buying to your lawyer by reference to a map.

Your lawyer will have access to the maps at the Title Deed Office (*Tapu Ofis*). Entering the plot number comes up with a Google Maps location. Brilliant! One of the best systems in the world.

Unpaid condominium (community) fees

This can cause a problem in two separate ways.

First, if the previous owner has not paid his condominium fees, they may become your responsibility.

The second is that, often, owners do not pay condominium fees because there is a problem with the apartments or in the administration of the condo. If this is the case, it's better to find it out before you buy the property and, possibly, to look elsewhere. A condo with unsolved problems will probably not have the money to spend on maintenance etc. and so tends to decay.

Developer finance

It is quite usual, as in most countries, for developments to be financed by loans made to the developer by banks. There is nothing wrong with that. However, your contract needs to make it clear that it is the obligation of the developer to clear that finance before handing over the property and its title to you and - just as importantly - you need to make sure that the amount that you're going to have to pay to the developer when you take delivery of the property is in excess of (and so sufficient to clear) any outstanding finance.

Safety first!

Don't become one of the people who simply drifts into the purchase of a property without making any checks.

For your own safety, insist on taking proper, independent, legal advice. Independent legal advice is advice from a lawyer not connected with the seller: someone whose duty lies solely in looking after you.

A sense of proportion

Remember that for every 'horror story' you hear, hundreds or thousands of people buy safely in Turkey.

The State of the Market

At the moment (2017), in most parts of Turkey, this is a buyer's market. There is lots of property on sale (though not as much as a few years ago) and there are relatively few buyers, especially foreign buyers. There are local exceptions to this rule. For example, there is great competition to purchase property in central Istanbul and there is a strong demand for property in well-respected coastal destinations. But in most of the tourist areas, you have the luxury of being able to choose from a number of suitable properties.

In all parts of Turkey, prices fell back from the heights they reached in 2007/8 but in some places - such as Bodrum - they have now risen again to virtually the same levels as prevailed at that time. In other places, prices are still well below 2008 levels. In some places, the prices are well below what it would today cost you to build the property: the direct costs, ignoring any profit. This is often a strong indicator that the property is a bargain.

The recent availability of mortgages for local Turkish people of modest means has generated lots of demand for properties of the type that they are wanting to buy - and that is also having a knock-on impact on other parts of the price range.

Are You Ready to Buy?

Going to look at houses should be the last stage in the exercise of acquiring a home in Turkey, not the first. The process of buying a property - whether it is for your personal use or for investment purposes - should start with thorough preparation.

This will save a lot of wasted time and money.

It is a good idea (though quite rare) to talk to your lawyer *before* you go to look at any property. That way, they will be able to take you through all the key issues (such as those listed below) calmly and clearly, before you get involved in the rush and pressure associated with buying a property anywhere in the world.

There are also certain steps that you can take yourself, just to make sure that you are ready to buy a property in Turkey: that you have the necessary paperwork and (if you're thinking of applying for finance) that you're likely to be acceptable to a mortgage lender.

We have a fuller checklist covering what you should be doing at **www.guides.global/checklists.php.** This is kept up-to-date and is therefore better than simply reprinting it in this book. You can a download a copy, free of charge. The main points are set out below.

Preparation checklist

Why are you buying the property?

Be honest with yourself. Do you and your spouse or partner agree why you are going to spend a lot of money buying a home in Turkey? This can often lead to some matrimonial moments!

Is this for retirement or long-term relocation, a pure holiday home, a holiday home that is also intended to make you some money, or a pure investment?

Which area will suit you best?

If this is an investment, where are you likely to make the most money? If it is for your own personal use, how easy will it be to get there?

Surprisingly, answering a dozen or so simple questions can narrow down the places likely to suit you to a radius of 50km or less (and that's in the whole world!)

Which type of property will be best for you?

A villa, an apartment, a townhouse, or something else?

How are you going to pay for the property?

Are you going to take out a mortgage? If so, where and for how much? What are you doing to guard against the risk of fluctuating exchange rates?

How are you going to manage the property?

Will you do this yourself?

Will it be done by local friends and neighbours?

Or will you use a professional property management company?

This question is nearly as relevant if you are buying a holiday home as it is if you are buying an investment property.

If you want to let the property:

- Who are your target tenants?

- Who will manage the lettings?

- How much money will you make?

Who should be the legal owner of the property?

The right choice here can save you a *lot* of money, even on a holiday home. See below.

Due diligence

The process of answering these questions is an essential part of your 'due diligence'. However, it is all too easy to skip over these points as tackling them might feel a bit complicated. That is a mistake.

The decisions you make will have a big influence upon your enjoyment of the property and the amount of money you make out of it.

It can be well worth speaking to your lawyer and/or someone who really understands the property market in Turkey to clarify your thoughts about these issues.

Who should own the property?

Getting this question of ownership wrong is probably both the most common and the most expensive mistake people make when buying property overseas. There are many people who could be made the legal owner of the property or, possibly, the shareholders in the company that owns the property. The best choice is often not obvious.

Making the wrong decision can cost you lots of money in totally unnecessary fees and taxes, both during your lifetime and on your death. Ask your lawyer for advice. It will be time and money very well spent.

Making the right choice can, in some cases, completely eliminate inheritance tax on the later passing of the property after your death and/or greatly reduce the taxes on any income from the property during your lifetime.

Some local lawyers will be unable to help you make this decision as it involves an understanding of both the Turkish and your own legal, tax and inheritance systems. In this case, there will be lawyers in your own country who will be able to help, possibly by working in conjunction with your Turkish lawyers.

Case study

André Redaud

Banker, French, 55

The problem

André wanted to buy a property in Turkey, with the intention to live in it for a couple of months in the summer and let it out the rest of the year. He was going to put it in both his and his wife, Sophie's, names but his friend told him this may not be the best option.

The solution

André saw an accountant, who confirmed that putting André and his wife's name on the property would not be the most tax-efficient solution. Sophie was a housewife, and so did not have any taxable income in either France or Turkey, whilst André had both. Because of the size of his income, he paid large amounts of tax at higher tax rates.

If he put the name only in the name of his wife, the income from it would be hers and not his. This meant that, if the house was in Sophie's name alone, any rental income would be taxed at a lower rate.

This would save the couple money under both the French and the Turkish tax systems. It looked like André would save about €3,000 per year in tax if he put the property just in his wife's name.

However, a few years ago André had been through a divorce and he was very much aware that, by putting the house in his wife's name, he could make things more complicated if his current marriage failed and, in the end, he decided that he would rather forgo the tax benefit and have himself registered as the half-owner of the property.

The best long-term decision is not always the one that brings the greatest short-term gain. Before you make any decision, you need a thorough understanding of your options, and their consequences.

What are the options as to ownership?

There are many ways to purchase a property in Turkey. These include:

- In your name alone

- In your name and the name(s) of your spouse or other co-purchaser(s)

- Wholly or partly in your children's names or in the name of somebody who you would like (eventually!) to inherit the property from you

- Via a Turkish company

- Via a Trust

Each of these methods has advantages and disadvantages. The one that will be best for you will depend entirely on your individual circumstances.

Getting advice

The choice is *not* obvious. Just because a husband and wife are buying the property does *not* mean that the best choice is always to put it in both of their names. Just because your neighbours bought the property in their joint names does *not* mean that this will be the right solution for you.

Please, seek advice. It will almost certainly save you money.

Is the Process of Buying the Same as at Home?

No. The systems in Turkey are likely to be very different from those in your own country.

In Turkey, you should be safe to buy property if you take some basic precautions - just as you would in your own country. Just remember that this is a different country where we speak a different language and have a different legal system. If you are not familiar with either of these, you definitely need proper legal advice.

Sometimes the procedure for buying a property in Turkey may be better (quicker, cheaper, safer, easier) than the procedure in your own country. Sometimes it may be worse. But it is always different.

This can be a little confusing.

If it's any consolation, a Turkish person buying an apartment in (say) Paris or New York would probably be just as confused, baffled and worried as you are!

The main things to look out for when buying property in Turkey

The important thing to understand is that there is no simple list of dangers that you need to check. For different people and different types of property, or for people who are buying for different purposes, the dangers will be different and so the checks needed will be different. It is part of your lawyer's job to work out the questions that need to be answered in your particular case.

However, there are some dangers that arise in every country and every transaction. For example:

- Does the seller have good legal title and the right to sell?
- Is the property affected by debts?
- Has the building been constructed legally?
- Will you be able to use the property for the purposes you desire?
- Does the property suffer from any defects?
- Is what the seller and the agent have told you about the property true?

In addition, in Turkey there are other issues that often need special attention. These include:

- Are you *sure* you have chosen the correct form of legal ownership?
- Is the property built in an area that is specially protected or where foreigners are not permitted to buy?
- If you are buying a 'ruin', will you be able to restore it?
- Are the boundaries of the property clear?
- Is the existing planning status of the property clear?
- Does the property have a habitation certificate, permitting its occupation as a dwelling?
- What is the price that will be declared in the title deed (*tapu*)? As we have already said, the price you declare as the price paid for the property should, legally speaking, be the full price paid. This is the value used to calculate all the taxes arising out of the transaction. Declaring any other value can lead to all sorts of problems, both locally and in the country where you live. Declaring any other value is also illegal.
- Are you aware of the rules of any condominium or Home Owners' Association of which the property forms a part? These can be restrictive.

There will usually be other issues that arise in the special circumstances of any particular transaction.

All of these issues should be discussed with your lawyers, who should then be instructed to make the enquiries needed to protect your position.

What is the role of the estate agent/realtor?

Most buyers will use the services of a real estate agent (realtor) to help them find a property. Most estate agents in Turkey are honest and competent, but there are some who are not.

It is always a good idea to seek out a personal recommendation about estate agents from friends or family who have been through the process, or even from your lawyer.

At the very least, make sure that your estate agent is registered with the Turkish Chamber of Agents. At the moment, there is no legal obligation to be professionally qualified before operating as an estate agent in Turkey, or for the agency to be licenced. Licensing may come shortly.

Many properties are advertised via several different agents, so even if - as most of us are - you are more concerned about the property on sale than you are about the agent selling it, you can still choose to deal with a 'better' agent. One who is recommended. One who speaks your language. One who has experience dealing with people of your nationality.

You may come across estate agents in your own country offering property for sale in Turkey. If they are legally entitled to work as an estate agent in their own country, they are legally entitled to offer property in Turkey for sale as far as the Turks are concerned. *However*, such agents must (and most do) work through a registered Turkish estate agent when it comes to negotiating or finalising the transaction. So, when you come to Turkey to look at the property, you will be dealing with an estate agent experienced in selling property in Turkey.

Estate agents in Turkey may operate differently from those in your country.

For example, they do not operate a multiple listing service (MLS). As a result, you need to wander from one estate agent's office to another to find everything that is on offer.

Alternatively, in many parts of Turkey, you can select the agent you would like to work with and they will liaise on your behalf with other agents in the area to show you both the properties that they have themselves been asked to sell and the properties on sale via all the other estate agents in the area. They will negotiate an arrangement whereby they will receive a part of the fee due to the other agent in return for introducing you to the property. You should not, yourself, have to pay the agent any fee for providing this service unless you specifically agree to do so in writing.

Another way in which the agents in Turkey will probably be different from the agents in your country is that they publish very little information about the properties they are selling. In places with a preponderance of sales to foreigners, you may find rather more detail than in other areas, but even then the information tends to be somewhat limited. There will be a picture. You will be told the number of rooms in the property, the number of square metres covered by the property and its approximate location. The rest is discovered by inspection.

You are not likely to find floor plans, the measurements of individual rooms, or any details about the facilities in the property, or in the condominium of which it might be a part, in the estate agent's publicity materials.

Are there other sources of property in Turkey?

Yes. There are a growing number of ways in which you can find your new home in Turkey.

Banks

Following the recession of the late 2000s, many banks have repossessed properties to sell. Prices can be low. Such properties sound attractive, especially if the bank will grant you a mortgage to help buy the property, which they might be more inclined to do if - by selling the property - they are solving a problem.

However, remember that many of the properties are in undesirable locations and that many will have been neglected pending repossession. Finding a property through a bank can also be more time-consuming than when you're using an estate agent as the estate agent will be able to help you filter the large number of areas and properties down to a few that you might really want to buy.

In fact, whilst some banks take care of the sale of these properties themselves, most put them in the hands of local estate agents. Even if you are interested in a repossessed property, you are probably better off sourcing one via an estate agent.

Private sales

A few private individuals sell their property themselves: advertising on the internet, by signs on the property and (sometimes) in specialist press. These people will, almost always, be Turkish. As a result, unless you speak Turkish, you may find dealing with them difficult. It is also, always, time consuming.

Auctions

Finally, some properties are sold by auction. Properties offered via auction are properties being sold upon the orders of the Court. Once again, the idea of buying property at auction can be superficially attractive but - unless you speak fluent Turkish and have the time to view lots of properties and attend lots of auctions - this approach is not, generally, a good idea for a foreign buyer. You can end up attending a lot of auctions where you are not the successful bidder. If you are paying somebody to do this for you, it can get expensive!

Visits to view properties

It is usual for the estate agent, or an employee of the estate agent, to accompany you when you visit the property. You may find them very reluctant to give you the full details of the property, to take you there or to give you the details of the seller until you have signed a document confirming that it is they who have introduced you to the property. Whatever the reason they give you for this requirement, the real reason is to protect their commission!

Always visit the property at least twice - preferably at different times of the day - before putting in an offer to buy the property.

Do you really need a lawyer?

If you speak fluent Turkish and understand both Turkish law and the system of buying and selling property in Turkey, you probably don't need a lawyer. Many Turkish people would not use one.

However, for most foreigners the use of a lawyer is essential.

The estate agent selling you the property might try to persuade you that he has the skills to do all this work on your behalf, and that this would save you money. Don't listen. Remember that the estate agent only gets paid if you buy the property - and that, in most cases, his client is the seller of the property, not you.

When it comes to finding a good lawyer, ideally, seek recommendations from people who live in the area: especially foreigners who speak your language.

If you don't know anybody, you may find recommendations on the website of your country's consulate in Turkey. Such lawyers will usually be experienced in dealing with people from your country and are likely to speak your language well.

Be very careful before using the services of the estate agent's 'own' lawyers. Are they the estate agent's brother? Are they looking after your interests or the interests of the agent who is providing all their work?

Find somebody who you are comfortable working with, who speaks your language and has experience of dealing with foreigners - preferably, foreigners of your nationality - who are buying property in Turkey.

Of course, we will usually be happy to help by acting for you!

Always make sure that you agree, in advance, a fee with the lawyer.

For the basic service, this will, typically, be an all-inclusive 1% of the price of the property (subject to a minimum of €1,200) plus any direct expenses that they incur on your behalf.

Should you arrange a survey/inspection?

You can do quite a lot for yourself. Having a look at the property in a slow and methodical way and checking some of the basics could result in you rejecting a property without the need for a formal survey.

However, if the property passes that initial test and - wherever you buy a property - it is sensible to have the property surveyed (US: inspected). We strongly recommend a survey, especially in the case of older or unusual properties, or properties that have been extended or modified.

It would be just as expensive to re-roof or re-wire a house in Turkey as it would be back home!

Surveys are still not common in Turkey, particularly amongst Turkish buyers. They will invest in a survey for high value properties, but often don't for more modest ones.

Surveys are carried out by licensed experts. They are inexpensive: perhaps TRY500-TRY1,000 (€121-€242/US$138-US$276/£107-£214) for a modest house.

It's also worth noting that it can be complicated (and expensive) to carry out a survey on an apartment, where the main walls and services can (and usually do) belong collectively to all of the owners in the block rather than to one individual apartment, and where a survey of just your part of the building can be pretty much meaningless in the absence of a report about the rest of the building.

A local surveyor or your lawyer will be able to tell you whether a survey would be realistic or useful in your case.

Structural surveys typically take between seven to ten days. The time and cost varies.

Note that there may be cheaper alternatives to full structural surveys. These involve a surveyor or other skilled person inspecting the property (but not pulling up carpets, removing kitchen appliances etc.) and producing a general report as to the property's condition. These tend to be about half of the cost of the structural survey. However, they offer less reassurance and come with fewer guarantees.

It is also possible to get some of the benefits of a survey - but not a full structural survey - by having a builder look at the property. This is usually particularly relevant if you are thinking of doing extensive repairs or alterations to the property. If you're going to virtually rebuild it, you may not care too much about its current state and care rather more about the cost of doing the work necessary to achieve what you want to achieve. Such an opinion by a builder is likely to be free if he thinks he's going to obtain a sizeable job because of it.

Strangely, surveys are relatively uncommon in the case of locals buying local property. As a result, it can - especially in a seller's market - be difficult to persuade the seller to wait a couple of weeks for you to get a survey before you sign some form of contract. Often, in reality, the pressure is coming from the agent (who wants to secure their commission) rather than from the seller! However, in today's buyer's market, this is less of a problem.

Where possible, if you want a survey the best way is to persuade the seller to take the property off the market for a few days to allow the survey to take place and for you then, very rapidly, to sign a Reservation or Preliminary Purchase contract.

If the seller will not do this, it is legally possible to negotiate a special clause in your contract allowing you to sign a contract there and then but making the contract conditional upon your receiving a satisfactory survey result. However, many sellers are reluctant to do this because of the complexity of specifying what is 'a satisfactory report' (meaning that the contract must go ahead) and what is an unsatisfactory report (giving you the right to cancel the contract).

What is the role of the Notary (*Noter*)?

The Notary plays a large role in lots of legal transactions in Turkey - including dealing with Wills and inheritances and authenticating all sorts of important documents. See page 280 for more details.

However, in Turkey (unlike in many European countries), the Notary does not play a major part in the process of buying and selling real estate.

If you're dealing with a property transaction in Turkey, the most likely involvement with the Notary will be drafting a Preliminary Purchase Contract (in order to make it fully enforceable: see above) or producing and witnessing a Power of Attorney (see page 288).

It is important to bear in mind that the Notary is not there to give you legal advice or to promote your interests at the expense of the other party. They are more a referee, to make sure the process is followed properly, than a lawyer acting on your behalf.

The Notary will usually know nothing about the law in your own country. Therefore, a Notary is no substitute for your own independent legal advice.

Communities of owners/condominiums

Many people who buy a property in Turkey, whether as a holiday home or for their own permanent use, will choose to do so in a development that shares common facilities. The classic example of this is a block of apartments, where there are shared access ways, gardens, parking areas etc. but these days it could equally be in a resort development comprising individual houses which share the use of pools, tennis courts, and a reception area.

If you do this, you will be buying into a development with a 'community of owners'. A community of owners is a legal structure, common throughout continental Europe and used in Turkey, which has been created to allow for the orderly management of blocks of apartments or groups of houses. This is set up by a document called the Management Plan.

If your house or apartment shares facilities with other owners, there must - by law - be a community of owners. Every block of apartments, by definition, shares facilities, because you will find that you are the owner of the internal part of your apartment but that the outside walls, the roof, the foundations and all the communal areas such as stairways and lifts will be shared with the other owners.

When you buy into a community of owners you buy not only your own house or apartment but also an undivided share of those common facilities. An undivided share is a share which is not physically apportioned to you.

In other words, you do not own (say) a piece of land representing 1% of the parking area but you and your fellow owners collectively own 100% of the parking area.

When you buy into a property that is part of a community of owners there are several consequences:

1.   You will own a share of the common areas.

    a)   The size of your share will, these days, usually be proportional to the size of your apartment or house compared to the total size of all the apartments or houses. In other words, if you have an apartment of 100m2 and your neighbour has an apartment of 200m2 in a block of 1,000m2, you will own 10% of the common areas and your neighbour will own 20%.

b) In some older developments, you may find that your share in the common areas is split equally between all the owners in the complex. In other words, if there are 100 owners you will each hold 1% of the common areas.

2. You will be responsible for paying your proportion of the expenses of maintaining those common areas. This could include, for example, the costs of electricity used to light the hallways, the costs of cleaning, the cost of gardening, the cost of redecorating the common areas and the cost of repairs to the roof, the outside walls, and the foundations. Your share will be proportionate to your share in the community.

3. You will be responsible for paying your proportion of the expenses of managing the community.

4. You will have the right to take part in the management of these common areas. A committee of owners will usually be appointed to coordinate this activity and, in all but the smallest complexes, that committee is likely to employ the services of a specialist management company who will take care of things on a day-to-day basis. The committee is elected, each year, by a general meeting of the owners, which you will have a right to attend and at which you will have the right to raise any issues of concern to you and vote.

5. The residents also elect a president. The president may have a number of duties under the terms of the community's constitution. The president must usually be a resident in the community.

6. If you do not pay the amounts for which you are responsible, there is a fast-track court procedure by which the community of owners can recover the sums due from you and - if you still fail to pay - there is a process by which they can seize and sell your property to recover the money due. To do this they are allowed to go directly to the Enforcement Court, rather than having to start a court case against you to prove the debt. You will also have to pay interest of 5% *per month* on the amount outstanding until payment.

7. You will have to abide by the rules of conduct agreed by the community. You should be given a copy of these rules and of the constitution of the community when you buy your property. These are important documents as they govern your rights within the community and your day-to-day conduct. Do not ignore the rules. They can cover everything from whether you're allowed to have pets, to whether you can use your property for business purposes, to the frequency with which you must mow your lawn. If you fail to comply with the rules, the community can take enforcement action against you, in the worst case obtaining a court order to ban you from doing what you're doing - and if you fail to comply with that, your property could be sold by the court!

This all may sound rather draconian, but some such rules and arrangements are needed if a group of apartments or houses is not to fall into disrepair and so that life is not extremely noisy and chaotic. This is particularly true in the case of holiday properties.

Most owners do not have any real problems in complying with their obligations but many do find that the community can become a bit of a den of intrigue in which there is a lot of petty politics.

Incidentally, even if you are a tenant you will also have to obey the rules of the community in which you live.

It is important that you check the rules before you buy or rent. It would be unfortunate if you moved into a new home only to find that you were not allowed to keep pets or - in extreme cases - your children.

It is also important to make sure that there are no outstanding community debts for your property and to check whether the community has approved, or is discussing, any major items of expenditure.

Items that have already been approved should be the financial responsibility of the old owner, but if the community is discussing, but has not yet formally approved, (for example) the complete renovation of the swimming pool, this could cost each owner quite a lot of money.

Cooperatives

The concept of a cooperative is, in some ways, similar to the concept of a community of owners but, in a cooperative, you and your fellow owners own the entire property between you in undivided shares. In other words, you do not have a separate legal title to your own apartment and then a shared interest in the community's facilities. You have, say, 1% ownership of the entire building.

Under the rules of the cooperative you will still be entitled to the exclusive use of your apartment, but the legal structure is different.

Cooperatives have long been a feature of property in Turkey. They were originally invented to allow groups of people to get together, buy some land and build some houses as a shared project. They're now much less used as the more recent community of owners' arrangements are generally better and more efficient.

State aid for improvements to the property

There is no state aid for the improvement of property in Turkey.

Preliminary Contracts to Buy a Property in Turkey

Once you have found a property that you would like to buy you will, almost certainly, be asked to sign some form of Reservation Agreement or Preliminary/Promissory Purchase Contract.

However, the market in 2017 is (once again) a bit of a buyer's market. As a result, although you will be put under some pressure to sign some sort of preliminary contract immediately, in order that the property can be taken off the market, you should not be in any great hurry to do so. It is better to get it checked by your lawyer before you sign. This can normally be done very quickly.

Why sign a preliminary contract?

Having said that, there will genuinely be some occasions when the property in question is in great demand and you may well want, immediately, to secure it by signing at least a Reservation Agreement. There is, in principle, no reason you should not do so.

The reason people want to sign some form of preliminary contract is that it reduces uncertainty; and uncertainty almost always equates to danger. If you have only a verbal agreement to the sale, either party can change their mind and it is then, at best, difficult (but usually impossible) to prove what was agreed and to do anything about it.

From the estate agent's point of view, it also helps him collect his commission!

However, remember that it is not strictly necessary to sign *any* form of Preliminary Purchase Contract, but it is almost universal practice to do so, especially in tourist areas.

Types of preliminary contracts

There are three main types of preliminary contracts that you might encounter, and two possible alternatives to them.

Each has its own advantages and disadvantages. They are significant. You should know what they are before you get involved in the process of buying a property in Turkey.

Estate agent's agreement

This is not, strictly speaking, a preliminary contract in relation to the purchase of the property, but it's worth mentioning here just for the sake of completeness. This is only an agreement between you and the estate agent.

In most cases, it will simply be an acknowledgement that this agent has introduced you to this property. This is more in his interests than in yours, as it's really designed to safeguard any commission he might earn from the sale of the property, particularly if the property is listed in the offices of several estate agents.

A second type of estate agent's contract is a contract where you agree to pay an agent a fee for helping you find a property. This is rare.

It is not usual to have these agreements checked by your lawyers, though there is nothing to stop you from doing so.

Reservation Agreement/Reservation Contract

Although estate agents in Turkey are not professionally qualified, it is very common for them to produce these simple initial contracts themselves.

This contract takes the property off the market for a short period.

It should contain little more than the details of the buyer and seller, the description of the property to be sold, the price agreed for the property and how long it will be taken off the market for you to complete your enquiries and sign a proper purchase contract. See the sample Reservation Contract at **www.guides.global/books/turkey/turdownloads.php**.

You pay a relatively small amount of money (typically €1,000 - we refer to euros here as many properties are priced in euros) to take the property off the market for a short time (typically two to four weeks) During this period your lawyer can carry out their checks to make sure that the house is safe to buy.

If it is safe, you then sign a more comprehensive Preliminary or Promissory Purchase Contract to buy the property, or even proceed directly to the signing of the formal Deed of Sale: the *tapu*. See below as to these options.

If your lawyer finds any problems and you do not want to go ahead, you stop the process.

If you do not go ahead with the purchase because you merely change your mind you will, almost always, lose the deposit you have paid. If you do not ahead because there is a legal problem with the property you will, in theory, be entitled to recover this payment. It can sometimes be tricky to do so unless the problem is clear and obviously the responsibility of the seller.

You should understand that a Reservation Contract does not give you any rights over the property. At best, it means that - if the transaction does not go ahead - you will be entitled to the refund of your money. You will not be able to take action to force the seller to sell the property to you. This does not mean that signing a reservation contract is without any merit, but it is of limited use. It is, however, a clear (if symbolic) statement of intent.

Once again, this contract is really of as much benefit to the estate agent as it is to you. If he later has any trouble with the seller, he holds at least €1,000 of his commission!

Preliminary/Promissory Purchase Contract

A Preliminary Purchase Contract or Promissory Purchase Contract is a true contract between you and the seller, under which the seller agrees to sell the property to you and you agree to buy it. In theory, it creates a binding obligation on both parties.

Until recently, these were used a great deal. Now their use is rather rarer. This is because it has become clear that these contracts are only really enforceable by either party if they have been notarised - and that costs money.

Notarised contracts

According to Turkish Law, promissory contract for the purchase of a property must be subject to the involvement of a Notary (*Noter*). Otherwise the contract is accepted only as showing a debtor-creditor relation between the parties - which takes you back to the position where you are only entitled to the refund of the money you have paid.

A notarised Promissory Purchase Contract (NPCC) can be fully enforced. Both parties can be forced to honour their promises. Any penalties agreed in the contract can be applied. The seller can be forced to sell the property to you and you can be forced to buy it from the seller.

The cost of a notarised Promissory Purchase Contract is not cheap. The combination of the Stamp Duty and Notary's fee will usually be 1.5% of the price of the property. In addition, when you finally sign the *tapu* (formal Deed of Sale) you will have to pay the usual property transfer tax (4%) and Title Office fee. See below for details.

Private (non-notarised) contracts

If you do not sign a notarised Promissory Purchase Contract but, instead, either sign a non-notarised Preliminary Purchase Contract or sign nothing and go directly to the Title (*tapu*) Office and sign a Deed of Sale (*tapu*), you will not have to pay this 1.5% - but you will still have to pay the Property Transfer Tax and Title Office fee when you sign the *tapu* at the Title Office.

Which to choose?

The top and bottom of it is that, if you sign a *notarised* Promissory Purchase Contract you'll be paying more fees and tax than would otherwise be the case but your contract will be stronger and more legally enforceable.

The upside of signing a preliminary contract of any kind (notarised or not) is that, although any penalties stated in the contract will not be enforceable unless it has been notarised, it still forms a basis for you to get your deposit back if things go wrong through no fault of your own, and the basis for some kinds of litigation in respect of the contact. As the deposit paid on this type of contract is, typically, 10% of the price of the property, it is reassuring to know that you have at least some protection.

This problem of notarisation - or lack of it - is particularly important if the contract provides for a long term payment plan for the property: for example, where a property under construction is being paid for by instalments.

All in all, for many people it is probably sensible:

- To *dispense* with signing a notarised Promissory Purchase Contract if you're only paying a small deposit such as the €1,000 you would pay under a Reservation Agreement. You can proceed directly to the signing of the *tapu*.

- If you're going to be expected to pay a larger deposit, or if there is going to be a significant delay before you can sign the Deed of Sale (*tapu*), to sign at least a non-notarised Preliminary Purchase Contract

- If you are going to be paying a lot of money (especially by instalments when buying a property under construction) you should probably sign a proper *notarised* Promissory Purchase Contract, paying the fees and taxes involved

Alternatives to preliminary contracts

Buying the land straight away

If you are buying an off-plan property (something still under construction) and the developer will agree to it, you can buy the land now (and take full legal title to it) and then agree to pay the developer for the construction of the property by instalments as the work progresses.

This gives you a lot more protection. As the owner of the land, you will benefit from the work done on it. However, few developers will accept this because, if you don't make the payments, they've already handed over title to the land and have a very weak negotiating position.

An Offer to Buy (*Fiyat Teklifi*)

An Offer to Buy is sometimes used instead of a Promissory Purchase Contract.

This is usually when your offer is subject to conditions or where the price or payment method is very different from that sought by the seller.

It a formal written offer to buy a property.

Your lawyers or, at least, an experienced estate agent should ideally draft it. This makes sure it contains the clauses needed to protect you. There are lots of possible protective clauses: for example, a clause saying that the contract will be cancelled if you do not receive a mortgage offer within a certain number of days; or if your survey shows defects in the property; or if the seller does not produce adequate proof of ownership and legal title.

The Offer to Buy will contain a closing date by which time the buyer must have accepted your offer.

If she does not do so, the offer automatically lapses and the document is no longer of any legal effect.

Offers to Buy are rarely used in Turkey except in major commercial contracts.

Which type of arrangement should I choose?

Whichever type of document you are asked to sign, it is a good idea to seek advice from your lawyer and to get your lawyer to have a look at it before you sign.

Is there a cooling off period?

There are some countries where the law grants buyers a period of grace, during which they can cancel their purchase contract without having to give any justification for doing so and without facing any penalty. Any money already paid must then be refunded.

Turkey is *not* one of these countries, so as soon as you sign a contract it is legally binding upon you.

It is, therefore, particularly important that you only sign a contract if:

1. You really want to buy the property
2. It is really necessary to sign a contract

It is also important that you sign the right type of contract - and one that is properly drafted to reflect your circumstances and those of your particular purchase.

What happens if I pull out of the deal?

This depends upon the type of contract you have signed. See above.

What happens if the seller pulls out?

Unless you have signed a notarised Promissory Purchase Contract, you will not be able to force the seller to sell the land to you and transfer legal title to you. The best you will be entitled to is the return of your deposit.

What if you don't want to sign any of these agreements?

You can proceed directly to the signing of the final Deed of Sale (*tapu*), simply on the basis of a verbal agreement to buy. You then complete your purchase of the property and the transfer of its ownership to you at the same time, by signing the formal contract of sale - *tapu* - at the Land Registry. This, of course, means that you do not part with your money until you have the opportunity of obtaining full legal rights over the property.

If you're going to do this, it is important that you and the seller really have agreed all the relevant details so that you don't get into an argument when it comes to the Land Registry preparing the formal contract (*tapu*).

Buying a house in this way can save you quite a lot of money in notarial fees and taxes, but it leaves you very exposed; the seller can change their mind or move the goalposts at any point. The might decide not to sell at all or they might try to bounce you into paying a higher price, sometimes on the actual day of the proposed signing and handover.

If any of this happens, doing without the notarised Promissory Purchase Contract can prove to be a very expensive saving!

What if I am buying directly from a private seller or developer?

Some people buy property directly from a private seller or developer, without the intervention of an estate agent. You still need to take all the same precautions and sign the same contracts.

In our experience, buying directly from a private seller is almost always more complicated than buying via an estate agent. Even ignoring the language issues - most private sellers are Turkish - which often create difficulties for our clients, the whole process tends to be more problematic.

- The sellers seldom fully understand the process.
- The houses are often being sold privately because there are problems associated with them.
- They are often sold in this way after they have failed to sell via an agent.
- They are often overpriced.

It is also worth remembering that even some major developers will sell property that is illegally constructed or, for some other reason, not safe to buy. This is sometimes by oversight and sometimes a calculated attempt to sell a property with problems.

If you're buying directly from a private seller or developer, it is *absolutely essential* that you use the services of a good lawyer.

The Legal Process of Buying a Property in Turkey

There are several stages in the process. It is probably worth summarising them.

The Preliminary/Promissory Purchase Contract (*Satış Vaadi*)

If you decide to sign a PPC, do so after your lawyer has carried out, at least, the following checks:

- A check to make sure that the person selling the property is its registered legal owner; and that the property is free from debts or other burdens (e.g. rights of way across the property) that might adversely affect you

- A check that the description of what you are buying matches the description in the title register. In the case of second-hand properties, it is commonplace for there to have been illegal or undocumented changes or extensions to the property

- A planning enquiry to establish the current planning status for the property. Ideally, this would show that there is (in the case of a new property) a construction licence for the building of the property or (in the case of a resale property) a habitation certificate authorising the occupation of the property as a dwelling

- Checks on the proposed contract of sale to make sure its terms are fair and cover all the necessary points needed to protect you

- Checking that, where these are required, the proper guarantees securing the completion of construction of the property will be made available

There may be other checks required in the particular circumstances of your transaction. Your lawyer should discuss these with you.

Survey

As we've already mentioned, surveys are rare when people are buying property in

Turkey - but this does not make them a bad idea.

If you have the property surveyed, you will at least know:

- That it is actually the property you thought you were buying

- What has been built tallies with the building licence that's been issued

- If it is a resale property, you will have some idea of the condition of the property.

Mortgage

This will also be the time to obtain an approval, in principle, of a mortgage. See page 409.

Potential changes to the property

If you wish to make alterations to the property (for example, to put in a swimming pool) this will also be the time to check that the authorities are likely to agree to them.

If you want to use the property for a particular purpose (for example, as a bar or office) you should check that this will be permitted.

Report

Once all the steps appropriate in your case have been taken, your lawyer should produce a written report setting out their findings, their general observations and their opinion as to whether they think that it is - from a legal point of view - safe to proceed with the purchase.

Signing the Preliminary/Promissory Purchase Contract

If everything is OK and you decide to go ahead with the purchase, you will then often sign some form of Preliminary Purchase Contract or Promissory Purchase Contract, so committing yourself to the purchase (see page 382).

You will then pay a part of the agreed price as a deposit. Typically, in the case of a resale property, this is 10% of the price. For property bought off-plan (not yet built) the deposit (often 30% of the price) is usually followed by a series of stage payments as the building work progresses. The triggers for these payments will be set out in the contract.

After you have signed a Preliminary Contract of some kind

Whether you sign some form of preliminary contract or decide to dispense with this step and proceed directly to the signing of the Final Contract of Sale (*tapu*), your lawyer will need to take various steps on your behalf.

Power of Attorney

In many cases they will prepare a Power of Attorney authorising someone in Turkey to sign the Final Contract of Sale/Title Deed (*tapu*) for you. This will be needed if you cannot or do not want to be in Turkey to deal with the formalities yourself.

The Power of Attorney can be signed either in Turkey or in your own country. It is much cheaper to do it in Turkey, if you happen to be in the country at the time. It is sometimes so much cheaper that it is worth making a special trip to Turkey for this purpose! See page 288.

The person having the Power of Attorney will usually also need to apply for a tax number for you, to open a bank account and/or to obtain other documentation needed to buy a property in Turkey.

If you are taking out a mortgage in Turkey, your lawyer may need the Power of Attorney to liaise with your lender.

If you need to give your lawyer a range of powers, it will all be done in one document, though you should note that, if two or more people are buying, a separate Power of Attorney will be needed for each buyer.

If you are taking out a mortgage to help pay for the property, you will need either to be present in person for the signing of the *tapu* or to give a special Power of Attorney to somebody who can sign for you. Most banks no longer accept the finalisation of such contracts via an ordinary Power of Attorney. At best, they will insist that the Power is drafted as per their template. Some will insist on your being physically present. If the bank *will* accept signature via a Power of Attorney, you and your lawyer will need to prepare the Power of Attorney in the agreed form.

Bringing the money to Turkey

While this is taking place, you and your lawyer will make arrangements with your bank for any mortgage funding to be made available on the day the *tapu* is signed. In order to do this, the wording of a deed of mortgage will have to be agreed.

You will then need to arrange for the rest of the money to be transferred to Turkey. This will usually be paid into your own bank account in Turkey, leaving you or your lawyer (using a Power of Attorney) to draw it out when needed. Remember that you will need to transfer not only the balance of the price but also the amount needed to pay all the fees and taxes, plus a small margin to deal with the unexpected. Your lawyer will give you a calculation showing the amount you will need to transfer.

Whatever that sum is, it is a good idea to add a bit extra to allow for fluctuations in exchange rate and the unexpected. We suggest 1-2% of the total to be sent. If this money is not needed, it will remain in your bank account and be available to pay bills, buy furniture etc.

Make the transfer via a specialist foreign exchange (FX) company, rather than via your usual bank. This is likely to save you a lot of money. See page 112.

Before you sign the Formal Deed of Sale (*tapu*)

After signing the preliminary contract, your lawyer will have to liaise with your seller and estate agent. When everything is ready, they will arrange for the Land Registry (*Tapu Ofis*) to prepare for the signing of the Deed of Sale/Title Deed (*tapu*).

To repeat, the *tapu* is the document transferring legal ownership of the property to you. It may be referred to in English in different ways: Deed of Sale, Title Deed, Formal Contract of Sale etc. none of these are strictly accurate. It is the *tapu*!

The *tapu* must, by law, be prepared by and signed in front of an officer at the *Tapu Ofis*, sometimes referred to (again slightly incorrectly) as the Land Registry. The *Tapu Ofis* must carry out various tasks to prepare for this. When everybody is ready to proceed, the *tapu* is signed.

Whilst this is being done, your lawyer will obtain approval from the municipality that the amount being declared in the proposed *tapu* is at least the minimum they assess the property as being worth.

Your lawyer will also obtain the compulsory earthquake insurance (DASK) from the government for around TRY500 (US$130/£100/€110).

The *Tapu Ofis* will require formal proof of your identity and other personal details, together with the relevant details of the property. They will then prepare the *tapu* document for signature by the seller and the buyer.

These days, the final preparation for the signing of a *tapu* is all a very slick process. Your lawyer will, online, make an appointment to sign the *tapu*, and they will usually be able to sign that day or the next day.

He or she will then pay the Property Transfer Tax due, immediately before the signing the *tapu*, using a special ATM in the *Tapu Ofis*… and that's really it.

The only real delay comes about if you need to obtain a military clearance (which can add three or four weeks to the process) or if you want to obtain a mortgage (which will also add several weeks to the process).

When everything is ready at the *tapu* office, your lawyer will receive an SMS saying that the *tapu* is ready for signature, giving a payment code and setting a time for the signing.

Signing the Formal Deed of Sale (*tapu*)

As already stated, this is either signed, in person, by each of the sellers and by each of the new owners or it is signed by people having Powers of Attorney on their behalf. As also already mentioned, you may not be able to sign via a Power of Attorney if you're taking a mortgage in Turkey.

If you attend in person to sign the *tapu* (which is an interesting thing to do and which could well cost you less than the price of preparing a Power of Attorney in your own country), a translator will also be required unless you speak fluent Turkish. In this case, you will be taken into a special room where the officer will read the title document to you (in Turkish) and where it will be translated for you (by your interpreter).

Once you or your lawyer have signed, you can collect your finished copy of the *tapu* - your proof of ownership of the property - about five minutes later.

Registration of title

This whole process is then registered in the Land Registry's computer system - TAKBIS - and forms the legal basis of your claim to ownership of the property.

One of the great joys of the Turkish system is that the *Tapu Ofis*, where you sign the Deed of Sale, *is* the Land Registry. So, by signing the Deed of Sale, you have complied with all of the steps that are needed to secure your title to the property.

This is a great deal faster, and somewhat safer, than the arrangements in many countries, which involve a signing before a Notary followed by a separate registration of title at the Land Registry office.

How Long Does This All Take?

The whole process from seeing the property up to the signing of the Final Contract of Sale will (in the case of a resale property with no mortgage) typically take about 12-16 weeks, though this can vary enormously.

If you are going to take out a mortgage, this will usually add about a month to the process. If you need military permission, allow an extra four to six weeks. In the case of a property under construction, the speed of construction usually determines the pace: typically, perhaps, 18 months.

What are the Fees and Expenses when Buying a Property?

The total of the fees and expenses is typically from 6.5-10.5% of the price paid for the property. See the table below.

The largest component of this is the Property Transfer Tax, paid to the Government of Turkey. The *Tapu Ofis* will tell your lawyer the exact amount that is required.

The lawyer will want to have your money in his bank account in order to pay this tax! They will, usually arrange this by withdrawing the money that you have sent to your Turkish bank account (using the Power of Attorney you have given them) or by getting you to transfer the funds directly into their bank account.

The total size of the total bill depends upon several factors. The most important is the price of the property.

There will be additional fees if you're taking out a mortgage (typically about 1% of the amount borrowed).

Item	Cost
Lawyer's fees	1% of the property price (minimum €1,200) + VAT (18%)
Lawyer's direct expenses	Varies
Notaries' fees - Power of Attorney	TRY800
Property Transfer Tax	4%* of the property price (usually 2% paid by the seller and 2% by the buyer but, in some cases, the seller will ask the buyer to pay it all, or vice versa)
Military clearance, if needed	TRY600
Tapu Ofis/Admin costs	TRY200-TRY300

*this was 3% until the end of September 2017 because of a temporary discount given by the government to help the property market

Things to Do as Soon as You've Bought a Property

As the new owner of a property in Turkey, there are various steps that you ought to take:

- Tell the local town hall that you have bought the house. This should have been done, automatically, as part of the purchase process, but it is a good idea to contact them. It's very important for the town hall that you register as an owner, because the grant that they receive from the government each year depends upon the number of inhabitants (local and foreign) registered as living in their area. By registering you will give them just a bit more money to spend on schools, roads, garbage collection etc.
- If your house is part of a community of owners, introduce yourself to the president and to the administrator of the community. Once again, they should have been notified about your purchase automatically but it is good manners to present yourself to them and it is helpful if, for some reason, the notification hasn't arrived. You will need to make arrangements to pay your community fees. In some cases, these are payable monthly and in others they are payable in one annual lump sum.
- Notify the utility companies - water, electricity and telephone - that you are the new owner of the property and arrange for future bills to be sent to you.
- Insure the property. Your lawyer or estate agent should be able to suggest a suitable insurance company. See our chapter on home insurance (p94) for more detail.
- Finally, while it's nothing to do with buying the house, this is a very good time to make a Will relating to your assets in Turkey. See our chapter on Wills (page 461).

Turkey: how things *really* work

We know this all sounds a bit complicated - and it is. But, in truth, it is probably no more complicated than buying a home in your own country. It just seems to be because the process is different and you are not familiar with it.

Buying a New Property

Many people prefer to buy and own new property. There are a number of reasons:

- They will be the first owner of the property. No-one will have used the kitchen or bathroom before. Strangely, this is the most common reason why I am told that people like to buy new property! It is probably the worst reason. It is also probably not true. Your builders will almost certainly have been making their tea and eating their lunch in your kitchen, and their bottoms will have sat upon your toilet seat.

- Repairs costs should be very low for the first few years. In fact, the property will come with a guarantee against any major defects for the first five or 20 years (depending on the nature of the defect).

- Running costs and, in particular, energy bills will be much lower than in an old property. This is because of ever-improving building standards and, in particular, increasing levels of insulation. This is especially true in Turkey, where older properties were often very poorly and cheaply built.

- New properties are better equipped than properties built a few years ago. Many will now come, as standard, with fitted air conditioning. Kitchens and bathrooms are of a far higher calibre than they were five years ago.

- The property will be built using the latest designs. Of course, in ten years, tastes will have changed and your house will look as old-fashioned as the one built ten years ago does to you today!

- Depending on when you agree to buy the property, you may be in time to get design changes incorporated into the property. For example, you may be able to choose the style of your kitchen or bathroom, to have a bedroom converted into a study, or even to combine two rooms into one.

- Depending upon how early you agreed to buy, you may get the best plot: the one with the largest garden, the best views, the easiest access to the communal pools etc.

- Depending upon when you buy, you may benefit from buying at (say) 2018 prices but take delivery of a property in (say) 2020, by which time it could have risen significantly in price.

The potential problems of buying a new house

There are three main problem areas when buying a new house:

Every new house has teething troubles

As it dries out, plaster will shrink a little, and small cracks will appear. You may get drips from taps or pipes. There will be bits of painting that have been missed. And so on. These are not a disaster but they do need to be fixed.

This process is called 'snagging' and you need to make sure that your contract sets out a clear procedure for dealing with these problems.

It will usually be the responsibility of the builder or developer to fix them (see below) and, in Turkey, they will generally be fixed quite quickly but it can be a problem if you're buying a new house for use as a vacation home.

This is because you will not be living there and so it may take time for you even to identify that the problems have occurred. It may then take time for you to liaise with the builder and then for you to arrange to get them fixed.

This shouldn't necessarily put you off buying a new property, but it is a factor to consider.

In practical terms, the most important thing is to make sure that the property is thoroughly inspected before you take delivery of it and pay over the balance of your money. This might be done by you personally, or you might have it done by a surveyor. In most cases, it's done by the owner in person in order to reduce cost but, unless you have special skills and knowledge, a professional is more likely to spot any problems.

When it comes to inspecting the property, do take a bit of time. Many of the things to look out for are on our Inspecting a Property checklist - downloadable for free from **www.guides.global/books/turkey/tur-downloads.php**. I am always surprised by just how slow and detailed a proper inspection is.

Bad developers and builders

Your biggest nightmare is if the developer or builder is a rogue or goes bust.

Fortunately, we do not have many rogue developers or builders in Turkey; but we do have some who go bust.

This causes you a problem because it is the developer or builder who issues the guarantee that your property will not suffer from any serious defects: anything substantial for the first five years, and anything very serious for the first 20 years (see below). This guarantee is not backed up by the government or any other organisation so, if the developer goes bust, the guarantee can become valueless.

Luckily, most people will take out insurance against this risk. It is fairly low cost, typically about €500 for the full ten-year period, but this is rising quite quickly.

The second problem if the developer or builder goes bust is that it is they who are responsible for sorting out all the little problems referred to above. These are not big enough to be caught by the guarantee.

Happily, these smaller problems tend to come to light quite quickly and so - with a bit of luck - the developer or builder will still be around to deal with them! If you're concerned about this, insurance is again available to guard against this risk. A typical policy on a three-bedroom home might cost €150.

Note that neither of these risks will be included as standard in your homeowner's insurance.

Falling prices

The moment you turn the key in your door, the price of your house will fall in value. This is just like a car. It will usually happen even if the general property market is rising in value.

This is because of people's liking for brand new property. They're prepared to pay a premium for buying it.

This is such a significant factor that some wealthy investors will buy investment property and then keep it, empty and un-let, until they see an opportunity to sell it on at a profit. This way it will still benefit from the 'new property' premium.

This fall in value may come as a surprise to you as many people assume that all property rises in value. Of course, after the initial fall, the property will rise or fall in value in the same way as the rest of the property market.

You can guard against this risk to a certain extent, but you can't eliminate it.

It is worth quantifying the potential loss. Check out how much properties more-or-less identical to yours but which are, say, 12 months old are selling for in your area and compare that price with what you are going to be paying for your new property. You can often do this online.

Until about two years ago, you could approach the developer and strike a hard bargain on price, so making a big dent in the loss. With the improving property market, there is now much less opportunity to do this. Nonetheless, it's worth having a go to see whether there is any possible movement on the price.

Guarantees

These are sometimes called warranties.

By law, the developer of a new property is responsible for fixing any 'major' defects that occur within the first 20 years from the date when the property is delivered to its first buyer.

'Major' is defined by Turkish law. Basically, it means any structural defects. In other words, if the house begins to subside (sink) or it develops major structural cracks (rather than tiny little cracks from the plaster drying out) or if the roof is defective, the developer will be legally obliged to fix it. This guarantee will apply both to the main structure of the house and to any ancillary buildings such as garages or swimming pools. It will not apply to things such as garden walls.

The developer will also be responsible for fixing any 'serious' defects during the first five years after the property was first delivered. These, more minor, defects are defects that are less of a problem than major defects but still more than you would expect from routine wear and tear.

Case study

Juan Moralez

Mechanic, Spanish, 43

The problem

Juan bought a new house in the countryside just outside Bitez (near Bodrum) in 2011. In 2012, a storm hit the area and the roof of Juan's house started leaking dramatically. He was unsure whether this fell under the ten-year guarantee or if it counted as an 'act of God'. If it was an 'act of God', would it be covered by his home insurance policy?

The solution

Juan contacted a surveyor to have a look at the roof. The surveyor concluded that a new roof should have been able to take the strain of what was a fairly normal Autumn storm in Turkey.

The surveyor explained that, normally, damage caused by a storm would be damage that would be paid for through the owner's household insurance and not something that you would claim from the developer but that, in this case, the quality of the construction had been poor and that was what caused the problem. He also identified other parts of the property that were not constructed to the standards required in Turkey.

Armed with the surveyor's report, Juan contacted the developers of his house, who accepted responsibility and fixed the roof. They were also forced to make good the other defects before anything broke or caused actual damage. The surveyor gave Juan a lot of unpaid support during this process. Juan had to move out of his house for a week whilst work was being done, but, luckily, his home insurance covered the cost of a hotel; as well as damage to his belongings from the leaky roof.

In the end, all Juan had to pay was TRY700 for an hour of the surveyor's time. The rest was only inconvenience.

So, for example, if the central heating plant or the air conditioning plant breaks down within five years, the builder will have to fix it. If the exterior paintwork develops serious problems - rather than just needing a bit of touching up - the builder will have to fix it.

Minor defects do not include things caused by routine wear and tear, by soiling or by damage outside the builder's control. So, for example, if the outside paintwork of your house becomes grey and discoloured this will not be covered. If the central heating stops working because you allowed the oil pump to run dry, this will not be covered.

These guarantees are transferable when you sell the house.

There are no guarantees if you buy a resale property unless it was built less than ten years ago. In that case, it will benefit from the residue of the developer's guarantees, if any. However, this benefit must be specifically transferred to the buyer when they buy the property. This is easy. Your lawyer will deal with it.

The guarantees are from the developer. This may not be the same as the company that actually built the house; though, if work by a sub-contracting builder was defective, the developer should have rights against the builder and you would inherit those rights if the developer went bust.

Buying an Off-Plan Property

An off-plan property is a property that you agree to buy before it is fully constructed. You might be buying when no work at all has been done: when it is a mere concept or architect's drawing. Alternatively, you could be buying when the building works are partly completed.

In the boom years of the property industry in Turkey - roughly from 2002 to 2007 - buying property 'off-plan' was extremely fashionable and extremely common.

This is because people were persuaded that there was money to be made by doing so. They were told that prices were rising so quickly that, by the time the property was finished, it would be 20-30% more expensive than it was today and - in any case - you probably wouldn't be able to find a newly built property to the exact specification that you wanted.

All this was true whilst the market rose sharply but, when the roundabout stopped, a lot of the people who had bought off-plan properties found they were in trouble as the developers went bust in droves and prices tumbled.

Sometimes - all too often - they lost all the money they had paid.

There is still a market for off-plan property, but this is mainly in Istanbul rather than in the coastal towns.

The benefits of buying an off-plan property

From the buyer's point of view, there are several main benefits to buying an off-plan property.

The first - and, perhaps, least important - is the potential to benefit from prices rising in the way described above.

The second is that you can often negotiate changes to the standard specification with the builder. For example, you may want your bedroom to be a little smaller and your bathroom to be a little bigger or to convert one of the bedrooms into a dressing room or to have a separate dining room rather than a large kitchen-diner.

The third is that you should have a better range of properties available to you than you would if you waited for the properties to be finished. By that stage all the ones in the best locations or with the best views could well have been sold.

From the seller's point of view, there is one massive advantage. He can use your money to build the property. That saves him a lot in project finance costs, which, in Turkey, would typically amount to, perhaps, 20% per annum in many cases.

The government, by way of an incentive to kick-start this industry, is also allowing foreign nationals and Turks resident abroad to buy new properties from developers VAT free - if the funds are being transferred from abroad.

The disadvantages of buying off-plan

There are few disadvantages from the seller's point of view, but from the buyer's point of view there are several:

It is often difficult to know what you're buying

Most people are not good at interpreting plans. This is particularly so if the plans are measured in metres and they are used to dealing with feet and inches!

Your 'large' living room can turn out, in reality, to be very poky.

The quality of the workmanship may not be what you expected

Your contract will, no doubt, contain certain clauses setting out the quality of work and the quality of the fixtures and fittings you can expect but they're usually too vague and, too often, open to debate. It is not uncommon for you to feel that what you have been delivered is inferior to what you were shown or promised. This may give rise to certain rights on your behalf, but it is always time consuming and inconvenient to have to deal with this sort of situation.

This is even true where you have been shown a property as a show house and think you're buying an identical unit. Surprisingly often, your contract will not refer to the show house by saying that what is delivered to you must be equal in size and quality to the show house.

Delay

It is quite common for building projects to be delayed. Sometimes this is because the builder misjudged the time needed to complete the project and sometimes it can be for reasons outside the control of the builder, such as strikes or the non-availability of some essential components.

In the worst cases these delays can go on for months.

It is very important that your contract should contain a completion date, a clause stating that builder will have to pay you compensation if he goes beyond this date (unless it is for reasons beyond his control) and a clause saying that, if he goes beyond a fixed later date, you will have the right to cancel the contract and have all your money returned to you.

The builder may go bust

If the builder goes bust before he finishes work on your house, you will have a whole host of problems. Even if you're protected by the law and you don't lose any money, getting your house finished will usually take months and a lot of time and effort. This is because other builders are usually reluctant to get involved in half-finished projects because they never quite know what they're going to find and so how much it is going to cost to finish the work. Unfortunately, before developers go bust they often start cutting corners and so the new builder can find that work that is apparently finished is substandard and has to be done again.

The worst-case scenario if your builder goes bust is that you could lose all the money that you've paid to him up to that point. You become just a regular creditor of the company and, when it's put into liquidation, you - like all the other creditors - may only receive (say) 2% or (if you are lucky) 10% of what is owed to you.

General problems associated with new properties

You will, in addition, face all the issues that face any buyer of any new property. See above.

Financial guarantees on off-plan property in Turkey

The law does not give any specific financial guarantees to people buying off-plan property in Turkey. Unlike in some other countries, there is no limit to the amount of money that the builder can take from you before the property is built, and there is no arrangement where money taken has to be placed in protected bank accounts or in some other way guaranteed so that it is safe in the case of a disaster.

Stage payments

Stage payments are usual in the case of a purchase of an off-plan property in Turkey.

These are payments made as the building work progresses. The size and staging of the payments is, in theory, a matter for negotiation. However, in practice, the terms are usually laid down by the builder - and there is little opportunity to modify them substantially.

Sometimes, the schedule suggested is unfair. It can also be dangerous in that it requires you to pay the developer far more at an early stage than the cost of the construction - meaning that, if the developer fails at the end of the project, there will not be enough money left to be paid to cover the completion of the building.

A typical schedule for payment might be:

- A 10% deposit when you sign the contract (if work has already started)

- A further 10% when the foundations of the property have been constructed

- A further 20% when the walls have been finished

- A further 20% when the roof has been put on the property and it is watertight

- A further 20% on the structural completion of the property

- The final 20% when the property is delivered to you and you take legal title to it

Mortgages on off-plan property

If you want to take out a mortgage on an off-plan property, you will have a cash-flow problem.

No bank will lend you money to pay for the initial deposit or the stage payments. They will insist on waiting until you get the legal title to the property and then, at the same time as you get that title, they will release the agreed mortgage money to you and take the protection of a registered mortgage (legal charge) over the property.

This is because, until that point, they cannot have any security for the loan they are making to you. You don't own the property, so you can't mortgage it to them.

You will, sometimes, be able to obtain a mortgage if the developer is able to give you an interim legal title to the property. This is the *kart irtifak tapu* (provisional title). See page 367.

Special steps to take if buying off-plan property

The two main special steps that your lawyers will need to take on your behalf if you're buying an off-plan property are to see that the proposed terms of the payment are reasonable and to make sure that, when it is built, you will be able to get a habitation licence for the property. Without this your property is considered as incomplete.

If the construction of the property has been properly licensed by the municipality and it is built in accordance with that construction licence, you should be able to obtain a habitation licence without difficulty but, all too often, builders make changed to the design (sometimes substantial) without getting the necessary approvals. In these cases, it can be difficult (or even impossible) to obtain your habitation licence. This is especially a problem if the size of the property has been increased without permission.

There are, of course, many other things for them to do, many the same as when buying any property.

Buying Commercial Property

Buying commercial property can be a little more complicated than buying residential property.

Commercial property is, in essence, anything that is not residential or agricultural. The definition includes shops, bars, restaurants, hotels, warehouses, car parks and the like.

Some buyers are buying such property purely as investors. They usually think that commercial property has less risk than residential property and that you tend to get far fewer problems with your tenants. It is far from clear that they are right.

Others buy commercial property for use in their own business.

It is still very difficult for foreigners to obtain a mortgage to buy commercial property in Turkey. In the last few years it has been difficult even for Turkish people to do so, but most banks will now offer local people a 60% loan-to-value mortgage. We expect that granting mortgages to foreigners will become easier over the next year or two - but you will probably, even then, not be able to borrow more than about 30% of the value of the property.

Should you buy or rent commercial property?

If you are buying commercial property for the use of your own business, you will usually have a choice between buying a suitable property or of renting one.

Advantages of buying

- You don't need to worry about rent increases

- If you manage to get a mortgage you may be able to fix your monthly mortgage payments for the whole duration of the mortgage, so giving you certainty as to your future outgoings

- Property tends to go up in value over time and, if it does, your business will benefit from any capital growth

- If the property goes up in value you may be able to re-mortgage it to release additional funds for your business or for yourself

- You will be more free to make alterations to the building to suit your particular business requirements and you will benefit financially if the property increases in value as a result of those alterations

- Under Turkish tax law, any mortgage interest payments will be tax deductible in the same way that your rent would have been

Disadvantages of buying

- Even if you can obtain a mortgage, you will have to pay a substantial amount of the property price yourself. This ties up money that could, perhaps, be used better elsewhere

- You must pay for the maintenance and upkeep of the property, though this is often also a requirement if you rent commercial property

- If mortgage rates change, your mortgage payments could go up, but so could your rent

- If the property loses value, as they did over the last few years, this will reduce the value of your business

- Owning the property restricts your flexibility, particularly if your business needs to grow into larger premises or shrink into smaller ones

- You are in business as (say) a plumber, not a property speculator!

Probably the most significant disadvantage of buying commercial property in Turkey is inflexibility. If you want your business to double in size quickly, it will be much more difficult (and expensive) selling your property and buying another than it would be finding another place to rent.

The advantages and disadvantages of renting are the flipside of the advantages and disadvantages of buying!

What kind of premises should you buy?

There are several considerations here.

- How much room do you think you're going to need now and in the foreseeable future?

- If you can afford to buy more space than you need now, will you easily be able to sub-let any excess?

- Do you need parking?

- Do you need your premises to give a particular image: stability, elegance, high-tech or whatever?

- Do you need lots of storage space? If so, it can be cheaper to buy one unit for your active business use and another (much cheaper and less well located) for the storage of things that you will only need to access rarely.

- Do you want a modern building or a traditional/historic building? Modern buildings are generally much cheaper to buy and run.

- What are your requirements for power and water? Will these be available in sufficient quantity in this building?

- Does the building already have a licence to be used in the way in which you want? If not, will a licence be easy to obtain?

- How much will it cost you to repair and improve the building?

Location

Location is as important for commercial buildings as it is for residential buildings: possibly more so. The price you will pay for the building can vary dramatically depending on its location. For example, a shop on the main shopping street in Istanbul or Bodrum can be five or ten times as expensive as a shop in a second or third-level location.

Do you have a requirement to be in a particular place? If not, you can save a lot of money by choosing a place only a few hundred metres away from the prime location, and often get the side benefits of easier access and a lot more available parking.

Finding the premises

Many of the estate agency firms in Turkey deal with commercial as well as residential property.

Commercial property in also advertised in the local press. However, you should bear in mind that the best commercial property is seldom advertised. It is passed on by word of mouth, often via the estate agent.

Legal steps and due diligence

A contract for the purchase of commercial property is likely to be more complex than the contract for the purchase of a house and so, unless you are very experienced and your Turkish is fluent, you would be foolish not to use a lawyer to assist you.

There are several steps that will need to be taken before you sign a contract:

- Your lawyer will check that the property has all the permits and licences necessary to use in the way in which you want or that they will be easily obtainable

- If the licences are not already in place you may try to negotiate a holding contract - either an option to buy or a contract with a 'get out' clause saying that you can cancel it if you don't get the necessary permissions

- You will probably need to do a survey (inspection) of the building. This will not only look at its structural condition but also at the questions of whether you will be able to obtain adequate electricity, water, drainage, broadband, telephone and other services on the site and whether your proposed use is likely to create any special environmental or other issues.

- You will be wise to obtain detailed estimates for any improvement works, repairs or decorating that you intend to do to make sure that the overall cost of the project is within your budget

- Depending upon what you intend to use the premises for, you may need other professional advisors such as hotel or restaurant consultants

Raising the money

As already indicated, you are likely to need to raise most of the price yourself, from your own resources. You will also need to find all the cost of improvements, repairs and redecoration and the legal and other fees involved in buying the property.

The legal fees and taxes, payable on top of the price of the property, are likely to amount to about 7% of its value but the exact sum will depend upon its size, type, and location. Your lawyer will be able to give you an estimate early in the process.

Which is cheaper - buying or renting?

Obviously, this all depends on your particular case, but there is a general rule of thumb that says that the overall cost of buying a property - mortgage, legal expenses etc. - will be higher for the first five years that you own it than you would pay by way of rent. For the second five years, the figures will probably be pretty much the same. For the third five years and beyond, ownership will probably be cheaper than rental.

This does not take into account and rise or fall in the value of the property.

Buying commercial property in Turkey as an investment

Recently, any property investment, including investment in commercial property, has been a bit of a rollercoaster ride. After years of steadily rising commercial property values, the crash of 2007/8 saw them fall by up to 50%, leaving lots of owners with large losses.

Prices in Turkey have now begun to rise again and the price of prime property - top quality office blocks, shops, hotels etc. in the best locations - is now almost back at 2007 levels. Other property in other locations is still a long way off 2007 values.

Is the increase going to continue or have the price rises gone too far, with the result that there will be a downwards correction? Frankly, nobody knows. The consensus of professional advisers is that commercial property prices will continue to grow for the next few years. This is based on the analysis that there is very limited availability of top-quality property and that the success of the Turkish economy and growing population is generating more demand than there is supply.

If you are thinking of investing in commercial property, you will need to decide which particular type of commercial property is of interest to you. Some smaller investors buy individual shop or office units in secondary locations whereas others swear by prime prestige stores and hotels.

Rather strangely, in Turkey the rental yield you can expect to obtain from commercial property is around the same whichever type of unit you buy. It averages about 10% per annum of the value of the property. However, those who sing the praises of prime property will tell you that they have less problem collecting the rent and fewer voids.

Of course, an alternative to making a direct investment in commercial property is to look at investing in a Turkish version of a Real Estate Investment Trusts (REIT) or something similar.

If you're thinking of investing in commercial property in Turkey there are four main things you need to bear in mind:

1. Volatility. The market has proven that it can go up and down violently.

2. Diversification. Because of the high cost of a lot of commercial property you have to be very rich to build up a diversified portfolio and so you're exposed to the danger of something going wrong with your only building.

3. Liquidity. It will always be slow - months not weeks - if you need to sell your commercial property. In bad economic times, it can be virtually impossible to do so.

4. Management. The success or failure of any commercial property project depends on good management. You will probably not be willing or able to manage the property yourself and so you will need to find a good, reliable local property management company.

Obtaining a Mortgage

Written by **Burak Orkun**
Managing Partner (Accountancy Department) at Orkun & Orkun
www.orkunorkun.com • info@orkunorkun.com

In the past, many foreign buyers of property in Turkey used to take a mortgage from a bank in Turkey to help with the cost of the purchase.

As you will see, the position has now become more complicated, but it is still possible to obtain mortgage finance in Turkey.

Can a foreigner take out a mortgage in Turkey?

Legally speaking, there is no restriction on any foreigner, resident or non-resident, obtaining a mortgage on a property in Turkey.

Nor is there any restriction on the type of property concerned.

Nor is there any restriction on the interest rate that can be charged, the length of the mortgage or its other terms.

This very free and easy approach to mortgages is, however, at the moment, far from the reality. Only lending institutions (banks) based in Turkey can take mortgages over property in Turkey. This, in effect, means that you are limited to dealing with the main Turkish banks.

The various Turkish banks (most of which are, in fact, foreign-owned) have substantially different arrangements when it comes to the loan-to-value ratios they will grant (especially to a foreigner), the interest rates you will have to pay, and the fees that they will charge. This variance is far greater than in many countries.

It is often helpful if you ask your lawyer or estate agent to introduce you to a bank, as they will probably know the foibles of the various banks and bank managers in their area and be able to select a bank that will work well with you.

There are no mortgage brokers in Turkey. Banks do not pay any commission to people who introduce mortgage customers to them.

How much can I borrow and for how long?

Traditionally, loans to foreigners were (for residential property) at 80% loan-to-value, which was the maximum permitted by law. In other words, the bank would lend you €80,000 on a property valued at €100,000. Remember that the bank's valuation will, most likely, be cautious and so lower than the market price. Remember, too, that the mortgage will not cover the costs (legal fees, stamp duty, Property Transfer Tax, etc.) associated with buying the property: say, 10% of the price.

So, in the real world, you might agree to buy a property for €120,000. The legal fees and taxes involved might be, say, €10,000. Total €130,000.

The bank might have valued the property, conservatively, at €100,000 and offered you a mortgage of 80% - €80,000. So, despite a headline 80% loan-to-value, you would have to find €50,000.

Total, you are likely to be offered a loan to value ratio lower than 80%, so you will have to find an even larger amount yourself.

The duration of any mortgage must be for a minimum of three years but, depending upon your age and the amount you're borrowing, would more typically be for ten or 20 years.

All conditions and limits on mortgages, except for interest rates, are governed by the Turkish Mortgage Code and Turkey's 2007 Mortgage Law, which is strictly enforced. Many banks, in the past, were fined for lending home buyers part of the required 20% deposit!

This means that Turkey, during the property boom of the early 2000s, did not have lenders offering mortgages at silly loan-to-value ratios or for huge lengths of time, unlike some countries.

Mortgage interest rates in Turkey

Mortgages are offered either at a variable interest rate or at a fixed rate. The detailed arrangements (including the currency in which the loan will be denominated) vary depending upon the type of buyer. See below.

Variable interest rate mortgages are not popular in Turkey. Consumers prefer fixed rate mortgages, as they can guarantee that their rates won't go up, and they can always jump ship to another bank if rates go down.

Fixed rates are offered either for the whole duration of the mortgage or for a period of, say, five years: after which a new fixed rate would be agreed or you could convert the mortgage to a variable rate mortgage.

Fixed rate mortgages, when available, are also popular with foreign buyers.

Note that, rather confusingly, in Turkey interest rates are sometimes referred to as a "rate per month" and sometimes as a "rate per year". Obviously, this makes a huge difference! Increasingly, rates per year are being used by the major banks.

In general terms, mortgage interest rates in Turkey have been increasing in recent years. They were around 0.7% per month in 2013, and have now reached almost 1.4% per month for a five-year loan.

Mortgages to citizens of Turkey

There is a range of mortgages available to citizens of Turkey. This includes foreign-born citizens. Typically, a Turkish person will take a mortgage over a period of ten years. Depending upon the bank they are using, and their personal circumstances, they will usually, at the moment, pay somewhere between 16% and 19% per annum interest for a mortgage denominated in Turkish lira.

Mortgages to foreigners who are resident in Turkey

Since the crash of the mid-2000s, mortgages have become more expensive. Banks also use more mechanisms for their own security, such as under-valuation of the property, better valuation experts and more stringent checks on potential customers' solvency.

Current interest rates (Sept 17) are about 16-19% per annum APR for mortgages denominated in Turkish lira.

However, unlike many countries in the EU, the Turkish government has not been discouraging foreigners from getting mortgages. Quite the opposite, in fact: the administration puts pressure on banks to fund foreign buyers.

Real estate development is considered to have been one of the saviours of the Turkish economy during the financial crash, and it is therefore one of the most supported industries in Turkey.

One persistent problem experienced by foreigners resident in Turkey is that many of them seek mortgage finance when they have little demonstrable income. These applications will not succeed. All of the banks insist that the applicant for a mortgage must show that they have sufficient income to repay the mortgage. In making that calculation, they do not take into account any income that you *might* generate by renting out the property concerned.

Mortgages to foreigners who are not resident in Turkey

Unlike the case of foreigners who are resident in Turkey, only limited mortgage finance is presently (in practice) available from banks for foreigners who are not resident in Turkey.

This is getting better, but it's unlikely that we will see plentiful mortgages, particularly with high loan-to-value ratios, in the near future.

At the moment (June 2017) a foreigner should not expect to be able to obtain a loan-to-value ratio of more than 70%. Having said that, headline offers of 75% are beginning to appear in the market.

Mortgages are all 'full status' mortgages. This means you produce proof of your means and ability to repay the loan, and a calculation is used to establish affordability. Your existing monthly liabilities, including your other existing mortgage commitments or rental payments, loans, credit card payments and family provision payments are taken into account, along with the likely payments under your proposed new mortgage. The total of these must, typically, not exceed 33% of your monthly gross income.

Mortgages are, typically, lent to non-resident foreigners denominated in foreign currencies: USD, EUR or GBP depending upon their nationality.

Interest rates are slightly different depending on the currency: 7-8% in GBP; 6-8% in euro, 7-8% in USD.

Mortgage interest rates can be compared online via websites such as **www.hangikredi.com/kredi/konut-kredisi** and individual banks announce their current rates at their own web sites and by signs at their branches. Note that mortgage interest rates are normally quoted as the monthly rate, not the annual rate.

Minimum loans are, depending upon the bank, about £50,000.

Maximum age at repayment is, typically, 70.

What types of mortgage are available?

There is only one basic type of mortgage in Turkey. This is a repayment mortgage: a mortgage where, over the period of the mortgage, you repay both the capital and interest to the bank.

What is the process for obtaining a mortgage?

When mortgages are available, the process is straightforward but involves quite a lot of paperwork. The person wanting to borrow makes an application to the bank. This will, often, be coordinated by your lawyer or estate agent.

Things to bear in mind:

- According to the banking law, the mortgage contract must be in the customer's language or translated by an official (sworn) translator. At the very least, contracts in English are available from all banks in Turkey. Many other languages may also be available, depending upon the branch's location. For example, contracts may be available in Russian at the Antalya branch or in Arabic at the Trabzon branch.

- Mortgage contracts must be signed personally. If the customer is married, the spouse must confirm his/her consent to the mortgage by signing another document.

- If you're applying for a mortgage it is sensible to do so in good time - at least two months before you need the money and preferably three or four. Otherwise the funds may not be available when they're needed. In theory, it can all be done in only two to three days, but it's best not to rely on that! Nowadays, some banks speed up this process by receiving applications via online banking.

Once you have provided the necessary documentation, it takes a few hours for a credit check to be carried out. "Interim approval" is then received from the relevant department of the bank.

Once the mortgage has been approved in principle, the bank will carry out its own valuation and survey of the property to check that it is sufficient to justify the amount being lent. This takes another day or two.

Once it has received the results, the bank will confirm the mortgage offer, which will then be legally binding - provided that the title to the property is good.

The offer usually remains valid for four months.

Your lawyer will carry out the various checks needed to make sure that the property has good title and otherwise satisfies your requirements. At the same time, the bank will carry out its checks on the title. Assuming all is in order, and when you are both ready to proceed, an arrangement is made for the signing of the formal Deed of Sale (*tapu*) in your favour and the formal mortgage by you to the bank. See above.

The Deed of Sale and the mortgage are both signed at the same time in front of an officer at the *Tapu Ofis*. At the time of the signing of these documents, the bank will transfer the loan funds to the seller's account.

Repaying your mortgage

You will need to pay your monthly mortgage instalments to the bank from a bank account located in Turkey. You will usually open a bank account in the same bank that granted your mortgage and then feed that account by regular payments from your home country.

Although it is usual to make your mortgage payments from a bank account in Turkey, it is permissible to make the payments directly from a bank in your home country or, indeed, even in cash but neither of these is really recommended as both can create problems further down the line.

The mortgage may be repaid early, but there is usually a penalty of 1% of the loan value (if the loan is for less than 36 months) or 2% (if the loan is for more than 36 months) if you wish to do this.

Building or Altering a House

Written by **Başak Yildiz Orkun**
Managing Partner (Legal Department) at Orkun & Orkun
www.orkunorkun.com • info@orkunorkun.com

Building a House

To build a house in Turkey, there are various requirements that must be satisfied:

Zoning

The land upon which you wish to build the house must be in an area that has been zoned for the construction of residential property.

If its permitted use is something else, you will need to make an application to the local municipality for the permitted use to be changed.

In some simple cases, this application can be straightforward - for example, if you wish to convert a small former hotel that is no longer economically viable into a dwelling - but, in most cases, the land usage plan will have already been approved by the government of Turkey and so the municipality may not be able to make the change that you want. If this is so, then the whole process becomes lengthy and costly.

Provisional approval

You must make an application to the municipality for provisional approval of your plans for the house.

What you intend to build must comply with the regulations in the area where you're building it. These vary from one part of the country to another. Typically, there will be limits on the minimum plot size upon which a house can be constructed, limits upon how close the house can be constructed to the border of the plot, limits on how tall the property can be and limits upon the overall size of a property that can be built on any given size of plot: so-called construction density.

Obtaining this provisional consent is usually straightforward and will, in most places and in a straightforward case, often take no more than four weeks.

Once you have your provisional approval, you or your architect (and it's almost always necessary to use an architect) will need to complete the design of the property and submit the 'project' to the municipality.

- The project is the full set of technical drawings and calculations used in the design of the house. It covers all aspects of the construction: walls, roofs, the water system, the electrical supply, the sewerage system and so on.

- The architect must be qualified and licenced in Turkey. If you want to use someone from your own country (for many reasons, this is not usually a good idea), your 'home' architect will need to engage a local Turkish architect to sign off and present the application.

There will often be some revisions negotiated in connection with the project submitted but, eventually, the project will either be approved or rejected.

- If it is approved, you will be given a building licence.

- This will be conditional upon you building exactly what was submitted in the project.

You must start work on the property no later than 24 months after the date the licence was granted.

- If you do not, the licence will lapse and you will have to start all over again.

- If you find any problems while constructing the house - for example, a geological fault that requires you to move one or more of the walls - you will need to apply for the project to be amended. In most cases this is simple if you have good reason for making the application and you stay within the overall size and other limits set out in the licence.

Whilst the property is under construction, you must have it inspected on a regular basis by a specialist building inspection company. These are licenced by the government. The purpose of these inspections is to make sure that everything has been built in accordance of the plans that were approved.

After the property has been built, you are required to notify the municipality so that they can inspect the property.

Once the municipality is satisfied that the property has been built in strict compliance with the licence and that it is ready for delivery, the municipality will issue a final habitation certificate for the property.

This is the document that authorises the building to be used as living accommodation. It is also needed in order for the electricity and water companies to connect to the property.

At each stage of your application to the municipality there are fees payable. They vary from municipality to municipality.

In addition, of course, you will have to pay the fee of any architects you involve in the process. They do not have a standard fee. In theory, there is a tariff of fees laid down by the College of Architects but, in practice, this is negotiable.

Altering a house

In Turkey, the rules regarding development of (alterations to) your existing property are a little complicated but, in practice - particularly in rural areas - often ignored.

Turkey: how things *really* work

It is easiest to start by explaining what you can do without obtaining any form of
permission. This is pretty limited. You may paint or decorate the inside of your
property and, unless there are specific restrictions, you may also paint or decorate the
outside of the property. Note, however, that there are restrictions in many places. The
aim of these restrictions is, generally, to maintain the cohesion of an area and protect
your neighbours from you painting your house a vibrant purple. For example, in
Bodrum, you are not allowed to paint the outside of any house in pink. The rendering
of any property must be either white or a natural sand colour.

In theory, anything else and, certainly, any extension to your property - however small
the extension might be - is treated as development of that property and it requires
permission from the municipality. This applies whether you want to add an extra
bedroom or you want to build a pool or a terrace.

An application is made to the municipality. This is fairly simple in most cases but the
municipality may require architects' and/or engineers' drawings to support and explain
the application. A fee, of course, is payable.

If your property is within a condominium, you will also need a licence from the
condominium if you intend to do any external work on your property. Generally, all
external parts of a condominium do not belong to the individual owner of the
apartment concerned but are owned, collectively, by all of the owners.

Property Development in Turkey

Written by **Başak Yildiz Orkun**
Managing Partner (Legal Department) at Orkun & Orkun
www.orkunorkun.com • info@orkunorkun.com

Property development is the process of building new property: homes, hotels, factories etc. It can either be the development of land into buildings - in which case it can either be previously undeveloped land (green field sites) or land that has previously been used for some other purpose - or it can be the re-development of existing buildings.

Making changes to your home or other property can also count as property development. For example, adding a garage or an extra bedroom or a pool. See page 414 for more detail.

Development Numbers

Development is a substantial industry in Turkey, and Turkey very much sees development - both for local people and for residential tourism - as a key factor in its future economic success.

In 2016, 1.34million homes were sold in Turkey and nearly 995,000 building permits were granted.

Who is Developing in Turkey?

Development activity in Turkey is pretty much evenly split between local Turkish companies and international development companies.

Where are People Developing in Turkey?

In 2016, the main areas for development were Istanbul, Izmir and Turkey's other large cities. There was some development in coastal areas, but the huge overhang of unsold residential properties built in the 2008/9/10 era has limited the commercial viability of new development other than in specialist cases. Having said that, there has been a lot of activity when it comes to the development of hotels and other tourist accommodation in tourist centres such as Bodrum.

Types of Property Developer

Property developers range from huge international companies to private individuals. There is a distinction between the developer of a property and its builder or contractor.

The developer is the person who has the idea behind the development and then coordinates the activities of architects, engineers, builders, and other specialists.

You do not need to have any qualifications in order to be a property developer in Turkey, but any construction company wishing to undertake work on new developments must be properly registered as a construction company before they can do so.

There is no restriction on foreigners resident in Turkey undertaking property development and there is no restriction on foreigners not resident in Turkey doing so - except that they will need to comply with Turkish company law when it comes to the appointment of a resident director etc.

Types of Property Development

Large-scale property development

By large-scale property development, we mean (for the purposes of this book) projects that comprise more than, say, 50 finished units. This is not a legal definition but a practical one.

Small-scale property development

Small-scale property development is usually either building an individual property on an individual plot of land or it is building a small group of properties on a single plot of land. For example, demolishing a large old house and building five smaller houses or apartments on the site.

Alterations to property you already own

This type of property development is very common but completely different in nature from the other two types. See page 415.

Large-Scale Property Development

The process

Whatever the size of the development, the process of developing a larger project tends to be similar, although individual parts of it will carry more or less weight.

Identifying an opportunity

Property development opportunities abound around the world; but to identify one that is going to suit your requirements you will first need to know about what is available in the marketplace. Generally, this means having a detailed knowledge of the country and area concerned. For someone who does not have that knowledge, lots of proposed development opportunities can be superficially attractive but doomed to failure as they are beset by lots of hidden (and expensive) problems.

This does not mean that you cannot execute a large property development project in a country or an area that is new to you. Many successful development companies have expanded into new areas. However, what it does mean is that you will have to be even more cautious than usual when selecting a development project and spend a lot more time and money on the process of due diligence before you commit to it.

Despite the fact that you can develop in unknown locations, most people would agree that it is easier, and usually more profitable, to stick to areas that you know. This applies both to geographic areas and to areas of activity - sticking, for example, to residential development or hotels or wherever your area of expertise lies.

This often leads foreign developers who see opportunity in Turkey to team up with experienced local people and companies. See page 209.

Preliminary feasibility study

Once you have a potential project that your instinct and experience tell you is viable, you will need to carry out a preliminary feasibility study.

The extent of this and what is included in it will vary enormously from one developer to another. Some very successful developers rely solely on their instinct before embarking on a full due diligence exercise. Others have a quite sophisticated process for preliminary feasibility studies, involving architects, financial planners, and the like - even at this very early stage.

The most important thing about a preliminary feasibility study is that you need to establish that there is a market for the project, that you can keep your costs under control and that the margins on it are substantial. Usually, the potential profit identified in your preliminary feasibility study is rapidly eroded as you get into full due diligence and so you need to make sure that the numbers look exciting enough to make it worth going any further.

In Turkey, feasibility studies are prepared either by architects or by project engineers. The latter tend to be cheaper and found more often in projects involving fewer than about 50 units. Whichever way you go about it, such studies are always quite expensive. For a project involving the construction of, say, ten homes on a fresh plot of land, you should budget €5,000-10,000. This is just for the feasibility study, not the detailed project design.

Expression of intent

Assuming your preliminary feasibility study looks positive, you will need to reach an agreement in principle with the person who is selling the land or project. This agreement, too, should always be subject to satisfactory due diligence.

Despite the fact that this is a very weak agreement (because there will be so many 'get out clauses' that it is almost always possible to cancel), the agreement is still important as it reflects a moral, and sometimes legal, obligation to proceed with the project and not to deal with others whilst the investigations are continuing.

Of course, any agreement of this kind is only as good as the person you're dealing with and so, before entering even this type of expression of intent, you should make sure that you are happy doing business with the other party involved. It can be worth doing, or getting your lawyer to do, some background checks on the person concerned. Business-orientated lawyers can usually help you with this.

The parties often prepare preliminary expressions of intent themselves, rather than getting lawyers to do it. This may be fine if both parties are experienced, but you should always use the services of a lawyer to produce even this basic document if you are relatively inexperienced and/or you are dealing with a country whose legal system is not familiar to you and/or you are not fluent in Turkish. If you do not, the danger is that something that you think of as a mere preliminary expression of interest may turn out to be legally binding upon you.

Due diligence

Due diligence is the process of making sure that what you have been told or believe to be the case is true.

The nature of the due diligence required in any project will vary, but it's likely to include (at least) the following headings:

- The local market

- Is there a demand for the proposed product?

- What are likely sales prices?

- Does the land have good legal title?

- Are there any restrictions on what you will be able to do on the land?

- Does the land have (or can you obtain) permission to build what you want to build?

- Will all the services that you require - water, electricity, roads etc. - be available?

- Is the professional support you need (architects, project engineers, etc.) available in the area and/or will you be able to use the professionals you have previously worked with to deliver this project?

- What will be the costs of construction?

- Where is the finance going to come from?

- How will you be able to sell the project?

- How well does the legal system work and will you be protected if anything goes wrong?

- How will you sell the units you are building - and at what cost?

Special points

In Turkey, there are some special issues that require particularly careful attention.

Building permission is complex

Each municipality operated within a legal framework of what can and cannot be built. There is sometimes a little room for manoeuvre but, generally, not very much. Your project might be brilliant and beautiful but, if it is not of the type authorised in the area where you want to build, it will go no further. Thus, it is usually important to clarify this issue before you embark upon detailed investigation of the project.

There is a practical problem here. The only person entitled to negotiate with the municipality is the current owner of the land. Most municipalities will happily have a general discussion about a proposed project: after all, if it goes ahead you will be bringing employment and wealth to the area. However, most will not commit anything to paper. You can get around this by having a limited Power of Attorney from the owner, permitting you to negotiate with the municipality (but not to enter a binding agreement) and little else.

Restrictions on the professionals you can use to assist with your project

Only architects licensed to work in the area can be used for a project in that area. If you choose to work with your own favourite architect from another area or another country, they must have all their work approved and signed off by a local architect. This can add significantly to cost. It also adds, considerably, to the risk of confusion.

Only legally authorised construction companies can build development projects. Many small builders do not have that registration.

Finance

There is no legal restriction of how much of the sale price a developer can take by way of advance payments. Nor is there any restriction on how the developer can use that money. However, the reality is that buyers are very cautious. This applies equally to local Turkish buyers and to people from foreign countries.

They saw a great many developments in Turkey fail during the period from 2007 to 2011 and they saw a great many buyers lose all or part of the money they had invested.

They are, therefore, now very reluctant to pay large amounts of money to a developer before they take delivery of their property - and, even if they have paid a deposit, they're very unlikely to be prepared to pay significant further sums unless they see real progress being made with the development. This has an impact upon how your contracts of sale will need to be drafted.

This means that you will need to raise more outside finance than would be the case in some other countries.

Who carries out due diligence?

The ultimate responsibility for carrying out the due diligence on any project rests with the person or company who is going to be the developer of the project.

Having said that, it is usual for a large portion of the due diligence - in some cases all of it - to be contracted out to various professionals.

If you are working in a place where you are unfamiliar with the legal and administrative system and, perhaps, where you don't speak the language it is essential to seek professional help in this way.

The main person putting together the due diligence pack is likely to be your lawyer or - in some cases - a project engineer but they will, as necessary and directed by you, liaise with and call in the services of people such as accountants, hotel consultants, architects, project engineers, banks and other specialists.

Selecting partners

Assuming your due diligence is sufficiently encouraging for you to want to proceed with the project; you will need to select architects, engineers, builders etc. There are over 40,000 registered architects in Turkey.

It is usual for a proposed developer to meet various companies with the necessary qualifications and decide which they would prefer to work with. These people are used to discussing possible projects in this way and, particularly for larger projects, they will usually be happy to spend quite a lot of time in these meetings and doing some preliminary general work in relation to the project in order to satisfy you that you could work with them and that they are capable people. This is usually at little or no cost.

The choice of partners is, of course, critical. When choosing the people you want to work with, make sure that you check out their reputations. It may well be that this is an area where your lawyer will be able to help by using his local knowledge and connections.

Contracts

You will need a lot of different contracts for a project of this kind. These will include:

- A contract for the sale of the land

- A contract with an architect

- A contract with a project engineer

- A contract with a builder or builders and other contractors

- Contracts for finance

- A contract with your sales agent

- Contracts with your individual buyers

It is absolutely essential that all these contracts are prepared by your lawyers.

To prepare them, they will need to understand your wishes very clearly. Expect this process of discussing what you want and need to take some time.

Once they have prepared the contracts, particularly the contracts with your individual buyers, you may want to take their words and convert them into your house style. If you do this, you need to get the lawyers to approve the final version.

Sales

Sales are, of course, essential to any project and you will usually want to test the water at as early a stage as possible to make sure that your offer appeals to the buyers you're aiming it at: and that your pricing is right.

Under the law of Turkey there is no restriction as to how early you can start your sales activity. However, if you are merely testing the water and have no immediate intention of building the project it would be illegal to take any money at this stage.

A key factor in making sales is choosing the right estate agents.

Whilst it is permitted for developers to sell their own properties, for example, from an office on-site, most developers will use the services of estate agents. It works better for all but the largest developers.

In Turkey, it is still not necessary for estate agents to have any professional qualification or licence, but a developer will wish to make sure that the agent or agents selling his property are perceived in the area to be reputable and well-established. This can make a big difference to sales, especially to local people.

Many developers who want to attract foreign buyers will also wish to undertake marketing and sales in the countries from which those buyers are likely to come. They can either do this directly (for example, by having their own sales offices in the countries in question) or they can use local real estate agents in those countries to offer the properties on their behalf.

Until recently, lots of Turkish developers had their own overseas sales offices but, since the crash, this has become much rarer.

Although an estate agent does not need a professional qualification in order to sell property in Turkey, if you want to sell through agents based in other countries, those agents will need to have whatever qualifications and licences are required in their own country.

In practical terms, even in you appoint agents in (say) Germany or Russia to sell to their citizens you will also need an agent in Turkey to deal with the buyers if they come to Turkey on inspection visits or just to look at your properties. You can either appoint the Turkish agent to be the managing or coordinating agent, or you can carry out that task in-house. Many experienced developers, large and small, prefer to keep in-house control of this crucial task.

Special development opportunities in Turkey

At the moment, the main excitement amongst the development community in Turkey relates to Istanbul generally and, elsewhere, to hotels and residential complexes that operate in the same way as a hotel.

These residential complexes have, for example, a hotel reception facility, bars, and restaurants - but they either offer apartments and villas instead of hotel bedrooms or in addition to conventional hotel bedrooms.

These individual accommodation units - whether villas, apartments, or hotel bedrooms - can be owned by individual investors, who then allow a hotel management company to let their properties as part of an overall project for the site. These developments have the twin advantages of having performed relatively well during the recession of the mid-2000s and of offering buyers a ready-made way of securing some sort of ongoing income from their investment.

However, they do need to be set up very carefully to ensure compliance with both Turkish law and the law of the country where the buyers live.

Another area of activity attracting a lot of attention is the renovation of old city property. In some places, this might be by way of a restoration of the old buildings, but it is, more commonly, by demolishing the old and building afresh, often to a much higher density.

The other main area of current (2017) development opportunity relates to small infill sites within existing developments. In essence, they are the properties needed to finish off that development. They may have been planned but not built when the developer was overtaken by the crisis of 2007-2011. These have been popular as the recession has come to an end, because the developers have been able to acquire the land cheaply and because construction costs in most places are currently (2017) at rock bottom.

Quite a lot of development by foreigners is now done by way of joint ventures with Turkish construction companies.

Small-Scale Developments

Pretty much the same process applies as applies in the case of large developments but there are two great differences.

The first is that the process of due diligence cannot take nearly as long or be nearly as costly if you are only building a few units. As a result, it cannot involve as many professionals. In many cases, the due diligence report will be prepared by your lawyer and your accountant with the only outside sources of information being costings from your chosen builder and information from your chosen estate agent. Even though due diligence must be more limited, you should not think that this means you do not need to do due diligence on a smaller development. It is still essential.

In general terms, it is a good idea for a new developer - even a developer with considerable experience in another country - to start their career in international development in Turkey with a small development. Even then, they will often not make a profit on that first development. They will, however, learn a lot of lessons and they will generally find that their later, bigger, developments will proceed more smoothly and more profitably if they take this path.

For a novice developer, starting small is almost essential.

Selling a House in Turkey

Written by **Başak Yildiz Orkun**
Managing Partner (Legal Department) at Orkun & Orkun
www.orkunorkun.com • info@orkunorkun.com

The process of selling a property in Turkey is much more straightforward than the process of buying a property in Turkey. So much so that most Turks would simply choose an estate agent and then, with the agent, look after the rest themselves.

However, unless your Turkish is faultless, and unless you are very well versed in the local culture, this won't work for a foreigner - and so this chapter is intended to steer you through this important, but still quite simple, process.

How to Find a Buyer

Simple. Choose an estate agent.

Make sure you use one who is experienced and well-respected in the area. Local friends or your lawyer should be able to recommend someone suitable.

Think about where your buyer is likely to come from. Is your property likely to appeal to a foreign buyer, to a Turk from Istanbul or Ankara, or to a local person. If it is likely to appeal to a foreign buyer, which country are they likely to come from? Choose an agent with exposure in the right places and the language and other skills to deal with those buyers.

Although many Turks advertise their properties privately (without an estate agent) via the local press and internet, a foreigner will always benefit from the services of an estate agent to find and deal with a buyer:

- They will know the market and prices, so securing you the best price for the property

- They will prepare the property information documents in the way that they would be expected in Turkey; essential if you are looking for a Turkish buyer and no disadvantage if you're looking for an international buyer

- They will show people around the property and, of course, if they're Turkish, be able to speak to them in fluent Turkish

- They will be able to negotiate the sale of the property. As you will know if you have spent any time in Turkey, negotiation is art that takes a form very different from its form in many other countries

- They will liaise with your lawyer, the Notary, the Land Registry etc. to complete the transaction as quickly as possible

We're not trying to create work for estate agents here, but it really is the most sensible course of action to use one.

Most estate agents in Turkey are reputable, but different firms do aim at different parts of the market and so it's worth doing a bit of research before you make your choice of agent. Research is, perhaps, a rather grandiose term for what you need to do. Normally you will only need to see which agents are selling most property in your area. There will usually be one or two clear leaders.

If your property is in a well-known and self-contained area - such as in central (historic) Istanbul or in a marina area such as Göcek - you need to decide whether to sell it through an agent that specialises in just that area or one with a wider coverage. Generally, the best advice is to sell the property via the agents dealing with the most properties of that type in the area in question.

Obviously, when choosing an agent, you need - if possible - to make sure that somebody in their office speaks your language fluently and, ideally, that there is a second person in the office to provide backup language skills when the first is out of the office.

The agent's fee will, typically, be 3% of the sale price.

Legal Steps

Who should deal with the sale?

You can have your agent both sell the property and deal with the resulting contracts and paperwork, or you can use the agent to sell the property and then use your lawyer to draft the contracts and deal with the other paperwork. This is likely to cost you a little more. The agent's fee will remain at, typically, 3% of the sale price and the lawyer will probably charge you 1% of the sale price (subject to minimum fee of €1,200) to deal with a fairly simple sale.

Whichever method you choose, you (or, more likely, your lawyer or estate agent) will have to do four main things:

Prepare a contract and document pack

Surprisingly, it is rare for a pre-prepared document or sales pack to be produced in the case of the sale of property in Turkey, but there is strong anecdotal evidence that having a proper document pack greatly increases the chance of a quick sale, and greatly speeds up the process of making that sale.

The document pack will comprise a contract, a copy of your proof of title, a copy of your planning permission for the construction of the building or of your habitation licence permitting it to be used, and (possibly) items about the safety of the property.

In Turkey, it is not common for the seller to produce a survey (inspection) report showing the condition of the property in anticipation of sale being made, if the buyer wants a survey, he will obtain one.

If you're going to have a document pack, it must be in Turkish but should ideally be accompanied by a translation into your own language and into the languages of other likely groups of buyers. This is most conveniently done by having the document in a two-column format.

Occasionally, we find clients from (say) China who speak neither Turkish nor English well enough to understand the contract. In this case we normally recommend that the contract is prepared, initially, in Turkish and English - the two dominant languages used in Turkey - and that we then provide a separate translation into Chinese. We can also provide separate translations into other languages, depending upon the language skills of the buyer.

Deal with any technical or other queries raised by the buyer

These can take many forms: from enquiries about whether the curtains are included with the sale and when the pool was last maintained to queries about the validity of your building licence.

Some of these enquiries will be dealt with by your estate agent. In fact, almost all of them are first directed to the estate agent. The estate agent will then refer the ones that need to go to the lawyer to the lawyer and the ones that need to come to you to you.

Attend to sign over the title to the property

This will be done in front of an officer from the Land Registry (*Tapu Ofis*).

If it isn't convenient for you to attend in person (remembering that each person included in the legal title will need to be there), they may appoint someone else to sign on their behalf by using a Power of Attorney. See page 288.

Receive the money

As the seller of a property in Turkey you will, mainly, be interested in the bit where you receive the money!

It is conventional that the buyer should pay over a deposit, usually 10% of the sale price, at the time when they sign the contract to buy the property and the rest of the price when you sign over the title to the property. The initial 10% is usually retained by the estate agent or by your lawyer until the final title has been signed over, at which point the whole of the price (less any fees and taxes) is released to you.

The Legal Process

This is very similar to the process when buying a property, but there is rather less to do. See page 388.

Fees & Taxes

There will be several fees and expenses that you must pay when you're selling your property in Turkey.

The main things you will need to deal with are:

- Paying all of your utility and other bills and cancelling your accounts.

- Bringing your general tax affairs up to date. This is particularly important if you are leaving Turkey.

- Agreeing who will pay the property transfer tax. This tax (4%) is, conventionally, split between the buyer and seller (2% each) but any arrangement can be agreed. Some sellers insist that it all be paid by the buyer.

- Pay your estate agent and your lawyer. They will, usually, make sure that they hold enough of your money to ensure that they get paid!

Item	Notes	Cost (% of price)
Estate agents' fees	If you require the agent's full service, including showing people around the property, and you appoint the agent on an exclusive basis	3-5%
Lawyers' fees	This will usually be subject to a minimum of €1,200	1%
Property transfer tax	This is usually split between the buyer and the seller (in total, 4%)	2%
Land Registry admin fee (*Tapu Ofis*)	This is usually paid by the seller	TRY200-300
Experts and surveyors' fees	These will depend upon the type of your property and the decisions that you make.	

Your Tax Affairs

When you sell your property, especially if you will be leaving Turkey, you will need to bring your tax affairs in Turkey up-to-date. For example, you must show that you've paid your property tax for the current year and that your personal tax filings/returns are up-to-date and that all other relevant taxes have been paid.

Taxes in Turkey

There will be tax to pay if you sell your property within five years from the date of purchase and make any profit on it. See page 248.

Taxes in Your Own Country

Depending upon your nationality and where you normally live, you will probably also have to declare the capital gain that you have made to the tax authorities in your own country and pay whatever tax they assess is due on that gain. However, in most cases you will find that there is a double taxation treaty between your country and Turkey with the result that, typically, you will be able to deduct the tax you've already paid in Turkey from any tax liability 'back home'.

You will need to check the details of the tax treaty between Turkey and your country. Your lawyer should be able to help you to do this. See page 262 for general information about double taxation treaties and which countries have signed a treaty with Turkey.

Other Things You Might Want to do When you Sell

If your property is in a community of properties (see page 380), it is considered courteous to notify the president of the community personally that you have sold it. This also avoids the risk of them chasing you if the new owner doesn't pay his dues.

You may want to cancel your insurance policy in relation to the property. You may be entitled to a refund.

You should tell your bank what you are doing. If you want to keep a bank account in Turkey, it may be necessary to change the type of account.

Renting a House in Turkey

Written by **Başak Yildiz Orkun**
Managing Partner (Legal Department) at Orkun & Orkun
www.orkunorkun.com • info@orkunorkun.com

Many people coming to Turkey decide to rent a property here. There are several reasons. They may just prefer renting property. They may be sent to Turkey for a fairly short time in connection with their work and find that renting a property in Turkey is more cost-effective than buying. They may decide to rent for a year whilst they look for a property to buy. They may decide to put their cash into a business rather than into a property in which to live.

Whatever their motivation for renting a property in Turkey, there are certain things they need to know if they are to do so safely and without undue stress.

There is a plentiful supply of rental property. These are of all types, from tiny apartments to huge villas.

How to Find a Place to Rent in Turkey

There are two main ways of finding a property to rent in Turkey.

Estate agents

Most estate agents in Turkey also act as the managing agents of property available for rent. Unfortunately, they will only have access to the properties on their own books - i.e. the properties they have been asked to manage. There is no MLS (Multiple Listing Service) for rental properties in Turkey. This means that you will have to contact each of the agents individually to find out what they have available.

Do not rely on their websites, which are likely to be out of date. The best rental properties are let very quickly indeed. The cynical might think that some of the attractive property left on websites for a long time is no more than a hook to capture new customers.

The estate agent's fee in connection with the letting is usually paid by the owner. However, under Turkish law, it is possible (though uncommon) for an estate agent to charge you (the tenant) a fee for renting a property to you.

A number of estate agents have started to offer a rental alert scheme. This means that if you register with them and tell them what type of property you're looking for, they will send you an email alert when a suitable property comes on their books. Of course, they could be sending that email to dozens of people. This is no substitute for maintaining regular contact with them in an attempt to get ahead of the queue.

Turkey: how things *really* work

If you find a rental property that you like, you should move quickly. The best properties do not stay on the market for very long.

Direct rentals

Many owners do not use an agent to rent out their property. They advertise it in the local paper (either the main Turkish-language paper in the area or, sometimes, in local foreign-language press) or on the local 'for sale and wanted' or 'bulletin board' websites. See the useful contacts section at the end of this book.

You will have to know the market, especially rental values, and speak good Turkish if you want to go down this route.

Whilst Turkey is a very safe place, as always be careful when it comes to arranging to meet strange people in empty properties.

What Type of Property?

We each have our own requirements when it comes to finding a property in which to live.

You may want to consider some or all of the following:

- Location. It is convenient for where you're working or the places you want to visit?

- Local facilities. Are there local shops, bars, restaurants etc. or are you prepared to travel to them?

- Is there parking? In most Turkish towns and cities there is a huge shortage of parking.

- Are you comfortable with the area? Is it too noisy? Is it too isolated? Is it safe?

- Are you looking for a property that is furnished or unfurnished? There are few unfurnished lettings in Turkey. Many people, if they want to use their own furniture, will take a furnished property and then (with the agreement of the landlord) put the existing furniture into storage until they leave the property. If you want to do this, you will be expected to pay an additional security deposit and to give the landlord written authority to remove any items you leave behind at the end of your tenancy.

- Are you prepared to share with others?

- Are you prepared to take an apartment that has only a shower rather than a bath; or are you prepared to take a property where there is no shower but only a shower attachment over a bath? Most smaller properties in Turkey offer only a shower.

- Does the property have all the appliances that you require? Smaller properties tend to be sparsely equipped: for example, no washing machine.

- Do you need a garden? In the towns and cities, most rental properties do not have a garden - although villas and properties outside the towns and cities do.

- Is the property accessible? Most of the cheaper apartments will be in buildings without lifts (elevators).

- Are there any schools in the area?

- Are pets allowed?

- Is smoking permitted?

- For how long is the property available and from when?

Viewing a Property to Rent in Turkey

When you find a property that interests you, you will need to see it. Viewings are arranged either with the agents or directly with the owner, depending on who is marketing the property.

When you're looking at a property for the first time, it's very easy to miss important features or forget to ask about something. Think about:

- How well is the property maintained and decorated?

- Who is responsible for the maintenance and decoration? In Turkey, for tenancies of less than 12 months, it is the landlord who is always responsible for the maintenance of the property and its decoration, but you will be charged for any damage you cause to the property other than what can be described as 'fair wear and tear'. For longer tenancies, the responsibility for maintenance and decoration is agreed between the landlord and tenant and recorded in the tenancy agreement.

- What kind of heating does the property have? For water? For space heating?

- Is the furniture in good condition?

- Is there enough storage space?

- Are there instructions for all the appliances? Are they in your language?

- Do things work? Turn on the taps and lights, flush the toilet. Do the windows open? Does any air conditioning work?

- If you're in a block of flats:

1. Is there any extra charge for community services - so-called 'community fees'? You will normally be expected to pay these on top of the amount of your rent.

2. What are the arrangements for mail?

3. Is there any security?

- Who will be responsible for coordinating maintenance and repairs and what performance promises are there?

- Are utility bills included within the rent? Usually, they are not.

Whilst you're visiting the premises, ask if there are any other tenants in the building or neighbourhood and, if possible, speak to them.

Being Accepted as a Tenant

At the moment, the property rental market favours the landlord in that there are lots of tenants searching for relatively few good properties.

You can give yourself an advantage by doing several things:

- Start looking as soon as possible: at least four weeks before you need to move in, preferably eight or even 12.

- Be prepared to pay an immediate rental deposit. You will usually be asked for two months' rent in advance, plus the equivalent of a further month's rent as a security deposit.

- Be prepared to sign a tenancy agreement quickly. This is a standard form agreement but it's likely to be in Turkish (although this is not required by law) and so you might need to get it looked at by your lawyer. A few of the larger rental agencies are now producing dual column rental agreements in Turkish & English, Turkish & German, and Turkish & Russian.

- Be prepared to sign a guarantee that you will leave and clear the property at the end of the lease

- Have proof of your ID (a copy of your passport) available.

- Have proof of your ability to pay the rent. For example, a bank account statement and salary slip.

- Above all, be polite!

The Cost of Renting a Property in Turkey

There is a huge range of rents within Turkey. There is no rent control.

In addition to the amount you're paying by way of rent you'll be expected to pay your utility bills, the charges in relation to any community within which the property is located and the annual property tax for the property (unless you're renting for a period of less than three months, in which case these are paid by the landlord).

Your Rights and Responsibilities as the Tenant of a Property

Your rights

- Your landlord must give you exclusive occupation of the property. He can only visit with your consent.

- Your landlord must honour his repairing obligations. See above.

- You must be allowed to stay in the property for the whole agreed period of your tenancy, provided you pay your rent on time. Your tenancy can be for up to ten years. It can then be renewed. During the period of your tenancy, the landlord can only recover possession if he needs the property for his own use, for the use of his family, or if the property is to be demolished.

- You must receive a written tenancy agreement containing certain key terms including: the full names of the parties, the amount of the rent and the rent deposit, when the rent can be reviewed and the address of the person responsible for repairs.

- Your landlord must ensure that the property is safe for your occupation of it.

Your responsibilities

- Pay the rent on time. Payment should be made by bank transfer. Do not pay in cash: it can lead to all sorts of problems.

- Look after the property by using it in a sensible way and causing no unnecessary damage to it. If you do not, you will have to pay the landlord compensation.

- Pay all of the bills relating to the property on time.

- Act reasonably as far as your neighbours and others are concerned. Not too many noisy parties and make sure you deposit the rubbish correctly.

- Use the property for the purpose that has been agreed. This will usually be as a place to live. If you want to run a business from the property, you will need your landlord's consent and (if it's in a condominium) you will usually also need the consent of the condominium.

- Tell your landlord when something goes wrong with the property. Note that you will be responsible, whatever the agreement says about maintenance of the property, for routine replacements such as lightbulbs, fuses, batteries etc.

Repairs

All major repairs are the responsibility of your landlord. These include all repairs to the roof, to the walls of the property and to its structure generally. They also include repairs to the bathroom and kitchen and to the electrical system in the property. In short, almost all repairs are the responsibility of the landlord.

When it comes to minor repairs - replacing worn carpets, dealing with a broken window or fixing a leaking tap etc. - the responsibility is decided between the parties in the rental agreement. In the absence of any agreement it will be the landlord who is usually responsible.

The tenant is responsible for minor repairs arising from the usage of the property. For example, replacing worn carpets, dealing with a broken window or fixing a leaking tap.

Deposits

Your landlord will almost certainly want to take a deposit from you. There is no standard system for deposits, nor any recognised normal size for a deposit. The deposit will, often, be in two parts: a rent deposit of the equivalent of two months' rent and a security deposit of the equivalent of one month's rent.

There is no form of deposit guarantee scheme, and so you have to recognise that it may be difficult to recover any deposit that you have paid.

As usual, if you're being asked to pay a deposit to cover the cost of any damage that you might cause to the property, it is a good idea for you to take plentiful photographs (and preferably a video) showing the state of the property when you took it over. Make sure you back them up in a safe place. It's embarrassing if, two or three years later, you have lost your phone with all of the photographs on it!

Checklist When You're Moving out of a Rented Home

- Has the rent been paid up to date?

- Has everything you own been cleared out? If you need to get rid of big items, be sure to arrange it well in advance.

- Have you returned the landlord's furniture etc. to its original place?

- If you put your landlord's furniture in storage, have you brought it back? This is your responsibility.

- Have you tidied any outdoor areas?

- Have you repaired or replaced any minor damage that was your fault?

- Have you paid the landlord for any major damage that was your fault?

- Can you be there when the 'check out' inventory is being done? If not, take photographs showing the state of the building. Make sure they are date stamped in some way. If your camera won't do this, the old trick of showing a copy of today's paper in the photograph still works. Then make your own detailed inventory.

- Have you paid all the bills - water, electricity etc.?

- What arrangements are being made for the repayment of any deposit due to you?

- Have you delivered the keys to the landlord or his agent and received a receipt confirming this?

Letting (Renting Out) Property

Written by **Başak Yildiz Orkun**
Managing Partner (Legal Department) at Orkun & Orkun
www.orkunorkun.com • info@orkunorkun.com

It's possible to make a good profit by letting (renting out) a property in Turkey. Just make sure you're aware of the issues. As always, we recommend seeking advice from your lawyer and accountant before going ahead with any big plans!

Will You be Letting Seriously or Casually?

About 60% of the foreigners who buy houses in Turkey let them. About half of those people rent out on a 'serious' basis. That is to say, they are trying to make money by letting their property and try to find the maximum rental income each year. The other half let casually: to family, friends and friends of friends. They are looking not so much to make a profit from renting but to defray some or all of the cost of ownership.

There are fundamental differences in the way these two groups should approach the task.

The first group should put themselves into the head of the person they want to rent their property. Which part of the market are they trying to capture? You cannot be all things to all men. The single person or childless couple wanting to enjoy Turkish culture will have very different requirements from the family wanting a cheap and quiet holiday in the countryside, or a visiting student.

Where would your target tenants like to rent? What type of property would they prefer? What features do they require?

This type of landlord should then buy a property, convert it, and equip it solely with their prospective tenants in mind.

The second group should make few concessions to their tenants. After all, theirs is - first and foremost - a holiday home for their own use. They will have to make some changes to accommodate visitors but they should be as few as possible. Perhaps slightly darker shades of upholstery, an area where the owners can lock away their valuables when not in residence, and more sets of bedding.

Most importantly, both groups should provide a 'house book' and a visitor pack. Both are a good idea whether you want to let on long term of short term lettings, though the contents will vary a bit.

The house book first gives visitors some guidance as to what tourist attractions and other facilities are available in the area and emergency contact numbers for the inevitable time when someone is ill or the plumbing springs a leak.

The visitor pack gives directions to the property, maps, and other information useful before they set off on holiday or start to live in it.

This chapter relates mainly to the first group (the 'serious' landlords). I will make some comments directed specifically at the second and they can pick and choose from the other ideas, depending on how far they are willing to compromise their personal wishes in order to increase rental income.

This chapter is also aimed mainly towards those looking to let their property to short-term tenants.

Should You Use a Letting Agency?

Strangely, the decision as to how you are going to let your property is one of the first that you are going to have to make. This is because, if you decide to use a professional management or letting agencies, it will probably alter (or, at least, expand) your target market and, therefore, the area in which you ought to be buying and the type of property to buy.

If you are going to let your property through a professional management agency, it is worth contacting such agencies before you make a final selection of the area in which to buy to see what they believe you can obtain in that area in the way of rental returns. Better still, they will usually also be able to tell you what type of property is likely to be most successful as a letting property in that area.

They might even come up with better suggestions about both the best area and type of property than those in your original plan.

See below for thoughts about how to choose and manage such agencies.

Do you want to use the agency both to find the tenants and to manage the property?

If you are thinking of finding the tenants yourself then you will have to decide upon your primary market. Most people letting property themselves let it primarily to people from their home country. There are a number of reasons for this. Lack of language skills and ease of administration are probably the most common.

Short-Term Lettings

Many people want to stay in apartments or houses (rather than hotels) when they visit Turkey. As more and more tourists flock to the country, the chance to make some money by buying a property and letting it (renting it out) becomes tempting.

Short-term lettings mean letting your property to several people over the course of the year (mainly during the tourist season) for holiday (vacation) or, occasionally, work accommodation. The lettings will, typically, be for no more than a couple of weeks.

You need to be aware that the world of property rentals is changing quickly. This is true not only in Turkey, but in most parts of the world. Countries are trying to come to grips with companies such as Airbnb, which have caused a huge increase in the number of properties available to let. They've also made it very difficult to control the quality of the property on offer and to ensure compliance with the landlord's tax and other obligations in Turkey.

At the moment, the legality of short-term rentals in Turkey is very debateable. This is mainly because it is very difficult for the landlords to comply with all of the rules surrounding these lettings.

In particular, you should note the following points:

- The short-term letting of property is treated as a business. The business activity should be registered and you should pay business taxes. This has, in the past, seldom been done; but there is a great stirring of interest in this field within the Turkish government agencies and there could well be trouble ahead.

- Under the current state of emergency, owners are required to declare the presence of people staying in their property to the police, daily. There is a fine if you fail to do so. The good news is that this declaration can be done online, but it is still a time-consuming task. The authorities are paying particular attention to lettings via Airbnb, which are relatively easy to trace and which the government feels "provide homes for terrorists".

- Complying with safety requirements: short-term lettings fall uncomfortably between the rules that govern hotels and the rules that govern the regular letting of a home on a long-term basis. This is another area in which the authorities are developing a keen interest.

  There is a perception that many apartments offered to tourists on a short-term basis are substandard in terms of the facilities they offer. Of course, the hotel industry is very powerful and so this is a great opportunity for them to take action, strangling their competition, and they are not slow in seizing that opportunity.

- Neighbours complain: neighbours are becoming increasingly vocal about complaining when there are short-term occupants in a property.

  This is, perhaps, not entirely surprising. Short-term occupants do not give your neighbours the same feeling of security as they have when your apartment is being occupied by someone for many months; and people staying in an apartment for just a few days or a couple of weeks are, perhaps, likely to be busy enjoying themselves and making more noise than normal.

  Complaints by neighbours are another justification used by the authorities for a crackdown on short-term letting.

  Make sure that, if your property is part of a complex or community, there aren't any rules against holiday rentals.

The 2016 law

Law 678 of 2016 lays down rules that owners must follow. Its stated aim is "to combat increasing terrorist incidents, to provide general security, to combat those who illegally enter Turkey, and to fight against the informal economy".

The law covers:

- Hotels, motels, inns, pensions,

- Single rooms

- Daily or short-term rented houses, camping grounds, holiday villages and the like

- All kinds of private or official accommodation

- Private health institutions and rest homes

- Operators of social facilities for religious and charitable institutions.

In other words, almost everybody renting out on a short-term basis.

Owners need to keep details of the identity and the arrival and departure records of every domestic or foreign citizen who uses their facility and to keep those details available, day and night, to law enforcement organizations.

They have to be connected, electronically, to those law enforcement agencies in a way that allows them instant access to that information.

Failure to do this attracts a penalty of TRY10,383 ($2,700/€2,200/£1,900) per day. That's a lot of money! Those who do not supply accurate data or delay in doing so face a penalty of TRY5,191 per day.

Fines have to be paid within one month.

Business licenses will be cancelled.

There is much discussion about how all this can be achieved.

The holiday season

Turkey has quite a short peak holiday season. The domestic demand lasts, in most places except Istanbul, for no more than about two (or, if you are optimistic, three) months and - to make matters worse - Ramadan usually falls within it. It is true that, for foreign tourists, there is some demand for a longer period, but - even for them - there is really only significant demand from June (late May, if you're lucky) to September.

Where Should You Buy a Property to Let?

The choice of the area in which to buy your rental property is by far the most important decision that you will make. This is especially true if, despite the problems associated with them, you want to let on short-term holiday lets. There are some, but not many, parts of Turkey where it is fairly easy to let your property sufficiently regularly to make it a commercially viable proposition. There are plenty of areas where this is a hopeless task.

The factors to take into consideration when deciding upon the area are slightly different from the factors relevant when you're thinking about buying a home for your own personal use. They will also vary depending upon your target clientele and your preferred way of administering the property.

Climate

The climate of Turkey varies hugely. You would expect no less in such a massive country. Most people looking at short-term lettings will be thinking about Istanbul or the Aegean and Mediterranean coasts.

Even on the coast, it can get very cold - and very wet - in the winter months.

Access

Just as important as the climate is the ability of tenants to get access to your property. This is true at two levels. The area in which the property is located must offer convenient access from the places where the tenants live and the property itself must be easy to find.

If you are thinking of letting to tourists, it is worth repeating the results of the research conducted, a number of years ago, by the travel industry. These show that 25% of all potential visitors will not travel if it involves travelling for more than one hour from a local airport at either end of their journey. If the travelling time rises to one-and-a-half hours, then the number that will choose not travel rises to 50%. This research was undertaken in the context of package holidays, but the principles must also apply to people renting holiday homes.

Of course, this does not mean that if your home is more than an hour's drive from an airport you will not let it. It is beyond doubt, however, that the closer you are to an airport, the easier you will find it to let your property to tourists.

Do not underestimate the importance of being able to find your property! Navigation in Turkey can be trying. There are few people to ask for directions (especially if you don't speak Turkish!) and there are few signposts of much help when it comes to locating a rural cottage or a house in the centre of an old Turkish town. The closer to a main road the better. Giving decent maps and guidance notes is also essential. Nothing is guaranteed to ruin the start of your holiday as much as cruising around for three hours to cover the last 500 yards of your journey.

If your property is difficult to find, it is a good idea to arrange to meet (or have your tenants met) somewhere easily accessible. This could be your rental agent's office or in a well-known hotel.

Tourist attractions

Governments are keen on tourist attractions because they attract tourists! The fact that they are prepared to invest millions of taxpayers' money in encouraging these attractions should persuade you that having one near to you is a good thing when it comes to letting your property to tourists.

'Tourist attractions' is a term that covers a multitude of things. It could mean being near to a championship golf course or a famous beach or sailing area. At the lowest level, the tourist attraction could be a lady in your town who teaches pottery classes or Turkish history. The point is that there must be something to bring people to your area so that they will need to use your accommodation. The mere fact that the house is a beautiful home in in the middle of some pretty countryside is not, of itself, enough to attract a significant number of tenants.

Facilities

Many people going on holiday (or renting long-term) want to eat out. Even those who will probably end up buying most of their food in their local supermarket and cooking at home *think* they want to eat out. It will be much easier to let your property if it is within easy distance, preferably walking distance, of one or more restaurants. It should also be within walking distance, or a short drive, of shops and other facilities.

Choosing the Right Property

The choice of property is almost as important as the choice of area. Not all properties rent to the same extent.

Location. Location. Location. Everybody has heard that this is what matters. It is trite but true.

What is special about the property you are thinking of buying that that will make someone want to rent it in preference to all the others on offer? This is the most important question to consider.

Pick a pretty home

Most people will decide whether to rent your property after they have seen only a brief description and a photograph. The photograph is by far the more important. Research that we carried out showed that 80% of a group shown 32 potential rental properties picked the same three properties. The common factor in these properties was that they were all pretty.

Make it attractive

Make sure the external decoration and garden/pool area are kept in good order. These are what will show up in your photographs and will create the first impression when your guests or tenants arrive.

New or old?

New property is generally cheaper to maintain than older property. However, for rural or beach-side properties, a new property is not nearly as likely to be perceived as attractive by potential short-term tenants. They like a bit of character. It is different in towns and cities, where modern properties are often preferred. The preference also varies depending upon the nationality of your tenant. The British are more likely to favour older, character properties: Germans & Russians new ones.

If you are seeking longer term tenants, they may appreciate - as you do - the relative ease of looking after and living in a more modern property.

Once again, horses for courses.

How Should You Equip Your Property?

If you market the property well, you will get tenants. You will only get repeat tenants and recommendations from existing tenants if the property meets or exceeds their expectations in terms of the facilities it offers and its cleanliness.

Repeat tenants and recommendations are your most profitable customers.

The facilities required will depend upon the target audience you trying to attract. Think about that audience and think about what you would want if you were part of it. For example, if you are trying to attract an audience of sailors they will appreciate somewhere to dry their clothes quickly so that they can be ready to get wet again the following day. Young weekend visitors will want high-speed broadband.

Presenting Your Property to Tourists

The top tips are:

Welcome

It is much better if someone is present, either at the property or in a nearby house or office, to welcome your guests when they arrive. This is, however, often an expensive service. Flights often arrive late at night or early in the morning and, sadly, they are also often delayed. This person may be hanging about - at your expense - for a long time.

Despite this, a welcome by a person is hugely important. They can show your guests how to use the property and sort out any minor problems. They can also help your guests with any special requirements and they can alert you if they think there might be a problem with the tenants.

Cleanliness

The property must be spotlessly clean. This applies, especially, to the kitchen and bathroom. This may require some training for your cleaner as our expectations when going into rented accommodation are more like what we would want to find when we go to a hotel than what we would expect in an ordinary home.

Kitchen & laundry

This must be modern, even if traditional in style. Everything should work. You should have a microwave. You should also make sure that there is sufficient cutlery and cooking equipment and that it is all in good condition. A cookbook giving local recipes is a nice touch.

A washing machine and drier in or just off the kitchen are now commonplace.

Bathroom

These days, more usually bathrooms. Shower rooms (where there is no actual bath) are perfectly acceptable and can save a lot of water. In fact, shower rooms are preferred by many when compared with a bath only and by almost everybody when compared with a bath with a shower over it.

En-suite bathrooms for each bedroom are ideal.

Some visitors will welcome a bidet, especially those from mainland Europe.

Make sure that there is, at the very least, soap and shampoo in the bathrooms - as well as plenty of toilet rolls! Guests will much prefer it if you provide towels as part of your service.

Research shows that hair dryers are appreciated so that people do not have to carry their own. If you are going to provide hairdryers, get a good dryer and say so in the pack you or your agents send to the tenant when they book. Otherwise, the gesture is wasted.

Bedrooms

The number of bedrooms you choose is very important. Generally, in cities and towns you will get a better return on your investment on properties with fewer (one or two) bedrooms - which will be cheaper to buy - than on larger properties. In rural areas, or by the seaside, where most your guests may well be families, a three-bedroom property is probably your best compromise.

A five or six-bedroom house may look great and seem massive value but it can be hard to rent profitably. Exceptions can be on a golf course or in a place with a convention centre, where groups are increasingly keen on larger properties with lots of facilities, including a pool. There is also a growing trend towards multi-generation family holidays (grandparents, parents and children), for which larger properties with a pool are ideal. Check with your estate agent how it is in the area where you want to buy.

Of course, larger properties are more flexible and open up a wider range of tenants.

You can always rent out a larger property to just a couple, but you will only receive a low rent for it and that makes it unprofitable.

Bedrooms should have adequate storage space.

Most importantly, bedrooms should have clean and comfortable beds. The only beds that last well in a regularly used rental property, where the people sleeping will be all sorts of different sizes and weights, are expensive beds such as those used in the hotel industry. Beds should be protected from obvious soiling by the use of removable mattress covers, which should be changed with each change of tenants.

Nothing except dirtiness produces more complaints than uncomfortable beds.

Always supply bedding as part of your service, rather than expecting clients to take their own.

Living areas

Furniture and upholstery should be in good condition. The style is a matter of personal preference but a 'local' style is often attractive to short-term visitors.

The furniture must be comfortable.

There should be adequate means of cleaning, including a vacuum cleaner.

Heating & air conditioning

If you want to let the property outside the period from June to September, heating is essential. Even for lettings within that period, it is highly desirable. It should be effective and cover the whole house.

In an ideal world, air conditioning is probably best avoided except in the most expensive lettings. This is because it can be expensive both to run and maintain. Yet, in Turkey, air conditioning is so necessary, particularly in the peak summer months, that it will probably be difficult to let the property at a decent rent without it. At the very least, you might want to put air conditioning in the bedrooms. Check your agent's recommendation for your area.

Swimming pool

For most holiday audiences, a swimming pool is highly desirable. In a rural area, it will significantly increase your potential number of tenants. A pool should be of reasonable size but need not be heated.

If your property is in a complex with a shared pool, you do not need a private pool as well, except (perhaps) in larger multi-bedroom villas.

Welcome pack

You should make sure that basic groceries such as bottled water, bread, milk, coffee, sugar, and a bowl of fruit are left in the house to welcome your guests. A bottle of local wine goes down well too, unless you are aiming at a Muslim market!

Documents

Make sure that all guests are sent a pre-visit pack. Tell them what they need to bring with them and what is supplied. The pack should include notes about the area and local attractions, a map showing the immediate vicinity, notes explaining how to get to the property, emergency contact numbers and instructions as to what to do if they are, for any reason, delayed.

A house book should be available in the property. It should give much more information about local attractions, restaurants etc. These are usually available, free, from your local tourist office. A place for restaurant and entertainment suggestions from previous tenants is a good idea.

Include a comprehensive list of contact numbers for use in the case of any conceivable emergency.

Also have a visitors' book. This will be a useful vehicle for obtaining feedback and a means of making future contact directly with the visitors, who might have been supplied by an agency. This can avoid having to pay commission to an agency for 'finding' repeat visitors.

How Much Should You Pay for the Property?

When buying a property as a business you want to pay as little as is possible for the property, consistent with getting the right level of rental return. If you are *only* buying the property as a business proposition, then this price/rental balance (or return on investment), together with your judgement of the extent to which the property will rise in value over the years, are the main criteria upon which you will decide which property to buy.

If you are going to use the property not only as a rental property but also as a holiday home, then there is an additional factor. This is the amount of time that you will be able to use the property yourself consistent with getting a certain level of rental return.

For example, if you bought a two-bedroom apartment in Bodrum Centre for €100,000, that property might be let for 52 weeks per year to local people and produce you a return, after deduction of all expenses, of (say) 3%. If you bought a three-bedroom apartment in Yalikavak (near Bodrum) for €100,000 and let that to visiting families for eight weeks per year, you might also generate 3% on your investment.

While the properties would be performing equally well financially, the Yalikavak apartment would allow you and your family to use the property for over 40 weeks per year, whereas the Bodrum apartment would not allow you to use it for yourself due to the longer-term rentals. This could make the Yalikavak property the more attractive proposition.

I hasten to say that the figures I'm quoting are simply examples to illustrate the point, rather than indications as to what is obtainable at any particular moment in any particular place.

Whatever way we look at it, paying the minimum necessary to buy the property is the key to maximising its financial performance.

Marketing a Rental Property in Turkey

Properties do not let themselves. You will have to do some marketing. In the early years, you will have to do more marketing than in later years because you will have no existing client base. As in any other business, the cheapest type of marketing is catching repeat clients (or recommendations from existing clients) and so some money spent on making sure that the property lives up to, or exceeds, their expectations (and so secures their return next year) is probably the best spend that you will make.

There seems to be no correlation between the amount spent on marketing and the results achieved. Much money spent appears to be wasted.

What are the key points?

- Choose the method of marketing most appropriate to your property and your circumstances.

- Follow-up all leads generated at once. Contact them again after a couple of weeks to see whether they have made the mind up.

- Send them your details again next year at about the same time, as they are likely to be taking another holiday. Do the same the following year and the year after.

Remember that your marketing is only as good as the quality of the response you give to people making enquiries. You will probably do better spending less money on advertising and paying more attention to following up the leads that you have generated!

Letting agents

Most people will benefit from using a local letting agent, certainly in their first few years. As a means of letting the property, the main benefit of these agents is that they can pick up local traffic (from people who are already in the area). This is not traffic you would otherwise be likely to capture. There is, surprisingly, quite a lot of this.

Your local letting agent may also serve as your letting management agent: meeting *all* your visitors, dealing with cleaning etc.

Printed directories

If your property is pretty and looks good in a photograph, you are likely to get good results from the various directories and magazines focusing on properties to let in Turkey. They only work if they are inexpensive because, for a private owner with only one property to let, you only have one opportunity of letting each week - and so a directory that produces, say, 50 enquiries for the first week in September is not particularly helpful.

There are far fewer of these directories in Turkey than there were, say, five years ago. This is a result of the internet.

Internet agencies

This is now, by far, the most common form of third party marketing.

Companies such as Airbnb (**www.airbnb.com**), HomeAway (**www.homeaway.co.uk**), HolidayHomes (**www.holidayhomes.com**) and **sahibenden.com** (for locals) provide comprehensive and affordable services to those wanting to let their home for periods from a few days to a few weeks.

They are, certainly, at the very least a sensible top up to your own marketing activity if you want to address this market. Many people let solely via these agencies. However, bear in mind the legal issues surrounding short term lettings (see above). Marketing via high profile agencies such as these puts your property on the government's radar.

Traditional advertising

The problems with advertising are its scatter gun approach and, in many cases, its cost. You only need a very small number of responses. You cannot afford to pay a large amount in advertising fees for each week-long let. Except for very expensive properties, traditional advertising is too expensive.

However, we have had reports of good results from the specialist property press - and even more from ultra-cheap advertising on your local supermarket notice board or in your church or school magazine!

Your own contacts

Your own contacts are, without doubt, the best and cheapest opportunity you have for marketing your property in Turkey. Remember how few people you need to rent it out for, say, 25 weeks per year. Given that many people will take the property for two weeks or more you will probably only be looking for ten to 15 lettings.

Remember that letting for 25 weeks would be a *very* good result.

The people who find this easiest are those who work for large organisations. If you are lucky enough to work for a major hospital or in a large factory, you will almost certainly be able to find enough people to keep your property fully occupied within your working environment and using your circle of family and friends. You will have the additional advantage of knowing the people who are going to rent the property. This reduces the risk that they will cause it damage or fail to pay you.

Even without lots of people from work, most owners will be able to find enough friends, neighbours, and relatives to rent a nice property in Turkey for ten weeks per year. This will leave only a relatively small number of tenants to be found by advertising or other marketing means.

When renting to family and friends, or indeed close working colleagues, you will have to learn how to raise the delicate issue of payment. Given that you are not going to be incurring any marketing costs and, probably, much less in the way of property management costs when letting to these people you should be able to offer them an attractive price and still generate as much net income as you would have done by letting through an agency.

Make sure that you address the issue of payment when you accept the booking as doing so later can be very embarrassing. Relatives and friends can expect stuff for free!

Some people find it more comfortable to have their property management agency deal with all rentals, including these referrals. They can then tell the people that the terms of their contract require this and so avoid any discussion about money. However, if you do this you will have to pay the agencies fee for processing those tenants.

The internet

The internet offers tremendous opportunities for bringing a specialist niche product to the attention of a vast audience at very little cost. It also offers the possibility of showing lots of pictures and other information about your property and the area in which it is to be found. As such it is ideal for the person wanting to rent out property in Turkey.

It is worth having your own little website, designed specially for this purpose. Not only can it be your brochure but it can also act as a way of taking bookings. It is much cheaper to have someone print off a copy of your brochure from their own computer than it is for you to send it by post.

You may have the expertise to create your own website. If you do not, it's quite fun learning. There are some programmes (for example, Wix or Wordpress) that allow you to create a very professional-looking website very simply.

If you have not got the time or inclination - or want functionality that free website-builders can't provide - a simple, but very effective, site can be put together professionally for about €250.

As well as having your own website, you should consider listing your property on one of the many international property websites. These listings are, generally, low cost. You will soon find the ones that work and the ones that don't. If you are trying to attract the Turkish market then the main tool is probably the Turkish equivalent of Gumtree, **sahibinden.com**. It, too, is inexpensive.

You will have to decide whether you want to use your website only as a brochure or whether you are prepared to take electronic bookings. You will be able to take payment only by cheque or bank transfer unless you are lucky enough already to be a merchant with a credit card account or you are prepared to incur the expense of setting up the facility. Alternatively, try PayPal. This is relatively low cost and it works.

Many people decide *not* to take bookings directly from the website. They like the opportunity to talk to potential tenants before committing to let to them. They feel that this is an important extra security feature.

Doing deals

Two particular forms of deal might appeal to you.

If your property is in a rural area, where there is somebody offering a very local tourist service, it can be sensible to make contact with them and to try to arrange for the people visiting that facility or attending that course to be introduced to your property. This can significantly increase your lettings, particularly off-peak. If you pay the person concerned, say, 20% commission you will be well ahead.

The second type of deal is worth considering if you know some other people in the area who also have properties to let. One of the frustrations of marketing your property is when you find four lots of people who want to rent the property for the same week! Getting together with others, in a mutual assistance group, will allow you to pass excess lettings to each other.

Letting Agencies and Property Managers

Letting agencies - or at least good letting agencies - will have the opportunity to capture clients from the domestic market as well as from various international markets. They will argue that the fee that you will pay them (typically 17.5-30% of your letting income) will be recovered by the extra lettings that they will make during the season.

This may or may not be true. In our experience, the people who are most successful (or, at least, who make the most money from) letting their property, are those who attract the clients themselves. This, however, assumes a level of commitment that many people simply cannot afford and a level of skill they do not have. It is simpler to use a letting agency. For most people, it will also be more profitable.

Even if you use a letting agency, keep on trying to find tenants yourself. The income from an extra five or ten weeks let per year is largely profit.

If you decide to use a letting agency, the choice of agency is critical. There are some excellent agencies in Turkey. There are also some crooks and incompetents. The difference in performance between the two will make the difference between making a profit and a substantial loss. Choosing a good agency can, easily, double your income.

The temptation is clear. If somebody comes into their office on a Friday in August and wants to rent an apartment, yours may be available. Will the agent put the rent - perhaps €1,000 - in your bank account or in his own pocket? Will the agent rent out your apartment or the apartment belonging to one of his 'special friends'?

In the past, too many agencies have thought that you would never find out, because you were 1,000 miles away, and so succumbed to temptation.

Selecting an agency

When selecting which letting agency to appoint there are various checks that you should make. Remember these people hold the financial success of your venture in their hands.

- If the agency is a Turkish agency, are they experienced? Many such services are offered as an adjunct to estate agencies.

- Check their premises. Do they seem welcoming and efficient? Is there evidence of significant letting activity?

- What marketing do they do? If they are reliant upon passing trade then, except in the most in-demand areas, they will not get you good results.

- Ask to see a sample of the information pack sent to a potential client. You will be able to judge a lot from this. Is it impressive? Is it the image you want to give of your property? Would you follow it up by booking?

- Inspect two or three properties that they are presently managing. If they are dirty or ill cared for, then so will yours be. Then it will not let, or it will let and generate lots of complaints.

- Ask for references. Preferably they should be from other overseas clients. Take the references up. Preferably speak to the people on the telephone. Ask whether there are happy with the agency's performance and whether the financial projections given to them have been met.

- What contract are they offering you? Unless you are familiar with Turkish law (and fluent in Turkish), it is sensible to get this checked by your lawyer before you sign it as some give you far more rights (and protection) than others.

- Make sure that the contract gives you an entitlement to full reports showing when the property was let and for what money. Do not accept a broad analysis by period (e.g. miscellaneous income, August to September). Insist on a breakdown week by week. Also insist on a full breakdown of all expenses incurred in connection with the property.

- Make sure the contract gives you the right to dismiss the agent on fairly short notice.

- How many weeks rental do they think you will be able to obtain in this area? How much cash do they think they would generate for you after deduction of all expenses, including their charges?

- What type of property do they think would be the best for letting purposes in this area? Each area has its own special opportunities.

Controlling the agency

Once you have appointed a letting agency you must control it.

- Check the report you receive from the agency and check that the money you actually receive corresponds to the amounts shown in the report.

- Let the agency know, in the nicest possible way, that you and all your friends in the area check each other's properties every time you are there and compare notes about which are occupied and the performance of your letting agencies. If they believe you, this is a deterrent to unauthorised lettings.

- Telephone the property every week. If someone answers the phone, make a note and make sure that there is income shown for the week of the phone call. Otherwise you need a very good explanation! Doing this justifies the cost of a phone in the property.

- From time to time, have a friend pose as a prospective customer and send for an enquiry pack.

- If you get the opportunity, call in to see the property without warning to see what state it is in.

All this may sound like hard work. It is. It will significantly increase the income you receive from your rental property.

Furnished or Unfurnished?

From the point of view of the landlord the safest type of letting is a short holiday letting of furnished property.

If a furnished property is let as a holiday letting, the tenant's rights to stay on at the end of the period of the tenancy are limited or non-existent. In any case, very few tenants of this type will want to do stay on.

However, again note the legal restrictions on letting in this way. See above.

The Letting Agreement

A suitably drafted tenancy agreement will take into account all these factors and protect you in the event of a dispute with your tenant and, in particular, in the event that he or she wishes to stay on at the end of the tenancy.

If your property forms part of a condominium or a coop, your tenants will have to agree to abide by the rules of the community and should be supplied with a copy of the rules or, at least, of the part of the rules that governs their conduct.

In the rental contract you should stipulate what things are going to be covered by your insurance and what are not. Typically, the tenant's personal possessions would not be covered under your policy.

See the sample contract at **www.guides.global/books/turkey/tur-downloads.php**

Insurance

Make sure that your property is properly insured. 'Ordinary' property insurance will probably not be sufficient. See page 97.

Fractional Ownership & Timeshare in Turkey

Written by **Başak Yildiz Orkun**
Managing Partner (Legal Department) at Orkun & Orkun
www.orkunorkun.com • info@orkunorkun.com

There are many things that we use infrequently: a holiday home, a boat, a luxury car or a 4x4. Even expensive jewellery.

For some people, the thought of sharing the use of those things is something totally unacceptable. Read no further.

Others can see a compelling logic in sharing the use of expensive items:

- It reduces the cost of ownership

- There is no need to worry about what is happening to it when you're not using it

- It is often better for the item to be used regularly than left standing (houses, boats and cars all fall into this category)

- It is better for the environment for something that has consumed lots of materials and energy to produce to be used more intensively

- In the case of holiday homes in Turkey and elsewhere, it is better for the local community. It is not a good thing for a community to have hundreds of homes that are left empty for a large part of the year

All these thoughts gave rise to the ideas of timeshare and fractional ownership.

In addition to mainstream timeshare, a number of timeshare arrangements have arisen in Turkey 'by accident'. These are, perhaps, projects which could not be sold in the usual way or developments where a group of owners have decided to use timeshare as a way of marketing their unsold parts of the development.

Worldwide, timeshare and fractional ownership have not taken off to the extent that they are dominant in any of the fields referred to earlier, yet both are used in Turkey and worldwide. In the case of property - houses and apartments - there are some 20million timeshare owners worldwide (only 7million of them in traditional timeshare resorts) and the number of fractional ownership programmes increases daily.

Timeshare has its problems. Timeshare developed a terrible reputation for overcharging, poor selling techniques and high running costs: so much so that it reinvented itself as "fractional ownership".

Timeshare was very popular in 80s but today it is relatively uncommon in Turkey. For example, RCI (the exchange organisation which is most important player in the timeshare industry) lists fewer than 40 timeshare developments in Turkey, as opposed to 110 in Spain.

Although Turkey has a specific type of Title Deed for timeshare, and the legal system tends to deal with timeshare very well, I believe the popularity may be declining because of the large number of short-lets and hotels available nowadays.

From a legal point of view, the most straightforward arrangement now tends to be for smaller timeshare projects where there are, say, 11 owners owning and sharing the use of a house. These are more properly classified as fractional ownership projects, rather than as timeshares. There are a number of ways in which their position can be protected quite satisfactorily and their rights recorded by a note at the Land Registry (*Tapu Ofis*).

Fractional Ownership and Timeshare: the Difference

Nothing and everything.

Fractional ownership can be seen, by the cynical, as a way of relaunching the very jaded concept of timeshare.

This is not entirely fair.

When timeshare was first conceived in the early 1960s - strangely, in the UK - it expanded upon an earlier concept, popular after WW2, called vacation home sharing.

Vacation home sharing had a political and ideological basis as well as an economic one. The idea was that four European families - for example, somebody from Germany, somebody from France, somebody from the UK and somebody from Italy would, together, buy a holiday home: let's say in Spain. Each would have the right to use it for three months of the year, either in one block or in several parts.

Today, this would be seen as a fractional ownership rather than timeshare. The owners actually *owned* the asset and simply shared the use of it.

The next stage in the development came when a UK company decided to offer properties divided not into quarters but into 1/50th shares. This allowed somebody to buy one, two or three shares and have one, two or three weeks' use of the property each year. The remaining two weeks were allocated for redecoration and maintenance.

With this arrangement came the need for a more rigid allocation of usage. Two patterns eventually emerged. Fixed weeks (where your share gave you the right to use the property for (say) the fifth week of the year, every year) and rotating usage (where, this year, you had the right to use the property for the fifth week but next year it would be the tenth week and the year after that the 15th week etc.).

The general ownership model for early timeshare was one where the timeshare owner actually owned the asset. For practical reasons, you couldn't have all 50 people's names on the title deed and so, generally, the owner owned indirectly. This means that either the property would be owned by a company (with the owners having a 1/50th share in the company) or the property would be owned by trustees (who held it 'in trust for' the 50 owners). In either case, the official owner had to maintain the property and manage it on behalf of the real owners, but in the best interests of the owners.

In either case, the owner could sell his or her week to another person and, in either case, if they jointly decided to sell the whole property then the net proceeds of sale would be distributed between them.

All these early arrangements would, today, be seen as fractional ownership - because the 'owner' actually owned the asset.

In the early 1970s the idea reached the US where, as is so often the case, an interesting idea was converted into a raging commercial success.

However, in the US they changed the ownership model. In those early American timeshares, the operator would, typically, own three or four resorts in different places. The buyer received a 'vacation licence' which gave them the right to use any of the resorts (usually on a first come, first served basis) for a fixed period of 25 years.

Most recent timeshares have used this model, or something similar to it.

Increasingly, timeshare is now the field of big hotels. The likes of Marriott operate several timeshare programmes. They realise that it is a way of ensuring customers come back to their group of hotels year after year. Needless to say, with such contracts, the owners of the timeshare weeks have no say at all in the decor or services provided.

Hence the real difference between timeshare and fractional ownership is the fact that, in fractional ownership, you actually own the asset; whereas, in a modern timeshare, you are likely to have only have a contractual right to use the asset for a certain period of time and for a certain number of weeks each year.

Just to confuse the situation, there are still one or two products sold as timeshare which *do* give the owner of the week the ownership (together with the other owners) of the premises, but this is now rare.

The Worsening Image of Timeshare

Timeshare promised to be a great way of enjoying holidays in high quality resorts at a cost far lower than you would pay if staying in hotels.

It was hugely successful as a concept, but then came to the attention of a number of very dubious characters who realised that there were enormous profits to be made. If you could buy an apartment for $100,000 and sell it to 50 people at $5,000 each you generate a gross profit of $150,000. You also have the ability to charge for (and make a profit from) the expenses associated with the use of the property each year. The size of this profit led to terrible and very high-pressure sales techniques, along with a lot of owner dissatisfaction.

Because of this, timeshare became regulated in most places around the world - including Turkey.

The timeshare operators seem to be smarter than the regulators, and so as soon as one abuse was closed they would come up with another.

So, timeshare developed a terrible image.

Relaunching it (albeit in its original and safer form) as fractional ownership helped to clean up the image problem.

Exchange Organisations

Exchange organisations allow the owners of timeshare weeks to swap the use of their weeks, not just for weeks in other resorts owned by the same group but for weeks in thousands of resorts worldwide. There are two major timeshare exchange programmes: RCI and II. Between them they give access to about 300,000 properties in 100 countries around the world. Both of the exchange organisations provide a comprehensive and reliable service.

If you want to exchange your week in Spain for a week in a resort in Mexico, you will have to pay the exchange organisation a modest fee for providing that service.

Most timeshare resorts belong to one or other of these programmes. It's worth looking at the rules of the exchange organisation associated with your development to see what they have on offer and what it will cost to use the service.

Maintenance Charges

It's important to note that, in addition to the price you pay for that right, you will also have to pay an annual charge (called 'the maintenance fee') for the maintenance of the complex and the cleaning and other services that you will use while you are there. This charge can be substantial - sometimes as much as (or more than) renting a local hotel room: though, in fairness, the accommodation is often more spacious and of higher quality than you would find in a typical hotel.

Second-Hand Timeshare

It's worth noting that timeshare weeks are often available second-hand, at a far lower cost than the original cost of purchase. This is because people's ideas change and the owner wants to get out of his timeshare contract and so avoid having to pay the ongoing annual maintenance charges for their weeks. Check, very carefully, the level of the annual maintenance charge and how much it has increased in recent years.

How Does Fractional Ownership Work?

Fractional ownership is, in some ways, more simple than timeshare. However, there are more ways in which it can be structured.

In the simplest of cases, a property will be divided up into four or six periods of usage each year and the owners of those periods of usage will be listed on the title deed to the property as the joint owners of the property itself. In some ways, this is the simplest and best form of ownership, although it can be more expensive when you want to sell your right to somebody else, as you then have to do a proper new title deed for your share. It can appeal, in particular, to members of the same family, a group of friends, or colleagues.

Other fractional ownership programmes put the property into the name of some form of company and then make the owners of the fractional shares the owners of the company. This can work equally well and it is usually simpler and cheaper to transfer the ownership of a share in a company than it is to transfer the legal title to a property.

A few fractional ownership programmes put the ownership of the property itself into trust and the trustee then owns it on behalf of the individual owners. This also makes the transfer of ownership simple and straightforward.

While these are the main methods of ownership offered, there are others.

Most fractional ownership programmes relate to only one property. Until recently, it was not possible to take advantage of the worldwide exchange facilities offered by RCI and II if you owned a 'fractional', but that has now changed. RCI has opened a new website called the Registry Collection to deal specifically with exchanges of fractional ownership.

Whereas fractional ownership (like timeshare) started off as a small number of small programmes, more and more big companies are now coming into this field and offering fractional ownership opportunities.

When it comes to the use of your time in your fractional ownership property the way things are organised is similar to the way in which they're organised for timeshare. In other words, you may have an entitlement to use your property (for example) for the month of April each year or you may have rotating rights to use the property (for example) in April this year, in July next year and in October the year after that.

However, in the case of small fractional ownership programmes, there is an additional way of organising the use of the property which is quite common. One of the owners becomes the secretary of the group and owners book, through the secretary, the time they want to use: on a first come, first served basis. Indeed, even where the constitution of the fractional ownership programme lays down fixed or rotating usage, owners sometimes ignore it and set up this kind of arrangement because they find it more convenient. Generally, if the property is divided up into four or six fractions, you will all get to know each other and become friends. It is often the case that, with this free and easy approach, people are happy for their period of use to overlap that of another owner. For example, you might agree to fly in on a Tuesday and that the other owner is not going to fly out until the Friday. That can work out well for all concerned!

As with timeshare, there will be an annual charge to pay for the expenses of maintaining, administering and cleaning the property.

Regulation of Timeshare and Fractional Ownership

As already mentioned, the abuses in the timeshare world led many countries to introduce legislation to regulate the industry. Within the European Union (EU) there is a directive: 'Directive 2008/122/EC on the Protection of Consumers in Respect of Certain Aspects of Timeshare, Long-Term Holiday Product, Resale and Exchange Contracts' dated 14 January 2009. Turkey has not adopted this legislation.

Why Does Timeshare Work?

For most people, there are three great attractions to timeshare.

First, the entry price can be low - though this is not always the case; there are some very high-end timeshare products.

The second is that the quality of the accommodation has, usually, been very high.

The third is that most timeshare resorts are members of an exchange organisation.

Due Diligence

You are well advised to do your due diligence about any fractional ownership or timeshare that you're thinking of buying to make sure that you really understand what it is you're buying, the facilities offered, the reliability of the operator and the overall costs involved - including the ongoing annual costs.

There are three main players of concern to the buyer: the company that owns (and sells) the project, the company that actually runs the development and any exchange organisation to which it belongs.

As I have already said, both timeshare exchange organisations are reliable and work pretty well.

So, when you are thinking of buying a timeshare or fractional ownership it is worth doing some due diligence about both the company promoting the timeshare and the company that operates your resort. They could be the same company.

Some have a very good reputation. Others are appalling. Needless to say, you should not buy in a resort run by a company with a bad reputation. A Google search for "problems [timeshare/fractional company name] Turkey" will often be revealing.

Making a Will in Turkey

Written by **Başak Yildiz Orkun**
Managing Partner (Legal Department) at Orkun & Orkun
www.orkunorkun.com • info@orkunorkun.com

Making a Will is one of the most important things that you need to do, especially if you own any property in Turkey. It can save you a huge amount of money. It costs very little. It gives you peace of mind. It is easy.

Yet very few people do it. Only about 50% of our clients make a Will when they buy a property and, because we always raise the issue, that is almost certainly a much higher percentage than will be the case for foreigners in general.

That is crazy, because failing to make a Will can prove to be a very expensive mistake.

You can put into your Will pretty much anything that you like, but you should note that there is no concept of Trusts under the Turkish legal system, although there are other ways of producing pretty much the same result as you could do under a Trust. If you want to make provisions similar to those you would normally put in a Trust, you will need to take legal advice.

Why Should You Make a Will for Use in Turkey?

There are four main reasons.

The first is that it can create a great opportunity for planning your affairs to reduce your liability to inheritance tax in Turkey and elsewhere. This can save you very large amounts of money.

The second is that it will make dealing with your affairs in Turkey much quicker. In Turkey, if you do not deal with an inheritance and pay the taxes due on it within six months (for non-nationals) there is a penalty to pay.

The third is that you can make sure that the people who will receive your property on your death are the people you *want* to receive it.

The fourth, and possibly most important, is that you will probably sleep more easily knowing that your affairs are in order.

What Types of Wills are Valid in Turkey?

The law of Turkey recognises any Will valid under the law of Turkey, valid under the law of the place where the Will was made, valid under the law of the place where you are habitually resident or valid under the law of your own country.

Case study

Jack Delaware

Retiree, American, 81

The problem

Jack had made a Will in America before he moved to Turkey almost a decade ago. He realised, though, that most of his assets were now in Turkey rather than in America - and so making a new Turkish Will might be a good idea.

The solution

Jack checked with his lawyer, who confirmed that it was very possible to make a Turkish Will for his main assets - his property, his car etc. - whilst having his American Will deal with any assets still in the States.

So, Jack made an appointment with a local Notary, who (unusually) spoke fluent English, thus saving on the need for a translator. His witnesses said he was mentally sound, much to his relief, and he quickly went through the process of making a Turkish Will.

Jack made sure that the Notary he used was aware of his American Will, and even brought a copy of it into the office.

He also wrote to his US lawyer and had him draw up a fresh US Will acknowledging that there was a separate Will in relation to his assets in Turkey.

Jack told his lawyer, his neighbour, and his daughter (back in America) where to find copies of both of his Wills and - just as importantly - gave his daughter an up-to-date list of his assets and copies of other key documents.

This means that Turkey will recognise pretty much any Will that you have made, whether it's a Turkish Will or a Will from overseas.

For most people, the choice will be between using their 'home' Will to deal with their affairs in Turkey or using a special Will drawn up in Turkey.

However, in some cases there is a third option and that is having a Will prepared in accordance with the Washington Convention on the Form of International Wills. Unfortunately, relatively few states are signatory to this convention and it generally seems easier to rely upon a will made in your own country or in Turkey.

If you have made a Will in your home country then, technically, you do not need to make a new Will in Turkey. However, there are good reasons for doing so:

- It will be far cheaper to deal with your affairs in Turkey using a Turkish Will that it would be using your home Will.

- It will also be far quicker.

- You can tailor each Will to take maximum advantage of the tax laws in the country concerned.

How do I Make a Turkish Will?

Any person over the age of 15 may make a Will, provided they have legal capacity: the ability to make fair and reasonable decisions.

In Turkey, there are three ways of making a Will.

A verbal Will

In certain circumstances, you may make a purely verbal Will, but this is generally a poor idea as it can be hard to prove your wishes when the time comes. We do not recommend it.

A handwritten Will

You may make a handwritten Will in Turkey.

It does not have to follow any particular form. Nor does it have to use any particular words. It does need to make it clear that this is your Will and it does need to be dated.

It must be entirely in your own handwriting. The Will must also be written in Turkish.

For various reasons, a handwritten will is not generally a good idea, even if you speak fluent Turkish. It is not even a good idea for native, Turkish-speaking Turks.

It is too easy to make a mistake in what you say or to be unclear as to your wishes and it is too easy for the Will to provoke all sorts of disagreements and arguments when you die.

It is much better to use a third option: make a Will in front of a Notary (*noter*).

A Will made in front of a Notary Public

Making a Will in front of a Notary Public in Turkey is very simple. It is also our recommended way of making a Will for use in turkey

You decide what you want to put in your Will. Because of the tax-saving opportunities offered by making a Will, it is worth taking advice upon this from your lawyer. This might cost €100-150. It could save you €200,000.

Once you've decided what you want to say in your Will, you go to the office of your local Turkish Notary. There are Notaries in most towns and cities, even small ones. It is helpful to choose a Notary who speaks your language, but this is seldom possible. You explain to them (or, more likely, their clerk) that you want a Will and what you want to put in it.

If you've sought legal advice about the contents of your Will your lawyer will probably write a letter to the Notary, saying what you want to do, or liaise directly with the Notary over the preparation of your Will. In this case, you won't have to attend at the Notary's office at this stage.

The Notary will then prepare your Will and tell you when it is ready to be signed. This will, normally, take two or three days. If you're going back home before then, you can tell then when you're going to be back in Turkey and the Will can be ready for signature at that time.

You must attend, in person, at the office of the Notary, at the agreed time, to sign your Will. You will need to take your passport with you as proof of identity.

You will also need to have two witnesses present at the Notary's office. They must be over 18. Any gift made in the Will to a witness is usually invalid.

When you arrive at the Notary's office either (if you speak Turkish) the clerk will go through the contents of your Will to check that it reflects your wishes or (if you don't speak Turkish) there will be an official translator present. The translator will be arranged by the Notary. The official translator will translate the Will for you and check that it reflects your wishes.

Either way, if the Will is not quite right, it will be amended whilst you wait.

You will then be taken into the Notary's room where the Notary will have a brief conversation with you. If they speak your language, the conversation will be in your language. If they do not, it will be via the official translator.

The Notary will then read to you the Will that has been prepared. It will be read to you in Turkish. If the Notary does not believe that your Turkish is good enough to understand fully what you have said, they will require the Will to be translated to you by the official interpreter.

The Notary will then examine your proof of identity (if they've not already done so) and you will then sign the Will in their presence.

The Notary will then witness the Will.

After you and the Notary have signed the Will, you will have to tell your two witnesses, in the presence of the Notary, that you have read the Will and that it is your last Will. The witnesses then sign a statement, attached to the Will, saying that they consider the person making the Will to be of sound mind and capable of making a Will, and that the person has acknowledged the document to be their Will in the presence of the witnesses.

The Notary will keep the original Will in their archives, lest it should later be needed.

The Notary will also supply you with an official copy of the Will.

The Will remains a private document and only becomes public after you have died and after the Court has issued a Certificate of Inheritance.

Once you have received the Will, it is a good idea either to let your children or other heirs have a copy of it (the better solution if you are not concerned about privacy) or - at least - to tell them where you keep your copy, and the name and address of the Notary who prepared it.

Whilst you're doing all this - though it's not strictly needed - it's an extremely good idea to put the Will in a big envelope marked 'Will' and to also place in the envelope a list of all your assets including, in the case of investments, the contact point for the investment and its reference number. Once again, this will make dealing with your affairs when you die very much easier and cheaper. Put the list in the envelope, but do not physically attach it to the Will. Most importantly, keep the list up-to-date!

Every lawyer will tell you that their heart sinks when a distraught son or daughter, following your death, brings into their office a suitcase full of old bank account statements, share certificates, correspondence about investments etc. The lawyer will then have to follow up every single one of these leads in case you have €1million in the account concerned; yet they know, in their heart of hearts, that most of the accounts will have long since been closed and the investments sold years ago. This can all cost a lot of money! From the lawyer's point of view, it is also very boring work.

This housekeeping is nothing to do with making a Will but something you really ought to do at the same time.

How Much Does a Notary Will Cost?

This depends on whether you need a translator. See above.

The Notary's fee for preparing a Will is usually about TRY750 (€170, US$200, £150). If an official translator is required, you will also be expected to pay the translator's fee. This varies upon the language spoken but is, typically, TRY200.

There will be an addition charge from your lawyer if you seek advice on the tax-saving opportunities presented by your Will. The amount will depend upon the complexity of your situation.

How long does it take?

Typically, the process takes several days.

In cases of urgency, the process from telling the Notary what you want to say in your Will all the way through to receiving the original signed version of the Will, can be completed on the same day: often within couple of hours!

In an emergency, the Notary can visit you - often on the same day - in hospital or at your home.

The Will is legally effective as soon as it has been signed in front of the Notary.

What Happens to my Will?

Unlike in many countries, where the Will itself is a valuable document, under the Turkish system it does not matter if you lose or burn your copy of the Will. The copy that matters is the copy that is held by the Notary.

That can be retrieved by your heirs.

What if I Want to Change my Will?

There are several ways of doing this but the simplest is to make a new Will. That, automatically, replaces the earlier Will.

It is also possible to change just part of your Will by way of a document known as a codicil (*vasiyetname eki*). In a codicil you expressly declare that the original Will remains valid but that you wish to change certain aspects of it. A codicil is made in exactly the same way as a full Will.

In general terms, we don't think codicils are a good idea. They create unnecessary confusion and, in our era of the word processor, it is no more trouble (and barely more expensive) to completely replace the original Will.

Although getting divorced does not automatically cancel your Will, your ex-spouse will no longer be your legal heir and will no longer benefit from any gifts made to them. In practical terms, you should take a new Will if you divorce. In that Will you could, if you wished, make a perfectly valid gift "to my ex-wife". Few people do!

What Happens When I Die?

The process for dealing with an inheritance in Turkey is quite straight-forward. See the next chapter.

Important Note!

It is vitally important that when you ask the Notary to prepare a Will you tell him if you have already made a Will somewhere else. It is equally important, if you're making a new Will somewhere else after you've already made a Will in Turkey, that you tell the person making the new Will that you have already made a Will *in Turkey*.

If you do not, the Notary or the other person making the Will is likely, almost automatically, to start it by saying that you, "revoke all Wills that you have previously made". If you're making a Will 'back home', this will (or, at the very least, may) cancel your Will in Turkey! If you are making a Will in Turkey, this could have the effect of cancelling your Will back home. This is not a good idea.

Instead, the Notary in Turkey should say that you "revoke all Wills that you have previously made in Turkey" or the person making a Will for you in another country should say that you "revoke all my previous Wills except for the Will I have made relating to my property in Turkey". They will use different forms of words depending on the circumstances, but that is the message.

Dealing with an Inheritance in Turkey

Written by **Başak Yildiz Orkun**
Managing Partner (Legal Department) at Orkun & Orkun
www.orkunorkun.com • info@orkunorkun.com

Inheritance and dealing with an inheritance are topics where you will find that a little bit of forward planning can save you a great deal of money.

There are two completely different issues. Who has the legal right to inherit your property is one thing, how much tax has to be paid is another. Forward planning can remove any problems about who can inherit your property (either 'back home' or in Turkey) and greatly reduce the taxes due in both places.

The system of dealing with an inheritance in Turkey is fairly simple but still has a few tricks to catch out the unwary.

Is a Foreigner Treated Differently from a Turkish Person?

Yes. You are treated more favourably!

In Turkey, foreigners (whether resident in Turkey or not) are only subject to Turkish inheritance taxes on the assets that they hold in Turkey. Turkish law does not tax any assets that you leave in any other country: for example, the country of your birth. However, and it's an important however, you may well find that those assets are taxed in that country. As a result, this concession may not be quite as beneficial as it first appears.

Inheritance is one of the most important areas of law where you really need to understand the interaction between what is happening in Turkey and what is happening in your own country.

It is worth repeating that the two most important aspects of this are the questions of who has the right to inherit in Turkey (and how those rights interact with the rights they or others may have in other countries) and the rules concerning taxation of inheritances in Turkey (and how they interact with the rules concerning taxation of inheritances in other countries).

What Happens to my Property in Turkey When I Die?

Turkish nationals

A Turkish person is not free to dispose of all the assets they own when they die ("their entire estate") as they see fit. Certain relatives have certain fixed rights to inherit a part of those assets. This concept - the 'reserved portion' - is commonplace in continental European legal systems but comes as a bit of a surprise to people accustomed to the freedom of Anglo-American law.

As few of our readers are likely to be Turkish citizens, we will only deal with the Turkish system briefly.

The reserved portion is a specific percentage of the total value of the estate. The percentage depends upon the number of people entitled to a share of the portion and the closeness of their relationship to the person who has died.

Any amount in excess of the reserve portions may be disposed of in whichever way you see fit, either by giving more to some or all of the people entitled to a share in the reserve portion or by giving things to other people altogether.

The people who have a possible entitlement to a reserved portion are:

Your children

The children must inherit a minimum of 50% of the amount that they would have inherited under the Turkish rules about intestacy - in other words, what happens if the person had died without making a Will. You can provide for them to inherit more than this, but they may not inherit less. See below.

Your parents

The reserved portion of your parents is one quarter each of what they would have received if you died without making a Will.

Your spouse

The reserved portion of your spouse is either three quarters or the full amount of what they would have inherited if you had not made a Will, depending upon whether you left any children or parents alive at the time of your death.

Inheritance on intestacy

If any Turkish citizen dies without making a Will ("dies intestate"), their property is distributed to their next of kin following a set of rules laid down by Turkish law.

If they have any descendants, only their descendants will become their next of kin, and so inherit any property. If they don't have any descendants, their parents and (through the parents) the rest of their wider family will be entitled to benefit.

The position of the spouse is weak under this system.

Foreigners

A foreigner who dies owning assets in Turkey, whether it's a home or a bank account or any other kind of asset, is dealt with totally differently.

Turkish law states that, when a foreigner dies, the rules that should apply to who should inherit what are the rules of that foreigner's own nationality, even if the foreigner is a resident in Turkey.

So, if a US citizen dies in Turkey then his assets in Turkey will be disposed of in accordance with the law of the United States and if a French citizen dies leaving assets in Turkey, those assets will be disposed of in accordance with the law of France.

In some cases (for example, in the case of a British citizen), this will mean that the assets may be disposed of in whichever way the person who has died stated in their Will. In other cases (for example, in the case of a French person or many other continental Europeans) the Turkish Court will apply the reserved portions and other rules that apply in that person's country.

All of this relates only to the question of who inherits what.

Whatever the law in your country says about *who* may inherit and *what* they should inherit, there is the completely separate question of what inheritance (and other) taxes are going to be payable in Turkey. Just because Turkish law accepts that foreigners should be free to dispose of their assets in Turkey in the same way that they could 'back home', does not mean that they don't want to get their fair share of tax out of the inheritance!

Why do These Rules Matter?

Let's take an example.

Let us imagine that a person owns a house in Turkey, a car in Turkey and a bank account in Turkey. Let's say the house is worth €500,000; the car €10,000 and (at the time of his death) the bank account contained €1,500. Let us also imagine that at the time of his death, he had debts of €1,500 in Turkey.

This means that the total value of his estate was €511,500 but that the net value, after deducting the debt, was €510,000.

He had no assets outside Turkey.

He had three children and a wife.

He would like to leave as much as possible to his wife.

Example

If he had Turkish citizenship
The distribution of his assets will be treated under the laws of Turkey.

If he made no Will
In this case, the wife will inherit 25% (€127,500). The children will share 75% of the assets, and so receive 25% (€127,500) each.

If he made a Will

The children would have the right to inherit, between them, a minimum of half of the legal portion (so 37.5% of the net assets). The surviving wife legal share (25%) will be reserved in full since she is an heir with children. The rest of the assets (35.5%) could be disposed of as he pleased. He could, for example, give it all to his wife, to his eldest son or to his mistress.

So, even for a Turkish citizen, making a Will makes a big difference to the outcome.

If he was a foreigner

In essence, the foreigners own law will apply.

If he was Euroslavian

Turkish law would apply the law of the fictional country of Euroslavia when deciding who should inherit his assets.

Euroslavian law says (let's say) that the assets should be divided amongst the children in equal shares but that the wife should have the lifetime right to use the assets.

The children would each inherit €170,000 and the wife would inherit nothing: though she would have the right to use the assets for her lifetime.

If he was a British citizen

If he made no Will

His wife would inherit the car and the bank account plus the first £250,000 (say, €270,000) of the estate and half of the balance of the estate: a total of €390,000. The children would share the rest (€40,000 each).

If he made a Will

He could leave the full €510,000 to his wife, so she would be better off by €120,000. Alternatively, he could leave to full amount to any person of his choice or divide the assets between any number of people in whatever proportion she saw fit.

Tax

All these calculations ignore the issue of tax but, as we will see later, they would each be responsible for paying their own tax on their inheritance.

Conclusion

Making a Will can, almost always and even in a simple case, get you a lot closer to achieving your wishes than reliance upon the law of intestacy.

However, in many common cases, it is essential in order to avoid major disaster.

The elephant in the room is any second wife and family.

It is increasingly common for a man in his 50s, with a wife and adult children, to divorce and either live with or marry somebody 20 years his junior and to have a new family.

The children of the first marriage will, in many countries, have rights greater than the rights of the second wife. There may well be no love lost between them, and so the position of the second wife can become very difficult.

If the couple were not legally married, her position can become impossible as she would, in many countries, have no inheritance rights at all.

The moral of this story is that if your personal life is in any way complicated - if you are remarried with a second family, if you have disabled parents, if you're in a same-sex relationship etc. - it is really important to get good legal advice about how to deal with the inheritance issue and how to make a suitable Will.

It is also important if you are lucky enough to be rich.

What Will Happen to my Property in Other Places?

Turkish citizens

The Turkish rules would apply to all your property, wherever in the world it is located.

In the case of assets that are 'immovable property' (land or houses) those assets will be dealt with in accordance of the law of the country where the land is located.

All other assets would be disposed of in accordance with the rules in Turkey.

Non-Turkish citizens

Turkish law only applies to the assets that you have in Turkey.

Any other assets will be dealt with either in accordance with the law of your own country or, in some cases, in accordance with the law of the country in which they're located.

Should I Make a Will?

Yes!

See the previous chapter.

See the Guides.Global checklist of things to do before you see your lawyer about making a Will. This will speed things up and make sure that everything is covered in your meeting. **www.guides.global/checklists.php**

What Taxes Will Have to be Paid When I Die?

This depends on a number of factors. See our chapters on taxes on death (page 259) and inheritance planning (page 476).

How do I Actually Deal with an Inheritance in Turkey?

What does 'dealing with the inheritance' mean?

When a person owning assets in Turkey dies there are a number of things that need to be done in order to transfer the ownership of those assets into the names of the appropriate people.

Part of this process involves paying any inheritance taxes due.

The process of transferring the assets and paying the taxes is what we mean by 'dealing with the inheritance'.

Do I need to use a lawyer?

In practical terms, the answer is "yes" because your heirs need to receive a 'grant of probate" document, stating the identity of your heirs, from the Turkish Court of Settlement in order to be able to re-register the assets in their names and pay the taxes due on the inheritance.

Many local people would deal with an inheritance without using a lawyer. The process is not particularly complicated but if you don't understand the system and you don't speak Turkish it becomes almost impossible.

What documents do I need?

In order to start the process of dealing with an inheritance in Turkey, the heirs will need to gather together the following documents:

- The deceased's death certificate or a certified copy of it

- The deceased's passport or a certified copy of it

- If the deceased was officially resident in Turkey, the deceased's residence card or a certified copy of it

- A list of all the assets in Turkey belonging to the deceased and the documentation relating to them: for example, title deeds, bank statements and the certificate of ownership of any vehicle registered in Turkey

- If there is a Will in Turkey, a copy of the Will. This does not need to be a certified copy as the original will be obtained from the Notary's registry, where it will have been in safe storage

- If there is a foreign Will, a certified copy of that Will and a certified copy of the official document giving effect to the will. This has different names in different countries but is usually some sort of court order

- A declaration by the heirs, stating that there is no contest over the Will/inheritance. This could occur if the Will is not satisfactory and/or clear to the Court of Settlement

- One or more documents evidencing the relationship between each of the heirs and the deceased. This could be a birth certificate, a marriage certificate or (if the person is a more distant relative) a series of birth certificates and marriage certificates showing the connection between the two. If no document is produce the person will be treated as unrelated by blood, with the adverse tax consequences explained earlier

- If the people who are going to inherit are resident in Turkey, certified copies of their residence cards

- If the people who are going to inherit are not resident in Turkey, certified copies of their passports

- If the inheritance is to be regulated by foreign inheritance law, a certified statement by either a Notary Public or by two lawyers qualified in that jurisdiction, stating the effect of the foreign law both in general terms and with specific reference to the situation in this inheritance

- If the people who are going to inherit are not going to be dealing with this themselves, each of the heirs must produce a Power of Attorney in favour of the person they want to deal with the inheritance. This must be someone who will be in Turkey to sign the necessary documents. This will usually be a lawyer but could me a member of the family.

  The Power of Attorney can be prepared either in Turkey or wherever the person happens to be located.

A certified copy means a copy where the original has been presented to a Notary, who then certifies that the copy is a true copy of the original. If the Notary is not located in Turkey, the Notary's signature will have to be apostilled.

Official translation means a translation prepared by a legally certified translator, either in Turkey or elsewhere.

The process of 'apostilling' a document is a process of official certification by the government in the country where the document was produced that the signature of the Notary matches that in their records. It is required for notarised documents that are going to be used internationally.

The process if there is a Turkish Will

If you are going to use a lawyer to deal with the inheritance, you can pretty much ignore this part of the chapter as the lawyer will take all these steps on your behalf.

However, the basic way in which things work is that:

1. The inheritance process is managed by the Court who, once the process has been completed, will issue a Certificate of Inheritance.

2. There will be a court hearing and the Will will be opened before the heirs or their representative.

3. Armed with the Certificate of Inheritance, the heirs may arrange for the title to any land or buildings to be transferred into their names; for access to any bank account; or to change the registered ownership of any shares or other assets.

The process if there is a foreign Will

The process is the same as if there was a Turkish Will except that, instead of producing the Turkish Will, you will produce the officially translated and apostilled copies of the certified foreign Will, officially translated and apostilled copies of any official documents recognising the validity of the Will, and the officially translated and apostilled statement of foreign law.

The process if there is no Will

The process of dealing with an inheritance in Turkey if there is no Will at all is more complicated but similar.

Instead of producing the relevant Will, you should produce the documents required in your home country for dealing with an inheritance where there is no Will (for example, a court order or a Certificate of Law stating the law that applies in circumstances where there is no Will, and stating the effect of that law in the case of the deceased).

So, for example, if the deceased was from the fictional country of Euroslavia, under Turkish law it will be the law of Euroslavia that applies to this inheritance.

The Certificate of Law would be a document prepared by a Notary in Euroslavia stating, briefly, the provisions of Euroslavian law that apply when somebody dies without making a Will. For example: "Under the law of Euroslavia, where a person dies without making a Will, 50% of their net assets after the payment of any debts will belong to the husband or wife of the deceased and the remaining 50% will be divided equally amongst any children of the deceased."

If the deceased had a wife and children, that is all that it would need to say about the general law.

If the deceased did not have a wife and children, then the Certificate would go on to explain what happens in those circumstances. In other words, the authorities in Turkey are not looking for a textbook about inheritance law but a summary of the key provisions that apply in this case.

The certificate would then go on and say something like, "In the case of John Doe the effect of this law is that his wife, Jane Doe, will be entitled to half of the deceased's assets in Turkey; and his children, Anne Doe, Bill Doe and Charles Doe will each be entitled to one sixth of those assets."

As an alternative to having the certificate of law produced by a Notary in Euroslavia, it can usually be produced by two lawyers practising in Euroslavia, who then attend before the Notary Public, produce proof of their licence to practise and swear that the statement of law that they have produced is accurate to the best of their ability.

It is, generally, cheaper to have the certificate produced by the Notary Public.

The rest of the process is the same as when there is a Will.

General Notes

These statements of what needs to be done look fairly simple and, in most cases, the process *is* fairly simple. But there is often a bit of a sting in the tail when the Court or one of the organisations who need to transfer the ownership raise a query or ask for something unexpected.

One of the most important things to remember when dealing with an inheritance is that you have only six months - as a foreigner - from the date of the death to file the necessary documentation with the Court, for the Court to process that documentation (which typically takes about a month) and for you then to pay any necessary taxes.

This is a good reason for having a separate Turkish Will dealing with your assets in Turkey. If you do not, you are likely to have to finalise the deceased's affairs in your own country before you can even start to deal with things in Turkey. That, of course, could itself take up all of your six months!

If any heir does not get to the point where he has paid those taxes within that six-month period, he will be charged a administrative fine for late declaration. This will not be a substantial amount.

Inheritance Planning

See our section on inheritance planning (page 476).

Investment Opportunities in Turkey

Written by **Başak Yildiz Orkun**
Managing Partner (Legal Department) at Orkun & Orkun
www.orkunorkun.com • info@orkunorkun.com

Nowhere in this book is our initial disclaimer more important than in this section. When thinking about your investment plans, everything depends upon your personal circumstances. There is, most definitely, no 'right' answer: no 'one size fits all'.

Having said that, there are some basic facts and general principles that you should be considering when deciding about your general investment plans. These apply just as much in Turkey as elsewhere.

See the section in our chapter moving to Turkey (page 50) as to whether or when you should move your money to Turkey.

See our section on foreign exchange (page 112) about how to move your money.

Cash

As in any country, you will need to keep a certain amount of your money available in easy-to-access form. There will always be the unexpected expense, such as the need to do repairs on your roof or flights to see a sick child in Australia. How much you should keep in cash depends upon your personal attitude to risk. Many people who are in the happy position of having quite a lot of money find that having a sizeable lump sum (€50,000 or so) in the bank is a great comfort blanket.

For most people of modest means, a good starting point might be to keep about €2,500-5,000 in instantly available cash - i.e. in the bank or available in some other way. However, many people feel that this is not strictly necessary if they have credit cards with a good credit limit and the ability to access other funds in a short period in order to pay off those credit cards. Of course, funds kept in the bank, at the moment, earn little or no interest if they are kept in euro, dollars or pounds and so people are understandably keen to minimise this wasted opportunity. However, funds kept in a Turkish bank in Turkish lira can earn good levels of interest - currently about 13%.

When it comes to funds that can be accessed quickly, many people will look to keep €10,000 in some form that can be accessed within (say) seven or 14 days. Some will increase that to €20,000-30,000. However, again, the point applies that any funds that can be accessed that quickly may, generally, pay you very little in the way of interest and so they do little to help your standard of living.

Finally, many will wish to keep funds that can be accessed reasonably promptly (say, within a month or six weeks). Around 10% of your available money is normal for this (less any money that they have more quickly available).

Case study

Joshua Chang

Lawyer, Singaporean, 58

The problem

Joshua had money to invest, and wanted to invest some of it in Turkish property. He was worried about doing so, however, as the Turkish lira had recently proved very volatile and was at a very low point (early 2009) against the Singapore dollar. This could be seen as a valuable opportunity or a big risk!

The solution

Joshua decided that the Turkish lira, and the Turkish property market, would recover. He bought a property in Göcek for TRY400,000. At the time, the Singapore dollar and the Turkish lira were of almost equal value, and so the property cost him SG$402,000.

Now, in 2017, the apartment is worth TRY700,000. So the property price has recovered well. However, the Turkish lira has fallen sharply in value against the Singapore dollar. TRY1 is now only worth about SG$0.38. So, Joshua's TRY700,000 is now only worth about SG$270,000.

So, this was not his best investment, not because of the fall in value of Turkish property, but because of the weakened Turkish currency.

He's now decided to make another property investment, this time in the UK: where the fall in value of the pound against the Singapore Dollar makes prices look attractive and where there is a strong underlying demand for property. He hopes his judgement is good this time but, at least, he will have diversified his investment portfolio.

Of course, if Joshua had made the right call he could have made money. Investing a lot of money in one place is always a big risk.

The Rest of Your Money

As to the rest of your money, it should be invested in ways that are going to generate you a sensible amount of income. You should choose to invest some in ways that can be accessed reasonably quickly - say, within three months - but other funds could be held in long-term investments which it might be difficult, slow, expensive or all of these to turn back into cash if you suddenly found you needed to do so.

As with several other sections of this book, the most important issue here is what you and your partner find acceptable: what you are comfortable with.

The stock market

Turkey has a stock market (the BORSA). Its key index is the BORSA Istanbul 100 Index.

The Index currently (July 2017) stands at an astonishing 105,633.88. There are proposals to reduce the Index by a factor of 100 to make it more manageable.

Over the last five years, the performance of the Index has been quite volatile but over the last year it showed a return of over 31%; and so far in 2017, a return of over 35%. However, it may be significant that, in May 2017, two of Turkey's richest families cashed in profits and sold over US$600million of shares.

Volumes tend to be in the region of 750million shares per day.

The number of participating companies has increased from 80 in 1986 to 413 in 2017, and its market capitalisation has, over the same period, increased from US$650million to US$29billion.

You can follow all the key figures, in Turkish or in English, at **www.BORSAistanbul.com**.

Offshore investments

Do offshore investments make sense for somebody living in Turkey?

The short answer is: yes.

However, it depends in part by what you mean by 'offshore'.

Taken in its strict sense, an offshore investment is any investment located somewhere other than Turkey and it is almost universal for foreigners living in Turkey to have some of their investments located elsewhere. There are many people who have investments in Eurozone countries or who hold some of their wealth in places such as the US, the UK, Japan etc.

However, 'offshore' can be used with a much narrower meaning. It can be used to suggest places - often called tax havens - where there is a combination of banking secrecy and very low tax to entice investors to put their money there. Whether such investments make sense for you depends entirely upon your personal circumstances.

When thinking about offshore investments, people will usually think immediately of places such as the Channel Islands, the British Virgin Islands, the Bahamas etc. - many of which have a pretty clean bill of health from the OECD regulators.

However, the OECD every year compiles a list of countries that are wholly or partially noncompliant with exchange of information for tax purposes.

The number of countries on these lists has steadily reduced over the years as more and more have bowed to the pressure to follow the rules laid down by the OECD.

In the 2016 report, the only fully non-compliant country is Trinidad and Tobago.

This suggests that the idea of holding your money in a place and expecting nobody else to know about it is no longer based in reality. It is, almost certainly, not a good idea to invest in countries on any of the blacklists or 'grey lists'; if for no other reason than that history has shown that most such countries eventually bow to the pressure of the OECD/EU and enter disclosure agreements.

However, many people invest in or via these offshore banking centres not for secrecy, nor to hide their money, but because they believe that there are better and more flexible investment opportunities accessible via these places than they can access from Turkey: for example, a much wider range of mutual funds in various other countries.

Whether you want to take advantage of these extra opportunities is entirely a matter for you. You may feel that the range of investment opportunities open to you through your local financial institutions in Turkey or those in your home country are perfectly adequate for your purposes and you may take comfort in the fact that they have been approved by the regulators in the various countries that you know well.

If you want to join the offshore investors, you need to check out - carefully - the strength and safety of both the places and the investments. There is a lot of material online to help you do this. Not all of it comes from reputable or authoritative sources.

You also really ought to take good financial advice from a specialist in the field.

Do not invest anywhere or in anything if you are 'cold called' or approached, unexpectedly, by email.

Should you have an offshore bank account?

The question of having an offshore bank account is completely different from the question of whether you should have offshore investments. Yet, for some people, the two become confused.

People have off-shore bank accounts even if they don't have the slightest interest in, or wish for, banking secrecy.

Many people who work internationally simply find it very convenient to have an offshore bank account: typically located in places such as the Channel Islands, Panama, Belize etc. These may be small islands but they have substantial banking activity and offer great incentives to those who bank there.

Even if you do not want to take advantage of the wider range of investment opportunities, there can still be good reasons for having an offshore bank account. It is, for example, often much simpler to operate accounts in a number of currencies if they are based offshore. For example, you might be from the UK and have some residual income coming from the UK, you might do some work in the US and some work in Singapore. In Turkey, by default you will have only a Turkish lira account. Whilst you can, sometimes, open accounts denominated in other currencies, the process can be rather tortuous and the process of transferring funds from one account to the other can be rather slow. By contrast, having accounts in various currencies opened in an offshore bank is simplicity itself.

Some people also find it convenient to have a credit card issued by an offshore bank, even if it's only for use in emergencies.

One feature of money held in offshore banks is that you will seldom have to pay any (or at least much) tax in those offshore destinations on the money you generate through the accounts or on your investments there. You will, of course, have to pay the charges of the bank for running the account but these are often modest and certainly often cheaper than the charges that would be made by your Turkish bank for providing the same service.

However - and it's a very important however - the fact that you do not have to pay tax in these earnings in the offshore country concerned **does not** mean that you do not have to pay any tax at all on them.

For people who are tax resident in Turkey, these earnings are part of your worldwide earnings and, as such, need to be declared to the Turkish Tax Department. You will then pay your normal Turkish tax on those earnings in exactly the same way that you would if they were paid into your local Turkish bank account.

If you are not tax resident in Turkey - if, for example you spend five months per year in Turkey but you are still spending most of your time in (say) Germany, the US or the UK, you will have to account for and pay tax upon those earnings in accordance with the tax policies in the country where you're tax resident. In most countries, this will mean that you have to pay tax on them in the country in which you are tax resident as part of your worldwide income. As a non-resident in Turkey, you will not be taxed on that income in Turkey.

So, using an offshore account does not (usually) have any legal impact on the amount of tax you have to pay.

What some people do, which is illegal, is fail to declare the money flowing into their offshore bank account to the tax authorities in Turkey or their home country. They may, for example, decide that they're going to spend €10,000 a year on holidays and travel and use their offshore bank account and credit card to pay for all of that from income that they pay into that account. They then conveniently forget about both the income and the expenditure when it comes to filing their tax returns in Turkey or elsewhere. This may appear very attractive but it is illegal and you need to be aware not only that it is illegal but that the risk of detection and punishment increases all the time.

First, you have the danger that the offshore centre concerned will sign an OECD disclosure agreement and then give the various countries concerned full details of the people who have bank accounts with them.

Your next danger is that a whistle-blower leaks that information. This has happened several times in the recent past and it has given much joy to the UK, US, German and other tax authorities who are now busily chasing the people concerned for large amount of tax that they have not paid over the years.

A further danger is that the government of Turkey finds out about your account from someone in Turkey. This will, typically, be your ex-wife or a neighbour with whom you've fallen out and to whom you've foolishly bragged about your clever offshore arrangements. The tax department rewards those who report people in this way.

In these circumstances, the approach of the Tax Department is very simple and very effective. If they find that you have (say) US$1million in a bank account in (say) Belize and that you have had income flowing into that account of (say) US$20,000 every year, they will very simply contact you and say, "We see that you have all this money in Belize. You've not told us about it in previous tax returns. Obviously, you would not have lied to us and so we can only assume that this is money that you have earned this year. We are therefore going to tax you on the US$1million as income in the present financial year. This will be at our highest tax rate and, in addition, you will have to pay us a penalty for late payment." Ouch! This is not a nice letter to receive.

Given the low tax rates prevailing in Turkey it is, in our view, simply not worth the risk trying to obtain a marginal but illegal advantage by the use of offshore bank accounts and investments.

Having said that, if you would, for perfectly genuine reasons, find it convenient to have an offshore bank account - perhaps to have accounts in various currencies - there is no reason why you should not do so but you will (in almost all cases) need to declare the account to the tax department in the country where you are tax resident.

Other investments

There are, of course, a vast range of potential investment opportunities both in Turkey and worldwide.

As ever, you need to choose opportunities that fit your personal circumstances. In particular, they should reflect your attitude to risk and reward.

It is worth repeating at this point that there are thousands of people around the world who make their living by persuading gullible investors to part with their money for investments that are hugely overpriced or of no value at all. So, if you are telephoned by someone offering you a great investment opportunity in shares in SleaseCo or you receive constant emails explaining the benefits of some investment that will produce you 40% (or 400% or 4,000%) per year, delete the email or put down the phone.

See our chapter about financial planning (p 271) for more information on this subject.

Investing in Property in Turkey

The Property Market

Written by **John Howell**
Editor & Founder of Guides.Global
www.guides.global • john.howell@guides.global

When you're looking for property in Turkey, the first thing you need to know is what's available: not the specific houses or apartments but the types of property commonly found. Just as important are the typical prices you will have to pay for any given type of property.

Obviously, within any type of property, prices can vary enormously depending upon all sorts of factors (such as location and condition) but an overview of the typical range of prices is still useful. It will help you navigate estate agents' websites.

The Turkish property market peaked - and crashed - along with the others in the Mediterranean in the mid-2000s. However, Turkey has enjoyed a stronger, swifter property market recovery than some of its neighbours.

The market in Turkey has suffered with the tribulations faced by the country itself: political uncertainty, some unrest, the influx of millions of refugees and wars in many of its neighbouring countries.

The size of the market

In 2016, 1,341,453 houses were sold in Turkey. This was an increase of 4% on 2015.

Of these sales, nearly 450,000 were made with the assistance of a mortgage. This number is increasing rapidly (for example, in December 2016, the number of sales involving a mortgage was up 21.8% compared with the same month of the previous year). Mortgages have become available to ordinary, middle class Turks, and this seems likely to further increase the number of sales in Turkey and put some upward pressure on prices.

In December 2016, there were 142,713 house sales. Almost exactly one half were to first time buyers.

Coincidentally, resales (second-hand houses) also made up almost exactly one half of the market.

The type of property being sold

Probably because of Turkey's growing population, and mass migration to the cities, the most common purchase is a new property.

Turkey: how things *really* work

Amongst foreigners, over 80% of properties bought in Turkey are new, or very recently constructed. The main exception to this is in Istanbul, where there is a strong market for older properties in the old part of the city.

There is a huge variety of property on sale: from large and very expensive villas down to tiny apartments.

By and large, the people buying the expensive properties tend to be Turkish. People buying middle-range properties tend to be from Turkey, the Middle East or the former Soviet Union. Western Europeans usually buy smaller holiday homes - either apartments or two- or three-bedroom villas.

Resale properties vs new build properties sold

In December 2016, the shares of new vs resale properties were almost even:

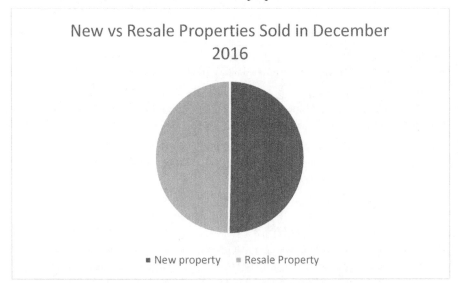

Average property prices in Turkey

House Price Index

Turkey's House Price Index is released monthly. You can view it here:
bit.ly/2ubNYMj

The historical data on the next page was taken from January of each year.

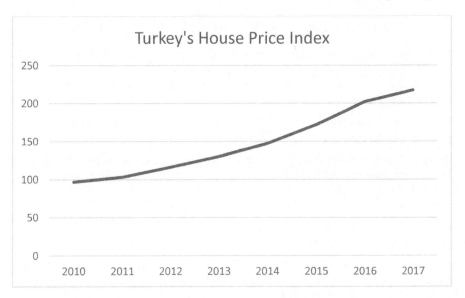

How many foreign buyers are there in Turkey?

In the whole of 2016, 18,189 properties were sold to foreigners. This was a decrease of 20.3% on 2015, and a huge reduction on the numbers in the peak years of 2006/7.

Of the sales to foreigners, 5,811 were in Istanbul and 4,352 in the province of Antalya.

Where are the foreign buyers coming from?

Of the foreign buyers, the largest single contingent came from Iraq (3,036), followed by other Middle Eastern countries. Russians bought 1,224 - almost the same number as people from Afghanistan.

The number of sales to Western Europeans were down substantially. Three of the big buyers have, historically, been the Germans, the British and the Dutch. The number of British buyers in 2016 fell to 827 from 1,054; the number of Germans to 714 from 869; whilst the number of Dutch remained more or less stable at about 200.

Interestingly, nearly 30% of houses in Turkey are bought by women.

Who sells property in Turkey?

There are no official statistics as to the different groups of people who sell property in Turkey but, anecdotally, the overwhelming majority of property is sold via estate agents or via personal contacts.

Foreign sellers vs local sellers

The number of foreigners selling property in Turkey dropped to almost nothing after the 2007 crash. However, their presence is slowly but surely making itself known again as the property market recovers. Once again, there are no official statistics.

Considerations When Investing in Property

Real estate has long been a popular option for those wishing to invest their money. It is tangible, you can use it yourself and many of us have ourselves made money in the property market or have heard stories about people making their fortune through property investment.

People take comfort from the fact that they can touch their investment. It will almost never simply disappear or lose all of its value overnight.

People also take comfort from the fact that they feel (not always correctly) that they 'understand' property and its investment potential. They themselves need somewhere to live. Others also need somewhere to live. There are more and more of them all the time. They will satisfy that need by buying or renting property.

However, as many people found out during the global financial crisis of 2007/10, putting your money in property does involve a risk.

In this chapter I will pose some questions for you to think about before investing in Turkish property. Always see a financial advisor and a lawyer before making a large purchase such as a house or apartment.

Why are you buying?

If you're buying property as a pure investment, then you will want to buy a property that is going to generate income (usually rent) and/or a capital gain (the amount by which the property increases in value): preferably both. You will want the results of your due diligence to indicate, clearly, that this is likely to happen.

In fact, many people would argue that a property (or anything else) that does not produce an income is a speculation rather than an investment.

If you're buying a property that you want to use as a holiday home but let for part of the time to cover all part of its running costs, then your analysis of its potential as an investment may be a little less rigorous but the analysis should still be done. In this case, you may attach more importance to how well the property suits your requirements as a holiday home and accept the limitations that flow from that: for example, because you wanted property located in the middle of the countryside knowing full well that such properties will not be as productive a letting proposition as a property located in the city or by the sea.

However, even if this is your plan, it might be as well to think about the extent to which you're prepared to make compromises in your holiday preferences if those compromises are going to improve the financial performance of the investment.

- Would you be prepared to buy a property located a little nearer to where there is popular demand?
- Would you be prepared to buy a property that is a more attractive letting proposition?

- Would you be prepared to buy a property with lower inherent running costs (for example, with smaller grounds or without a swimming pool)?

What is your attitude to risk and reward?

Every investment carries some risk. Some carry a great deal more risk than others.

One of the most common misapprehensions amongst the people that I see is that they misunderstand the nature of risk and reward. They assume, because it seems intuitive to do so, that the greater the risk, the greater the likely reward. This is simply not true. There are many property investments that carry truly astronomical amounts of risk and yet come nowhere close to providing the potential for reward appropriate to the level of risk that you are taking. Conversely, there are many property investments where the risk factor is relatively low and yet the likely rewards surprisingly high. For most people, this second type of property will be the better bet.

I encourage potential buyers (and, if they are a couple, they should do this separately) to rate themselves on a scale of one to ten. A person with a score of one is truly risk averse: the sort of person who throws out a can of food on the very day it reaches its 'sell by' date. A person with a score of ten is happy to go bungee jumping. Often, you will find that the two people in a couple have very different scores. In these cases, it is not simply a question of working out the average. It is a question of working out the level of risk with which both will be comfortable. This is usually much closer to the lower score than the higher.

What is your attitude to diversification?

Some investors are content to have all their eggs in one basket. For some, the one property that they're buying will be their only investment of any size. Such concentration of your funds is probably not a good idea and it is certainly not something that would be recommended by most investment professionals. Yet some investors have only limited funds and really like the idea of investing those funds in real estate. In this case, limited or no diversification might be the price they have to pay and that they are prepared to pay. However, even these investors would be well advised to think about the possibility of a co-ownership scheme (perhaps with friends or relatives) with a share in several properties rather than the outright ownership of one property.

Other investors are absolutely insistent on diversification of their investment portfolio. Some have rigid percentages from which they will not deviate. Often, those percentages will change as the years go by to reflect their changed investment objectives and financial situation.

One of the percentages will be the percentage of their total assets that they wish to see invested in real estate. Another might be the percentage that they wish to see invested in overseas real estate. Another might be the maximum amount or the maximum percentage of the overseas real estate pot that they would wish to see placed in any one investment or in any one country or in any one type of property. This might sound a little complicated, and a certain amount of flexibility is a good idea, but the basic principle is sensible.

For the investor in overseas real estate who is wanting to build and diversify his portfolio of international real estate, there is a whole separate topic of how to choose real estate assets in different parts of the world that mesh together and form a sensible, balanced whole: taking into account the investment prospects in those different parts of the world, the currency prospects in those countries and the relative merits of the different categories of real estate (residential, commercial, land etc.) that are available. This is beyond the scope of this book.

If building a diversified property portfolio, it can make a lot of sense to take some professional advice. This can help you filter the masses of information (much dubious) that are available and choose the most beneficial combinations of countries, areas, and types of property. Doing the research necessary to make the best decision yourself takes far more time than most people are prepared to invest and there are simply too many choices and too much information for most people to process. This advice need not be expensive, especially bearing in mind the benefits than can flow from it.

What is your attitude to liquidity?

An investment in real estate is, by its nature, an illiquid investment. In other words, it cannot be sold quickly if you need the cash. In bad economic times, it could take a very long time to sell.

Many people are not too worried by this. Provided they have other investments in cash, or which they can turn to cash quite quickly, they are prepared to accept the illiquidity as the price they have to pay for the other attributes of real estate investments that appeal to them.

Yet, even within the category of real estate investments, there are some that are much more illiquid than others. An apartment in the centre of Istanbul might sell quite quickly, even in bad times, whereas a rural property in central Turkey, ten miles from the nearest road, might take years to sell if there is a lull in the property market. Right now, the property market in Turkey is in gentle recovery, but these things are cyclical.

If you can accept the basic fact of illiquidity but need to limit that illiquidity as far as possible then you must factor this into your choice of property.

What is your investment strategy?

If you are thinking of buying a property as an investment then you have, clearly, included real estate in your investment strategy but that does not bring the matter to an end. There are many different sub-strategies within the category of real estate.

Investing for income

Some people are investing for income. They might be retired and using the income as (or to add to) their pension. They might like the idea of the property increasing in value but that is not their primary aim. They want income. They want secure income and they want an income that is likely to be strong and reliable in the future.

A common solution in Turkey is buying a shop on a high street. You won't expect big capital gains, but it's reasonable to assume a decent rental income (perhaps 10%) paid (usually) on time.

See page 438 for more about letting property.

Investing for growth

Others are not concerned about income. They perhaps have plenty. They want a place where their property is likely to grow in value to the greatest extent possible. In other words, they're looking for capital growth. In Turkey, you might buy land close to a growing city, a new airport, or a beach that's rising in popularity. You won't get any monthly income, but capital could ("could", of course, being the operative word) double or triple within two to three years.

Some would argue that this is not *real* investment: investment is about generating income; looking for capital growth is speculation. That is, perhaps, a bit unkind - given the track record of property price rises over long periods - but it is worth a thought.

As is always the case, some investors will be looking for a bit of both.

Long- or short-term?

Some will be looking to invest for the long term. For example, the pensioner or the pension fund. They want to buy a property that will perform now and that is likely to perform equally well in ten or 20 years' time. They do not want to go to the expense and trouble of having to sell their property and buy another (or even to change it for a completely different category of investment) in a few years' time. They have often done their maths and worked out that the costs of acquisition and sale are substantial and will dramatically reduce the net performance of their investment.

Others are happy to buy and then sell at a profit. Some will wish to do so very quickly. In other words, they will be looking for a real bargain, which they can sell on without delay; possibly not even getting to the stage where they take legal title to it. Of this group, some will wish to rent out the property for the period between the time when they buy it at the time when they sell it whereas others will wish to keep it in its pristine new condition until sale.

Buy to improve

Others will want to buy the property and then add value by improving it before selling it on. That could be by way of a simple clean up and redecoration (often surprisingly effective) but, more usually, it involves a full update, restoration, or extension of the building.

Buying 'off-plan'

What about buying 'off-plan'? This means buying property before it has been fully built and, in many cases, before construction has even started. In thriving markets, such purchases can produce large rewards. It is not uncommon for the launch price to be 40 or 50% lower than the price will be at the time (perhaps three years ahead) when the properties have been fully built. This can be for several reasons. Developers need money to launch the project and, very often, they cannot raise bank finance to fund this. They, therefore, sell their first few properties at very heavily discounted prices in order to generate the necessary funds. Developers (and their banks) also like to see confirmed sales as this shows that the project is attractive. That, in turn, makes other sales easier and raising outside finance less challenging.

There are two obvious, but often underestimated, risks in pursuing this strategy. The first is that the project never raises all the finance necessary and so never gets built. The second is that, contrary to expectations, the property does not rise in value during the construction period. This could be because the general market does not rise during this period or it could be because the property was overpriced when initially put on sale and only sold at all because of the huge discount.

The danger, in either case, is that you lose all or a large part of the money you have invested. In many countries, there is no protection for the funds invested by initial buyers in this way. In Turkey, there *are* some protective mechanisms that can be used to secure the money you have invested in these cases but those mechanisms don't work very well. As a result of bitter experience, many people have decided to steer well clear of off-plan developments.

If you are looking to invest in an off-plan project, you should be looking (with your lawyer and financial adviser) - and very carefully - at the precise terms of the protection being given to you. If the development is not eventually completed and legal title delivered to you, is it absolutely guaranteed that you will get your money back? Who is giving the guarantee? Do you trust them? Do they have the financial capacity to repay you if the shit hits the fan?

See page 400 for more about buying off-plan.

Combining business with pleasure

Many property investors also like the idea that they can have some personal use of the property in which they're investing. For the pure investor, this should be an irrelevance. They should be looking for the property that is going to perform best as an investment and care nothing about whether they can use it themselves; or even whether they like the property.

However, there is - without doubt - a hybrid category of people who are both investors and who want personal use of the property. They face special issues. See page 438. For these people, there are opportunities, whether they are looking for a holiday home that can also make them some money, or a property that is clearly and primarily an investment property that they might be able to occasionally occupy between long-term tenants. But there is no doubting that mixing business with pleasure in this way does usually diminish the ultimate performance of your investment. For them, the questions should be: by how much is the performance diminished; and do the benefits of personal occupancy outweigh that reduction in performance?

Property investment funds

Some investors are put off by the idea of owning real land, bricks and mortar. They dislike both the potential cost of buying and selling property and the reality that each such purchase will often tie up a large part of their available investment funds. Yet they like the concept of investment in real estate. So, they look at investment funds.

There are many of these and of many types. The same three great risks attach to all of them. How good was the choice of the property upon which the fund was based? How expensive is the fund's management? How readily can your investment be cashed in and returned to you? In many cases, the choice of property leaves a lot to be desired. In just as many cases, the administrative charges associated with the fund seem very high. Often, the arrangements for the disposal of the asset can be a little optimistic. All three of these faults dent or destroy the performance of your investment.

Development

There is money to be made in property development and so some investors are tempted to cut out the middle-man by becoming developers themselves. In my experience, few succeed: at least in their first development. They find that being a property developer is a lot more complicated than they thought and that there are a lot more hidden costs than they expected. Most lose money, at least on their first investment. Property development is not a game for amateurs.

However, genuine opportunities for making substantial profits do exist. If you are prepared to do your homework, be patient and start small this can be an interesting option, especially if you have relevant existing skills and have time to invest in the project.

Many will drift into 'real' property development after a couple of 'buy-improve-sell' projects, which are a good way of building expertise in the area.

See page 417 for more about property development.

What about 'below market value' (BMV)?

Some properties are marketed as being 'below market value'. Sometimes this is true and sometimes they can present spectacular bargains. On other occasions, much more frequent, such claims are nothing more than an unethical marketing ploy. Do not take them at face value.

Why would somebody be selling at less than market value? There are many reasons.

It may be that they have bought a number of units in a development and secured a substantial discount by doing so. If they can sell quickly, they can afford to pass them on as individual units at rather less than the price of such an individual unit in the marketplace. The speed of the sale is an essential part of their business plan and the discount produces the speed.

On other occasions, the sale might be by somebody who is in serious financial difficulty or whose personal circumstances mean that he wants to get rid of the

Turkey: how things *really* work

property quickly. For example, his employment might have come to an end and he is now leaving the country or he is in the process of getting a divorce and he and his wife need to turn their house into cash and buy two smaller properties before one of them kills the other.

If you want to buy in the BMV market, make sure that you are dealing with a good and reputable seller or agent and crosscheck the value claimed for the property.

What about 'distressed property'?

In the last few years there has been a lot of talk about 'distressed property'.

Distressed property is property that is being sold because the seller is in difficulty. The seller could be a private individual who has bought a property - either a holiday home or his primary residence - that he can no longer afford or it could be a developer who is unable to clear the units in his development and is in trouble with his bank. I have touched on the issue of distressed property in the section on properties that are sold below market value, but it's important to understand that, whilst distressed property is often being sold at below market value, this is not always the case. It is certainly not always the case that below market value property is distressed property. They are first cousins, not identical twins.

There is a whole range of levels of distress. At the lower level, you find the person who is merely anxious to sell and who is, therefore, prepared to lower the price a little in order to do so. At the top of the range you find the person whose house will be repossessed in a few weeks' time if he does not sell it and who knows that any equity he has built up will simply disappear into the pocket of the banks. He will be a far more motivated seller and prepared to take a much bigger hit on the price of the property. Sadly, somebody's misfortune is always somebody else's opportunity.

Developers often find themselves in a slightly different position. Sometimes, just like private individuals, they know that if they do not sell the units very quickly, the bank will repossess them or put the company into administration.

However, on many other occasions, the position is not quite that dire. The developer may have sold 90% of the project and covered his costs but he is not capable of selling the last few units, which generated his profit, in the normal way. Without the profit, he cannot go on to his next development and so the inability to sell may be losing him not just the profit on those units but the potential profit on the whole of the new development. This will usually be much higher. Add to this the fact that he may need sales staff on site (who are costing him money every single day) and you can see that he will be motivated to dispose of these last, troublesome, units at significant discounts.

In some cases, the developer may not want to give cash discounts because he feels that that would be breaking faith with his earlier buyers, whose properties could be seen as being thereby devalued. In these cases, he may well be prepared to give you a substantial alternative incentive: a complete furniture pack, a new car, a two-week cruise etc. During a recession, more developers are prepared simply to cut the price of the last units in their development.

Distressed sales offer a major opportunity to buyers though, as Turkey's property market recovers, they are becoming scarcer.

The mere fact that the property has been reduced substantially in price does not, of itself, make it a good buy. How does it rate in comparison to other similar properties in the area? Using the internet to visit property portals and local estate agents' websites can give you a good sense of real current market values and, of course, going around agents' offices and looking in their windows also works.

There is another test of value which I find very useful. If the house is on sale at less than the cost of construction: that is to say, the cost of the bricks, mortar, timber, and labour used to build it - ignoring the cost of the land - this is a good indication of value. Barring a complete collapse in the economy and wages, nobody is going to be able to come and build another property for the price you are paying. The cost of construction is also usually fairly easy to establish by local enquiry.

Whilst talking of distressed sales I must also make mention of 'short sales'. Short sales are sales of property that is under threat of repossession by a bank but where the bank permits the owner to sell the property and to sell it at a price less than the amount outstanding on the mortgage. They agree to write off the balance. Turkish banks will often do this.

They do so for a number of reasons. In some cases, this is, for them, a cheap and quick way of getting most of their money back. In many other cases, dealing with the property in this way can avoid it appearing as a distressed loan in their accounts and, as a result, can avoid the need for them to write off all or part of the value of the loan and weaken their balance sheet. This is becoming more important as banks all over the world are having to strengthen their balance sheets by introducing more capital. The introduction of the Basel III rules for international banking (which increase the amount of capital required by banks) made this problem even more pressing.

There are special procedures to be adopted if you a buying a property on a short sale. The process also takes longer than usual, typically an extra two months.

What is your timescale?

This will greatly affect the property that you're going to buy. Are you looking to make money over five years, ten years, or 20 years? As a rule, real estate investments do not work well for timescales of less than five years - although there have been some exceptions. This is because the costs of both acquisition and disposal are high in Turkey: perhaps, 10% on the purchase and 5% on the sale.

What's going to happen to the currency?

When you buy a property in another country it is quite likely that, in that country, they will use a different currency. This adds another level of opportunity and another level of risk to the transaction.

Currencies can change in value quite dramatically, sometimes over a relatively short period.

If this works in your favour it can be hugely beneficial. If you buy a property that goes up in value by 30%, that is good news. If, during the same period, the currency has also risen in value against your own - say, by 20% - this is a huge added bonus. On the other hand, of course, if the currency has fallen in value against your own then when you come to sell your property and convert funds back into your own currency you will not make nearly as much money and, in the worst case, you could even show a loss on the deal.

This may be obvious, but what can you do about it?

Nobody can predict, with any accuracy and in detail, what is going to happen to the value of any two currencies over the next few years but a little bit of study can help you understand whether it is likely that currency A is going to rise or fall against currency B.

There are several things that you can do. A good starting point is to look at the history of currency values. These can be found at many points on the Internet. I normally use xe.com (**www.xe.com/currencycharts**) because I find it easy to understand and you can present the information in simple graphs showing up to ten years.

You can also gain from a foreign exchange (FX) company's expertise and reduce your risk through their services. They will usually be happy to have an exploratory chat with you.

How are you going to pay for the property?

At the moment, it can be difficult for a foreigner to get finance to buy investment property in Turkey. Many foreigners buying such property in Turkey will have to use their own cash. However, mortgage finance is no longer impossible to obtain. See page 409. If you can produce documentation making your case for a good income abroad, and you're asking for finance that's considerably lower than the valuation of the property, you might be in luck.

The advantage of borrowing is that, if you can borrow in the same currency in which the property is valued, if the property rises or falls in value against your own currency, so will the value (in your currency) of your loan.

Do you want to let (rent out) the property?

Most people who buy property as an investment want to rent it out. This is how they generate income from their investment. Although property prices are rising in Turkey, they are not doing so quickly enough to generate a high enough capital return for most investors to rely upon that alone.

The question is, who are they going to rent it to? There are two main tactics.

The first is to rent it out in short-term lets, typically to people taking their holidays. The rent per week will usually be much higher than you would obtain on a long-term let and you will be able to use the property yourself for the periods when it is not occupied. However, there are drawbacks. The administration is more complicated. The property management is more expensive because of the number of handovers required.

There may be more wear and tear on the property. There will be longer periods when nobody is paying you any rent. There are legal restrictions. See our chapter on letting out property - page 438.

The alternative is to let the property on long term rentals. This will be less attractive if you wish to use the property, in part, as a holiday home but it can be a much less complicated way of generating rental income. In Turkey, many people have to rent rather than buy, due to a big gap between salaries and house prices. Teachers, bank managers, doctors, and lawyers all rent property. As a result, there are many quality tenants looking for quality property.

A hybrid approach is to rent out to visiting academics or seasonal workers. Academics come to our universities on year-long placements, starting in September and ending in June or July. You can, therefore, rent to them but still have the property available for your own use (or to rent to others) during the peak holiday season of July & August.

The choice of the property you buy should be greatly affected by your choice of target tenant. For example, if you a looking to rent to visiting academics you are likely to want to buy a house or apartment close to the university and you will find that, for younger teachers, the preferred type of property is a two-bedroom apartment with air conditioning.

What is your exit strategy?

How (and when) are you going to turn this investment into a profit?

Do you have a clear strategy about bringing the investment to an end? What is going to trigger the sale of the property? Is it going to be the expiry of a certain number of years (an easy option if there are a number of you investing in the project and you want certainty) or is it going to be when the property makes a certain amount of potential capital gain or, dare I say it, loses a certain percentage of its value?

If you are buying a property with a view to selling on at a profit, exactly who is it who is likely to want to buy the property from you at the time when you want to sell it? Is there a clearly defined target market? What evidence is there that it exists? What evidence is there that they will pay you the mark-up that you wish for?

In every case, why will the buyer want to buy your property rather than the hundreds of others on the market? You can help by buying the best property of its type: the best location, the best views, a corner site, good internal layout, and an attractive community.

Financial & Investment Planning in Turkey

Written by **Burak Orkun**
Managing Partner (Accountancy Department) at Orkun & Orkun
www.orkunorkun.com • info@orkunorkun.com

For the purposes of this book, the terms 'financial planning' and 'investment planning' are used interchangeably.

Basically, financial planning is all about working out what assets you currently hold and then deciding how the value of those assets should best be invested in order to give effect to your personal investment targets.

Financial planning arrangements are well beyond the scope of this book but the important thing we need to stress here is that, if you're becoming involved with Turkey, this is a great opportunity (and reminder) to carry out a thorough fact finding mission and to make a thorough financial/investment plan. This might be a revision to your existing plan or, all too often, it is the first time that our new clients have made such a plan.

It is very likely that the investments that you hold at the moment, bought for all sorts of reasons and at a time when you were resident in another country, will no longer be suitable to your needs. Or (at the very least) that there will be better opportunities available to you in your new circumstances.

Unfortunately, there is a great temptation when you're involved with all the issues associated with moving to a new country to acknowledge that you need to do this but then put it on the back burner. That is a mistake. When you're moving country, some of your best investment and financial planning opportunities arise once only and at the time when you're making your move. These opportunities can disappear completely once you have made your move to Turkey. It is, therefore, a good idea - however busy you are - to devote a little bit of time to this now.

Inheritance Planning in Turkey

Written by **Burak Orkun**
Managing Partner (Accountancy Department) at Orkun & Orkun
www.orkunorkun.com • info@orkunorkun.com

Inheritance planning (sometimes known as 'estate planning') is a concept that does not have a universally agreed definition. Here, the two terms are used interchangeably. It is different from, but related to, general financial planning.

Most people would agree that inheritance planning is a process by which an individual (or, in some cases, a whole family) arrange their affairs so that, on a death, there is a sensible transfer of assets to the people who they want to inherit and one which preserves as much of their family wealth as possible, usually by reducing to the minimum the taxes that would have to be paid.

Many people would also agree that a part of inheritance (estate) planning is preserving as much flexibility as possible for the individual up to the time of their death.

A much smaller number of people would add that the process should consider the administrative and practical issues relating to dealing with a death, and to arrange for as many of these tasks as possible to take place where they are simple and inexpensive.

Whichever definition you might adopt, this is most definitely an area where the right solution will depend entirely upon your financial position and other personal circumstances. Something that worked well for your brother or next door neighbour could well prove disastrous for you.

Skilled professional advice is essential. The more complex your circumstances, the more essential it becomes.

Indicators that your situation might be complex are:

- Being in a second marriage

- Having children by several relationships

- Having foster children and some adopted children: they may not be recognised as children under the Turkish inheritance formula

- Living with someone to whom you are not married

- Having assets in several countries

- Being wealthy

- Family discontent, particularly if you want to 'cut out' one or more of your children from any inheritance

The Importance of Inheritance Planning

Inheritance planning has four huge advantages.

Making sure the right people inherit

If, for example, you are a same sex couple, or an unmarried heterosexual couple, you may find that Turkish law (or the law of your own country) does not gave you the right to inherit from each other in the way you might like. On the contrary, the law might oblige you to pass the ownership of your property to (for example) the children of a previous relationship.

In this case, inheritance planning would focus on how to pass your wealth on the person you wish to inherit.

This could involve (for example) taking a large loan against the assets - so that they have little net value) and making arrangements for that cash to pass, on your death, to the person you wish: perhaps by using some form of Trust.

Sometimes, it might even involve marrying, taking up a new nationality (and renouncing your old) or moving so as to take up residence (and to have property located) in a place with more flexible rules. However, you do not usually need to take such drastic action to solve most problems.

Saving money

Good inheritance planning can save you huge amounts of money. Do not underestimate the amounts involved. They can be hundreds of thousands of euros.

For example (and it is a very simplified example), if you were thinking of buying a TRY2million (€442,000) property in Turkey (2018):

1. If you put the property in just your name, and left it to your wife, they would inherit TRY2million. They would have an allowance of TRY404,556, so they would pay tax on TRY1,595,444. This would amount to a tax bill of TRY58,722 (€ 12,639).

2. If you put the property in your name only, but left it to your wife and two children, they would have a tax free allowance of TRY606,462 so they would pay tax on TRY1,393,538. This would amount to a tax bill of TRY48,677 (€10,468).

3. If you put the property in the joint names of you and your wife, and left it to your two children, they would inherit only TRY1million on your death and would have a tax free allowance of TRY404,556, so they would pay tax on TRY595,444. This would amount to a tax bill of TRY13,063 (€2,809).

As I have said, this is just a small example of how some minor adjustments to your plan can produce significant tax savings on your death.

Flexibility

You could make an even bigger saving (depending upon where you and the children lived) if you gave away some or all of your assets before you came to Turkey. If, for example, you were British and gave your children the money with which to buy the house in Turkey in their names, then that gift would be a potentially tax-free gift (in the UK), and would be tax free provided that you survived for more than seven years. There are restrictions on your ability to do this, particularly if you are going to live in the house yourself but they (and similar opportunities) deserve investigation.

As the children would always have owned those assets as far as the Turkey Tax department is concerned, there would be no inheritance in Turkey, and so no inheritance tax, when you died.

However, this is not flexible. Once you've given the assets away you've given them away and, if you later need them, tough luck: unless the recipient will give some of the money back to you. That could, itself, give rise to a tax liability.

It is a much more flexible approach to give away small parts of your assets when you are sure you will not need them and leave the rest to be dealt with on your death.

Most people find that flexibility is very important.

There are many ways of ensuring flexibility. Cash gifts, Wills, Trusts and so on. Which is right for you will depend upon your personal circumstances and that is something upon which you will need proper professional advice.

Simplicity

The fourth objective of inheritance planning, at least under my definition, is to make it as simple as possible to deal with your affairs when you die. It is stressful enough when a loved one dies without you having to make trips half way around the world to deal with mountains of paperwork.

Although the legal responsibility of dealing with a death in Turkey rests with the individuals who inherit, it is sensible - in advance - to make arrangements for a local lawyer to deal with these things on their behalf. You can also take the opportunity to prepare Powers of Attorney authorising (again, in advance) somebody to sign all the necessary paperwork on the heirs' behalf.

Part of your inheritance planning should be to do this - which means briefing the lawyer as to your circumstances and then keeping them up to date with any changes - and then to tell the people who you want to inherit that you have done so. They're not bound to use the services of this lawyer if they don't want to do so, but most will be grateful to you for making the arrangements in advance and so simplifying their lives at a time of great stress.

Part of keeping things simple also involves telling your heirs what you want to happen on your death. Do you want to be buried or cremated? Do you have any special wishes? Is there anything that you particularly do *not* want to happen? I remember a Turkish client who insisted that his coffin should not be carried in a Mercedes!

Make these decisions and tell all the relevant people so that they do not have to worry about them when the time comes.

Another aspect of keeping things simple is to make sure that you, your heirs and your lawyer all know about your assets and liabilities. Some people are reluctant to tell their heirs about their financial circumstances and, if that is so in your case, there is a simple solution: tell your lawyer.

Of course, your financial circumstances will change all the time and so the best way of dealing with this is simply to have a file (paper or digital, preferably both) in which you keep an updated list of all your possessions and liabilities. Say in the list where the paperwork relating to them all is stored. Put the paper list in the same envelope as your Will - but not physically attach it to the Will.

Tell your lawyer and your heirs where the file is kept.

Most importantly, do keep it up-to-date. Having this list can save large amounts of time (and so cost) but it has precisely the opposite effect if you say that you have (for example) 1,000 Rolls Royce shares and that the certificate is in your filing cabinet when you have actually sold them.

Conclusion

There is no escaping the fact that proper inheritance planning requires professional help. Because of the way in which international legal and tax systems interact it will usually require help from someone familiar with the laws of Turkey and with at least a passing knowledge of the laws in your own country - or at least with a contact over there who does know them.

If your affairs are complicated - particularly if you've been married several times and/or have children by multiple relationships - it can be complicated getting such advice. That can make it somewhat expensive, but the savings you are likely to be able to make are likely to be many, many times the cost of the advice.

The good news is that if your affairs are relatively simple, your adviser - usually your lawyer or your financial adviser - will be able to identify this very quickly and so the advice can be very inexpensive.

Trusts in Turkey

Written by **Başak Yildiz Orkun**
Managing Partner (Legal Department) at Orkun & Orkun
www.orkunorkun.com • info@orkunorkun.com

As in many countries, Trusts can be a very useful tool when managing your affairs in Turkey. They're useful for both foreigners and native Turks. They are especially useful when managing your inheritance but they have other applications too.

What is a Trust?

A Trust is an arrangement under which a person or a group of people are made responsible for assets for the benefit of another person or group of people.

The people responsible for the assets and who administer the Trust are known as 'trustees' and those who benefit from the trust as 'beneficiaries'. The person who sets up the Trust is known as the 'settlor'.

The arrangement is set up in a way recognised by law and the Trustees are subject to legal controls. It is, often, set up by a written document called a 'Deed of Trust'.

The assets are then held in the trust and will be dealt with and released as directed by the Deed of Trust. For example, they might be used for the benefit of Mr A until his death and then for the benefit of his children, or kept safe by the Trustees until someone reaches the age of (say) 25.

Why Should You Think of Using a Trust?

There are a number of reasons. Trusts can reduce inheritance tax, simplify the inheritance process, protect your assets from attack by creditors, safeguard young children or people with limited life-skills, make sure assets are properly looked after and do many other things. However, they are definitely not for everybody.

What is the Downside of Using a Trust?

Cost and complexity. Setting up and administering a Trust both cost money and many people like a simple life, where their affairs are easily understood by them and their families.

Sometimes, if Trusts try to be too 'clever', they can be attacked by (for example) the tax authorities. The cost of that can outweigh all the benefits.

Can You Use a Trust in Turkey?

Turkey recognises the concept of Trusts. You can set up a Trust as per the Civil Code of Turkey; this should be a legal entity registered with the Directorate General of Foundations.

However, the definition and operation of "Trust" in Turkey and your home country will differ. Trusts in Turkey cannot be used in the wide range of circumstance in which they can be used, for example, in the US.

This does not mean that Trusts cannot be used in Turkey at all. There are occasions on which it is convenient for assets to be owned on behalf of a group of people but not directly in the names of each of the members of that group. This could be for many reasons, not the least of which could be the size of the group.

In these cases, the asset could be owned by (for example) a Turkish limited company, the official shareholders of which were a few individuals who held the shares on trust for the rest of the group. Owning the shares in this way would have no impact in Turkey. The owners would be treated as the full and beneficial owners of those shares. However, if the shareholders (the Trustees) came from a place where Trusts were recognised, then the rights of the rest of the group could be enforced in the country in which the official shareholders were resident.

If the beneficiaries were also resident in that country then this could be quite a neat and cheap way of reducing complexity.

Foundations

Turkey also has the concept of Foundations (*vakıf*). These have some of the same characteristics of Trusts, but Foundations are usually established for charitable purposes or for the management of immovable assets (land and buildings) belonging to big families.

How Do You Find Out More?

You will need to consult a financial adviser who is familiar with the use of Trusts. This could be an adviser in Turkey or one in your home country.

Appendix 1 - Useful Contacts

Please see **www.guides.global/books/turkey/tur-contacts.php** for a list of useful contacts (including embassies, government contacts, medical professionals, vets, Notaries, lawyers, accountants, etc.) We've organised the list online as we are forever adding to it - and contact details often change.

Appendix 2 - The 100 Words

I am sorry but I don't speak Turkish		Pardon, Türkçe konuşamıyorum	
My name is		Adım…	
How far is …		…….ne kadar uzak	
What time is…		….Ne zaman	
I don't understand		Anlamıyorum	
I understand		Anlıyorum	
I would like		……. istiyorum	
Do you have…		…….. var mı?	
I am hungry		Açım	
I am thirsty		Susadım	
I must		…….. yapmalıyım	
Hello	Merhaba	To have (verb)	Sahip olmak
Goodbye	Hoşçakal	To be (verb)	Olmak
Please	Lütfen	To go (verb)	Gitmek
Thank you	Teşekkürler	To give (verb)	Vermek
Yes	Evet	To think/believe	Düşünmek
No	Hayır	To walk (verb)	Yürümek
Me	Ben	To take (verb)	Almak
My	Benim	To read (verb)	Okumak
You	Sen	Now	Şimdi
It	O	Soon	Yakın zamanda
He	O	Later	Sonra
His	Onun	Always	Hep
And	Ve	Never	Asla
But	Ama	Today	Bugün
Also	Ayrıca	Tomorrow	Yarın

With	ile	Thing/item	Şey
Without	onsuz	Friend	Arkadaş
Because	çünkü	Man	Erkek
From	…..'dan	Woman	Kadın
To	…..'ya	Child	Çocuk
Until	Kadar	Country	Ülke
Near	Yakın	Your nationality	Nerelisin?
Far	Uzak	Food	Yemek
Inside	İçeride	Drink	İçecek
Good	İyi	Water	Su
Bad	Kötü	Beer	Bira
Big	Büyük	Wine	Şarap
Small	Küçük	Petrol/Diesel	Benzin/mazot
Very	Çok	Police	Polis
Much (a lot)	Daha çok	Doctor	Doktor
More	Çok	Hospital	Hastane
Less	Az	Pharmacy	Eczane
Other	Diğer	Consulate	Konsolosluk
Sick	Hasta	Airport	Havaalanı
Well	İyi	Car	Araba
For (purpose)	İçin	Taxi	Taksi
What?	Ne	Telephone	Telefon
Where?	Nerede	Bed	Yatak
Who?	Kim	Towel	Havlu
When?	Ne zaman	Toilet	Tuvalet
How?	Nasıl	100	Yüz
Why?	Neden	1,000	Bin
1	Bir	1,000,000	Bir milyon
2	İki	None	Hiç

Turkey: how things *really* work

3	Üç	Few	Biraz
4	Dört	Many	Çok
5	Beş		
6	Altı		
7	Yedi		
8	Sekiz		
9	Dokuz		
10	On		

Appendix 3 - Document Library

A library of sample documents is available for download at
www.guides.global/books/turkey/tur-downloads.php.

We are constantly adding more documents.

In some cases, these documents are designed to be used 'as is'. In others, they form a template for a document that you can prepare.

Readers have found the 'Letters to Lawyers' section and the various checklists particularly useful.

Appendix 4 - Glossary

Please see **www.guides.global/books/turkey/tur-glossary.php** for a list and explanation of common legal terms, both in general and specific to Turkey.

We've put the glossary online as we are forever adding to it - and legal definitions sometimes change.

Index

Printed in Great Britain
by Amazon

19841480R00302